British Muslim Fictions

G000168601

First published 2011 by
PALGRAVE MACMILLAN

Palgrave Macmillan in the UK is an imprint of Macmillan Publishers Limited, registered in England, company number 785998, of Houndmills, Basingstoke, Hampshire RG21 6XS.

Palgrave Macmillan in the US is a division of St Martin's Press LLC, 175 Fifth Avenue, New York, NY 10010.

Palgrave Macmillan is the global academic imprint of the above companies and has companies and representatives throughout the world.

Palgrave® and Macmillan® are registered trademarks in the United States, the United Kingdom, Europe and other countries.

ISBN 978–0–230–25233–2   hardback
ISBN 978–0–230–30878–7   paperback

This book is printed on paper suitable for recycling and made from fully managed and sustained forest sources. Logging, pulping and manufacturing processes are expected to conform to the environmental regulations of the country of origin.

A catalogue record for this book is available from the British Library.

A catalog record for this book is available from the Library of Congress.

10 9 8 7 6 5 4 3 2 1
20 19 18 17 16 15 14 13 12 11

Printed and bound in Great Britain by
CPI Antony Rowe, Chippenham and Eastbourne

British Muslim Fictions

Interviews with Contemporary Writers

Claire Chambers
Senior Lecturer in Postcolonial Literatures,
Leeds Metropolitan University

palgrave
macmillan

For Joash and Derry

Contents

Contents

Acknowledgements

I could not have written this book without the financial, intellectual, and emotional support of many institutions and people. Financially, I am indebted to HEFCE's Promising Researcher Fellowship, the British Academy's Small Grants, and the Arts and Humanities Research Board's Early Career Fellowships for providing funding for the sabbaticals and resources which made it possible to undertake this research. I thank them for their generous support.

I am very grateful to colleagues and former colleagues at the School of Cultural Studies at Leeds Metropolitan University (especially Ruth Robbins, Caroline Herbert, Mary Eagleton, Christer Petley, Kristyn Gorton, Rachel Farebrother, Babita Bhogal, Melanie Chan, Lisa Taylor, Emily Marshall, Rachel Rich, and Kenyetta Cohen), for their academic and administrative support, help with funding applications, and, above all, their advice on general and scholarly matters. Sections from the introduction have appeared in an earlier form in my article, 'A Comparative Approach to Pakistani Fiction in English', *Journal of Postcolonial Writing* 47(2) (April 2011): 122–34. The interview with Leila Aboulela was first published as 'An Interview with Leila Aboulela', *Contemporary Women's Writing* 3(1) (2009): 86–102. Thanks to the editors of these periodicals for helping me develop my ideas in print.

Intellectually, I have too many debts even to begin to repay. The book would not have been possible without the enthusiastic participation of the thirteen authors interviewed here. They deserve my thanks for the fiction, non-fiction, conversations, political insights, and innumerable kindnesses. I would also like to thank the writers Bina Shah, Tabish Khair, and John Siddique for their friendship and patient proofreading.

Bart Moore-Gilbert provided advice and a welcome research base at Goldsmiths College in the early stages of the project. James McGrath, James Dodge, and Gareth Bell helped me with invaluable transcription and other work. Warm thanks go to Sameena Choudry of Education Leeds for working with me on the education project described in the Introduction, and for sharing her wide knowledge of South Asian writing. I am very grateful to Nukhbah Langah, Muneeza Shamsie, and Shadab Zeest Hashmi for their friendship and intellectual insights in Pakistan, cyberspace, and elsewhere. Of the community groups I've worked with, thanks go to Zahid Hussain (again) of Manchester Muslim Writers; Irfan Akram of Muslim Writers Awards; and Waqas Tufail and Nasreen Mansoor of Greater Manchester Diversity Researchers' Forum (GMDRF), University of Manchester.

I have also received great intellectual and emotional support from my academic friends. Of these, five deserve special mention. My thinking about this book has greatly benefited from lively discussions with Peter Morey, Amina Yaqin, Anshuman Mondal, and Stephen Morton. Most importantly, I doubt I would have been able to cope with the pressures of juggling teaching with research, had it not been for Susan Watkins's friendship, collegiality, and sense of proportion.

The most heartfelt thanks go to Rob, Joash, Derry, Susan, and Richard. I benefit so much from your belief in me and unconditional love and support. I hope the finished book is worth all the benign neglect (don't worry: you don't have to read it!).

British Muslim Fictions is supported by the Arts and Humanities Research Council (AHRC).

Arts & Humanities Research Council

Introduction

Background

This book of interviews with writers of Muslim heritage is the first in a two-book project, to be followed by a monograph on artistic representations of British Muslims, 1966–present. In terms of the selection criteria for this book, the interviewed writers are resident in the UK, of Muslim heritage, and have produced literary fiction in English widely considered to be high quality and influential.[1] The second book focuses on representations of Muslims by writers who are often, but not necessarily, of Muslim heritage. Both books analyse the term 'Muslim writing', which has recently come into currency, in order to complicate and contest it.

There has long existed high demand for author interviews as resources to supplementing understanding of contemporary literature. Three recent volumes of interviews illustrate this point: Susheila Nasta's edited volume *Writing Across Worlds* which contains interviews with writers broadly considered 'postcolonial';[2] Philip Tew, Fiona Tolan, and Leigh Wilson's collection of interviews with specifically British, but mostly White and Christian/secular writers, *Writers Talk*;[3] and *The Big Bookshelf*, an anthology of thirty interview transcripts from Sunil Sethi's Indian television show, *Just Books*.[4] However, my book differs from these collections, given its exclusive focus on writers with Muslim backgrounds in Britain and beyond. This is important because their excellent writing, while rarely discussed in relation to religious identities, is increasingly gaining recognition from critics, literary prize boards, and research students. The volume is also distinct from the first two in that all interviews are conducted by me as the single researcher.

1

In recent years there has also emerged great interest in sociological interviews with British Muslims in order to shed light on communities that are marginalized and little-known beyond the stereotypes. For me, the most important of the many books in this area are Philip Lewis's *Young, British and Muslim* and Anshuman A. Mondal's *Young British Muslim Voices*.[5] Despite their similar titles and publication within a year of each other in 2007 and 2008 respectively, they put the interview format to different use. Lewis presents his interviews (with both well-known and unfamiliar young Muslims) alongside readings of novels such as Hanif Kureishi's *The Black Album* and Zahid Hussain's *The Curry Mile*, discussion of intergenerational tensions and *biradiri* networks, and analysis of Muslim websites, mailing lists, and magazines. Mondal uses the interview format more extensively, talking to young, practising Muslims from many walks of life, and presenting their arguments within a journalistic, self-reflexive framework. His main, insightful conclusions are, firstly, that younger Muslims tend to be more religious than their parents and that this is creating conflict between the generations. Secondly, and contrary to the stereotypes, Mondal argues that despite many young Muslims articulating oppositional politics, they are not disengaged from society, with far more of them doing voluntary community work than non-Muslims of the same age. He concludes, 'Principally, I have learned to speak of Muslims rather than Islam.'[6] This is also a maxim I have drawn from my interviews with writers of Muslim heritage, especially given the heterogeneity to be explored shortly. My interviews differ from these two important monographs because, rather than excerpting respondents' comments amid sociological discussion, I provide edited interview transcripts in order to project their voices as fully as possible.

Especially since the 1980s, feminist, postcolonial, and Critical Race Theory scholars have directed attention towards methodological and ethical concerns when conducting research on, with, and for Others, whether these be othered through race, gender, class, or a combination of these. My own PhD thesis on the Bengali author Amitav Ghosh was grounded on the theories of Foucault, Said, Bhabha, and others, to the effect that knowledge is something that society 'produces'.[7] As Said points out repeatedly in his work, knowledge is not culturally transcendent, but is often deeply dependent on the political and economic processes of colonialism and now neo-colonialism/globalization. In our awareness of the imbrication of knowledge in power structures, we need to situate the researcher in the process of knowledge production. As such, and despite all efforts to ensure openness and probity in the interviews, there are still ethical issues in representing cultures and religions that are not, narrowly speaking, my own. My research into British Muslims in contemporary society and cultural representations is shaped by my locatedness as someone who grew up in a British Asian Muslim milieu in Leeds. As clichéd as it may sound, my worldview has also been crucially shaped by my gap year, 1993–4, which I spent teaching English in Peshawar, Pakistan, at the age of 18. I went on to specialize in South Asian literature in English as a postgraduate and continue to fuel my interest by return visits to the region and by engagement work with diasporic communities.

A turning point for me, as a Yorkshirewoman of Northern Irish heritage, came when news of the London bombers' identity broke in 2005. I was in Canada at the time and people kept asking about my city of Leeds in West Yorkshire, where it emerged that three of the four bombers also lived. Even though I had grown up with many Asians and Muslims and had lived in Pakistan, the people I knew tended to be from an elite or middle-class background and so I'd been unaware that in a place like Beeston in South Leeds there existed such politicized rage among a tiny minority of Muslims. It goes without saying that I and all the interviewees would condemn as horrific the violent, nihilistic path the bombers chose. A desire better to understand the range of issues facing Muslims in the UK led me to embark on this two-book research project, which is inflected with a sense of regional, northern English identity. Some of the

3

interviewed authors have written about hardline Muslims who may (or may not) be violent. For example, Mohsin Hamid, the author of probably the most famous of these texts, *The Reluctant Fundamentalist*, argues in interview that 'we're left with [...] a gaping hole where spirituality used to be [...] and a new politics that's calling itself religion' (p. 190). However, one key finding is that terrorism tends not to be the most pressing concern amongst writers of Muslim heritage in the current political context of heavy-handed surveillance initiatives such as the Prevent agenda, and vociferous, often Islamophobic debate about integration and lack of community cohesion. Yet the writers also do not shirk self-scrutiny of problems within Muslim communities in Britain and abroad, with many of them being extremely outspoken about abuses directed from some dominant Muslim groups and figures towards minority groups, especially women.

Literature and religion

In this section, I scrutinize a long quotation from Nigel Williams's comic novel *East of Wimbledon*, which centres on its protagonist, Robert's, inept attempts to pass as a Muslim in order to get and retain a job at the fictional Wimbledon Independent Islamic Boys Day School:

> He [the School's headmaster, Mr Malik] spread his hands generously. 'You, of course, among your other duties, will be teaching Islamic English Literature.'
> Robert nodded keenly. His floppy, blond hair fell forward over his eyes, and he raked it back with what he hoped was boyish eagerness. [...] 'In that context,' he said, 'do you see Islamic English literature as being literature by English, or Welsh or Scottish Muslims?'
> They both looked at each other in consternation. Perhaps, like him, Mr Malik was unable to think of a single Muslim writer who fitted that description.

'Or,' went on Robert, struggling somewhat, 'do you see it as work that has a Muslim dimension? Such as … *Paradise Lost* for example.'

What was the Muslim dimension in *Paradise Lost*? Robert became aware that the room had suddenly become very hot.

'Or,' he went on swiftly, 'simply English literature viewed from a Muslim perspective?'

'You will view English from a Muslim perspective,' said Malik with a broad, affable grin, 'because you are a Muslim!'[8]

Robert's three approaches to Muslim literature are indicative of some of the themes, problems, and approaches I have grappled with in this research project. In the early 1990s, when Williams's novel was written, the very idea of talking about 'Islamic English literature' or – my preferred term – 'literature by writers of Muslim heritage' appeared ripe for satire, but now all the questions posed by Robert in this opening passage are being seriously interrogated.

The first question, 'do you see Islamic English literature as being literature by English, or Welsh or Scottish Muslims?', concerns an apparent dearth of Muslim writers in the different nations that make up Britain but, since *East of Wimbledon* was published in 1993, there have emerged countless authors of Muslim heritage based in England – mainly London – and the majority of the 13 interviewees in this book are from this group. Many other writers, including two of the interviewees, Leila Aboulela and Robin Yassin-Kassab, live in and/or write about Scotland. Playwright Afshan Malik, poet Imtiaz Dharker, and memoir writer Sara Suleri Goodyear have all resided in and written about Wales.[9] Unfortunately, as this interviews book deals with literary fiction, none of these writers with connections to Wales but working in other genres is included. However, I have published an interview with Dharker (and fellow poets John Siddique and Moniza Alvi) elsewhere, and there will be chapters on poetry and memoir in the monograph.[10] Despite the small numbers of Muslims in Northern Ireland,[11] there is even a novel about this community, *Mohammed Maguire*, written by the non-Muslim author Colin Bateman.[12] I will shortly outline variegation within the category of 'Muslims', but this discussion of regional identities indicates that it would be wrong to assume that 'Britain' itself is homogeneous. The recent move towards devolution has highlighted the fact that Britain is made up of discordant communities. Even within the national unit of England there are tensions between the regions, particularly the once industrial north and the wealthy, technologized south.[13]

Of course, even in the early 1990s when Williams was writing, there were some fine authors of Muslim heritage working in Britain (Ahdaf Soueif, Abdulrazak Gurnah, Tariq Ali, Hanif Kureishi, and Salman Rushdie are the most obvious names, all but the last being represented here), although Robert is oblivious to this fact. However, since Kureishi and Rushdie at least are sceptical towards conformist Sunni Islam, is it cultural background or belief that makes writing (or identity) Muslim? In a talk entitled 'Great Muslim Writers', Zahid Hussain, one of the interviewed writers, interestingly reframes this problem: 'Is there a difference between "Muslim" and "Islamic"? Can non-religious literature be Muslim?'[14] Given Hussain's choice of great Muslim writers, which includes mostly male non-fiction authors such as Mohammed Marmaduke Pickthall, Allama Iqbal, Ghulam Sarwar, and Moazzam Begg, he seems to lean towards the religious interpretation of what constitutes Muslim writing. This is a perfectly valid understanding, but not one that is available to me, as a fellow-traveller rather than a believer. Robert Gleave has a different approach still, questioning the very validity of a division between interpretations of Islam as a civilization and as a religion. He argues that if we classify Islam solely as a religion, we risk buying into the Salafi argument that positions religion as blameless and represents culture as constituting negative accretions. On the other hand, Gleave criticizes social scientists and area studies experts who are interested in the culture, belief, and practice of Muslims, but not in broader doctrines and belief systems of Islam. A better way, he suggests, is to problematize a binary understanding of the apparently separate categories of religion and culture and instead explore their commonalities. As Gleave argues, scholars need to move 'from an uncritical acceptance of the category of "religion", towards a critical interrogation of "religion" as a category'.[15] This position reinforces Timothy Fitzgerald's wider analysis in *Discourse of Civility and Barbarity* that 'religion is a modern invention which authorises and naturalises a form of Euro-American secular nationality. In turn, this supposed position of secular rationality constructs and authorises its "other", religion and religions.'[16]

This book is more susceptible to Gleave's social scientist than his Salafi indictment, as there are fewer discussions of Islam than of the reified figure, and cultural category, of the Muslim. Following Amin Malak, I draw a distinction between the Muslim, 'who espouses the religion of Islam or is shaped by its cultural impact',[17] and the constructed religion of Islam. My theoretical framework is informed by religious studies scholars including Philip Lewis and Seán McLoughlin, who – influenced by the Community Religions Project[18] – conduct ethnographic research into the faith practices of subjects from specific locations. As such, the book's approach to religion is sociological, rather than metaphysical. Literary analysis is informed by discussions of the material culture – places of worship, organization of prayer, pilgrimage, fasting, and so on – of Muslims resident in Britain. Interdisciplinarity is at the heart of the project, and I draw upon insights from media, film, religious studies, politics, and history, as well as area studies and literature. Perhaps this is inevitable given my ten happy years in the School of Cultural Studies at Leeds Metropolitan University, but I should emphasize that the book does not aim towards *multi*-disciplinarity, in which there is a 'simple juxtaposition of two [...] disciplines' and 'the relationship between the two disciplines is merely one of proximity'.[19] Quite the contrary, for *British Muslim Fictions* interdisciplinarity has been entirely 'transformative',[20] whereby something new is created through the productive, if scabrous, encounter between disciplines.

In the quotation, Williams exposes his flimsy assumptions about the supposedly doctrinaire nature of Muslim intellectual thought. He makes Malik simplistically equate a Muslim background with a Muslim worldview: 'You will view English from a Muslim perspective [...] because you are a Muslim!' However, the furore over Salman Rushdie's novel *The Satanic Verses* from 1988 onwards indicates that Malik's circular reasoning can prove unreliable. Written by an author from a Muslim background, the controversial novel is about Indian, mostly Muslim, migration to the UK; multicultural London; and the loss of religious faith. It contains a notoriously intangible section in which a character, who is a borderline psychotic, has a dream about a character called 'Mahound' (an insulting Orientalist term for the Prophet Mohammed).[21] Whether by Rushdie himself, or the character Gibreel, or as a byproduct of his illness, it is difficult to say, but Mahound is portrayed as an almost paedophilic libertine, who is also a ruthless businessman. Drawing on the myth of the satanic verses, suggestions are made that sections of the Qur'an were dictated by the devil, and prostitutes impersonate the real wives of Mohammed. As Robin Yassin-Kassab indicates in the interview in this volume (p. 198), Rushdie is playing with early derogatory representations of the Prophet Mohammed and his co-religionists from within Christendom. Tabish Khair incisively describes these kinds of representation:

> From the 19th century onwards, th[e] perception of [Muslims'] sexual permissiveness was increasingly overshadowed by the discourse of Islamic conservatism, rigidity, intolerance and misogyny. Today, for instance, dominant or vocal discourses present Muslims as anti-female, anti-gay, sexually repressive etc., even though subterranean traces of the fear of 'Muslim' sexuality remain and are often encountered in perverted or demagogic terms: 'Muslims have too many children'.[22]

Rushdie plays on such Janus-faced modes of representation, presenting his Khomeini caricature, the Imam, as a sexually

8

repressive, autocratic figure, but also casting Mahound as a cynically libidinous impostor.

Despite Rushdie's polite refusal to be interviewed, and his statement at the height of the *Satanic Verses* Affair that he is '*not a Muslim*',[23] students and scholars of Rushdie should nonetheless find that this book sheds important light on his perception among other writers of Muslim heritage. While the references to Rushdie are sometimes – though by no means always – critical, they are also detailed and given weight by coming from a range of authors interviewed individually. In many cases, the writers brought up Rushdie of their own volition, while in others I asked specific questions about his writing or the *Satanic Verses* Affair. As a result, his significance is fascinatingly represented here. I do not mean to denigrate Rushdie, whose early work in particular, has subtlety and political responsiveness. The fact that his work continues to generate so much debate indicates the form-changing importance of texts such as *Midnight's Children* and *Shame*, as well as the paradigm-shifting centrality of the Rushdie Affair on contemporary representations of British Muslims. I will discuss these issues in greater depth in a chapter on *The Satanic Verses* in the second book.

Rushdie's representations caused great offence to many Muslims, particularly those from the subcontinent, where the Prophet is held in especially high veneration. It should be noted that many other Muslims were perplexed and angered by the protests against the novel.[24] As the controversy spread, *The Satanic Verses* was banned in India and burned in demonstrations in the United Kingdom and Pakistan, before the Ayatollah Khomeini seized a political opportunity by issuing a *fatwa* (a legal opinion, not a law) in February 1989 against Rushdie and his publishers. Rushdie was compelled to go into hiding until the late 1990s, and several people died in connection with the *fatwa*. The *fatwa* rightly generated opprobrium,[25] but commentators are increasingly recognizing that the hegemonic liberal response to ordinary protesters against the novel was also suspect.[26] The Rushdie Affair was a watershed moment both for an upsurge in stereotypes of Muslims, and for Muslims' perceptions of themselves as a simultaneously powerful and vulnerable community, distinct from other religions and secular groups, and not to be easily installed within the capacious but perhaps insufficiently specified category of 'British Asians'.

Without the Rushdie Affair, too, Williams would probably not have had the impetus to write the final novel in his Wimbledon Trilogy as a comedy about an innocent secular Christian and his encounters with religious zeal in a Muslim faith school. In the passage, Malik's simplistic statement that a Muslim will view literature from a Muslim perspective by dint of his/her religion, and Robert's subterfuge in pretending to be Muslim invites the question: is it possible to evince a Muslim perspective even if an individual is not a Muslim? Many significant Pakistani and Arab writers are secular, agnostic, atheists, or (like Pakistani American novelist Bapsi Sidhwa; Pakistani British poets Moniza Alvi and John Siddique; Lebanese artist, writer, and publisher Mai Ghoussoub; and the late Palestinian-American theorist Edward W. Said) were not brought up as Muslims or come from other religious communities. They all have in common, though, a Muslim civilizational heritage. In relation to my own positionality and interest in this field, as a non-Muslim who has nevertheless been shaped by South Asian Muslim culture in Britain and Pakistan, I often think of a statement by Amin Malak: 'Islam constitutes not only a cardinal component of Muslims' identity but also becomes a prominent feature in the identity of the non-Muslims (be they Hindus, Zoroastrians, Jews, or Christians) who happen to live in Muslim communities.'[27] Therefore, I take a broad view of the category 'Muslim', rather than examining texts for their religiosity or piety.

Indeed, and as can already be observed, I deploy the term 'writers of Muslim heritage' more commonly than 'Muslim writers' (and never use the schoolteacher's term 'Islamic literature'), in order to subvert stereotypical representations of 'Muslimness' as a unitary, unchanging identity, and to eschew problematic judgements about whether or not writers are sufficiently religious. As Kamila Shamsie ironically remarks, 'You can't see into someone's heart or mind for their views on religion, but you can see the length of their beard and how covered up they are' (p. 220). This book does not attempt to place the writers on a scale according to the perceived ardour of their religious beliefs. However, the term 'heritage' is itself far from ideal, because it connotes the heritage industry and a somewhat fossilized sense of history, but on a positive note, it also suggests something of value gifted to us from the past which should be preserved. 'Heritage' is preferred to terms such as 'identity' or 'roots' because, as Mai Ghoussoub illustrates,

> identity and root presume a settled or pure essence; they thrive in times of trouble, often preceding them [...] 'A carrot is a root,' says my friend to her husband, who keeps nagging her about returning to his country, to his roots. 'I am not a carrot!' she keeps screaming back at him.[28]

This issue of identity will be discussed at greater length in the monograph, but for now suffice it to say that the participating writers are certainly not root vegetables. Indeed, as will be seen from the interviews, they often express highly original and/or oppositional views with passion. I should say from the outset that I record the authors' ideas without comment in the following chapters, and that readers are invited to form their own opinions about the views expressed in the interviews (views which I do not always share with the respondents).

While all of them to a greater or lesser extent see themselves as being influenced by Islamicate civilizations, only Leila Aboulela, Robin Yassin-Kassab, Aamer Hussein, and Zahid Hussain explicitly self-identify as religious Muslims. Yet even the declared atheist Muslims like Tariq Ali, Nadeem Aslam, and Hanif Kureishi, are very well-informed about Islam and express fascinating responses to the post-9/11 treatment and representations of Muslims. I wish to complicate the concept of authenticity, which has dogged ethnic-minority writers, leading to many feeling that they shoulder a burden of representation.

As Ana María Sánchez-Arce observes, the concept of authenticity is problematic because '[a]n object remain[s] "authentic" for as long as it perform[s] the task it [i]s supposed to and los[es] its "authenticity" as soon as it stops functioning in an expected way'.[29] This can be seen when writers of Muslim heritage write about topics not associated with their communities, as in the case of Monica Ali's *Alentejo Blue*, her follow-up novel to *Brick Lane*, which centred on Portugal and was received badly by critics,[30] partly because of the uneven quality of the writing, but also because it did not operate 'in an expected way'.

The second approach to literature adumbrated by Robert in the quoted excerpt is to examine Western literary classics that have a 'Muslim dimension'. To take Robert's specific example of *Paradise Lost*, there have been several attempts to explore Milton's depiction of Islam.[31] In my monograph, I will explore the simplistic and sensationalist 'Muslim dimension' found in recent texts by such mainstream writers as Martin Amis, Ian McEwan, and Sebastian Faulks.[32] As I discuss in the interview with Tariq Ali, in the post-9/11 climate many writers appear to think that writing about Islamist terrorism will help them to gain recognition as serious novelists (pp. 45–6). Yet most, if not all, of the writers interviewed here fascinatingly challenge this new strain of Orientalism and, ten years on from the attacks on America, more literary voices than ever before are expressing nuanced and complex thoughts about Muslims' positions in contemporary societies. As Fadia Faqir puts it, with a nod to Marx and Said, 'cultures and races are beginning to speak for themselves, rather than as people who can only be represented' (p. 65).[33]

The fictional Robert's third strategy of critically interrogating canonical Western texts from the perspective of Muslims and other Others is a major part of Edward W. Said's research in *Orientalism*.[34] Said writes, '[t]he European encounter with the Orient, and specifically with Islam, strengthened [the] system of representing the Orient and [...] turned Islam into the very epitome of an outsider against which the whole of European civilization from the Middle Ages on was founded'.[35] Given

Said's huge influence on postcolonial studies, but no doubt to the fictional character's amazement, Robert's three approaches to 'Islamic literature' which begin the slight, unempathetic, and under-researched novel *East of Wimbledon*, neatly dovetail with much of recent theory. To adapt John McLeod's admirably succinct summary, postcolonial critics (and, in parallel, scholars working in other contested areas, such as women's, Jewish, or Muslim writing) firstly examine classic English literary texts for evidence about imperial (sexist, anti-Semitic, or Islamophobic) attitudes. In an act of recovery termed 'gynocriticism' by feminist thinkers, they also study and draw wider attention to texts by women, postcolonial, Muslim, or Jewish writers.[36]

Amin Malak suggests that 'Muslim narrative writers [...] project the culture and civilization of Islam from within',[37] and many of the texts epitomize this notion of an insider's view of Islam. By removing Muslims from the position of Other, these novelists create various possibilities for Muslims' depictions. In this century's climate of Islamophobia, wars of questionable legality, and oppressive counter-terror legislation, many writers are exploring Muslim identity. Whereas non-Muslim authors tend to zero in on the figure of the terrorist, drawing upon a tradition in literature stretching back to Conrad, Muslim writers have often looked at Islam in complex, multifaceted ways. The writers in this volume assert the right to explore their religious background, but equally to disregard, satirize, challenge, and praise it. Apparently emblematic Muslim themes, such as the Qur'an, justice, *djinns*, and compassion do recur in many of the texts and interviews, but so do issues not widely associated with Islam, such as feminism, cosmopolitanism, and literary experimentalism.

Methodology

The interviews are qualitative, using a semi-structured methodology, and no questionnaire was used, because the respondents are eloquent speakers and creative thinkers, and their insights would have been lost if quantitative methods were employed. The discussion is primarily about the writers' work, their literary techniques and intertexts, but we also frequently consider media/literary representations of Muslims in relation to debates about the veil, the so-called war on terror, and *sharia* law, among other themes. Through analysis of the interviews as a whole, I suggest that approaches to literature which accord due importance to religious identities will be central to future directions in literary studies.

To provide one example from Pakistan and its diaspora, first of all: Pakistani authors tend to be analysed as part of broader South Asian trends and considered alongside their peers in India, Bangladesh, and Sri Lanka. There is of course some logic to this, but Pakistan differs from India in that it has concerns and links in the Middle East, Central Asia, East Africa, and beyond, that derive from its Muslim identity. I am no cheerleader for the idea of a unified global Muslim community, or *ummah*, and know that exaggeration of this concept can lead to the very real tensions between different Muslim groups within an equally divided Britain being underestimated. Indeed, it is important to emphasize that no clear separation between 'the Muslim world' and 'the West' exists. Each is a constructed entity marked by permeable borders, a far cry from Samuel Huntington's 'clash of civilizations' thesis,[38] which several of the writers attack, while recognizing that constant emphasis on the supposedly ineradicably opposed 'sides' of Islam and the West is to some extent leading to a self-fulfilling prophecy. However, my approach has the advantage of bringing together writers from a broadly imagined, absorbent 'Muslim world' to shed light on each other. British Arabs, Africans, and Asians are discussed together, because of their shared religious heritage, without overlooking their vast contextual differences.

The interviews book enables Muslim writers to articulate their concerns in relation to current events, themes, and literary strategies. I hope the insight that this provides will be useful to Muslims and non-Muslims alike, in providing a contradistinction to the dominant discourse on Muslims in common currency today. Muslims of South Asian extraction tend to experience greater poverty, social exclusion, and racism than do other minority groups in current British society.[39] This is in part fuelled by Islamophobia,[40] which has gathered pace since the attacks on America in 2001 and the ensuing 'war on terror'.[41] Derald Wing Sue *et al.* argue that stereotypical views of groups designated as Other (including, although they do not discuss this group, people of Muslim heritage) damage the mainstream community as well as the marginalized, in that they 'lower empathic ability, dim perceptual awareness, maintain false illusions, and lessen compassion for others'.[42] Rather than reinforcing existing preconceived notions as to what a Muslim writer chooses to write about, this project intends to open up understanding of the catholic nature of Muslim-heritage authors' political concerns and literary representations.

In Paul Auster's recent novel, *Sunset Park*, his character Morris describes the author interview as 'a debased literary form, which serves no purpose except to simplify that which should never be simplified'.[43] This attitude overlaps productively with poststructuralist theory, as Barthes, for example, famously argued that the author is dead, and that of much greater value than his or her views is consideration of the writer/author as a writing subject; the reader as part of the text rather than a real person; and texts interacting with other texts through intertextuality.[44] Foucault also questions our most basic arguments about literature, posing the provocatively bland question, 'What is an Author?'[45] According to the poststructuralist argument, novels do not involve people speaking to people, but items of text speaking to and through other texts. This has been challenged by Seán Burke, Liz Stanley, and Reina Lewis, among others, who respectively call poststructuralism into question from philosophical, feminist, and queer perspectives.[46] In my view, and at the risk of embodying what Foucault calls the 'author-function',[47] there is great value in the interview form. Although writers can and do sometimes misrepresent their own work, presenting more limiting viewpoints than their ambivalent, multifaceted fiction, they can also shed light on conscious and unconscious intertexts, political agendas, and stylistic intentions. It is particularly important to examine authors from the subjugated Muslim community because, to repeat Liz Stanley's acerbic feminist critique of the poststructuralists' death of the author thesis in a new context: 'you want to claim a self, to speak your oppression, to name oppressors'.[48] A collection of interviews by its nature becomes a sociological as well as a literary endeavour, in that one converses with people as well as books.[49] In an emerging field like the study of texts by Muslim-heritage writers, this book of interviews acts as a sourcebook, if only to stimulate curiosity, debate, and dissent. There is also an element of canon formation here, and I hope through this book to draw attention to the connections and divergences between these writers of Muslim heritage, who are producing some of the most complex, politically engaged writing in the UK today.

Muslim Writers Awards

The research is also connected to my work as a judge for the Published Non-fiction category of the 2009 Muslim Writers Awards (hereafter MWA), a not-for-profit company. MWA not only offers prestigious literary prizes (its four main categories are Young Muslim Writers, Unpublished, Published, and Journalism) but, through its outreach work in schools, the organization also aims to inspire young and older Muslims to begin writing, enter competitions, and get into print. Literary prizes, most of them corporately sponsored, have of course come to dominate the literary scene since the late nineteenth century, partly due to a withering away of state subsidy in the arts.[50]

Prizes that are awarded to writers from particular social or political groupings are simultaneously inevitable and controversial. For example, the Orange Prize goes only to female writers, which has caused disquiet amongst many,[51] while writers such as Amitav Ghosh have criticized the Commonwealth Writers' Prize for subsuming the myriad concerns of fiction under the residues of imperialism, and because it is awarded only to writing in

English, thus excluding many important 'Commonwealth' languages.[52] MWA too has raised eyebrows for its arguably exclusionary emphasis on the emerging and contested category of 'British Muslims'. As is well known, Muslims in Britain were described in the 1980s as being 'Black', part of a political move to cement solidarity between different groups on the receiving end of racism. In the 1990s, this term began to be seen as too broad, so 'Asian' became the preferred moniker. Since 9/11 and 7/7, there is a perceived need for greater specificity still, so the term 'British Muslim' is now in common currency.[53]

However, it should be noted that 'British Muslims' form a minority group that has been demonized, and the term has largely been foisted on them from outside. In my view, it is important to look at this group, but there is a problem of slotting writers into a category of Muslim which may be nominal and defined by outsiders. It could also foster new partitions between beleaguered communities, forcing people to prioritize one part of identity over others, or sidelining them in a communalist cul-de-sac, so the issue is quite complex. As Low and Wynne-Davies put it, 'The increased utilisation of separate categories, such as "British Asian", "Asian British" or, more importantly, the politicized constructions of a religious and ethnic identity such as "British Muslims", has begun to mark a new phase in the politics of culture and the culture of politics.'[54] The Awards attracted particularly heavy criticism for its censorious directions not to submit 'offensive or unacceptable' material to the Unpublished prize category, including prohibitions on 'vulgar, explicit, pornographic, violent and obscene content', gratuitous blasphemy, and hate speech.[55] Such perceived censorship attracts criticism from writers and journalists,[56] and I was discomfited when I found out about these restrictions myself. (I had not been aware of these prohibitions when I agreed to act as a judge, as I was involved on another category, Published Non-fiction, the terms and conditions of which contained no such stipulations).

At an event at the London Book Fair 2010 to promote Muslim readers as 'Britain's biggest untapped commercial market',

Irfan Akram, MWA's Director, argued that because many elders in the Muslim community are new to this area of literature, it was important to take careful 'baby steps', so as not to repel them, with a view to making the Awards more inclusive and free in its expression in due course. In many ways this argument is convincing, and any practitioner introducing Islamicate writing into the classroom would do well to give careful consideration, for example, to the hurt and anger in the Muslim community over the publication of Salman Rushdie's *The Satanic Verses* as well as to the novel's strengths and the issue of freedom of speech. Because of current divisive geopolitics, there is a growing and often greatly exaggerated anxiety about Muslims, Islam, Islamism, and terrorism, which terms are often unhelpfully conflated. I would argue that organizations such as MWA which, despite their problems, indicate the great breadth of the 'Muslim world', are broadly a positive thing. To paraphrase a speaker at the MWA Ceremony in 2009, 'home-grown terrorists' are currently under scrutiny, but the Awards (and my education project, discussed later) draw attention to a rich array of home-grown Muslim art.

The outreach strand of MWA has been brought to the north of England, with the inauguration of Manchester Muslim Writers, based in Chorlton-cum-Hardy and run by Zahid Hussain, and the subsequent development of Lancashire Muslim Writers and Yorkshire Muslim Writers. I am involved with these organizations, particularly Manchester Muslim Writers, at which I delivered a paper in 2010 to the group's early-career writers about contemporary trends in writing by Muslim-heritage authors. Affiliated with MWA, Manchester Muslim Writers is a collective that was set up in May 2009 'to support the developments of writers in the widest sense and [...] weave the narratives of Muslims into the tapestry of British life'.[57] The group's emphasis is firmly on encouraging good writing, and I find it diverse, welcoming, and inclusive. When I first contacted Manchester Muslim Writers in 2009 and explained that I was neither a Muslim nor a writer of fiction, Zahid Hussain went out of his way to encourage me to come, and through that I interviewed him (Chapter 13) and met many other interesting aspiring writers of various ages, genders, backgrounds, and religions. In 2011, I will visit the new group Yorkshire Muslim Writers in Sheffield for the first time.

The writers and reasons for their inclusion

Writers of Muslim heritage have won or been nominated for many literary awards, even if, like the multiple winner of literary awards, Salman Rushdie, they have repudiated Islam. To describe those interviewed in this book, in no particular order, the groundbreaking English-language fiction of Ahdaf Soueif, which documents British–Arab cultural encounters, earned her a nomination for the Man Booker Prize for her second novel *The Map of Love* (1999). Another Booker nominee, Abdulrazak Gurnah, was born in Zanzibar in 1948, but emigrated to Britain in 1968 and has written eight relatively neglected but excellent novels. Mohsin Hamid, the Pakistan-born, US-educated, and now British-resident novelist, caused something of a literary sensation with his Booker-shortlisted *The Reluctant Fundamentalist* (2007), as it does not, as the title might suggest, trade in lazy stereotypes about Pakistani terrorists, but rather scrutinizes the corporate world of asset-stripping that is another, often overlooked, 'fundamentalism'. Kamila Shamsie's five novels to date have gained increasing recognition, with the latest, *Burnt Shadows*, having been shortlisted for the 2009 Orange Prize and MWA's Published Fiction category. Robin Yassin-Kassab (another nominee for MWA's Published Fiction category) is an exciting young British Syrian writer, whose first novel, *The Road from Damascus*, was published by Hamish Hamilton to great acclaim in 2008. Multiple award winner Nadeem Aslam is a lyrical chronicler of religious abuses both in his native Pakistan and neighbouring Afghanistan, and in South Asian communities in England.

First known for his short stories, Aamer Hussein has now moved into the production of uncluttered novellas and novels, and his fictional *oeuvre* is especially notable for its international cast of characters, not just from his native Pakistan or adopted nations of Britain and India, but from almost every continent. Leila Aboulela is a writer of joint Sudanese-Egyptian heritage, who currently resides in Doha, but has set her four books in Scotland, London, and Sudan. British Pakistani film-maker, fiction writer, and playwright, Hanif Kureishi, was one of the first writers to chart the experiences of Muslim and mixed-heritage characters in contemporary Britain. Fadia Faqir is a Jordanian writer based in County Durham, whose fiction is a fiery blend of feminism, anti-racism, and literary experimentalism. Tariq Ali is a prolific producer of fiction, non-fiction, and dramas for screen and stage, and his writing is always inflected by his Trotskyite politics, internationalism, and wicked sense of humour. Tahmima Anam is a cosmopolitan Bangladeshi writer living in London, who is two-thirds of the way through writing her pioneering Bengal Trilogy. Zahid Hussain's first novel, *The Curry Mile*, was published by the small independent publisher, Suitcase, and is a streetwise account of young British Pakistanis in Manchester.

All the interviews in this book were conducted through private face-to-face contact, except for Fadia Faqir (whose interview was held in public at Sunderland University's *Islam and Postcolonialism* conference[58]), Leila Aboulela (interviewed over the telephone and by email), and Ahdaf Soueif (by email). Unfortunately, there were many great writers who had to be left out, due to confines of space, time, or availability. As mentioned earlier, Salman Rushdie is the most conspicuous by his absence, but Monica Ali also declined to be interviewed, perhaps unsurprisingly given her eagerness not to be pigeonholed as an 'ethnic', let alone 'Muslim' writer.[59] Qaisra Shahraz, the Pakistan-born and Manchester-resident author of *The Holy Woman* and *Typhoon*, unfortunately did not receive two emailed invitations to interview. Iranian writers are not included, because I was unable to trace Yasmin Crowther,[60] and another of the most interesting UK-based Iranian writers, Shusha Guppy, tragically died in 2008. The Bangladesh-born writer

Manzu Islam is a lecturer at the University of Gloucestershire whose writing is increasing in assurance all the time, and he was not interviewed for this book, but his work will be analysed in the monograph. His latest novel, *Songs of our Swampland*, about the 1971 war and floods in Bangladesh, was only published by Leeds independent publisher Peepal Tree in autumn 2010. Similarly, Nadifa Mohamed published her novel about war in Somalia, *Black Mamba Boy*, towards the end of the fieldwork for this book, and so couldn't be included.[61] Mirza Waheed, who has lived in the UK since 2001, brought out an acclaimed novel about Kashmir just as the book was going to press.[62] Hisham Matar kindly agreed to do an email interview, but had to postpone it because of the recent outbreak of protest and extreme counter-violence in his nation of Libya, so his interview will appear as a separate output. Rukhsana Ahmad, Shahrukh Husain, Almas Khan, and Moni Mohsin are four of the most interesting writers of Pakistani heritage who had to be excluded due to the sheer quantity and quality of those based in the UK. Likewise, the Sudanese-British writer Jamal Mahjoub and Palestinian-British, but Beirut-born Tony Hanania were not interviewed, but are discussed in Geoffrey Nash's searching monograph *The Anglo-Arab Encounter*.[63]

No attempt is made at complete coverage of 'British Muslim writing' in either of my books – this would in any case be impracticable, given the burgeoning amount of high quality fiction being produced by writers of Muslim heritage – but the authors under study are illustrative of recent trends. In their different ways they 'write back' to inimical fictions created about Muslim communities by several leading non-Muslim writers (most famously Martin Amis), and by sections of the print media.[64] Fiction by some writers of Muslim heritage has also caused controversy, so non-Muslims need to thoughtfully scrutinize textual details which, while they are easily passed over by secular readers, may be seen as inflammatory by practising Muslims. There have been incidents in Britain comparable to, though less publicized than, the Rushdie Affair, such as protests over the US screening of Hanif Kureishi's *My Beautiful Laundrette* in 1986. Kureishi explains:

> They weren't complaining that the film was anti-Islamic, but that it was gay. They threatened to blow up the cinema [...] long before the *fatwa*. [...] They just wanted to shout, and I was rather sympathetic. If there aren't any films about Pakistanis, and then a film comes out at the centre of which is a gay Pakistani, I can see how they'd think 'Fuck! This was my chance to be shown as a nice fellow.' (pp. 241–2)

More recently, there have also been demonstrations over the filming of Ali's *Brick Lane* in the Spitalfields area, when it was felt by some members of the Bangladeshi community that she misrepresented them.[65]

While Nadeem Aslam and Hanif Kureishi cite him approvingly, other interviewees display distate for V. S. Naipaul's portrayals of the 'Muslim world' in his 1981 travel book, *Among the Believers*. In this book, Naipaul describes being encouraged to attend prayers in Pakistan soon after the Iranian Revolution:

> 'Stay for our prayers,' [my companion] said. 'It sometimes has an effect on newcomers, seeing us all at prayer.'
>
> But that was what I didn't want to stay for, and was anxious about: the prayers, the sight of a hundred thousand – or was it 200,000? – bowed in unison, in the avoidable desert of Raiwind.[66]

The narrator is reluctant to take part in the massive display of faith because of the apparent threat of conversion, alluded to here in his interlocutor's portentous statement '[i]t sometimes has an effect on newcomers'. Elsewhere in the text, he describes Islam as 'an imperialism as well as a religion',[67] and criticizes the religion's *sharia* law, its alleged tendency towards despotism, and failure to produce anything like a Renaissance in the modern age. From the opening page onwards of Naipaul's later text, *Beyond Belief*, he articulates even more controversial views of Islam, which he describes again as a religion that 'makes imperial demands', but goes further to criticize Muslims as '[p]eople [who] develop fantasies about who and what they are', suggesting that 'in the Islam of converted countries there is an element of neurosis and nihilism'.[68] Abdulrazak Gurnah criticizes these kinds of statements as 'appalling' in his interview in this volume, and in his novel *Desertion* he to some extent satirizes Naipaul through the portrayal of Sundeep, an Indian writer said to have become 'famed for his mockery of Africans and Muslims'.[69] In 2010, Naipaul pulled out of attending the European Literary Parliament in Turkey after a group of Turkish writers protested against his inclusion because of his Islamophobic views.[70] Both Abdulrazak Gurnah and Nadeem Aslam also castigate the Nigerian writer and playwright Wole Soyinka (who has studied and worked in the UK) for Islamophobic remarks in his non-fiction.

I confine my purview to literary fiction for the purpose of this book, but I will also explore popular fiction, auto/biography, poetry, film, and the politics of the publishing industry in the monograph. Of course, literary fiction is something of an elitist form, and when I presented at the Manchester Muslim Writers group, one questioner raised the issue of the creative work that is being done to combat stereotyping of Muslims in other media, such as social networking technologies, blogs, alternative media, graphic art, video sites such as YouTube, and so on. These are on the periphery of my vision; for example, I enjoyed the audacious wit and wordplay of such videos as 'Halal: Is it Meat you're Looking for', a British Muslim parody of Lionel Richie's 'Hello',[71] but I have to confess my lack of expertise in these new media. However, anyone who doubts the legitimacy of researching in the field of literature need only look to the *Satanic Verses* Affair to see the significance. As discussed, since this controversy it has become evident that even such an apparently rarefied form as the postmodernist novel has the potential to polarize street opinion about the position and status of British-based members of this transnational faith group.

This book is entitled *British Muslim Fictions* because it seeks to provoke thought about whether we can or should categorize literature according to religious identity. Some commentators and several of the interviewed writers are uncomfortable with the idea of using religious identity to categorize literature. Other books which discuss Muslim writing, such as those by John Erickson, John C. Hawley, Amin Malak, and Peter Morey and Amina Yaqin[72] deal with a global context, whereas this volume offers in-depth analysis of representations of Muslims in Britain. Additionally, an increasingly complex debate is taking place about what it means to be 'British Muslim'. Is a British Muslim someone who was born in the UK? If so, only three of the writers under study qualify: Hanif Kureishi was born in Kent, Zahid Hussain in Lancashire, and Robin Yassin-Kassab in London. Alternatively, does it include British citizens or residents (most of the writers interviewed have, or have had, a British passport)? Or does it concern Muslim writers who took asylum in Britain? In the post-war on terror world, more even than when critics Suhrke and Kabbani were arguing this,[73] the vast majority of refugees and asylum seekers are either Muslims, or come from Muslim-majority states. Many writers of Muslim heritage including Abdulrazak Gurnah, Tahmima Anam, Robin Yassin-Kassab, Nadeem Aslam, and Kamila Shamsie dramatize issues relating to asylum, migration, and discourses of Otherness in their fiction. One of the most intriguing discoveries in this research was that the writers fall into three categories: the first being the British-born group outlined above. The second and largest group (Fadia Faqir, Ahdaf Soueif, Nadeem Aslam, Abdulrazak Gurnah, Tariq Ali, and Aamer Hussein) comprises writers who arrived in Britain at an impressionable age, in their teens or early twenties. The third group (Kamila Shamsie, Leila Aboulela, Mohsin Hamid, and Tahmima Anam) is somewhat exilic, using Britain as a perhaps temporary base to write their fictions which explore other nations in more detail than Britain, and involve a renegotiation of the writer's relationship with the home country now that he or she is no longer living there. This perhaps should not surprise us, given the fact that writers are often adept at border crossing and tend to be well-travelled, with multiple, well-stamped passports. However, categorization is not nearly so clear-cut as the three group demarcations suggest, as at least two of the British-born writers, Yassin-Kassab and Hussain, have spent long periods of time overseas and are multilingual, while supposed exiles like Anam and Shamsie are routinely included in discussions of a specifically British writing scene.[74] The majority of these writers, therefore, neither has hyphenated identities, nor can be considered émigrés, but writes in liminal positions between West and East.

The term 'British Muslims' is relatively new, and is currently hotly contested by many commentators, in part due to the divisive questions often posed by opinion poll organizations which invite Britons of Muslim heritage to prioritize one component of identity over another. As Anshuman Mondal points out, '[w]ould it not be futile to ask if someone was a woman first and British second or a man if he was husband first and father second?'[75] My title *British Muslim Fictions* is designed to question whether the term 'British Muslim' is itself a mirage, and whether it is possible to talk about fiction in relation to this term. Finally, I want to suggest that representations by many mainstream writers and journalists of such issues (assumed to relate to Muslims) as 'offence', veiling, the 1989 *fatwa*, and the concept of *jihad*, may be viewed as constituting other kinds of fictions. In a 1997 introduction to his *Covering Islam* (1981), Edward Said writes, 'the term "Islam" as it is used today seems to mean one simple thing but in fact is part fiction, part ideological label, part minimal designation of a religion called Islam'.[76] More than a decade later, Robin Yassin-Kassab writes:

I suppose if you can have Black writing and Gay writing and London writing you can have Muslim writing too. The label,

25

like any other, is limiting if it's used as a box, but liberating if we use it as a springboard. The point is, that as Muslims in Britain, many fictions are being written about us. Many are presented as fact. [...] So we should write back.[77]

In this book I explore this issue of whether Muslim literature is a germane label; and, if so, what characterizes this writing; what religious, political, and social methods of 'writing back' it presages. With several respondents I also examine the related topic of whether the marketing category is a constricting 'box' to which Muslim writers are consigned, or an enabling 'springboard' from which they can launch global careers. However, as the examples of Rushdie, Kureishi, Monica Ali, and the more recent case of Sherry Jones's *The Jewel of Medina*[78] indicate, even fiction writers can be criticized for misrepresenting or producing 'inauthentic' accounts of the subjects they portray.

Recurring themes

I will now read across the interviews, drawing together common themes and debates; contextualizing the authors' varied situations; and describing ways in which the interviews contribute to current literary, cultural, and political debates. The book provides important interventions into current debates on postcolonialism, multiculturalism, and Black British writing. By positioning these writers together I do not wish to suggest that writers of Muslim heritage represent a closed group; my aim is rather to showcase varied voices as well as making subtle and important distinctions between them. To some extent, my interviews draw attention to an absence of univocality, indicating that – notwithstanding the attempts in sections of mainstream fiction and the media mentioned earlier to portray Muslims as a monolithic group – these creative writers are highly heterogeneous and sometimes conflicting thinkers. Despite lively differences of opinion, I will argue that certain shared tropes recur in the writing.

Key themes to which writers often return include Muslim Spain, the war on terror, gender, racism, class, language, and representation. The destruction of the syncretic, liberal Muslim civilization of al-Andalus by Christian intolerance is frequently used by writers of Muslim heritage to figure forth the migrant condition and contemporary dispossessions more broadly, such as those in India and Pakistan in 1947, and the current situations in Palestine and Kashmir. Texts by writers of Muslim heritage which explore the cosmopolitanism of Moorish Spain in their work include Tariq Ali's *Shadows of the Pomegranate Tree*, Salman Rushdie's *The Moor's Last Sigh*, and Mahmoud Darwish's and Agha Shahid Ali's 'Eleven Stars Over Andalusia', among others.[79] It is also noticeable that several of the texts discussed, such as Hanif Kureishi's *The Black Album* and Robin Yassin-Kassab's *The Road from Damascus*, explore the apparent dichotomy between 'freedom of expression' and 'fundamentalism' foregrounded in the Rushdie Affair. Additionally, the war on terror was an important turning point in the lives of Muslims in Britain. The war on terror, more than 9/11, pushed people's 'Muslimness', if not 'Islam' to the fore in the ways in which they are identified by others and their self-identity. Violently Islamophobic incidents like that experienced by Fadia Faqir's brother (pp. 64, 70, 72–3), have had devastating impact on some Muslims' safety and health.[80] For writers of Pakistani descent, at least, the war in Afghanistan represents a watershed which has had a devastating impact on Pakistan and its diaspora, and which is discussed in the recent fiction of Kamila Shamsie, Nadeem Aslam, and Feryal Ali Gauhar, among others.[81] Palestine is the wound to which all the Arab writers refer, but is also evoked to varying degrees among the writers of other Muslim heritage. The Gulf Wars have received relatively less attention, in literary fiction at least, but Aamer Hussein and fellow Pakistani writer, Uzma Aslam Khan, are exceptions to this rule.[82] Even in the Arab world, there have been surprisingly few sustained fictionalizations of the Gulf Wars,[83] although in *The Road from Damascus* Robin Yassin-Kassab foreshadows the conflict through his character,

Marwan, who was extensively tortured by Saddam Hussein's regime.

The diversity of Muslims' religion and culture is well represented in the interviews, across nations as well as centuries. Both as a whole, and at specific moments, the writers give strong and learned rebuttals of what Tariq Ali calls the shallow 'belligerati' caricatures of Muslims which currently dominate.[84] The number of references to artistic influences from many different nations, continents, centuries, and forms amongst the interviewees is particularly interesting. This eclecticism seems to form part of the writers' identity concerns, and they not only clarify misconceptions about Muslims in Britain (to be discussed shortly), but also record first-hand information about their experiences, bridging Muslim and non-Muslim culture/identities/religions. Muslims are frequently construed as being the archetypal Other to discourses of cosmopolitanism. Writing before 9/11, for example, Mandaville identifies and censures

> a belief that existing within this seemingly similar and undifferentiated religion were certain innate features that [...] legitimized such activities [as terrorism and anti-Western propaganda]. Islam came to be a registered trademark of illiberalism – the ideational source of countless malignant practices. In sum, when dealing with Islam, labels and stereotypes are the norm; this is by now almost a truism.[85]

Clearly this totalizing view of Islam is misleading and detrimental to the religion and those associated with it. Analysis of the spoken words and literary production of writers of Muslim heritage reveals an entirely countervailing image of pluralism, tolerance, sophistication, and hybridity, which I will analyse in the monograph as 'Muslim cosmopolitanism'.

Since Islamophobia often caricatures gender relations, the very reflective interview discussions of Islam and feminism from both male and female authors here are of great relevance to debates about feminism more broadly. Tariq Ali, for example, describes the long history of women's rights and proto-feminist perspectives within Muslim civilizations, while Fadia Faqir argues in favour of the term 'womanism' and the need for egalitarian movements genuinely to prioritize human rights, outside of Eurocentrism. The writers also have much to say about contemporary as well as more longstanding attitudes towards race, nation, religion, literary form, and (as in the Kureishi interview) popular culture, including film. Racism is a central concern for many of the writers, both colour prejudice and various forms of cultural racism, including Islamophobia. As Tariq Ali convincingly suggests, 'Islam has replaced communism' as a bogeyman (p. 43). Several of the writers compare the growth in Islamophobia with the 1930s' persecution of Jews, and Zahid Hussain appropriates the term 'neo anti-Semitism' to describe the current rise in anti-Muslim sentiment. Class is also an important issue, and Fadia Faqir points out that Britain inflicts a 'double whammy' (p. 68) on its citizens of class hierarchy and racial prejudice. Nadeem Aslam self-identifies as a working-class person, arguing that 'I'm more aware of my class than my race or religion' (p. 151), while Robin Yassin-Kassab phrases it slightly differently as convergence: 'race is also about class' (p. 195). Finally, Hanif Kureishi points to the 2000s' financial collapse as evidence that class has never gone away, even though during the boom years it was possible to forget the primacy of social rank. Another theme is language, whether this is explored through reflections on the mother tongue and multilingualism, the decision to write in English, or linguistic colonialism.

A final recurring image that several writers use concerns them not being able to find people like themselves (from a Muslim background) in the mirror of fiction. For example, Abdulrazak Gurnah argues that until recently Muslims have been excluded from African literature: 'I couldn't find myself in the mirror of fiction' (p. 125). Other writers extend this complaint to different art forms. Nadeem Aslam, for example, describes the first time he went to a gallery and saw paintings of 'people who looked like me; people who read the Qur'an, rather than the Bible' (p. 145).

Hanif Kureishi similarly acknowledges that before *My Beautiful Laundrette* few Pakistanis had appeared in films shown in the West (p. 242). Aamer Hussein observes that in his youth, he 'wanted to see on paper things with which [he] could identify (p. 96), and the title of his first collection, *Mirror to the Sun*, suggests that once art begins to reflect Muslims' and other Others' stories, the effects may be dazzling, even painfully so. Although she does not explicitly use the trope in our interview, Ahdaf Soueif's succinct answers recall the well-known phrase from her collection of essays, *Mezzaterra*, on Muslims 'doing daily double-takes when faced with their reflection in a Western mirror'.[86] Also without explicitly using the image, Fadia Faqir writes of the same phenomenon: 'you fail to recognize the truth of your experience in the Western perception and representation of it'.[87] In her interview, Faqir compares her fiction to broken, mosaic-like mirror-work, which reflects multiple perspectives and refutes an easy cohesive narrative. Taken together, all these writers suggest, firstly, and in parallel with Charles Taylor's identification of the 'politics of (mis)recognition', that 'a person can suffer real damage, real distortion, if the people or society around them mirror back to them a confining or demeaning or contemptible picture of themselves.'[88] Secondly, and more positively, these writers imply that fiction should hold up a mirror to the times and societies it sets out to describe. However, on finding that Muslims tended not to be reflected in literature, many of the texts discussed here act as magnifying glasses, concentrating the light and heat being produced by under-represented communities.

Pedagogical possibilities

I turn now to the relevance of this research to pedagogical practice. Through my interviews, encounters, and, in some cases, developing friendships with writers from Muslim backgrounds, I became determined to communicate the quality and diversity of this emerging canon. In addition to disseminating the research through my undergraduate and postgraduate teaching, in 2010 I was involved in organizing creative writing workshops with Year 9 pupils in Leeds. These were taught by acclaimed South Asian, Muslim-heritage novelists and poets, resident in the north of England, several of whom were also interviewed. They are John Siddique, born in 1960s Rochdale to an Irish Catholic mother and an Indian Muslim father, who has written four volumes of poetry;[89] Zahid Hussain, the interviewee in Chapter 13 of this volume;[90] Shameam Akhtar, winner of MWA's Best Poetry Award in 2008 and 2009; and Nasser S. Hussain, the British-born and Ontario-raised poet, academic, and teacher.

The project was particularly aimed at Muslim-heritage secondary school pupils, but was of course inclusive of people of all faiths and none. Muslims as a demographic group have tended to be discouraged from pursuing an arts education, but are expected to be the fastest growing sector of the book-buying public over the coming years (data available from MWA). Pakistanis are Britain's second largest BME (Black and Minority Ethnic) group after Indians, comprising 16.1 per cent of the total minority population, and Bangladeshis come sixth at 6.1 per cent[91] with both groups being largely Muslim. Furthermore, 43 per cent of England's 1.6 million-strong Muslim population traces heritage to Pakistan alone, with most having been born in the UK.[92] Despite their large numbers and their established history of settlement in Britain, Pakistani- and Bangladeshi-heritage children under-attain across Key Stages 1–4, notwithstanding their largely positive attitudes towards education, with girls outperforming boys, but still achieving less than other females nationally.[93] These inequalities seem to be connected to class and deprivation rather than cultural, family, or religious influences, although further research in this area is needed. English and literacy are particular areas of concern in the curriculum for pupils of Bangladeshi and Pakistani heritage, so the workshops are designed to encourage students' performance in these subjects, but in a fun and imaginative way. Pakistani and Bangladeshi students (along with Black Other), are also under-represented at universities when compared to the broader 16–24-year-old population, and '[i]n aggregate, [...] are better represented [...] in certain subjects (the more vocationally/professionally orientated ones such as medicine, IT, business studies and law)'.[94] As such, another aim was to embed a widening participation agenda in the project.

The initiative was particularly aimed at introducing pupils from British Muslim, other religious, and secular backgrounds to an excellent and growing canon of literature, and we introduced young people to role models who have helped them develop their talents and raise aspirations. At the same time, we hoped to increase the understanding, knowledge, and skills of the wider group of teachers, parents, and community leaders to meet the needs and aspirations of the local Muslim community. My research and the creative writing project thus coexist symbiotically, with the research informing the practice-based workshops and vice versa, in ways that I hope will be mutually beneficial for the research community and the wider populace.

1
Tariq Ali

Born in pre-Partition Lahore, Tariq Ali describes himself as a 'red-diaper baby'[1]: the son of Marxist parents, but from powerful Punjabi feudal stock. Politically active from a young age, he was encouraged to leave Pakistan by an uncle who was head of military intelligence, on account of his defying martial law and demonstrating on the streets against the killing of Patrice Lubumba in Congo, and later his unremitting hostility to the military dictatorship of Ayub Khan.[2] He went to Exeter College, Oxford, in 1963, where he became president of the Oxford Union, invited controversial figures such as Malcolm X to speak, and organized teach-ins against the Vietnam War.[3] To his disappointment, he was awarded a Third in Politics, Philosophy, and Economics, rather than failing outright, after deliberately courting failure by writing several inflammatory finals exam answers linking every question to the Vietnam War. Rather than enjoying the 'Swinging London' of fashion and music when he moved there, Ali's 1960s were characterized by activism and travel to the world's hotspots, including Prague, Hanoi, Bolivia, and Pakistan. Famously the inspiration for the Rolling Stones song 'Street Fighting Man', Ali also co-interviewed the Stones' arch-rival Beatle, John Lennon.[4] Between 1969 and 1971, he was instrumental in persuading Lennon openly to support the Left, seeing in the singer's popularity with both students and workers possibilities for cementing solidarity.

In 1968, year of revolutions, he helped relaunch and became an editor of the nineteenth-century radical cultural and political broadsheet, *The Black Dwarf*. Following a schism between him and other *Black Dwarf* intellectuals including Adrian Mitchell and Clive Goodwin over his sympathetic stance to the International Marxist Group (IMG), Ali left to become first editor of *The Red Mole* (1972–3). He then became, and continues to be, an editor and adviser to the *New Left Review*, and its publishing house, Verso. The key to understanding Ali's Trotskyism lies in his reading of his intellectual mentor, Isaac Deutscher, whose analysis of the USSR, acerbic critique of Israel,[5] and three-volume biography of Leon Trotsky proved highly influential.

After the fall of the Berlin Wall, Ali moved away from his role as a historian and political activist/commentator and became increasingly productive in television, film, theatre, and fiction. In the last few decades, while still believing in Marxist politics, which Ali argues were firmly relegated to 'the family vaults' after communism's collapse,[6] he seems to come close to recognition that communism shared certain features with religion, but that it failed to take into account the centrality of God in many people's worldview.[7] Nonetheless he continues to support communist and socialist governments, most notably Hugo Chavez's Venezuela.[8] From 1984 to 1998, his and Darcus Howe's Bandung Productions made programmes such as *The Bandung File* and *Rear Window* for Channel 4, presenting a hybrid view of world culture. With Howard Brenton, he wrote three plays, *Iranian Nights* (1989), which responded to the *fatwa* against

Salman Rushdie, and a theatrical work dealing with the overturning of Gorbachev, *Moscow Gold* (1990). Soon after Tony Blair's election as prime minister, Brenton and Ali penned *Ugly Rumours* (1998), a satirical unmasking of New Labour while it was still the toast of media pundits. Ali went on to write *The Illustrious Corpse*, another assault on New Labour values.[9]

Ali was close friends with Edward Said from 1972 until the latter's death from leukaemia in 2003. Lamenting Foucault's influence on Said's work, Ali argues that '[h]is quarrel with the political and cultural establishments of the West and the official Arab world is the most important feature of Said's biography'.[10] Ali suggests that the Six-Day War in 1967 marked an important watershed in Said's consciousness as an Arab and a Palestinian, and that his writings on Palestine politicized his view of literature and empire, moving him away from the earlier influence of poststructuralism. Although already very politically active, Ali too was affected by the 1967 conflict, travelling to Palestinian refugee camps in Jordan and finding himself shocked by the suffering there (he has continued to speak out on Palestine up to and beyond the murderous Israeli attacks on the Gaza flotilla in 2010, and writes 'Israel is the only remaining colonial power – on the nineteenth-century model – in the world today'[11]).

In the 1990s, he began his 'Fall of Communism Trilogy' and 'Islam Quintet' of novels (the latter was completed in 2010). He only returned to non-fiction after the turning points of the first Gulf War, the Yugoslav War, and finally 9/11, when he began again to write commentaries in order to counter what he sees as the West's increasingly virulent stereotypes of the 'Muslim world'. Over the years, he has written three books on Pakistan alone, which correctly predicted the break up of the country's two wings into Pakistan and Bangladesh in the 1971 civil war, and described the increasing volatility of the nation's four unevenly developed provinces.[12] In 2002, he published his non-fictional masterpiece, *The Clash of Fundamentalisms*, which became a book read by people seeking to acquire a post-9/11 perspective on geopolitics that was neither imperial nor Islamist.

Now he divides his time between fiction and non-fiction, has just finished what he describes as 'a short, sharp book on Barack Obama'[13] (whom he also fictionally renders as a cancer[14]), and is planning another fiction set in seventeenth-century England.

Brought up as an atheist, but sent against his will as a teenager for tutorials in Islamic history to enable him to argue against religion,[15] Ali has become one of the predominant thinkers on the place of Islam in current geopolitics, declaring his aim

> to write about Islam, its founding myths, its origin, its history, its culture, its riches, its divisions. Why has it not undergone a Reformation? How did it become so petrified? Should Koranic interpretations be the exclusive prerogative of religious scholars? And what do Islamist politics represent today?[16]

He compares early Islam to radical political parties, even Bolshevism; hails Mohammed as a 'visionary political leader'; and describes Mohammed's controversial youngest wife, Aisha (Ali's daughter with his partner Susan Watkins has the same name), as a powerful proto-feminist leader.[17] His exploration of such issues is particularly prescient given that he began writing the Islam Quintet in 1992, long before such discussions became commonplace. Ali discusses the rich multiplicity of the House of Islam, writing, '[i]n considering the meanings of Islam, Western analysts would do well to recognize it for what it is: a world religion that is in no sense monolithic. Both as a religion and a culture it encompasses numerous local traditions.'[18] While demonstrating sympathy to syncretic Sufism, vulnerable 'born-again Muslim[s]' such as *Night of the Golden Butterfly*'s Neelam,[19] and to previously secular Muslims propelled towards Islam by 'Euro-crassness',[20] he is nonetheless highly critical of Islamism and many men of religion. For example, he describes 'mullahs' as one of the four curses of Pakistan, along with 'America, the military and corruption',[21] and repeatedly satirizes Pakistan's Jamaat-i-Islami. He is also alert to longstanding divisions and lack of unity in the *dar al-Islam*, one of the main reasons why medieval Spain and Sicily were lost. He is non-partisan in his acerbic criticism of comparable Evangelical, Catholic, Orientalist, and capitalist fundamentalisms[22] and the fact that America sponsored Islamists during the Cold War.

Ali is a non-fiction and creative writer of great worth, but his novels to date have generated relatively little sustained criticism. Rather than attempting a comprehensive survey of his vast corpus,[23] the rest of this introduction represents an attempt to fill the critical gap on his Islam Quintet and its historical and geographical contexts. These non-sequential five novels are connected by theme rather than character and, with the exception of the second novel *The Book of Saladin* (which ends with Salah al-Din's spectacular, though shortlived triumph of reconquering al-Quds or Jerusalem), they are all narratives of Muslim societies in decline. His writing is rich with literary allusions to Arab writers including Naguib Mahfouz, Nizar Qabbani, and Abdelrahman Munif; to Western literature from Stendhal and Dostoevsky to Shakespeare and Greek mythology; and to Urdu writers such as Habib Jalib, Faiz Ahmed Faiz, and Allama Iqbal, whose interest in '[p]olitics as love[,] [l]ove as politics' he approvingly evokes.[24] Yet, perhaps the greatest value of the novels lies in the implicit comparison Ali makes between contemporary stereotypes of a supposedly moribund 'Muslim world' and his nuanced representations of specific sophisticated Muslim societies. As Madeline Clements observes, Ali's fiction is suffused with 'contemporary "resonance"'.[25] Ali makes a strong argument for bringing reason, *ijtihad*, and interpretation into secular and Islamist fundamentalist thinking about Islam. He also draws attention to early Islamic civilizations' progressive views on questions relating to women, sexuality, and good living, suggesting that the Muslim dissent, scepticism, and even heresy of earlier centuries has been lost.

Set in fifteenth-century Spain, *Shadows of the Pomegranate Tree* (1992) centres on the repercussions of Queen Isabella's adviser, Archbishop Ximenes's, notorious burning of Moorish books, which 'condemn[ed] a unique chronicle of a whole way of life to the obscurity of the flames'.[26] In the aftermath of Granada's fall, many Moors are forcibly expelled or converted in the rapacious Christian Reconquest. The Banu Hudayl family tries to stay on as Muslims, although clan member Zuhayr bin Umar finds that Allah fails to protect him when he fights back.[27] Zuhayr's younger brother, Yazid, is given a chess set, the pieces of which caricature Spanish historical figures (including Ferdinand and Isabella) in monstrous forms more commonly found in Orientalist writings of the period. The novel can be interpreted as an extended elegy for the extirpation of the tolerant, intensely hybrid societies of al-Andalus, with their 'interfaith marriages, cultural intermingling and family links',[28] by the ruthless Catholic purity of *conquistadors* such as Hernán Cortés, with whose repression of Aztecs in South America the novel ends.

In *The Book of Saladin* (1998), Ali provides a counter-history of the Crusades from Muslim perspectives, prefiguring George W. Bush's 'Crusader' rhetoric by several years. In his reading, the Kurdish warrior Salah al-Din (lambasted as Saladin in Christian annals) is portrayed as a complete man: brave, some-times indecisive, selectively abstemious (he is the butt of many jokes for his predilection for bean stew), but a womanizer. In contrast, Christians are represented as treacherous, idolatrous barbarians, and England's much-lauded Richard I is known as 'Richard the Lion-Arse' to Salah al-Din's revisionist foot-soldiers. The novel's climax, as mentioned earlier, comes in the reclamation of al-Quds/Jerusalem, which is interpreted as a dazzling triumph for the Believers. Unspoken comparisons with recent history are invited, as when local Jews are portrayed as preferring Muslim rule to Christian. This novel develops the bawdy, visceral humour evinced in *Shadows of the Pomegranate Tree*, and two of its most successful characters are Halima and Jamila, intelligent, sceptical women who meet and begin a sexual relationship in Salah al-Din's harem.

The Stone Woman (2000) provides an account of the decline of the Ottoman Empire, which is mirrored in the decline of a family. Set in Turkey in 1899 though with a few flashbacks, the novel depicts Islam as a secular religion: a cultural system rather than a spiritual belief system. The pagan statue, the Stone Woman of the title, is in effect the recipient of prayers or confession, and Allah is seldom mentioned. Greater emphasis is given to the tolerant Sufism of wine-drinking, relative gender equality, dervishes, and the state of ecstasy than to orthodox Islam, and as a youngster Iskander is particularly influenced by Sufism. In Iskander's library, works from the French canon sit easily alongside Ottoman books, and Michelangelo is compared to a Sufi: 'the Italian who should have built us a bridge across the Bosporus'.[29] A Committee forms with the aim of overthrowing the Sultan, and its more radical members, Selim and Iskander, give praise to the rationalist French philosopher, Auguste Comte, rather than Allah. The novel concludes with a portentous passage in which Iskander's daughter Nilofer watches the full moon set in the West and the new day rising over the East.[30]

In *Under Crescent and Cross*, Mark Cohen demonstrates that the medieval Arab-Islamic world was far more religiously tolerant than Christendom, but also cautions against what he calls the 'interfaith utopia hypothesis'.[31] In his Quintet, Ali highlights the cruelty of Christian rulers from the Crusades to the present, while never idealizing the Muslim societies he describes. In *A Sultan in Palermo* (2005), he reverses the Orientalizing gaze when Idrisi declares of an imagined Muslim conquest of England, 'We would have shone the light of learning on them.'[32] As the violence implicit in this quotation suggests, Ali draws attention to bombast, divisions, and brutality in Muslim Sicily at this time. The novel starts with echoes of Edward Said's *Beginnings*,[33] but from a religious perspective, as the protagonist wonders whether or not to begin his story by conventionally evoking Allah, or with the scientific ideas that preoccupy him. This protagonist, the Sicilian geographer Muhammad Idrisi, allows Ali to engage in a remapping of cartographies of Europe, and Philip argues that maps of the mind are more important than the science of geography.[34] Although Palermo and its Sultan at the time of the novel's setting are nominally Christian, and al-Andalus is Muslim, hybridity and interchange between Christian–Muslim worlds are regularly emphasized.

Night of the Golden Butterfly brings the Quintet up to date, providing a post-9/11 narrative familiar to readers of recent fictions by writers of Muslim heritage. The novel contains many semi-autobiographical details about life in Pakistan (here rendered as 'Fatherland'), which are also explored in Ali's non-fiction book *The Duel* (2008), including a trip across a bridge built by Alexander the Great, the convivial café culture of 1960s Lahore, and a vacuous swimwear model strutting the catwalk during the uprising of 1968. Yet the novel also represents many fascinating female characters: Jindié, the titular Chinese Punjabi butterfly; Zaynab, a woman married off to the Qur'an in order to give her inherited land and property to the family's patriarchs;[35] and the tragic but foolish Khalida 'Naughty' Lateef. Through the latter's transformation into the playfully named 'Yasmine Auratpasand',[36] Ali suggests that there is currently a high demand in the West, particularly Israel, for autobiographies by Muslim women, telling of the 'horrors' they suffer.[37] As Clements rightly points out, despite some sharp political observations, the novel is somewhat lacking in character development and central narrative focus.[38] However, the conclusion brings together characters from the earlier novels, 'the great scholars of al-Andalus and the Muslim world',[39] Ibn Maymun (Maimonides), Ibn Rushd (Averroës), and Muhammed Idris. These thinkers meet again in Plato's hyperreal painting triptych, alongside other influential figures that lurk behind the novels, including James Joyce's Stephen Dedalus, and South Asian poets, Sahir Ludhianvi, Waris Shah, Bulleh Shah, and Shah Hussain. The triptych, with its three panels, 'Fatherland', 'The Obscure Soul of the World', and 'My Life', is a satisfying artistic representation of Ali's three major themes: the ongoing destruction of Pakistan, world politics, and auto/biography.

CC: In an email to me, you responded to this book's structuring principle of interviewing writers of Muslim heritage

by saying that you have always resisted being stereotyped as anything but cosmopolitan. Your fiction celebrates the cosmopolitanism of cities, especially Lahore, although you argue that the city became a 'monocultural metropolis'[40] after Partition. Yet cosmopolitanism can imply an elitist conversance with the world of the frequent flyer, so to what extent does the word accurately describe you?

TA: It describes me in the sense that until recently, identity has never played any part in my life. My identity has essentially been formed by my politics, which are Marxist and internationalist. I have never been too sympathetic to nationalism except for Arab nationalism in a particular context. If people asked me about my identity when identity became huge in the academy and in culture (with New Labour especially playing on it), I described myself as a 'rooted cosmopolitan'. By this I mean that I don't privilege the country, or even the culture, in which I grew up, as being special, or *ipso facto* better than others. For me, seeing an incredibly beautiful piece of architecture, which happens to be a mosque, creates strong emotions, but so does a wonderful church or synagogue. I once saw a fifteenth-century synagogue in Cochin, India, built when the Jews were fleeing Spain. The Maharajah of Travancore-Cochin had given them a *firman* of land, which belonged to them in perpetuity. It was wonderful to see tiles on the floor of that synagogue which had been imported from fifteenth- or sixteenth-century Canton. That's what I mean when I say that I am a cosmopolitan.

Curiously, the more I write about the history and culture of Islam, the more I find that it is a very cosmopolitan religion. It's astonishing to think that by the time Mohammed died, the religion had already spread to China and the Atlantic coast. Islam, as a culture and a religion, learnt from the ancient and mainly written cultures which it encountered. Islam grew out of an oral culture, and met ancient civilizations, such as Persia, China, and India. When the Muslims arrived at the African coast, they found that civilizations had existed there for a long time, in Timbuktu and Senegal. This is why I don't think it's possible to describe Islam as one big blob. There are lots of different elements within Islam: Senegal and Indonesia are entirely distinct from each other. The dominant image people have of Islam is the Middle East and Saudi Arabia, because that's where the riches are, but this is misleading. Islam has always been cosmopolitan in its outlook, picking things up and reusing them. During the whole period of Islam in Europe, Muslim scholars translated ancient Greek texts and kept them in circulation, indirectly helping to fuel the European Renaissance. That is the sense in which I feel cosmopolitan, and not in this bogus sense of cosmopolitan-*ism*, which I find to be nothing more than a vehicle to promote the current world order. That is elite cosmopolitanism, and it's fake, because when it comes down to it, the United States with its EU poodle dominates that 'cosmopolitanism'. The word I prefer to 'cosmopolitan' is the traditional, old-fashioned word 'internationalist', which indicates that our cause is universal. Today more than ever, the things we are fighting for are things that are needed in most parts of the world. It's strange how a word like 'cosmopolitan' gets taken up, and I don't like the way it can be used as a hammer, to justify military interventions, or so-called humanitarian interventions. In 1999, for instance, NATO argued, 'you can't be opposed to the bombing of Belgrade because we're defending cosmopolitanism'. That's total nonsense; they were defending Western strategic interests.

CC: You make a distinction between Islam as a civilization, which you admire for its synthesis of cultures, and as a religion. Could you expand on your attitude towards Islam?
TA: Every religion, including Islam, has strong civilizational aspects to it. I regret that people conflate al-Qa'ida with Islam, and recently, over 50 per cent of people questioned in a British survey, said that the word 'Islam' conjured up images of terrorism. This is a tribute to Western media networks, which have worked hard to promote this connection and justify Western

occupation of Muslim lands, such as Iraq, Somalia, Afghanistan, and no doubt others. Islam has replaced communism as the enemy in people's minds. As readers of my work know, I have no time for small bands of terrorists, whether they're Muslims or anyone else. However, it's inaccurate to say that they are crazy people, unrelated to contemporary politics, who have fallen from the sky. These are people who believe that their world is being damaged and occupied by the West; terrorism is their revenge. I call them Islamo-anarchists, because there was a strong tradition in one brand of anarchism which believed that the way to make an impact was to kill people, blow up buildings and go for heads of state. Some Islamist groups have taken up this way of thinking in their propaganda for *tawheed*, what anarchists called the propaganda of the deed, but others haven't. I tire of pointing out to the Western media that Islam is like a rainbow, containing many different colours. It would be odd if there weren't any Muslim terrorists, and there are. Then you have Muslim Brotherhood types, who are moderate Muslims.[41] Additionally, you have many people from within Muslim culture who are secular, atheists, or other types of non-believers, but they are never talked about.

I don't accept this way of looking at Islam exclusively through the prism of the current need of the West to vilify Islam. Islamophobia is rampant in Europe and not exclusively on its far-right fringes but in the mainstream, as is borne out by these absurd opinion poll responses. I remember speaking at a litera-ture festival in Italy a few years ago, and a genuinely frightened old lady put up her hand and said, 'You sound very reasonable to me, but many Muslims aren't.' I pointed out that there are many Christians and Jews who are not reasonable either. She replied, 'No, but what should we do when there's an honour killing in Italy?' I told her to condemn it, as you would any-where else, and pointed out that honour killings are not unknown to Catholicism: Gabriel García Márquez wrote a whole novel about it.[42] She shut up, but it's irritating having to answer such simplistic questions so often.

CC: **You gave a speech on Islamophobia recently, an extract from which *The Socialist Worker* published,[43] and you argue that it is a relatively recent construct, which can be unmade. Do you trace the roots of Islamophobia back to the first Gulf War?**

TA: Very much so. Earlier, during the Cold War of 1950–91, the United States and the West decided to use reactionary Islamist organizations to fight communism on a global scale. They used the Saudis to send money via Wahhabi networks, which were set up everywhere. In Iran, they used local Islamists to create the necessary atmosphere to allow them brutally to topple a democratic government in 1953. This was a central strategy in the Cold War, and if you look at US Political Science textbooks from the 1950s and 1960s, they're fervently pro-Islam for that reason. Indonesia was the most shocking example, as it was the world's largest Muslim state, where they used Islamist vigilantes to wipe out over a million communists. They created this huge vacuum in the Middle East, Indonesia, even parts of Pakistan. Then they felt surprised and betrayed when the people they were backing turned on them. Yet, all these terrorist groups mirror their stance, saying things like, 'Once we were fighting a common enemy with the United States, but now they've betrayed us.'

You have postmodernist Muslims, like Tariq Ramadan, who isn't a bad guy personally, but what he really believes in I don't know, because his writing deliberately uses obscurantist postmodernist concepts to explain Islam to non-Muslims. When you are amongst unbelievers, it is considered acceptable by Islam to put on a mask, but I wish Ramadan wasn't constantly engaging in obfuscation. For example, he was once debating on French television, and some nutty group in Nigeria had decided to implement *sharia* law which, they said, meant chopping off hands of thieves and stoning people for adultery. Sarkozy, who was then Interior Minister, asked about Ramadan's attitude to that, and instead of saying it was a disgrace he said that he would ask them to impose a moratorium.[44] People get irritated by this because, as a believer, he should have said that these interpretations were totally unacceptable under *sharia*'s laws, or giving several other possible answers.

There are different Islamist political parties, which in some cases promise social justice, and because there are no other alternatives people turn to them, as with Hamas in Palestine which won because it was not seen as the den of collaboration and corruption that was the PLO. Then we have the Turkish Islamists, who are in power and are NATO's and the US's favourite Islamists, who, despite some disagreements, recognize and work with Israel and conduct joint military manoeuvres. The point I'm making is that religious identity isn't enough to identify people or movements. Neither an individual nor a party has a simple identity. The complexities have to be understood. When women, fed up with Islamophobic rantings and bans, especially in France and Turkey, decide to wear *hijab* to be oppositional: personally, I would advise them not to, but I defend their right to do so. I also denounce the imposition of the *hijab* in countries like Iran and Saudi Arabia, because the state has no right to tell people how they should dress, for God's sake.

CC: Your term 'the belligerati',[45] is used to describe writers who play on Islamophobic stereotypes, such as Martin Amis, John Updike, and Salman Rushdie. It seems that to make your mark as a hard-hitting novelist these days, you have to describe an Islamist terrorist. Does Rushdie make an appearance in *Night of the Golden Butterfly* as the 'uncongenial and bloated novelist, permanently high on his own fame or shame'?[46]

TA: A number of people have asked me that, but it's a novel and all the characters are composites. I don't like to say that it is based on Rushdie, and it's only a tiny, rather stereotyped character. People have also asked if Naughty Lateef is based on Ayaan Hirsi Ali. She isn't, because Naughty is quite a sympathetic character in many ways, unlike cynical Hirsi Ali, who is desperate to be used, and who now says that all Muslims in Europe should be forcibly converted to Christianity.[47] When Ayaan Hirsi Ali and Rushdie pose together for photographs, it says something, because she is not very bright and he used to be. It's sad when you see people like him going downhill. Becoming a celebrity is like a drug for him, and it's affected his literature. He used to be a very good novelist, but hasn't written a decent novel for years, and I don't know whether he ever will again. In *The Protocol of the Elders of Sodom*, there's a 'Postscript' on Rushdie, in which I explain why he 'was no longer the same person' or as good a writer after the Affair.[48]

You asked about the term 'belligerati', that I first used to denote the friends of Christopher Hitchens, whose decision to turn his coat and boast about becoming a supporter and adviser to Bush and Wolfowitz, influenced some who took Hitchens as a political guru. Amis doesn't know the first thing about politics, but he was prepared to be a mouthpiece. He didn't support the Iraq war, it has to be said, but his Islamophobia is extremely pronounced. When you hear people talk like that, you can understand very easily what happened to Europe in the 1920s and 30s, because it's exactly the same mentality. Lots of people in France, the rest of Europe, even Britain, used to ask if fascism was such a big problem, since it was hurting Jews, who were the Other. Islamophobia today is similar, with middle-class people endlessly competing at dinner parties about who lives near the worst Muslims. Yet Amis's mistake was to come out publicly and say that he wouldn't care a damn if every Muslim was strip-searched and had their fingerprints taken.

CC: He was a bit cleverer than that, because he framed it extradiegetically: 'There's a definite urge – don't you have it? – to say, "The Muslim community will have to suffer until it gets its house in order"…'[49]
TA: Exactly. That is very similar to anti-Semitism. I have never been able to read Amis, but people who admire him should be completely shocked by his saying such things.

CC: Your fiction displays great fondness and knowledge of Urdu poetry.
TA: Poetry played a big part in the culture I grew up with, as it was recited at the drop of a hat in Lahori cafés, public poetry

readings, and private chats. The reciting of verse, usually from a famous subcontinental poet, such as Allama Iqbal and Faiz Ahmed Faiz, was part of that Muslim culture which had little to do with religion. Lesser-known poets also shaped one's youth, such as Sahir Ludhianvi, who wrote a poem 'Taj Mahal', in which a lover proposes a clandestine meeting outside the Taj. This little poem is a brilliant, Brechtian reproach to her for suggesting this meeting-place, and the poet basically says, 'A great emperor, using his wealth as a crutch, built this mausoleum for his wife, but what has it to do with the love of us poor?' The poem asks how many died building the Taj, and begs the beloved, '[f]ind for me another place for rendez-vous'.[50]

CC: Both *The Book of Saladin* and *Night of the Golden Butterfly* contain the trope of a scribe writing a biography. You have yourself acted as an often highly critical biographer.[51] Several of your characters condemn hagiography, and in *Golden Butterfly*, Dara declares, '[I]n writing about [Plato] I would, of necessity, have to resuscitate the lives of others [...] [H]e did not and could not have then existed on his own.'[52] Is yours a communitarian view of biography?
TA: In order to understand the story of one person's life, you need multiple stories and voices like guests at a dinner table. In *The Book of Saladin*, when the Jewish scribe is requested to write Salah al-Din's history, he agrees, but with the audacious condition that he is also allowed to talk to other people.[53] The scribe is successful because he doesn't only portray Salah al-Din from his own point of view, but also from the perspective of his life-long servants, wives, and enemies. This is the method to employ in writing biographies, whether fictional or actual, otherwise they become useless and banal. Within the Islamic tradition, and every other culture, there are many awful hagiographies, consisting only of blind praise and eulogies in the most flowery language. In Pakistan, we call such writers *darbaris*, or courtiers. We must break this tradition of praising the master or mistress with what they want to hear, so that's why I strongly

47

insist on this method, as do many others. The other side of this coin is, of course, an empty narcissism.

CC: You seem to be pushing against the individualistic autobiographies of 'Naughty' Lateef, and against the trend you mentioned earlier of memoirs about apparently oppressed Muslim women.

TA: I'm challenging stereotypes about Muslim women, because when Naughty is murdered, most people believe that the culprits are fundamentalists, when in fact it's her relatively modern husband and sons who killed her, for money.[54] When I was doing a book tour for *Saladin*, an angry American lady said, 'I'm not saying I don't like your book, but you present Muslim women as if they were West Coast feminists, when we all know Muslim women are oppressed.' I responded that Muslim women may not have the same rights that men have. Women in the West did not have the vote until the twentieth century, and were heavily dependent on their husband and denied legal rights, but they struggled and won. In many parts of the Muslim world today, women struggle, but Muslim women have been asserting feminist arguments since the eleventh century. The woman argued that I was fictionalizing, and I agreed. However, I illustrated that my fiction was based on truths by reading some of Valada's poetry, written in Islamic Spain in the tenth century. She was stunned to learn that it was written by a woman, and so were a few bearded Muslim gents also present.

CC: I enjoyed *The Book of Saladin*'s narration of the Crusades from a Muslim perspective. In this novel and in *Shadows of the Pomegranate Tree*, you demonstrate that the fanatics who were destroying books in the medieval period tended to be Christians, although this is a phenomenon now usually associated with the post-Rushdie Affair Muslim world.

TA: I was also trying to show young Muslims here that burning books is deeply shocking and unproductive, and that Islamic culture has suffered heavily from books being burned. I argued with the mullahs at a public debate in Edinburgh at the time of *The Satanic Verses* Affair. None of them had read the novel, so I said, 'For your own benefit, just read it, before you decide to hate it.' I later ran into some of them, who argued that now Rushdie had backed the war on Afghanistan and made numerous pro-Western remarks, they had been proven right. I said no, threatening to kill authors or burning books is never right.

CC: You speak out powerfully about recent erosion of civil liberties in Britain, writing, '[m]y own politics are totally removed from those of the prisoners [Muslims detained in Belmarsh] – or of the more moderate versions of Islamism cultivated by Blair – but that is irrelevant. What we have is a gross violation of civil liberties: torture and imprisonment without trial.'[55] Do you have any optimism about the British Conservative-Liberal coalition government's recent announcement that they'll curb police stop-and-search powers introduced under New Labour?

TA: I don't have much confidence in the Con–Dems' announcement that they will curb police stop-and-search powers, but if they do it, I'll be very pleased. Just because they are Tories, it's foolish not to recognize that they are doing certain things better than New Labour. The fact that they are not going for identity cards and say they will reduce the constant surveillance, is positive. And yet, I wonder how deep it goes, and whether it will make a difference, or if it's part of cost-cutting, rather than civil liberties. Certainly, on civil liberty issues, this coalition is marginally better than the New Labour gang and many people live in that margin, but let's judge them by what they do rather than what they say. Neo-cons like David Goodhart of *Prospect* supported New Labour, pleading with them to become a proper nationalist party and come down harder on immigration.[56] These are the same people who have been bashing Islam non-stop. New Labour created an unpleasant undercurrent to show that they were just as tough as Thatcher, and finally ended up believing their own nonsense. Now they are confronted with a Tory–Lib coalition which, on some issues, promises to be on the left of them, like Ken Clarke denouncing the Build-More-Prisons culture of New Labour. The latter have a choice either to admit the coalition is right, or to denounce them and become even more entrenched in their securitization position. If David Miliband is elected leader it will be Blairism as usual. A great pity that New Labour was not destroyed at the polls, so that they were forced to rethink a few things, such as wars and neo-liberalism.

CC: You were probably the first English-language novelist to explore the theme of Muslim Spain, in *Shadows of the Pomegranate Tree* (1992). How do you account for the recent preoccupation with al-Andalus among writers of Muslim heritage?

TA: I can't account for the others, but for me it was very simple. During the first Gulf War, I was angered by a so-called expert on BBC television legitimizing the war by saying that the Arabs were a people without a political culture. My response, as someone who had never been interested in religion of any sort, was to research what European Islam was, and explain why and how it was defeated. Islam was forced out of the European continent by bloodshed, torture, killings, and forced conversions. Around the same time, I made a related documentary called 'Islam in Spain: The Final Solution' for our Channel 4 programme, *Rear Window*, and travelled around Spain for the first time, not having gone throughout the Franco years when we boycotted it. Seeing these old monuments that had survived was incredible, and I began to imagine, over the weeks I spent there, what life must have been like. I recognized that feeling from Lahore, where my parents would point out places where people with Hindu or Sikh names used to live. While travelling in southern Spain, *Shadows of the Pomegranate Tree* emerged, with the aim of reconstructing the lives of people in the last days of that civilization. I learnt a great deal by reading and talking to people. I met an Egyptian writer, Radwa Ashour, who had written a novel about it,[57] and some poetry already existed. Rushdie's *The Moor's Last Sigh* came out afterwards, so he got in on the act. Those were my motives and I'm really glad I wrote it.

As for *A Sultan in Palermo*, I got a call from an Italian friend who said, 'Are you going to forget Sicily altogether?' Unlike Spain, on which there is a lot of literature, there's virtually nothing on Sicily, and yet the island is rich in Arab culture. If you read Guiseppe Tomasi di Lampedusa's *The Leopard*, one of my favourite novels of all time, there is not a single reference in it to Islam, and Leonardo Sciascia's short stories are wonderful, but contain no references to that past.[58] That is how *The Sultan of Palermo* emerged later, as an act of recovery for this lost civilization. The problem with researching Sicily is that there are no monuments left, although if you travel to some parts of the island, you see that the Normans used Sicilian-Arab architects. For about a hundred years, most of the Norman period, Arabic was the language in which Sicilians learnt mathematics, algebra, logic, astronomy, and, when they were presiding over their Arab friends, they dressed in Arab robes.

I didn't write *Shadows of the Pomegranate Tree* or *A Sultan in Palermo* out of empty nostalgia, of which there is too much in the world, nor sentimentality, but to recover a history lost and rarely talked about. At that time, Spain had hardly examined this aspect of its past, but now Andalusia is a hot topic. A friend of mine in Granada created an amazing exhibition, using a map which lights up to show that Islamic culture was all over the peninsula, not just in the south, as is the accepted view. When *Shadows of the Pomegranate Tree*, which isn't by any means my favourite, was first published in Spanish and it was awarded the Castro Prize for best foreign language fiction, it was moving when people in Spain would whisper, 'We were hardly taught anything in school about this.'

CC: You are a great chronicler of Muslim and other cosmopolitan cities, such as London, Lahore, Cordoba, Paris, Palermo, and Basra. *The Book of Saladin* is even constructed

around a tripartite city structure, of Cairo, Damascus, Jerusalem. Where does your interest in cities stem from?

TA: From the fact that Islamic civilization was an urban civilization. Historically, the Bedouin Arabs were nomads who yearned for cities and, once they arrived, fell in love with them and never left again. Cities such as Cordoba were enormous compared to those in Christendom and Western Europe. The nomadic trading culture which produced Islam concentrated on cities, because that was where they sold, and that gave them strength. However, they ignored the countryside, and this lent fragility to Islamic civilization because, like ancient Greece and Rome, they could never build feudalism proper, which might have given them a more lasting base.

I could never live in the country, because I'm a city person, who likes the liveliness and that sense of community the remnants of which still exist. The café is a great Arab invention, and persists as a space in which everything can be discussed without fear of God or the ruler of the day. A few years after 9/11, a television producer asked me what hypothetical programme I'd make if I were still working in television. I said what I would really like to do would be to give a twist to the current obsession with awful reality television shows, by setting up crews in cafés in Damascus, Cairo, New York, and London. The idea was simply to film them for two months, and compare what the people are discussing in the Arab world with what they are discussing here. It would be an effective way of showing how ordinary people live, work, think, drink, eat, and what they talk about, but it never got commissioned. I'd be prepared to bet that in the Arab cafés, a lot of the talk is about politics and culture in one form or another, and that in the cafés in our world, it's consumerism, lifestyles, celeb-obsession, because Westerners have forgotten politics. Anyway, I'm interested not just in individual metropolises, but types of cities, and what happens to city life and culture under different forms of rule and economies. We're here in London's Soho, which is known for its prostitution and strip bars, but also, nearby, Karl Marx lived and wrote, and the magazine with which I'm associated, *New Left Review*, was born 50 years ago. The way in which cities become multilayered, how they change and grow, is always fascinating.

My favourite city of all time, in some ways, is Istanbul, which is the perfect place to be a *flâneur*. Here you can sense and see a palimpsest: the Byzantines, Constantine, the birth of Christianity, and the victory of Mehmed the Conqueror, all in one city. There was also one of the largest Jewish populations in the Muslim world. After they were expelled from Spain, many Jews moved to Istanbul, and often in the twentieth century, scholars used to go there to hear Ladino (Judaeo-Spanish) spoken, because only the Jews of those families knew it. It's a city which is rich in history and culture, and that can't be replicated in the countryside. That's not to say that village life can't be rich, but it's always limited.

CC: You are well known as a frank chronicler of sexual practices, including hetero- and homosexuality, bestiality, adultery, and incest, so to what extent would you describe Islam as encouraging open sexual civilization?

TA: If Islam had come later and women had had the same rights as men, it would have been the most balanced religion on sexuality. Islam's laxity on these matters is very different from the Pauline tradition in Christianity, of holding back, being repressed and puritanical. If one believes all the *ahadith*, which have been written – I don't, but many people take them very seriously – there's one *hadith* in which the Prophet is quoted as saying that sex isn't only about procreation, but also pleasure, and that foreplay is very important. He is represented as telling men to make sure that they ensure that they give women with whom they sleep pleasure, too. Even if it's an invented *hadith* (and there are many) it indicates that advanced talk like that existed at that time. Compare this to the Pauline tradition: here I know which side I'm on.

CC: Could you discuss what we might term 'hybridity' in your writing; for example, interchange between Christian and Muslim culture in the Middle Ages and the admixture of English and Punjabi vocabulary and idioms? Perhaps this cultural intermixing is best exemplified in Plato's triptych canvas in *Night of the Golden Butterfly*.

TA: That painting also contains all the characters from the previous novels, so it's my way of concluding the Quintet. As I was finishing the book, all these characters came into my head again. I speak in *Night of the Golden Butterfly* about Punjabi not being used as a serious language. Certainly it's the language closest to my heart, as it's the language I grew up speaking, and which I still speak in three different dialects. Punjabi poetry, when it is written or sung, continues to have a deeper impact on me than poetry in any other language, even though I write in English. If the French had taken India, one would have been writing in French, as a lot of Algerian and Moroccan writers do. History is responsible for hybridity, and history is hybrid itself. The entire world has been formed by migrations of one sort or another. The United States is a country of migrants and, for a while, adopting German as their national language was a real possibility. It also applies when the cultures are more similar. Joyce had to invent virtually a new language to write about the Ireland in which he was growing up, and it wasn't Gaelic, because English had taken over. He used English and altered it in genius ways. He couldn't bear Catholic Ireland – narrow, limited, restrictive – and went abroad, where he became increasingly crazy, so his last novel was virtually incomprehensible.[59]

CC: Please discuss *Night of the Golden Butterfly*'s representations of China, from the character Confucius's Maoism, to the thwarted Yunnanese desire to create an independent, secular state for Muslims and non-Muslims.

TA: Writing that was a real challenge. I've read quite a lot of Chinese novels over the last 15 years, and find them sensational. Once Chinese Punjabis had been introduced – and these people did and do exist – then it wasn't a big leap from that to uncover how they first got to India. In so doing, I came across an uprising, which was the subject of a few isolated monographs, one of which is the best account of what took place and from which I plundered shamelessly.[60] The deeper I went into that Muslim uprising in Yunnan, the more shocked and ignorant I felt. An advanced ruler wanted to unite with the non-Muslims to keep the Manchus at bay, and who knows what would have happened had he survived and not been betrayed from within. It's the same in Islamic Spain and Sicily, and would have been the same in the Middle East, had Salah al-Din not somehow managed to keep the unwieldy and unruly masses and nobles together. The whole history of Islam can be explained as a history of faction and conflict, so to discover a similar pattern in China was wonderful. Most people think of Chinese Muslims as Uyghur living in the border territories of Xinjiang, not in the heart of China. There's a whole tradition in Chinese Islam, in which the Prophet Mohammed is said to have appeared to an early Chinese emperor in his dreams. While I was researching, I began thinking that the section on China could perhaps have been a book in itself, but then I decided no, in it goes and the Islam Quintet is done.

2
Fadia Faqir

Fadia Faqir is an acclaimed writer who was born in Jordan in 1956, and is currently an Honorary Fellow of St Mary's College and Creative Writing Fellow at St Aiden's College, both at Durham University. Faqir studied for an MA in Critical and Creative Writing at Lancaster University in 1984. She returned to Jordan for a year before moving to East Anglia in 1986, where she wrote the first PhD thesis in Critical and Creative Writing, awarded in 1990, and where Angela Carter and Malcolm Bradbury were two of her advisers.[1] In a semi-autobiographical piece, 'Stories from the House of Songs', Faqir writes of her character Shahrazad, who is, and is not, herself:

> She sings with Achebe 'The Song of Ourselves', celebrating differences and similarities, rejecting absolute truths about herself and others, welcoming disruptions of linear narratives,

embracing debate, uncertainty and dissent. Standing outside the whale, 'in this world with no safe corners', she sings for bridges, those destroyed and those to be built. The truth is that there is no house apart from the fragile, strong house of writing.[2]

This comment, with its suspicion of grand narratives and linearity, and belief in the power of literature, doubt, contradiction, and oppositional politics, epitomizes many of the concerns of Faqir's *oeuvre* as a whole.

Never one to shy away from controversial or difficult topics, Faqir is unflinchingly critical of distorted misogynist cultural practices that attach to Islam. At the same time, she writes of being appalled by misrepresentations of Arab culture in the media, art, and academia, arguing 'you fail to recognize the truth of your experience in the Western perception and representation of it'.[3] This is a recurring complaint of artists, intellectuals, and scholars of Muslim heritage, but Faqir is also an impassioned chronicler of marginalized subjects, such as women, Palestinians, and migrants. She has also written a number of academic papers on gender, Islam, and democracy,[4] and is an impassioned opponent of 'honour killings', on which she has written extensively.

I have already quoted from Fadia Faqir's influential collection, *In the House of Silence: Autobiographical Essays by Arab Women Writers* (1998), which she edited, contributed to, and for which she did some translation work. For this work of non-fiction, and the Arab Writers' Series, she received the Women in Publishing 1995 New Venture Award. However, Faqir is best known as a novelist, although she has also written short stories, and plays which have been staged in prestigious locations in the UK and Denmark. Her first novel, *Nisanit*, was published by Penguin in 1987 and has been translated into Arabic. It came out of her journalism about Palestinian prisoner release, and is narrated in three voices: those of a young Arab girl; her lover, a Palestinian freedom fighter; and an Israeli implicated in his torture. Her second novel, *Pillars of Salt*, part of her PhD thesis written while at East Anglia, also has a tripartite narrative structure. In this text, images of spinning and weaving loom large, and seem to function as metaphors for matrilineal storytelling techniques. The three narrators are Maha, a Bedouin woman who married for love and is now widowed and being pursued by her abusive brother; Um Saad, who lives with Maha in a psychiatric hospital in Jordan and was forced to get married to a butcher who later takes a second wife; and Sami al Ajnabi, 'a self-styled guardian of morality gradually revealed as an unreliable sto-ryteller'.[5] Of the five translations of this novel, the Danish version was a runner-up for the ALOA Literary Award, 2001.

The work for which she is best known, *My Name is Salma* (North American editions of which go by the title *The Cry of the Dove*)[6] was published in 2007, and has a vast international audi-ence in 13 different languages. This is Faqir's first novel to deal with Arab migration to Britain and, once its protagonist Salma begins to cope with the exclusion and invisibility she faces as an asylum seeker in Britain, she starts work as a seamstress, con-tinuing the theme of fabrications first explored in *Pillars of Salt*. The fact that Faqir's writing tends to involve multiple narrative voices, skilfully intertwined in a dense tapestry which – rather than a linear trajectory – involves lateral shuttling between char-acters, suggests the efficacy of this image. The prologue of her eagerly anticipated fourth novel *At the Midnight Kitchen*, which Faqir describes in this interview, was published in the USA by Weber Studies and won their fiction prize in 2009. This was the only one of my interviews to be publicly recorded as a keynote for the *Islam and the Postcolonial* conference at the University of Sunderland in April 2010. This is an edited version of it.

CC: I'll begin by asking you how you negotiate your femi-nism with your alertness to Orientalist pressures to stereo-type the Arab Muslim.
FF: This is a tightrope I walk every day, really. How do you criticize the Arab and Muslim world, without your words being used by Orientalists to justify dropping bombs on Baghdad, or continuing the war in Palestine? It's a very difficult position to be in, but

I am a believer in turning a critical face both ways, to the new country and the country of origin. The offence is two-sided, and dissent has to be two-sided. Yet, not a single media organization is going to accept that position or me saying, 'Well, I'm not an Islam-basher, and I would like to qualify my statements, please.' And, the minute I started saying that, post-Rushdie Affair, I was dropped by so many media outlets. 'Please, can I not make generalizations about Muslims?' I removed one of your questions – about developments in Jordan – because I haven't lived in Jordan since 1984, and I can't pontificate about a country I haven't lived in for years. This isn't because I don't follow developments and how things are changing on the ground in my country of origin, but because I don't want to encourage the army of journalists and commentators to go there for a week then write about the Arab world and, in so doing, disseminate generalizations and instant impressions. I've been quite careful, and it's a constant battle. I don't think I win all the time, but I try – I'm aware of the dangers.

CC: There's a recurring focus in your writing on the construction of Arab/Muslim identity in the Middle East, and latterly, in its diaspora, and your view of identity is quite pessimistic and traumatized. Several of your characters, such as Um Saad in *Pillars of Salt*, and Salma, who's also known by the name of Sally and Sal in *My Name is Salma*, desire to slough off their former identities and become new. In the case of Um Saad, she wishes to become the film star Hind Roustom[7] whereas Salma longs to be a White woman with pale, unobtrusive nipples.[8] At one point, Um Saad exclaims, 'Can you cast off your identity like dirty underwear? [...] What is identity?'[9] How would you respond to her question?
FF: I don't know. Don't you feel like that some days? Don't you feel tired of being a White, middle-class female one morning? Don't you want to be given a break – a coffee break – from the stereotypes projected onto you? I am a Muslim woman 24/7. I get tired! When I go to conferences I become a representative not only of the Muslim and Arab world, but of the whole southern hemisphere.

I got asked strange questions about, for example, 'medical procedures in Indian hospitals'. What do I know about medical procedures in Indian hospitals? There is a desire to get out of the restraints and constraints on you, and perhaps a desire to overcome and surpass the human condition. We're all hostages; there are restrictions on us because we are human and the bus we are on is heading in one direction, which is frustrating sometimes. Slipping out of who you are for a short period seems desirable, a luxury, but we are prisoners of our pasts and the choices we have made.

CC: Is this issue of identity something that Muslim women get asked to theorize more than do other groups?
FF: Yes! We're typecast, aren't we? We are 'oppressed', we are 'covered'; we can't speak for ourselves, but must be represented. When I go to conferences, I stand on the podium and say, 'I am a Muslim woman and I can speak for myself', and *then* I start my talk. You have to overcome the barrier of being cast as a silent other, a mute subaltern. But what is identity? It's a fluid process. One day, I wake up craving Arab coffee and jokes, and wanting to wrap myself in the beauty of the Arabic language. Other mornings my English education kicks in, and I crave English books, the English language, maybe even an afternoon tea. So identity is composite and is dependent on context and positionality; it's fluid, and is continuously evolving. Identity is also in the eye of the beholder, not in my eye: it's how people perceive you. People think I've got an accent, but I cannot detect it in my speech. Identities or stereotypes are other people's expectations and fears projected onto us. We are either all of these things, or none of the above, or some of the above, depending on the web we find ourselves in at that particular moment.

CC: It interests me that images of disciplinary institutions abound in your writing. In *Nisanit*, the torture victim Shadeed is incarcerated in a hospital/detention centre;[10] there's the psychiatric hospital in *Pillars of Salt* in which Maha and Um Saad are confined as the supposed victims of female madness

in *Pillars of Salt*;[11] and in *My Name is Salma*, prison and detention centres for asylum seekers are important locations.[12] Could you talk about your interest in these spaces?

FF: I didn't find the answer to this question until very recently, when I allowed myself to face up to what I had been denying for years and years. The fact is that my father was arrested, thrown in an army camp somewhere, and tortured. He spent years in prison, and the family blocked this out: 'My life is beautiful. No one took my dad away.' I didn't want to face up to that, but recently I did an interview, and it all came back. That's why I feel paranoid some of the time, because I think there will be a knock on the door and I will be taken away. Guantanamo looming at the end of the horizon does not help. Institutions became an important part of my mental landscape: prisons, mental hospitals, asylums. It relates to my loss of my sense of safety when I was young after that rupture in our family. Someone once said to me – in my novel, I actually repeat it – 'Oh, Arabs are so moody.'[13] Do you know what we go through to become moody? How many knocks on the door turned us into 'moody'? How many members of our family have been 'disappeared'? The oppression continues in many countries, despite the promise of the Arab Spring. Now they're talking about controlling Google, controlling the skies and the earth, controlling bread, water and regulating the very air we breathe. The legal justice system is corrupt and you are guilty until proven innocent. It is effing [*sic*] complicated, as one of my characters says in *My Name is Salma*,[14] being an Arab Muslim today. You are hounded on both sides of the divide. These are some of the conditions that made the Arab Spring possible and I explore them properly in *At the Midnight Kitchen* and in my fifth novel *The Terrorist's Daughter*.

CC: Have you been influenced by theorizations of these disciplinary spaces, by thinkers like Foucault, or is it a purely political issue of specific people being taken away that interests you?

FF: I think the latter. Something happens in your life, a personal tragedy, and then you try to look for an explanation or a justification. To make sense of it you read around it, and that might help you understand it a bit more. When I went to East Anglia, the books I have read helped me contextualize, and perhaps even to deal with, many of the issues I encountered before coming to Britain. This includes feminism, Foucault's work on madness and institutions and 1960s psychologists like R. D. Laing. Loss of control and sanity are themes that run throughout my work.

CC: Staying with space, you also explore urban–rural contrasts and tensions, whether played out between Ammanites and country Bedouins,[15] or between the southern English city of Exeter and the north-eastern village of Aycliffe.[16] How do you think the problems and advantages of the city and countryside compare?

FF: My mother comes from somewhere called the Republic of Adygea or Kabardino-Balkaria in the south-west of Russia. My father is Arab, Bedouin, Ajrami, but he wears a suit and a tie and refuses to associate himself with the Bedouins. He is urban; he's an *effendi.* However, it's my White Circassian mother who loves the Bedouins, and adores their nomadic lifestyle. She used to take us to live with them in the summer, and I'm lucky to have experienced the end of a semi-nomadic period in Jordan. I spent a long time with my tribe, and that was so beautiful. It was secular, egalitarian, and there was something regal about the members of the tribe. I was lucky to have had that childhood and to have seen the tensions between city and village. I also witnessed the last session of storytelling. A number of storytellers entertained us with their stories, punctuated with the soulful music of the *rebab*. Then television came, and that tradition regressed and was squeezed out. I saw the tension between the urban and rural, and that, again, comes out in my writing and you see it clearly in *Pillars of Salt*. Living in a village is idyllic, utopian, and beautiful. Reflections and apparitions of the amazing summers I spent in my village Um il-Basatyn can be seen in most of my literary work.

CC: Would I be right in thinking, then, that you privilege the rural over the urban in your writing? That seems to be so in your portrayals of the British context as well as the Middle East, because the north-east of England is depicted as being a nicer place to the south (which it is!).

FF: I read somewhere that great art can only be born in the metropolis. I disagree with that because the most exquisite shoots grow in the shadows. I should know, because I am an immigrant, who lives in the margins. I have reservations about the arrogance of London. Most of my London friends wouldn't cross the M25 to see me, because it's too far! These kinds of tensions multiply and resurface in different ways in new contexts. And that's why I created a man from Aycliffe, who is perceived as uncouth by southerners. You see parallels with racism in the discrimination against the poor White people of Aycliffe. One interesting fact is that in Aycliffe they treat me beautifully. No racism! In the most marginalized and deprived communities I am treated so well. And in Durham, the most urban, and among academics, I get treated badly by some. Racism has nothing to do with education or its lack, or how far you've travelled; I think it comes from somewhere else. I wanted to reproduce that in *My Name is Salma*, and that is why the ostracized lecturer comes from Aycliffe and Salma identifies with him. People think such rivalries only involve foreigners against natives. But there are tensions between the natives themselves, and there is a hierarchy in Britain and a rigid class system. *My Name is Salma* explores all of that.

CC: At a recent talk you gave in Manchester,[17] you declared, 'I am a Black Arab writer', aligning yourself with writers such as Toni Morrison, and ideas of political Blackness. Could you discuss this powerful statement further?

FF: I feel Black. Within feminism, there are strands that are Eurocentric and exclusive, rather than inclusive, and I don't think I belong there. I am not against Arab men: at this juncture in history, I sympathize with Arab men. It's the worst thing – and maybe the most exciting thing – being an Arab man today. So I couldn't see myself sitting there entirely comfortable within feminism, and then I remembered Toni Morrison and Alice Walker, and the movement called 'womanism',[18] which has an eye on equality and another on community: how the group is perceived, and how the minority is interacting with the majority. In other words, it focuses on human rights, society, and equality, and I am more comfortable with that than with calling myself a feminist. Perhaps labels are too large or too small for anyone, but if I have to, then I will say I am a womanist, which means that I align myself with Black American women writers.

I am discriminated against in Britain. My family was subjected to racist acts. My brother was attacked in Oxford three years ago – he was smashed to smithereens. Why? Because a White guy on drugs thought he was a Pakistani. It was an unprovoked, racially moti-vated attack. And *we* had to report it to the police, deal with it, and clean up the mess afterwards. I had the pleasure of telling my parents that their handsome, 42-year-old son had been attacked, had stitches around one eye and inside his mouth and that he was suffering from post-traumatic stress syndrome. He spent two years sitting in the garden of our house in Amman, refusing to venture out. That shattered my belief that England is essentially benign. Now I see myself as Black, the underdog, the down and out, *A MUSLIM* in a political sense. 'Black' and 'Muslim' are not used here literally because that would be problematic. They are used as a stance against racism and Islamophobia.

CC: On the issue of womanism, how do you feel about people who are trying to create a Muslim feminism?
FF: I have no problems with that. I think that Muslim women are capable of finding a way forwards for themselves, whether they call it Islamic feminism, egalitarianism, or womanism. What they call it is unimportant. People will use whatever tools come to hand, and if they want to call themselves Muslim fem-inists, that's fine. What is important is for that movement to be fundamentally egalitarian, in favour of equality and equal

opportunity, and genuinely for *human* rights, rather than just women's rights.

CC: In *My Name is Salma*, migrants are almost invisible to indigenous residents,[19] doing their dirty work and suffering their racist abuse. You recognize that migration, whether within the Arab world, or from there to the West, often involves coercion, neo-imperialism, and painful displacement. In 'Stories from the House of Songs', the phrase 'Exile is a sad country' is repeated.[20] Could you talk more about your representations of migration, racism, and hybridity?

FF: [Laughing]. One of my English friends said to me 'You know Jane? She couldn't finish reading your novel, because it's so anti-British.' And it wasn't Jane who couldn't finish reading the book: it was her. It took me a while to understand some people's struggle with *My Name is Salma*, because it holds a mirror up both to British society and the society Salma had left behind. If the society she left behind has a conservative, strict code of honour, then the society here has its own constraints as well. I wanted to be even-handed: 'Don't think you're superior; you've got problems specific to Britain.' The fact that the family has disintegrated; casual sex; the objectification of women; the fact that if you are not beautiful, with long legs, there is no space for you in this media-driven and controlled society. Women, and men, have to go out every day and 'sell' themselves in what Guy Debord called 'The Society of the Spectacle'.[21] There are restrictions on you in Britain – and then you have other types of restrictions back in the old country. Perhaps I am more optimistic about future hybridity, because I see more diversity slowly seeping in, and people of different backgrounds, cultures, and races are beginning to speak for themselves, rather than as people who can only be represented. They are starting to tell their own stories. The future is multi-ethnic and diverse. And we minorities have to rise up to the challenge.

CC: You used a metaphor of holding up a mirror to British society, and that suggests a sort of mimesis. Your writing's

very far from being realist, and I'm intrigued by your non-linearity and references to Arab sources and storytelling. Geoffrey Nash observes that there is an exceptionally 'close connection to Arabic narrative forms' in your *oeuvre*.[22] For example, your own prose frequently gives way to snatches of verse and song, both folk forms and also 'high art' by Arab writers, such as Nizar Qabbani[23] and Mahmoud Darwish.[24]

FF: When I was writing *My Name is Salma*, I thought yes, I'm an Arab author, but there is no harm in experimenting with form. Why can't Arabs be experimental? When we want to sell a publisher an experimental Arab book, we're told that it has to be linear. It has to be, 'Ah, I was beaten up, I am oppressed.' We can't give them something a bit more modern or complex. Perhaps my novel could have two endings: a happy ending – end number one – and then end number two. Not a single publishing house would accept that, because it was too experimental for them. What a shame! I wanted to show that there are two possibilities for Salma: a happy one, and, perhaps, a tragic one. Recently, the novel was translated into Danish and the publisher wanted to leave it open-ended. How prescriptive! The response from Danish readers has been: 'What happens to Layla, the daughter? Are you going to write Layla's story?' So they want a sequel!

I do not believe in linear narrative: it doesn't appeal to me. You cannot represent the truth in 'this happened and then this happened'. You simply need causality, complexity, a multitude of perspectives to capture the whole picture. My narrative is always fractured. The glass is held in the hand then dropped on the floor. A fractured narrative could perhaps become more tragic and more beautiful than the whole. Maria Assif, speaking at the 2010 conference of RAWI (Radius of Arab-American Writers Inc), said that non-linearity and silences in some contemporary Arab American writers' fiction are expressions of the rupture or trauma that may have been experienced by the authors. In *My Name is Salma*, there is linearity, but the novel keeps shifting between past and present. The character, a woman with serious baggage, takes one step forwards then two steps back, and is torn between her past and present. Maybe this goes back to the chain narrative of *The Arabian Nights*. You have one story, within a story, within a story. You don't get the resolution quickly. When I was a student, I was fortunate to interview Toni Morrison and I learnt so much from that encounter and her writing style, where the events are presented as skeletal, and are then revisited and fleshed out. Morrison's *Beloved*, for example, is not a linear tale, told from beginning to end. The novel is, in essence, written in fragments, pieces shattered and left for the reader to place together. The juxtaposition of past with present serves to reinforce the idea that the past is alive in the present, and by giving us fragments to work with Morrison melds the entire story into one inseparable piece. Every character, even the dead ones and half-alive ones, tell parts of the tale. Morrison's use of both verse and stream of consciousness writing, which she employs where necessary, is unsurpassed.

CC: It sounds as though it would have been more accurate to say that you hold up a *broken* mirror to British society. Both Salman Rushdie and Derek Walcott talk about the relevance of fractured perspectives to the postcolonial experience,[25] and I think of your fiction as utilizing a mosaic structure.

FF: A few critics used the word 'mosaic' when they reviewed *My Name is Salma*, because you can't see the whole construction unless you take a step back. This is exactly what I wanted to create, and I guess 'mosaic' is a perfect description. I'm Arab, so there has to be a mosaic somewhere in my DNA! I aim to create something as intricate, detailed, and exquisite as Palestinian embroidery. Attention to detail; multi-perspectival; in-and-out of narrative lines, random images, where you have to take a deep breath and connect the dots to see or perceive the whole. Perhaps the walls of Alhambra in Granada are imprinted on my soul.

CC: Could you say more about the politics of publishing and of your work's reception?

FF: I wrote about this in my article 'Dalek in a Burqa',[26] because whatever I write, even if I write about creatures from outer space, the publishers will put a veiled woman on the cover. *My Name is Salma* was translated into 13 languages. We are negotiating the German translation. If you look at most covers you will see Salma wearing a veil, although in the book she takes it off to be able to get a job. Only in the Indonesian translation Salma, head uncovered, in a sleeveless dress, is reclining on a sofa in an erotic yet troubled position. In Italy she has no veil. In France, they chucked out the whole Orientalist concept and created a fantastic cover comprising a decorated glass of Moroccan mint tea next to a mug of English coffee with a Union Jack on it. To me, that sums up the novel. In publishing, unfortunately, we have to deal with editors, some of whom have either not been to school, or have been but were not educated properly. As an author I enter into debates with publishing houses all the time. I have to confront stereotyping, reductionism, a-historicism, a-everything. Somebody said to me, 'Why do you agree to reductive covers?' Most of the time I don't see them! Some publishers publish covers without my approval. You even get translated without your consent. Apparently *In the House of Silence* was translated into Turkish without my permission. The author is the last to know.

Claire, you asked me about the politics of reception, and the honest answer is that I don't know. You need to ask the recipients. In the United States, *My Name is Salma* was number 19 on the Independent Publishers Bestseller List and was reprinted three times. It sold well in Brazil, in Australia in hardback, France and Italy. So there are some countries where the reception is quite good; in others, the reception is not so good. Britain has a double whammy of two things that govern reception: it's a class-based society, and it's subtly racist. This works not only against me, but against the indigenous British, because the class system is so rigid. However, it's promising that ethnic authors are being studied now, and we are slowly swimming towards the mainstream. We're beginning to register a little bit on the radar. I don't think our texts and vision have become mainstream yet, but things will change in the fullness of time.

CC: To come back to what you said about your moving towards a greater optimism in your work, could you describe the novel you've recently completed, *At the Midnight Kitchen*, which, I think, may not be so optimistic, but also the memoir, *My Father the Fundamentalist*, and the novel, *The Terrorist's Daughter*, which you're currently writing?

FF: [Laughing]. *At the Midnight Kitchen* is grim. I wanted to write a cheerful tale and I failed. It's about a group of Arabs living in a block of flats in Hammersmith, London. There is violence, self-hate, guilt, and the pursuit of redemption, compassion, and forgiveness. A shady figure in flat number two is stabbed to death and then the narrative unfolds. The main character finds solace in cooking and offering food to strangers. Arab immigrants to the UK are normally perceived as medieval, ignorant, and rich. *At the Midnight Kitchen* challenges these preconceptions and shines a light on the lives of ordinary Arabs who seek shelter in this country. Their subculture with its colours, smells, sights, and food is evoked and placed against the foil of British culture. Their interactions in the new country, which are sometimes rewarding and sometimes disappointing, are enriching for the natives and the newcomers. 140 Osman Road is a fictitious address in the city of London, but through following the lives of its residents during the Arab Spring, challenges that lead to extremism or its opposite, and conflicts within the human heart, are explored. Ultimately, survival has its price and reward.

A key point I wanted to make is that Arabs and Muslims are not all the same; there is huge diversity, because they come from different countries, cultures, and backgrounds. After one of this morning's papers, somebody was being prescriptive about who is and is not a Muslim, and I felt like saying, 'No, we're all Muslims, all the way from the secular to the very religious.' Being Muslim is a matter of degree and interpretation, and some of us are cultural Muslims. In my case, I call my religion Granada. I know that Granada has a greatly contested history, but what I read about it appeals to me, so I wish it into being. That co-existence, harmony, respect for the creative mind, acculturation, openness, crossroads, caravans meeting – it might be a dangerous place to be, but it's *beautiful*: bridges are my home.

I wanted to show how diverse we are in the novel. But when I found out about the attack on my brother, and the way he was let down by everybody – the police, his boss, some of his friends, the National Health Service, this country – it somehow seeped into the narrative. I didn't realize until I finished that that was the elephant in the room of my book. The violence, racism, Islamophobia, and tense atmosphere in today's Britain found their way into the novel. Yet there is also humour, sex, lies, and food.

As for *My Father the Fundamentalist*: I was brought up in a Muslim house. My father used to knock on the door calling, '*Salah! Salah!* Prayer!' It was early and sometimes very cold. Teeth chattering, I would throw down the mat and pray. But my father had a cunning plan. He thought, 'If I recite multiple verses from the Qur'an loudly and frequently, something will seep into my children's minds.' I was brought up in that environment, and my father turned out to be right. There is something about the beauty, poetry, and musicality of the Qur'anic verses that is magical, and it found its way inside me by osmosis.

But I could not survive in that oppressive milieu. So I became an expatriarch, a woman who left her country mainly because of her father. I distanced myself from him and everything he stood for – like many of you, probably – but lately I began to re-examine my position. In an article for the *Guardian*, I called him a 'reluctant tyrant'. I'm getting old, so I want to get to know my father, and why he prioritizes Islam and the Muslim cause over *us*. We came second in his life; we still do. He spends all his time talking about Islam and leafleting. He went through hell because of his beliefs. He was an absentee father. Now I want to understand what motivates him, fuels his life mission. That is one part of writing 'the book of memory'.

Recently I received a grant from the Arts Council of England to write my fifth novel, *The Terrorist's Daughter*. There's something else I want to understand. Books are attempts to explore and perhaps forgive. 'What is Al-Qa'ida?', I get asked, 'What do you think of terrorism post-9/11?' I honestly don't know much about that and it has nothing to do with me, but I *want* to understand Al-Qa'ida, who they are, what they stand for and what motivates them. The book is also an attempt to document the history of Arab-Afghanis; fighters of Arab ethnicity, who travelled to Peshawar, crossed to Afghanistan and joined Al-Qa'ida. According to some sources many of them were medics,[27] and they had become very important in the movement and helped shape it. The novel will document their history and follow them on their journey from the Arab world all the way to Afghanistan. It will recount the massacre of Mazar-e-Sharif in 2001 from the Other's perspective. There will also be heart-rending choices. Any act of violence devastates the family, and it's really hard for the community to deal with having a member who belongs to Al-Qa'ida, or similar groups. There are repercussions for the people nearby, which will be explored. The narrative will find its way back to Britain, to a high security prison where all the so-called 'terrorists' are kept, either because they are criminals or because there was some miscarriage of justice. Then the father has to make a devastating choice. It will be a novel of discovery and self-discovery.

CC: I'm struck by this term, 'reluctant tyrant', which evokes Mohsin Hamid's novel, *The Reluctant Fundamentalist*. Are you doing a similar thing to Hamid: playing with the term of the 'fundamentalist' and also questioning who the fundamentalist actually is (see p. 186)?
FF: Definitely. *My Father the Fundamentalist* isn't a serious title; it's done tongue-in-cheek. It will raise many questions: Is he a 'fundamentalist'? What is that? Is this term, stripped of all nuances, still viable? My grandmother died when my father was just over a year old and soon after his father got remarried. He was brought up in a strict house that ticked like a Swiss clock. He also felt unloved, yet stood on his own feet and became a prominent member of the opposition and a businessman. He

didn't know how to handle us and was curtailed and limited by his blueprint, his upbringing.

CC: You mentioned Granada a little while ago, which suggests decline, but also regeneration through an energizing force, so I wanted to ask more about what that history means to you.
FF: I spoke at the Alhambra, as part of the Hay Festival of Literature and the Arts. It was very emotional, because – ask any Muslim – Granada fills us with awe and something happens to our hearts and resolve when we stand on its hills. In Mahmoud Darwish's 'Eleven Stars Over Andalusia', he writes, 'I am the Adam of the two Edens, I who lost paradise twice. / So expel me slowly, / and kill me slowly, / under my olive tree, / along with Lorca'.[28] Darwish allied himself with Lorca. The loss of Spain was an important rupture for Muslims. Perhaps the Arab world will somehow come out of this current situation stronger; renewed. Anyway, I was in Granada feeling this oppressive sadness; it was in the midst of the problem with my brother. I wasn't crying over land, because land means nothing to me! I wasn't crying over the loss of houses and palaces. I was crying over that enlightenment; that moment in history, if it ever happened; over that beauty, that openness and absorption of cultures and civilizations; that *inclusiveness*. All of that meant so much. It was a moment of reflection as well – Who am I? Why am I here? What am I writing about? Whom am I writing to? Is it permissible for this tongue to speak in English, or should it revert back to Arabic? Should I go back, or should I stay in this racist yet tolerant West? And *my* Spanish inquisition started. Although I flogged myself with questions, it was somehow cathartic.

CC: My last question – appropriately enough given the typically tripartite structure of your novels – has three parts. What does it mean to you to be a Muslim post-9/11? Do you think the way that Muslims are treated has changed? How are these issues reflected in your fiction?
FF: Before 9/11, religion meant nothing to me. It was something like water or air just there. It never mattered in Jordan and it never mattered much in the UK. If you said, 'What is your

religion?' I would have opened my passport and read, 'Muslim'.
It didn't mean much, really. After 9/11, everybody started label-
ling me and wherever I went I was told I was a Muslim. That
identity, or that affiliation, was inflicted on me by *you*, this
society! *You* define *me* as a Muslim. Therefore, I am a Muslim.
And I use 'Muslim' as a political term. If you want to knock on
the door and arrest me please do. We are used to our doors being
knocked on. I wear orange. I'm ready. I'm a Muslim. If I refuse
to define myself as a Muslim at this juncture in history it will
be an act of cowardice, a cop out. So I'm a Muslim. Waterboard
me, do whatever you want to do with me, I will not succumb or
ally myself with you. That's one development post-9/11.

Somebody said, 'You can't write about trees if the world is on
fire', referring to the Second World War, I think. As a Muslim,
I don't have the luxury to write about trees, flowers, the different colours of the seasons. I don't have that option. Art for art's
sake is not for me. I'm not going to write about trees, but there
is an urgent need to write about trees burning down. Somebody
has set fire to the whole forest.

In the UK and USA, innocent members of my family were dev-
astated by 9/11 and some of the details shall remain private. My
brother was attacked in Oxford by a young White man because
he thought he was a Pakistani – as if that is an excuse. His dark
skin was the only reason for that act of violence inflicted upon
him. Do you know what is hardest? The hardest thing for me
is not to forgive the assailant, the person who attacked my
brother; it's to forgive myself, *us*. Because something happens
to us when there is violence. Anger turns into fear, guilt, shame.
When a member of your family is violated, you blame yourself
for not protecting him or her. So now I don't seek *forgiveness* for
others, because I've already done that – I had to – but I seek it
for myself. I look for ways to be able to sign a peace agreement
with myself. To survive I must reclaim some of my lost innocence and that fake sense of safety in today's Britain.

I want to conclude with something I wrote post-9/11. Do you
remember when Tony Blair claimed that Saddam Hussein had

'weapons of mass destruction'? At that moment I wrote this, and I think it represents a turning point for me; in my history and who I am. From that point on I started calling myself 'Muslim'. I also realized that as a British Muslim I was guilty until proven innocent. If they push you into a corner, and then there is no way out; you write your way back to sanity.

Weapons of Mass Destruction
'We found two oranges in your suitcase.
We also found some fresh thyme;
A can of olive oil;
And a packet of ground coffee with cardamom.

We could not find a rosary,
But you must have one in your heart.
Please follow me, madam.'

3
Aamer Hussein

Aamer Hussein describes himself as 'a third-generation Karachiite', because he, his father, and paternal grandfather were all born in Karachi. However, his mother, the feminist activist and translator Sabeeha Ahmed Husain's cultured landowning family comes from Indore in Madhya Pradesh, India, from where she came to Pakistan as a bride in 1948. Hussein's family had a peripatetic lifestyle when he was growing up in the late 1950s and 1960s, with his father making regular visits to London before moving there permanently in 1968. The young Aamer spent many summers in Bombay, which city he writes about in such stories as 'Last Companions'[1] and 'The Blue Direction'.[2] Delhi is also a presence in his fiction, in stories such as 'The Angelic Disposition'.[3] He first visited the city several times in his twenties, and returned after a long absence when his sister moved there a few years ago. One of his sisters, Shahrukh Husain, is also a writer (of fiction and non-fiction for children and adults, and screenplays),[4] and is married to the Urdu expert, Christopher Shackle.[5]

Hussein left Pakistan in 1968 to attend boarding school in the Nilgiri hill station of Ootcamund, South India, and subsequently moved to Britain for further schooling in 1970, aged 15. After an attempt at undergraduate study, Hussein worked for a year in a bank. He later studied Persian, Urdu, and History at London's School of Oriental and African Studies (SOAS), graduating in 1981. As well as English, Urdu, Persian, and Hindi, Hussein is also strong in the romance languages of Italian, French, and Spanish. After graduating, Hussein was briefly employed as a research assistant for film and television, before starting to work full-time as a writer in the mid-1980s. He now divides his time between writing and academic work, having recently been awarded a professorial fellowship in creative writing from the University of Southampton, where he has worked since 2006. He lives in London's Maida Vale district and writes, 'many of my London stories, coming from lived experience, couldn't perhaps have happened anywhere else'.[6] Although Hussein's London of Bloomsbury, rain, symposia, pubs, and multicultural populations is evocative, and his description of the city as 'an imperial dowager without a future'[7] wryly accurate, it is limiting to categorize him as a writer of 'postcolonial London'.[8] Rather, he is a chronicler of many cities, particularly Karachi, 'that open city teeming with strangers like himself',[9] with its complex class divisions, violence, cultural intermixing, and arid beauty.

Aamer Hussein is a widely read, transnational Pakistani writer who wears his Islam lightly. One of the aspects of Hussein's work that I admire is his attention to the ways in which characters' religious affiliations intersect with other signifiers – such as gender, socio-economic status, age, and national origins – and assume varying degrees of importance in different situations. As Hussein says, 'I don't write about British Muslims as a community as my knowledge of them is limited, but religion (both in the sense of "origins" and of spirituality) is a quietly integral part of my stories, and I include subtle representations of Islam, or Islamic imagery, in my work.'[10] There is no naïve extolling of a united Muslim *ummah* in his fiction, but he does describe connections between characters of Muslim heritage, as when the narrator in 'Hibiscus Days' studies 'anti-colonial francophone fiction, in which I saw parallels to some pre-Partition Urdu poetry', and describes listening to Sufi Muslim folk songs as 'rip[ping] out something raw from the hollows of my ribcage'.[11] His characters often come from the Muslim world, and include Palestinians, Malays, Indonesians, Arabs, and Iranians.

Hussein's first collection of stories, *Mirror to the Sun*, was published in 1993, and is a promising, if uneven, debut, including excellent stories such as 'Your Children' and 'The Colour of a Loved Person's Eyes', but also rather impenetrable stories such as 'Dreaming of Java'.[12] It was followed by *This Other Salt* in 1999,[13] which contains a folkloric poem-within-a-story, 'The Lost Cantos of the Silken Tiger'. This story alludes to the Qur'anic tale of Yusuf (Joseph), which narrates Yusuf's betrayal by, and eventual return to, his family; his exile into slavery; and attempted seduction by Zuleikha (the name popularly given to Potiphar's wife in Muslim tradition). The Yusuf story is one of the myths common to Jewish, Christian, and Muslim traditions and, in Hussein's retelling, Yusuf is figured as a poet, challenged to a recital contest by the fiery, but ageing Zuleikha, during which they fall in love. This story gives way to discussion amongst Pakistani émigrés in London about the fictional Pakistani woman writer, Aarzou, said to have written the tale about her lover, the poet Yusuf Reza, in order to 'stage [...] herself as Potiphar's wife – an early feminist struggle to present a woman mad, bad and dangerous'.[14] As with many of Hussein's Russian-doll-like stories, 'The Lost Cantos of the Silken Tiger' incorporates hypodiegetical material, in this case a poem which gives Zuleikha the chance to 'write back' towards the end of the story.[15] In the early 2000s came *Turquoise* and the Pakistan-published *Cactus Town: Selected Stories*, which includes stories from both *Mirror to the Sun* and *Turquoise*, and which Hussein describes as being 'too big, but still in print'.[16] Hussein has an enthusiastic following in Pakistan, and some of his earliest reviews were in Pakistani newspapers and journals such as *Dawn*, *She*, and *The Herald*. *Insomnia*, in many ways his quintessential collection, was simultaneously produced by Telegram, an imprint of Saqi in London, and Sama Books in Karachi.[17] Hussein's relationship with the publishing house Saqi is long and loyal, and he was close to the publisher's co-founder, the Lebanese sculptor, writer, and artist Mai Ghoussoub, whom he describes as 'unforgettable' in the dedication to *Another Gulmohar Tree*.[18] Hussein's stories have been translated into several languages, and he is particularly popular in Italy, where a selection of his stories was published as *I Giorni dell'Ibisco* (2009), and *The Cloud Messenger* was first released in 2010.[19]

Hussein is prescient in being one of the only writers of Pakistani heritage to address the Gulf Wars in fiction, alongside Uzma Aslam Khan.[20] As mentioned in the Introduction, Pakistani writers have paid a great deal of attention to the Afghan conflict and its impact on neighbouring Pakistan[21] but, perhaps because they took place in Iraq, a country geographically and culturally distant from Pakistan, the Gulf Wars have been somewhat neglected. However, Aamer Hussein's story about the First Gulf War, 'Your Children', was published just a year after the invasion, in 1992.[22] Another story that tangentially discusses the Second Gulf War, 'The Book of Maryam', was collected in *Insomnia*,[23] but was originally published in 2004. These two stories touch on the issues of Saddam Hussein as a dictatorial Great Leader,[24] and the ethical and political concerns raised for Muslims by the US-led invasion. As a character in 'Your Children' remarks, the First Gulf War 'isn't a Muslim war',[25] and different national groups engage in constant debate about its legitimacy.

Hussein's novella, *Another Gulmohar Tree*, was published in 2009, and is partly inspired by the life of the Urdu writer Ghulam Abbas (author of the children's book *Moon and Star*[26] among other works) and his enigmatic wife Christian Vlasto.

'Chris' was of Greek-Scottish-Romanian ancestry, but chose in 1950 to follow Abbas to Pakistan and become his second wife, renaming herself Zainab, and later C. Z. Abbas. Chris Abbas's hybrid identities – British, Pakistani, Christian, and Muslim – are indicated in her multiple names. The relationship between the Pakistani writer and his translator-painter-illustrator wife allows Hussein to explore Urdu and English languages and artistic traditions, mixed-heritage relationships, and tensions precipitated by colonial history. C. Z. Abbas was one of several Western women working in the postwar Pakistani arts, probably the most famous being Alys Faiz, the journalist and poet wife of Faiz Ahmed Faiz. However, Hussein explains that he draws more extensively on the 'anonymous type of Western suburban Karachi wives' he met as a child. His character is called Lydia, but converts to Islam on her marriage, taking the name Rokeya, which is an allusion to the daughter of the Prophet, who married the Prophet's companion (later Caliph) Usman. Although *Another Gulmohar Tree* centres on a 'mixed marriage', it does not present this as being primarily about culture clash. Quite the contrary, Lydia, like many other European women who married Pakistanis, is happy in Pakistan and enjoys its thriving art scene, staying on after her husband, Usman's death. The novella falls into two parts, with the early section 'Usman's Song', presented as Usman's Urdu fables, about a boy feeding a frog; Rokeya befriending a deer; and a girl becoming a crocodile's bride. This synopsis indicates Hussein's interest in Pakistani women artists, and it should be noted that he has also edited, introduced, and co-translated a collection of short fiction by Pakistani women, *Hoops of Fire* (1999), which was revised and retitled *Kahani* [Stories] in 2005, with the addition of newly translated stories by Amtul Rahman Khatun and Hijab Imtiaz Ali.[27]

His latest novel, *The Cloud Messenger*, economically touches on many aspects of love, literature, and exile. To some extent it may be interpreted, like the book its protagonist, Mehran, is writing, as an 'autobiographical novel'.[28] Like Hussein, Mehran is taught Persian at an institution that resembles SOAS, by the eccentric squash-playing Orientalist Professor Lambert, who closely resembles the historical Ann Lambton.[29] Yet there is an ironic warning to academics about making category mistakes when Mehran's first story is published as he turns 40 (nearly a decade older than Hussein was when his debut story appeared), and the guest editor of a journal of postcolonial writing wrongly assumes a memoir piece about his Italian-Argentinian lover, Riccarda, to be fiction.[30] Mehran's modest description of his novel as 'a handful of reflections [and] [i]mpressions of people and places',[31] has some bearing on *The Cloud Messenger*, but the latter also evinces a rich intertextuality, through folk tales (such as the story of Prince Benazir); the Sindhi poetry of Shah Abdul Latif; Persian and Urdu literature; Enid Blyton; Tolstoy; and, above all, Kalidasa's *Meghaduta*, which gives the novel its title and wistful cloud imagery. *The Cloud Messenger* is also a travel narrative, containing subtle depictions of the cities that loom large in Hussein's own biography: Karachi, Bombay, Indore, London, Rome, and Delhi. Finally, Mehran's tragic relationships, one with the older, married Riccarda, and the other a 'slow suicide'[32] of a love affair with the disabled, alcoholic Pakistani economist, Marvi, are compelling and carefully plotted.

Mehran and *Another Gulmohar Tree*'s Lydia, along with several of Hussein's other characters, work as translators, and Hussein himself has translated at least four short stories, and small excerpts of poetry hidden throughout his work. The translator is always, for him, an alter ego of the bilingual writer. Figures of authors, critics, teachers, and academics also abound in his very literary fiction. One of Hussein's strengths is his sensitive yet discomfiting cultural translation, which, almost with an anthropologizing tendency, reveals the strangeness of British culture, as in discussions of Scottish Catholics' disapproval of abortion in *Another Gulmohar Tree*.[33] Similarly, Hussein's depictions of the English enthusiasm for strawberries in 'The Lark' suggest that quasi-religious rituals are not the sole preserve of the subcontinent.[34] In the first chapter of *The Cloud Messenger*, like Graham Huggan, he suggests that 'the exotic is not, as is often supposed, an inherent *quality* to be found "in" certain people, distinctive objects, or specific places',[35] because the Pakistani children find Selfridges, crumpets and strawberries 'insufferably exotic' compared to their own 'provincial' mangoes and papayas.[36]

CC: I'd like to start by asking about form, specifically your extensive *oeuvre* of short stories, and the more recent transition to the novella and novel form, with *Another Gulmohar Tree* and *The Cloud Messenger*, respectively.
AH: I started writing short stories in the mid-1980s, because I was taken by what I was reading at the time. I was interested in what we called 'Third World literature', and read very widely, particularly short stories. In Chinese literature; to an extent in Latin American literature; and especially subcontinental literature, short stories were a major form. I began to find that my head was crowded with several stories, and saying everything you wanted to in just a few pages was crucial. Over time, I conceived *Mirror to the Sun* (1993) and my more thematically controlled second and third books (*This Other Salt* [1999] and *Turquoise* [2002]), and realized I was on a path. My books all contain long stories of 7,000 words upwards, and several of my stories were novellas by some standards.

Another Gulmohar Tree grew from a short story, and took a little longer to write than some of my earlier work, because when it reached 7,000 words, the poet Ruth Padel said she thought I hadn't yet said everything I wanted. So it continued, and finally the story of Usman and Lydia reached 17,000 words, but it never got any longer. The opening sequence is something of an afterthought, as my editor liked the 17,000 words, but later, she asked, 'Would you consider adding one of the stories that Usman's said to be writing?', so I wrote the sequence of fables in one morning. Oddly enough, people say that putting the two together in that way has made it seem more like a novel than a novella – with two realms, as it were, which are together and apart. You can read Lydia's story without the fairy tales; however, you'd read the fairy tales quite differently if you read them by themselves. Each character from the fairy tales has a role in the main narrative. In the tale, Usman is the one who sings for his lost love. Rokeya's the one who's able to carry his frog back to him, which means giving him back something he's loved and lost. Umar is ready to campaign for the world, for justice. Jani, in marrying the crocodile, buys into power. The crocodile tale is a traditional story that was in the novella right from the start, because when I wrote the first draft, Usman writes that story as a parable to represent the system under Ayub Khan's dictatorship. However, I've never felt that inset stories work within the body of linear narratives, as they have to be compressed and synoptic.

I'm writing short fiction at the moment. But I think the *short* short story was never my strength. Yet, prolonging a story beyond 10,000 words presents an endeavour that I did not envisage making. I like to edit a short piece much more than I like wading in a morass of pages and files. Working with lengthy prose at the moment is a slog, and its pleasures are largely incidental. When people learn that I've managed to write 35,000 words in under a year, they're astonished, because many writers don't. But the short story writer is able to produce a compact narrative, even if it's multifaceted, within a shorter span of time.

CC: You mentioned that you are interested in the world literatures in which the short story form is dominant, such as Chinese and Urdu traditions.
AH: I came to Urdu later, because I had a block with my mother tongue, and I always felt it would be atavistic to turn to that before I'd done my work, as it were, with 'world literature' – not that I like that term. I always read the odd Urdu short story, but in 1991 I started to read them *seriously*. At this time I was teaching Urdu, and it was a practical decision: I didn't want to teach students to learn the language without some knowledge of contemporary literature, so I started researching what I hadn't been taught at university, which were stories from the 1980s and

early 1990s. There was a dynamic tradition of writing surreal stories, by Pakistani writers, many in their fifties or sixties at the time, who had been practising for 20 or 30 years. To some extent that influenced me, but you can't really see formal influences on my stories – except when I deliberately present pastiches of what these other writers were doing, in *This Other Salt* more than in any other book. My reading brought me closer, I think, to the notion of Pakistani literature, rather than subcontinental or Third World literature; it made me realize where my roots lay.

CC: On this issue of language and coming to Urdu quite late as a written language, in *Another Gulmohar Tree*, Usman says, 'you don't choose the language you write in, it chooses you'.[37] Is that how you feel about your choice of English?
AH: Absolutely. In relation to language choice, there was a whole series of historical circumstances, such as the fact that I was taught how to read and write English at five. I made a little autobiographical bow in *Another Gulmohar Tree*, as the young son of an English mother, which certainly I'm not – my mother is very well read in Urdu, English, and Persian, but she writes English best – but I had the same problems learning Urdu as the character, as I could not master the script. Then I went to India and learnt Hindi, which I learnt really fast, but as a language I felt it was never quite mine. I loved Urdu poetry and listened to a lot of songs, but didn't read Urdu fiction. I studied Urdu literature at university, and by the 1980s, I could read Urdu as a very strong second language. And now I'm pretty much a bilingual reader. I read many other languages, too. It's strange how comfort with reading Urdu just came to me, but it was far too late for me to write in Urdu, as there'd be too great a sense of artifice and hybridity.

CC: In *Another Gulmohar Tree*, Usman views Partition in a more positive light than do most Indian writers (Rushdie, Amitav Ghosh, *et al.*), arguing that Pakistan was created by people 'in pursuit of their dreams'.[38] Pakistani writers tend

not to subscribe to the myth of Indian secularism,[39] so what is your own opinion of these debates about Partition?

AH: The pursuit of dreams was what we were *supposed* to bring to Pakistan: it was intended to be a postcolonial state which brought together the best of all the worlds that had been left behind. Jinnah argued that everybody would live together equally, and people had no fixed idea of what Pakistani culture was going to be like. However, an equal number of influences later came into play: the Middle East, the indigenous Islamic culture which emerged, and Indian influences should also not be discounted. If you look, for example, at the cinema, or the new Pakistani literature, it's still closer to all things Indian. Early Pakistani artists were more cosmopolitan than their Indian peers, who were trying to create something Indian. In addition, there were various regional cultures that asserted themselves, and later came the demand for specifically Pakistani identity, which could either be regional, or religious, or both, and which disregarded Indian influences. When the dreams began to fade, then any cultural consensus that said, 'This must not be done, this must not be used, don't be too Indian, don't be too foreign, create a *local* idiom', created certain pressures to which some intellectuals reacted very positively, and others moved right away from, like novelist Qurratulain Hyder and modernist Islamic scholar Fazlur Rahman.

The Progressive Writers Association was never terribly Westernized.[40] Early Progressive writers were impressed with Bloomsbury, but regionalism mattered more to them than modernism. After Partition, they kept on writing in a fairly dogmatic *and* Leftist way about poverty and so on. The problem with the Association was that it treats the people it's supposed to be representing as objects of an upper middle-class gaze. The idea that people are victims of their circumstances and can never break away is perhaps deterministically naturalistic rather than Marxist. Thus Progressive writing worked within an outdated Leftist model, rather than Soviet or Chinese approaches, which usually show people escaping and transcending their background. My character Usman rebels against Leftist literary strategies, saying that he doesn't want to write in a prescriptive voice of any sort, or to wallow in the mud. However, there was another trend in Pakistan that was quite different and, I think, equally important, which translates as something like Arbiters of Elegance. They were trying to create a Pakistani aesthetic that was a strange mixture of a European notion of modernist grandeur and borrowings from the *Arabian Nights* and Islamic culture, and in its way it was quite effective. There were also modernist tendencies all the way through the twentieth century, with Qurratulain Hyder, who wrote *River of Fire*, as a card-carrying modernist, although she ended up being very postmodern.

CC: Please discuss your representations of hybridity. The gulmohar tree comes from Madagascar, but it becomes very much a part of Pakistani foliage, and your migrant figure, Lydia, also embraces Pakistan.

AH: Lydia tries hard to be Pakistani, for example decorating her house in a modern Pakistani style. Eventually, she gives in to what she really is, which is hybrid. She accepts that she's seen in stereotyped ways, and sometimes plays along with these and sometimes questions them. Is she hybrid, or is she assimilated? I don't know; she's well adjusted. She doesn't reproduce Pakistani material culture and art in bad faith; they're part of her. If you're asking a question about the contribution that migrants make to a culture, then, without appearing to be imperialistic or hegemonic about it, Lydia does, and that is also true of many South Asians living in the West.

CC: Yes, we see cultural mixing from the other direction in your short story 'Sweet Rice',[41] in which a British Pakistani woman attempts to create this subcontinental dish in response to a mid-life crisis. As well as describing hybridity, you're also sharp on racism in Britain. In 'This Other Salt', the narrator is beaten up by a Black man, as a result of racism.[42] Lydia's friend is patronizing towards Usman in *Another Gulmohar Tree*,[43] and

English characters exoticize the protagonist Hassan Khan in 'The Lark', stereotyping him as a Black Prince.[44]

AH: The idea behind 'Sweet Rice' came when my mother asked if I could find the recipe from a recipe book we had at home. A migrant friend of mine was in a similar dilemma to that experienced by Shireen. 'The Lark' is inspired by my father, during the Second World War. I tried to imagine what my father would have done in the circumstances that I had been in and vice versa. So the boy who is served the eel is me, aged 39 – not as a boy – when I went to a meal to a country house in Kent and was offered this fare; my hostess asked if she'd done something wrong, are 'Islamics' not meant to eat eel? And I said *I* certainly didn't, but didn't know whether or not we were allowed to. The story of his photograph is basically the way my father saw my mother's picture before they married, although the character was only 19, while Daddy didn't see my mother's pictures until he was perhaps 25. I'm working with family stories.

In terms of my own experiences of racism, I was incredibly peripheral here – very privileged. The worst comment I might have had was an Irish schoolmate saying, 'your skin is dark because your livers work differently'. For me, racism was cultural: I felt the people who asked silly questions were under-educated and ignorant. I used to love surprising people who would ask, 'Are you Greek? Spanish? You're not very dark, you don't look foreign or "Paki"', by saying where I was from. Most people in London didn't know where Pakistan was, and associated the whole nation with East Pakistan. But racism on the street? No. Maybe the odd veiled remark. Englishness has changed a lot, and people would say, 'As a visitor to our country, you perhaps need to know that we...' This was supposed to be a nice welcome: 'How long have you been here? When do you think you'll be going back?' It was all polite, upper-bourgeois. The most racist thing I ever encountered, and the most pervasive, is the glass ceiling. I'll tell you how it operates: if for example you're working as a literary academic, the first question you will be asked is, 'Oh, but of course you teach the students postcolonialism?' If you want to teach

English, you are given a dossier of texts to teach which includes ten African and five Caribbean novels. I'll say, 'I'm not an African scholar, but an arbitrary postcolonialist.'

If English ways sometimes seemed a little quaint to me, I was perfectly prepared to accept that some of my ways not only seemed quaint to them then, but still seem so *now*. When I tell friends that I don't eat pork, I know that we cook for vegetarians and people with all kinds of dietary quirks, but pork as a cultural signifier has become a marker for me. It seems to surprise hosts far more than when people say, 'I don't do dairy' or 'chocolate gives me a headache'.

CC: To what extent has being a Muslim become more of an issue than being Pakistani since the Rushdie Affair, or since 9/11 or 7/7?

AH: *The Satanic Verses* was the first event that made me identify as Muslim rather than South Asian. Until then we were all in it together, and we didn't make overt differentiations between, or amongst ourselves. After the Affair, a whole rhetoric of Otherness emerged around *The Satanic Verses*. I'm not saying that every critic was insensitive, but many were. For me, that was when the Muslim community first began to stand out. I noticed that in discourses like human rights rhetoric and, say, social work, South Asian women suddenly started saying things like, 'As an Indian woman, I would like to talk about the position of Muslim women', and the veil became a signifier and all that. Rural Punjabi groups – Sikh, Hindu, and Muslim – had norms about the position of women which I, as an urban Sunni Muslim, don't share, but now it was all about Muslim women. There was all this Othering, but Othering can sometimes be positive, because it teaches you to affirm something, even if this is only the creation of provisional cultural markers for yourself.

CC: To what extent has this affected you and your writing?

AH: I pray once a week, if that; but it's about my pact with the sacred. I don't know if you can actually put this in a way that makes sense to anyone, but I carry belief with me all the time. There's not a moment when I don't feel that we live in a giving world, a world that is in some way generous.

CC: In 'What Do You Call Those Birds?'[45] and *Another Gulmohar Tree*, you evoke the Qur'an's Surah Rahman, The Beneficient, with its famous refrain, 'Which is it, of the favours of your Lord, that ye deny?'[46]
AH: I'm very Muslim, in that I find it hard to choose from His many mercies which to enumerate. Somebody asked me the other day whether I believe in the infallibility of the Qur'an and whether it's possible to keep on interpreting it. The fact is, we're fallible readers, so how can we talk about fallible or infallible texts? I suppose then that mine is a very secular approach, which makes you constantly question really deeply held beliefs: the only response is your own interpretation built on a deeper knowledge of the texts.

CC: Your writing takes it for granted that Islam is a positive thing, despite the extremists that exist on the fringes of all religions, whose practices you criticize. Am I right in thinking you highlight justice, compassion, and community, and other constructive aspects to Islam?
AH: That's very central in my writing. Compassion, because when we talk about God we say *Bismillah al-Rahman al-Rahim*, 'in the name of God, the Compassionate, the Merciful'. Compassion is the maternal aspect to God. I would call myself, probably, an intellectual Muslim. The Muslim cultural heritage is where I come from, more than the Urdu language, which people keep thinking of as my primary cultural marker. It's actually my emergence from four generations of a Muslim intellectual family. As I advance through middle age, I'm increasingly more interested in Islamic philosophical writing, than in mystical and Sufi poetry. This is not so much theistic or theological discourse, but rather metaphysical and philosophical discourse about *us* and our place in the world; what our nature is and

how we relate to the cosmos: a kind of existentialist Muslim discourse.

CC: Do Muslim visual arts influence you aesthetically?
AH: More so than ever. It is less evident in *The Cloud Messenger*, but yes, over the last few years Muslim art has been an influence. However, while writing *Another Gulmohar Tree*, the person whose pictures I was looking at most was Mary Fedden.[47] She's probably about 90 now and a very established English painter. So perhaps we should talk about English influences as well.

CC: Yes, there are many English references in your work, including to Somerset Maugham, Agatha Christie, Dickens, and Georgette Heyer. *Another Gulmohar Tree* is rich in influences, both high and low culture, Urdu and English. You've mentioned visual artists, but who are your inspirations in English writing?
AH: Well, *Another Gulmohar Tree* contains an affectionately irreverent bow to the work of Persephone Books (a publisher that reissues neglected classics by mostly women writers). An editor of reprints once told me when I asked how she made her selection: 'We are publishing books for the Laura Ashley classes. We don't want to rock the boat.' What I wanted to say was that there was a kind of English writing, a lot of it from the north, that was bourgeois, but at the same time slightly close to the bone and discomforting, in the sense that it talked about physical and emotional distress. My book is a tribute to a powerful English tradition of women's writing: of reclaiming forgotten things and not forgetting domesticity in painting or in writing. My friend Lynn Knight, in a beautiful introduction to a novel called *Celia* by a forgotten writer called E. H. Young, wrote, 'home truths are the most disturbing of all'.[48] I feel that my book – although it's impossible to extricate it from its Pakistani moorings – is equally an English book about an English person who goes to Pakistan, looking at what her conscience says about the place that she goes to, trying to reclaim a decent relationship with an ex-colonial

terrain, without the deciding discourse of Orientalism. As such it belongs to an English tradition of writing about people who live abroad and discover something there.

In some ways, *Another Gulmohar Tree* is my most English book yet, although *Insomnia* and 'The Lark' also belong to this tradition. There are English male writers – three come to mind immediately – who are just as domestic and domesticated as women writers: for instance, H. E. Bates, Edward Upward, and V. S. Pritchett. When these writers look at a man, they regard him as being smaller than patriarchy, smaller than masculinity, and working in an almost post-Kafkaesque way in a world that's too big for him. Those writers are, perhaps unconsciously, strong on the vulnerability of the English male. *Another Gulmohar Tree* is a book that's written by someone who has lived in England for a long time and therefore perhaps has an English sense of restraint, caution, and diffidence.

CC: Could you tell me more about the Urdu writer, Ghulam Abbas, whose life story helped you to conceive *Another Gulmohar Tree*?
AH: The idea for *Another Gulmohar Tree* was in my mind throughout the early 1990s. It was always going to be about a female artist and her Pakistani husband, and was called 'A Falling Leaf' at that time. I put this story away for years, because my friend, the writer Hanan al-Shaykh, told me it was similar to many other things that had already been done. But then I read a short story by Ghulam Abbas, written in the 1950s, about a man who meets an English woman at a dance. I did some research and realized from a dedication he wrote to her that Ghulam Abbas's wife Zainab, whom I'd always thought was Pakistani, was actually English. Their story fell into what I was writing in that they did a picture book of rhymes together, *Moon and Star*, using Ghulam's poems and Zainab's pictures. But echoes and reflections of the novella very much come from my own imagination, and the development of their marriage is absolutely fictitious too. I use the event of the Abbases' mixed marriage more as social history.

Ghulam Abbas was 50 years older than me, and I was almost able to construct the character I loosely based on Abbas, Usman, as my opposite. As a writer, my eyes are very important, whereas he's a 'blind' writer. I started with an image of Chris Abbas's picture of children playing on the street, and various pictures of children in Karachi and at fruit markets. The actual picture is a picture of children using a skipping rope near a pond with ducks and two trees. And I thought yes, my Lydia will be drawing such scenes.

CC: As you say, Usman is not a visual person, because near the end, he realizes he's not been noticing or thinking about the gulmohar tree's blossoming and changing colour.
AH: Lydia and Usman are equal in their difference from me: that was the only way for me to deal with a woman artist of another culture. I don't see writing about women as a different thing from writing about men. Whether or not she is the centre of the book is up to the reader. You read from your own culture and literary background, which affects whether you want to see a person who is perhaps transplanted and struggling, or whether you want to see a person who is rooted in Pakistan. A lot of South Asian *women* identify more with Usman, whereas most English people, regardless of gender, see it as Lydia's book. Having said that, the *Times Literary Supplement* reviewer saw it primarily, or solely, as Usman's book, and she doesn't mention that Lydia has a perspective, or that there is a fairy tale there.[49] She saw a realistic portrayal of a man who is struggling with his world, his life. *I* feel it's a double-centred book: you can read it as her narrative, and you can read it as his in parallel. If you read them separately, you'll see that their weightings are carefully done, because they have almost equal numbers of chapters and pages. I don't really talk in any kind of triumphalist way about my works, but what I have achieved here is to create a little text that opens up to almost every kind of identification, never just Usman. The only thing that I would disagree with is when readers occasionally interpret Lydia as passive, to

which I say 'No, she's a woman of her time or slightly ahead of it, but she loves what she has, and wants to make it better, non-aggressively.'

CC: How do your dual roles as academic and writer intersect?
AH: They don't. I teach people to love books: that's mainly what I do. I'm not really a critic in any academic sense. I write essays about things I love and, more and more, they just come to me, on aspects of Urdu literature, or overviews of the work of writers I admire. About 20 years ago, I had things to say about forgotten trends and writers, and fervently argued the invisibility and the importance of Third World literature – you know: we ought to be reading more Chinese and Arabic writing, there ought to be more translations. However, I have no real points to make any more as a critic: frankly, when I listen to discussion at symposia, it sometimes bores me because I've been there and I wonder, 'Are we still there? Haven't we moved?' I could play devil's advocate either way: on the one hand, I'd argue that compared with years ago, when we had nothing, now we are so much more visible, and there is greater awareness of world writing. On the other hand, I would say 'Yes, but in the 1980s, we had five translations from the Chinese in any given year, and now we have almost nothing, so translated fiction has become more scarce than ever.' So I don't know; I just feel it's becoming a circular discourse.

CC: Please could you tell readers about your latest book, *The Cloud Messenger*.
AH: *The Cloud Messenger* is about a man who, rather like me, attends SOAS, reading Persian and Urdu. To begin with, there is a sense of order and chaos in his studies, and he finds that it's the order that helps him through. Facing life after graduation, he eventually finds work teaching Urdu at a university. We meet him when he is 50-something, and has just produced a book that might be the one we are reading. The very last thing he writes is a paper on Sufi poets, not in Persian but Sindhi and Siraiki, and you get the sense that he is moving his intellectual

horizons in that direction. *The Cloud Messenger* is also about Sufi poetry, specifically a love poem about a man and a woman at her death. Love takes the place of anything called 'God' here, and if we think of true love as being the discovery of something deeper and bigger, then it is a very emotional, probably early Islamic, Sufi notion of God.

In popular Sufism, to put it very simply, when you have known extreme love for a real person, that is very much a projection (I have been reading *The Interpretation of Fairy Tales* by the Jungian scholar Marie-Louise von Franz[50] for a dissertation I'm supervising on fairy tales, and that influences my terminology today). When the projection is removed, and that depth is lost, either your body or soul has, in a sense, died. Rebirth comes only through love as an absolute. If you tried to decode *The Cloud Messenger*, and the arch of Sufi poetry within it, you would find something like that. The character has these two terribly tragic relationships, and there's no explanation given, until at the end, you see Mehran stripped of all attachments. You are left to draw your own conclusion. I asked my editor, 'Where is the end of the book?' She said, 'When Mehran smiles and says that he has not decided what the title of the book is.' He leaves us with an enigma, and perhaps that enigma is something that connects with Sufi poetry in a secular world. You realize that you cannot live in the extreme state of passionate love.

What I am trying to suggest is not that every kind of love is actually a mystic experience; it is that the peak of experience, and the extremity of passion, make you realize that there are worlds beyond even that. It awakens you to them. It can make you extremely restless, make you break down or suicidal. We can also say that sometimes love inspires you to be greater than you are. You see that in *Another Gulmohar Tree*, where Lydia wants to paint better and better. Whichever way we look at it, these are what I am talking of as profane aspects. They do not necessarily have keys that lead to a mystic experience. But the stripping away of these earthly desires or attachments, or the loss of something that is very important to you, can leave you denuded in a way that is similar to what happens to the mystic or the dervish.

CC: What do you think of Nobel Prize-winning author, Doris Lessing's, Sufism?

AH: Lessing's best writing on Sufism is her concise introduction to a book on the life of Rabia of Basra, the great ninth- and tenth-century mystic.[51] In comparison to the muddle-headed earth mother Doris Lessing who evokes garlic and organic bread, this is another Lessing, who can say critical things in a terminology which isn't meta-language. She talks about Rabia in that way, and she knows a lot about religions. Writers on Sufism tend to be viewed as charlatans, but they're not. If you look at what has been kept in print, much of it is not esoteric or wishy-washy, the kind of thing that's supposed to have led to innocent Westerners becoming Sufi and not having a religion, but just floating around. These books are actually very hard, whether they are classics like *A Tale of Four Dervishes*, or *The Life of Rabia of Basra*, or Shah Waliullah,[52] who some people think of as an arch-conservative, and others think of as a great enlightened Muslim thinker of the eighteenth century, who prefigures other great progressives. This is the kind of publishing in which Doris Lessing is mentioned, and to which she is very close. I don't take her Sufi predilections with a pinch of salt. She has been interested in Sufism for more than 40 years – longer than she was involved in the Left – and we are very lucky to have her contribution.

CC: Could you say a little about your connection with British Indian writer Attia Hosain, author of *Sunlight on a Broken Column* and *Phoenix Fled*?[53]

AH: I was very close to Attia. She was an early South Asian expat in Britain. I would say that if she hadn't kicked and pushed me, I wouldn't have written. Attia was drop dead beautiful. She said other people can write criticism, but people like us, we've had our bodies and hearts broken, our country torn apart and, as part of the generation that inherited all this, we have to write creatively about that burden. One of the themes in *The Cloud Messenger* is feeling torn between the two countries of India and Pakistan – not emotionally, because I feel a lot for both of them – but mentally and politically. Put it this way, my mother's family is from one side, and my father's, from the other. Mine was the first generation to suffer that. My parents married six months after Partition. My mother's entire family stayed on in India, where they had vast land holdings. It would have been ridiculous for them to leave. A lot of people who went to Pakistan really left because they could make new lives for themselves there. Others left because they were forced out, but my mother's family wasn't compelled to go. It then meant that with wars and all kinds of things, many people couldn't travel back and forth freely. Nowadays, with my British passport and Pakistani birth, I have more trouble going to India than if I had one straightforward nationality; that's how it works. Attia knew Ghulam Abbas well. She said he was a colleague of hers at the BBC, though she never mentioned Chris Abbas and I don't know whether she knew her.

CC: With *Granta 112* attracting a lot of attention,[54] Pakistani literature is currently in the international literary spotlight. Do you find this focus on what is sometimes termed 'new Pakistani writing' helpful?

AH: Occasionally I feel like distancing myself from it all and saying that I was a Pakistani writer long before any of this. I was included in Pakistani anthologies in the 1990s,[55] so it's a label that hasn't suddenly come to me because of new interest from magazines. But it was only one of many labels; now, suddenly, I'm expected to react differently, as if the label has come to me because of a group. I don't want to sound egotistical, because in a way the identification was a recipe for being ignored, but there was a time when I was just about the only one in Britain with a book and that label. Then Kamila Shamsie came and shouldered the burden. Nadeem Aslam was seen as British Asian until fairly recently. His first novel was very Pakistani, but he was a British writer in terms of how he was received. I'm not British Asian because I didn't come here during my formative years and, unlike Nadeem, I know nothing about monocultural migrant communities, as I never lived in one. I'd love to know, but by the time I might have been interested, it was far too late.

CC: You rightly say you're not British Asian, but there is a Britishness that may not be hyphenated in your writing, and you also have American and European influences.
AH: As far as the short story is concerned, the first writers I really liked were Flannery O'Connor, Tennessee Williams, Jorge Luis Borges, and Elsa Morante. I rate Eudora Welty very highly and liked the writers from the Deep South very much. I was writing my life in one sense and, like Toni Morrison, I wanted to see on paper things with which I could identify. Very soon, I was finding the Western writers I was reading didn't go far enough in terms of representing what I wanted. My way of going about finding what I needed was to read Chinese fiction in translation, and fiction by many Arab writers including Naguib Mahfouz (who is a subtle though abiding influence) and African American writing in the original English.

I was also reading French literature about traumas experienced during the Second World War, when France was being assailed. I love Italian writer Cesare Pavese's *The Moon and the Bonfire*,[56] about the Partisans and the Italian fascists. When I think of this, I think in terms of Partition, though I didn't realize it at the time. To me, the novella form is a very French form so, in *Another Gulmohar Tree*, I reference Flaubert. His *A Simple Heart* is an exemplar of the perfect novella,[57] which has influenced Urdu as well. In my writing, I read all these kinds of texts and they send me down different routes, trying to find my own voice.

4
Leila Aboulela

Credit: Vaida V Nairn.

Leila Aboulela is a Sudanese writer, previously resident in Britain, who now lives in Doha, Qatar. Writing is her main career, and she also brings up her youngest child. The daughter of a Sudanese man and an Egyptian woman,[1] Aboulela was born in Cairo in 1964, but grew up in Khartoum. Egypt and Sudan were both colonized by Britain, although they had very different experiences of colonial occupation, which are discussed in this interview and in Aboulela's most recent novel, *Lyrics Alley* (2010). It should be noted that Egypt has had long cultural and migratory interaction with the Muslim Arab people of northern Sudan,[2] and Aboulela, with her dual parentage, is more aware than most of this shared heritage. Recent Sudanese history has been marked by ferocious civil wars between the powerful northern Arab Muslims, the subjugated southern African Christians, the communists, and *sharia*-endorsing religious parties.[3] Now the genocide in the western region of Darfur, the discovery and exploitation of oil resources, the designation of Sudan as a state assisting international terrorism, and the referendum on southern Sudanese secession receive much critical attention.[4] However, Aboulela writes that she wishes to counter these 'stereotypical images of famine and war' by depicting Sudan as 'a valid place' in her writing.[5]

Aboulela studied for a Masters degree in Statistics at the London School of Economics before moving to Aberdeen for her husband's work, in which city much of her writing is set. She has also lived in Indonesia, Abu Dhabi, and Dubai. In an early essay 'And my Fate was Scotland', she writes, in a comment which anticipates many of the themes in her writing:

> I moved from heat to cold, from the Third World to the First – I adjusted, got used to the change over time. But in coming to Scotland, I also moved from a religious Muslim culture to a secular one and that move was the most disturbing of all, the trauma that no amount of time could cure, an eternal culture shock.[6]

Her short story 'The Museum' was awarded the first Caine Prize for African Writing in 2000 and is an economical, yet unobtrusively impassioned narrative, which touches on the exploitative impulses which even today lead African artefacts to be displayed in Scottish museums. The story was later anthologized in her first collection, *Coloured Lights* (2001), which explores issues surrounding cultural hybridity; the question of whether to assimilate in a new culture or maintain cultural distinction; and the alternative lifestyles encouraged by faith and secularism. 'Coloured Lights', the story from which the collection takes its name, prefigures the bereaved Sudanese protagonist of *The Translator* and the postcolonial London location of *Minaret*.[7] Other stories discuss intercultural relationships, *halal* food requirements, abortion among non-Muslims, and White Muslim converts. The final two stories in the collection, 'Days Rotate' and 'Radia's Carpet', are two allusive, but arguably unsuccessful, incursions into the realm of science fiction. They are set in the twenty-second century, after a Great War, in a world that now has no countries or borders, in which nature is respected, and machines are banned. To some extent these stories depict a Muslim utopia, with banks not charging interest, angels consorting with humans, and where 'all power was spiritual power, all struggles spiritual struggles'.[8]

Aboulela's first novel, *The Translator* (1999), was longlisted for the IMPAC and Orange Prizes, and concerns a love affair between the eponymous Sudanese translator, Sammar, and her employer, the Scottish lecturer of Postcolonial Politics, Rae Isles. Recently widowed, Sammar lives a modest and lonely existence in her rented room in Aberdeen until she forges a closer friendship with Rae over the telephone one Christmas holiday. However, the stumbling block in their relationship is that Rae is not a Muslim and, after an argument about his lack of faith, Sammar returns to her family in Sudan. Months later, Rae pursues her there, having said the *shahadah* (declaration of faith) and converted to Islam. The novel ends happily, with Rae and Sammar planning to marry and travel to Egypt then back to Aberdeen. As this summary suggests, and as the title makes clear, this is a novel all about translation: not just the literal linguistic translation that Sammar is involved in, from Arabic into English, but also cultural translation. Sammar's view of her translation work is that she is involved in 'moulding Arabic into English, trying to be transparent like a pane of glass not obscuring the meaning of any word'.[9]

Minaret was also longlisted for the Orange and IMPAC, and traces the central character, Najwa's, descent from her privileged position as a Sudanese minister's daughter to exile in London when a coup dislodges her father from power, and eventually to the life of a domestic servant to a wealthy Arab family in the former imperial capital. Unlike many diasporic novels, where racism tends to be depicted as stemming from colour prejudice, Aboulela portrays overt Islamophobia in post-9/11 London (although interestingly the events of September 2001 are never explicitly mentioned). Najwa is referred to as 'Muslim scum' and has a soft drink thrown over her veiled head on a London bus in 2003.[10] Furthermore, when she spends time with the devout son of her employer, Tamer, she notices the unease with which Londoners regard his beard and Arab profile which they stereo- typically associate with terrorists.[11] Yet ironically, Najwa, Tamer, and their South Asian, Arab, and White convert friends from the mosque are not interested in politics. Educated as most of them were in English medium schools, they are equally opposed to anti- American feeling as to the West's neo-colonial activities in the Middle East. For them, Islam is far less an ideology than a code of ethical behaviour and a central marker of identity in the fragmen- tary world of migration, asylum, and family disintegration.

Aboulela's most recent novel, *Lyrics Alley* (2010), is set in Sudan in the early 1950s. This was the time leading up to Independence, so one of the things the novel reflects is the favourable relation- ship between the head of the family, Mahmoud Abuzeid, who is an important businessman, and the colonial authorities. Yet a tragic accident hits the affluent Abuzeid family, leaving Mahmoud's eldest son Nur disabled, and causing the break-off of Nur's engagement to his childhood sweetheart Soraya. The novel charts the unexpected ways in which the family comes to terms with the accident and how, in Aboulela's words, 'new avenues and new hopes can, mercifully, take root'. Once confined to his bed by paralysis, Nur discovers lyric writing and poetry. This strand of the novel, as Aboulela tells us in the interview, is based on the bio- graphy of her uncle, Hassan Awad Aboulela, who was a promising student left quadriplegic by an accident, well known for the lyrics he wrote for popular singers in Sudan. The teacher Badr provides a counter-narrative to that of the largely secular Abuzeid family, as he is deeply influenced by Islam.

In Aboulela's four fictional works to date, she is concerned to probe the ethical dilemmas faced by Muslims all over the world, and provides gradated descriptions of members of the transna- tional Islamic *ummah*. Her fiction is linguistically composite, incorporating words from Arabic alongside English, Scottish street slang, and colonial discourse. Aboulela is also a highly intertextual writer, and her texts allude to the Qur'an, Sudanese writers such as Tayeb Salih, Western romance fiction, and Arab poets. Finally, Aboulela deftly evokes three very different locations in her prose: the snowy, remote cities of Scotland (particularly Aberdeen), the teeming multiculturalism of London, and the heat and conviviality of Khartoum. A face-to-face interview with Leila Aboulela proved impossible, so this conversation initially took place over the telephone in July 2008 and has continued by email over the subsequent two years. It is the only interview to have been published first elsewhere,[12] but the original interview has been revised and expanded to incorporate the new novel, *Lyrics Alley*.

CC: Could you describe your latest novel, *Lyrics Alley*?

LA: It's a historical novel, set in Sudan in the early 1950s at the time leading up to Independence. Sudan was not technically part of the British Empire nor was it administered by the Colonial Office. This was because it was an Anglo-Egyptian Condominium. When Britain invaded Sudan, it did so alongside Egypt, and relations between Sudan and Egypt have long been fraught. I became interested in this era, because my mother is Egyptian and I myself emigrated to Britain. Therefore, the three countries that made up my identity – Sudan, Egypt, and Britain – came together in this book. The novel was inspired by the life of my father's cousin, the poet Hassan Awad Aboulela[13] who wrote the lyrics for many popular Sudanese songs of the 1950s. Like my father, Hassan was educated at Victoria College in Alexandria. If it was not for the accident, he would have gone on to attend Cambridge University (my father himself graduated from Trinity College, Dublin). So as I was writing *Lyrics Alley*, I was drawing on my father's youth and the stories he used to tell me.

CC: What's it like writing a historical novel?

LA: It's something very different for me. I had to do a lot of research, although most of the novel is based on things my father had told me, and his friends and generation. It's easy to get sidetracked with the research; I had to pull myself back and not put too much information into the novel. My priority was to keep the story going, rather than retaining every historical detail. The 1950s was a fascinating and pivotal time in Sudanese history. With British rule coming to an end, Sudan was at a crossroads. In the novel, the head of the family, Mahmoud Abuzeid, who himself has Egyptian roots, supports a proposed union with Egypt. However, this union fails as the majority of Sudanese opt for an independent Sudan free of any foreign influence.

CC: Please discuss the novel's juxtaposition of Sudan/Egypt; 'tradition'/'modernity'; and the position of the novel's mixed-heritage, or 'half-caste' characters, who have one foot in each nation.
LA: Because of the Anglo-Egyptian Condominium, Sudan's independence from Britain was also an independence from Egypt. Despite the strong fraternity between the two neighbouring countries, Egypt did pursue imperialistic interests in Sudan and, in the popular Egyptian imagination, Sudan existed as a back door to Egypt. It was also Egypt which bolstered the Arabic character of Northern Sudan and, it could be argued, stunted the natural integration between North and South Sudan. The Egyptians in *Lyrics Alley* see Sudan from a colonizer's prejudiced point of view but (unlike the British) they interact closely with the Northern Sudanese. This is because of the shared language, religion, and culture. Marriages between Sudanese and Egyptians were and are very common and the attitude of regarding the Sudan and Egpyt 'as one' was prevalent at the time, notwithstanding that the Sudan was consistently regarded as the lesser of the two. (One way of looking at the relationship between Egypt and Sudan is to see it as resembling the relationship between the United States and Britain in the late nineteenth century.)

In the novel, the biggest clash between modernity and backwardness is reflected in the conflict between Mahmoud's two wives: the illiterate, traditional Waheeba, mother of Nur; and

Mahmoud's younger wife, the sophisticated Nabilah who longs to return to cosmopolitan Cairo. The two are well-matched, with neither being a clear victor. The 'half-caste' children do have a foot in each nation but, with Sudan rejecting a union with Egypt and asserting its national character, the children (unless they assimilate either way) are poised towards a somewhat disadvantaged future. In the Sudan they would not be Sudanese enough and in Egypt they would be held back because of their Sudanese origins.

CC: The novel is perhaps not as religiously inflected as your previous texts and, with the exception of Badr, most characters are secular or even atheist. Did you make a conscious decision to move away from the '*halal*' credentials of your previous books?

LA: Not at all. The character of Badr is central to the novel. He is the one who sets out to make sense of the dilemma 'Why does Allah Almighty make bad things happen to good people?' As a believer, he worships an All-Powerful, All-Compassionate God and, in exploring this question from a theological point of view, I feel I have gone deeper in writing about Islam – and about the meaning of faith – than in my other novels. By moving the setting of this novel to Sudan and choosing an all-Muslim cast, I naturally lost the juxtaposition of East/West and the tension between Muslim/non-Muslim that was prominent in *Minaret* and even more so in *The Translator*. The situation in *Lyrics Alley* reflects Muslim cultures in a Muslim setting and I wanted to present characters with different shades of religious devotion. It was also important to show how the traditions that affected women adversely (such as polygamy and segregation) were not tied to religious observance. Urban Muslims in 1950s Cairo and Khartoum did not particularly feel the need to assert their religious identity. In the streets of Cairo, very few city women wore *hijab*. And prestigious schools such as Victoria College were strongly secular, discouraging their Muslim students from practising their religion or speaking in any language other than English. Privileged Sudanese people, who were trained to take over from the British administration, were encouraged to distance themselves from the pre-colonial rule of the Mahdi[14] which was heavily religious in nature.

Later on, after independence, rural–urban migration was largely responsible for bringing a more religious character into the cities. The inhabitants of faraway villages had continued with their traditional Islamic lifestyle and were not, from a cultural point of view, greatly influenced by colonial rule. In that respect Badr, who comes from this group, is the most contemporary of the novel's characters, the one who projects into our present day. He sees how Khartoum changes from having eight churches and one mosque to having more and more mosques, and his own move from the outskirts to central Khartoum illustrates this historical direction.

CC: Could you discuss the fairly frank representations of sexuality in *Lyrics Alley*, especially your outspoken but balanced discussions of the fraught topic of female genital mutilation, as practised in parts of North Africa?
LA: The Sudan was one of the first countries in Africa to outlaw female genital mutilation. However, the law, passed by the Anglo-Egyptian administration, was neither enforced, nor influential, and the procedure continued unabated. Only urban, educated families distanced themselves from this practice. And it was largely men rather than women who were keen for the practice to end. The situation described in *Lyrics Alley* where the father/grandfather is opposed to the procedure and the women strongly in favour, is sadly typical, and stories abound of wives who take advantage of their husband's absence to enforce the procedure on their daughters. With time, and greater education and empowerment of women, the rates of performance have dropped, as has the severity of the type of mutilation itself. (In order to protect girls from the adverse physical side effects of the procedure, Sudanese doctors developed less radical, clinically safe methods. These measures found popular support, although they did not, as was hoped, eradicate the practice altogether.) I intended to shock the reader with the episode of female genital

mutilation in *Lyrics Alley*. Nabilah's view of the 'backward' Sudan could be so easily dismissed by the modern reader as prejudice and even racism, but I wanted to bolster her position and illustrate the challenge she faced from a traditional society's perverse adherence to what was harmful and unnecessary. Nur's accident was an act of Fate, but I also wanted to show an alternative example of suffering inflicted by one person on another.

CC: The term 'Muslim writing' is seeing expansion in usage. How do you feel about being referred to as a Muslim writer?
LA: Yeah, I mean, I'm OK with it. I feel as though this is the type of question where I should answer, 'I don't want to be labelled or tagged as a Muslim writer; I want to be seen just as a writer', that's the right answer today, I suppose, and it's true. But at the same time, when I get appreciated by Muslims themselves, it's nice, because then it feels that they are saying to me, 'yes, you are authentic, you are part of the community, you know what you're talking about', so it's good to have this recognition, but at the same time it does constrict you. And certainly, in terms of literary circles in the Sudan, they don't like me having this tag of being a Muslim writer; they think that that's not an appropriate label to have. So I have mixed feelings about it, but I don't mind it too much, because there's some truth in it.

CC: Speaking of enjoying being appreciated by Muslim readers, what did you think about the description of you as a '*halal* novelist'?[15]
LA: Well, people are appalled by that in Sudan. In Sudan, writers and intellectuals are usually very liberal, leftwing, and so on, and people want me to be like that, they want me to be the liberated woman, so they are appalled at this *halal* writer thing. But when this was written in *The Muslim News*, it was written meaning that 'she's authentic, she's one of us'; it was meant positively, so I take it as a compliment.

CC: In *Minaret*, Najwa is from a secular family; she parties, wears short skirts, and is quite Westernized, and it's only

later when she comes to Britain that she becomes religious. I wondered when I was reading the novel if there's anything of that in your own background, if you were brought up in a secular way?

LA: Yeah, but I exaggerated it a lot in *Minaret*. In *Minaret* I made it very dramatic: Najwa was highly secular and then she became very religious, whereas in my own life it was more in the middle. But yes, I mean, I started to wear the *hijab* when I came to Britain; I didn't wear it in Sudan. In Sudan, all my friends at university were liberal and left-leaning, and they would have been just shocked if I had started to wear the *hijab*; they would have talked me out of it in a couple of hours [laughs]. Like Najwa in the novel, I used to look with a kind of admiration at the girls in university who wore the *hijab*, but it was only when I came to Britain that I felt free, that I wasn't surrounded by my friends or my family, and I could do what I wanted. And ironically, when I first came, and when I started to wear the *hijab* in 1987, nobody even understood what it meant. In London it just had no connotations whatsoever, so it was really a very good time to begin covering my head, without it having any repercussions.

CC: I'm interested in this point that you felt free to wear the *hijab*, because now veils are often interpreted by Westerners as markers of a lack of freedom. In contrast, for you, the *hijab* seems like a symbol of liberty.

LA: Yes, because I always had this shyness when I was younger; I grew up feeling a little bit bashful. I didn't like it if men looked at me or complimented me; I would immediately withdraw. Wearing the *hijab* sorted this out, because men didn't pay me the same kind of attention that they paid me before I wore the *hijab*. Actually, there's a word I use in the novel that seems to have been misinterpreted, because Najwa says that she becomes 'invisible' when she wears the *hijab*, and men don't look at her any more. I think people read it as being invisible in a very negative way. However, I meant it in an entirely positive way, that she was no longer having to put up with the way men were looking at her, and all that. I don't know, afterwards I wondered whether I should have used the word 'invisible'.

CC: There are several words in the text that are quite ambivalent, but that provides a richness as well. At one point in the novel, Najwa describes the *hijab* as a 'uniform',[16] which is another word that could be read in both a positive and negative light.

LA: The *hijab* does in a way feel very much to me like a uniform. I'm always struck if I meet a Muslim woman for the first time who wears the *hijab*; usually I'll first meet her outside, wearing the *hijab*, then after a while, as I get to know her better, maybe I'll meet her in her own home without the *hijab*, and I realize, 'Oh, this is the real her.' I feel that I don't really know her properly unless I see her without the *hijab*. So it is a kind of uniform, it does put a distance between you and other people. Something is hidden.

CC: What did you think of the debate that emerged when a member of the UK parliament, Jack Straw, said that he asks female constituents who come to see him in his surgery wearing the *niqab*, or face covering, to remove it?[17]

LA: Well, I understand how he feels, yes, that talking to someone with the face covered is awkward. I feel the same way, that it is awkward when I speak to another lady and her face is not visible, especially if I don't know her at all. There is a precedent in Muslim countries of requiring veiled women to show their faces for identification purposes. On a personal level, I wouldn't dare request that from another lady if she's decided to cover her face; I don't feel that I would have the courage to ask her to do that.

CC: Or the right to ask it, really?

LA: Or the right, yes, exactly. Well, Jack Straw has the right, of course, because he's a powerful person, in an official position, and this is going to give him the right. These political things are all about power, who is stronger than whom, and who can tell the other person what to do; that's what happens when things become politicized like that. But yes, I do feel that it is awkward when someone covers her face. I know very few ladies who do that, but I have one relation by marriage who does, and I find that I prefer visiting her at home, where I can see her face uncovered, rather than meeting her in public or having her come to my house. I feel more comfortable going to her where I can see her face.

CC: Do you think there's any Qur'anic justification for covering the face?
LA: From what I understand, from the Islamic point of view, it is a choice: to cover your face or not to cover your face. It's like a hat for men, wearing a hat or not wearing a hat. But on our holy journey to Makkah, the Hajj, you have to uncover your face, you can't cover your face when you go on Hajj. In the same way that men on Hajj aren't allowed to wear a hat, women when they go on Hajj have to cover their head, but aren't allowed to cover their face. Generally, I think face covering is an optional thing in Islam.

CC: To go back to the British Muslim label, I was wondering whether you read any other British Muslim writers.
LA: Oh, a lot. I mean, there's Kamila Shamsie, I read all of her novels; Ahdaf Soueif, I've read her books as well. But many of these writers prefer to be considered nationally, as a Pakistani writer or an Egyptian writer. I feel an affinity to them, except that maybe in my books the Muslim ingredient is a bit more prominent. I do feel that I'm like them: I'm a Sudanese writer; they're Pakistani, Egyptian, and so on. But for me, instead of having Islam as part of the culture, I'm consciously presenting it as a faith. There are many Muslim writers and they're writing different sorts of Muslim novels, but maybe in my case this religious element is heightened. Having said that, there are many distinctively Muslim writers on the international stage. I admire the work of the French Algerian Faiza Guène, Afghan-American Khaled Hosseini, Saudi Rajaa AlSanea, Pakistani American Mohsin Hamid, and Egyptian Alaa Al Aswany.[18]

They are a younger generation of writers who include Islam in their work much more than their predecessors did.

CC: Turning to *Coloured Lights*: in that collection you include stories about abortion ('Make Your Own Way Home') and heavy drinking ('Majed'), and perhaps a somewhat stereotypical portrayal of the pitfalls of British life, although Britain is explored with greater subtlety in 'The Museum'. I wondered if you could say a bit more about that collection.

LA: Well, the drinking is in a story where a father ends up urinating in his son's cot when very drunk, and it's shocking but this sort of thing happens. However, the character himself is a Muslim, a Sudanese, so it wasn't a comment about British life, nor was I trying to say that he'd been corrupted by British life. Heavy drinking is very much part of Sudanese culture. There's a clash between the ideals of Islam and the drinking lifestyle in Sudan. It's illegal, but people still drink. It's a major issue, because alcohol is a central part of African culture and it's been there a long time. Every time they try to bring in Islamic laws and try to Islamize the country, this tradition is the main thing that they hit against, and the restrictions annoy people very much. In other areas, the culture in Sudan is generally conservative, but when it comes to drinking it's different. It's a male thing in Sudan, though. Women don't drink; it would be shocking for a woman to drink and yet it's OK for men, so there's a double standard. As for the representations of abortion in 'Make Your Own Way Home', I wanted to present it as an inevitable and coldly practical solution to an unwanted pregnancy resulting from premarital sex. Nadia's parents are strict because they want her to follow Egyptian customs and to stay a virgin until she gets married. When she visits Tracy in the abortion clinic she sees what her parents were trying to protect her from.

CC: Why did you choose to make the protagonist of your first novel, Sammar, work as a translator?

LA: I felt that it was important for the theme itself that Sammar's translating. She's not only translating Arabic into

English, but is also translating Islam for Rae. She is the agent for his change. She shows him that Islam is relevant for him too and points out that he needs it. She makes Islam attractive by presenting herself as the prize or reward for his conversion. Her insistence (which is immature and egotistical) that if Rae loves her, he will love Islam, has strong impact on him.

CC: At one point in the novel, Yasmin calls Rae an Orientalist, which makes Sammar quite distressed. To what extent do you see the character as an Orientalist?
LA: Because Rae doesn't speak Arabic and never studied the language Arabic, he's not really an Orientalist. An Orientalist would usually study languages and be very much immersed in Arabic and so on. But yes, he has got this academic interest in the Middle East. Middle Eastern culture is not something that he's ever thought of, personally, for himself, though: it's mostly been an academic concern for him. I've always been fascinated by that, because there's no equivalent in the Arab or Muslim world. In the Middle East, nobody is an expert on the West or on Christianity, but in the West plenty of people are. Universities have Middle East Studies departments and we don't have that in the Middle East. We don't have Occidental Studies, for example; it just doesn't exist. I've always been interested in how there are all these Middle East experts, and how they have this kind of distance and authority. I've wanted to challenge them and shake them and say, you know, does this only go as far as being an expert, or can this be something more personal in your life, as in the case of embracing Islam? But he's not an Orientalist in Edward Said's sense, as someone who stereotypes the East and is coercive in his knowledge practices. No, I think he's basically one of the good guys [laughs].

CC: There are quite a few references in *The Translator* to *sharia* law, as when the mourning period for a widow is described as being kinder under the *sharia* than in secular society. *Sharia* is of course a concept much misunderstood

in the West, so could you explain a bit more about your thinking on *sharia*?

LA: Well, one of the misconceptions is the idea that *sharia* is a law enforced by the government or by an authority. In fact, for a Muslim, *sharia* is something personal as well, something you would follow yourself. It doesn't need anyone else to implement it. It also covers personal affairs; there's a blurring between personal and public affairs. I wanted to show that from the point of view of Sammar, a devout and practising Muslim, following the *sharia* for the period of mourning – which is four months and ten days, a specific period laid down by the *sharia* – she would see it as a very positive thing. It's not something that society's forcing on her; it's something that she herself believes in. This point is very important in all of my writing: Islam isn't just part of the culture in my fiction; it's not a social norm or something like that, but has to do with the individual and their faith, beliefs, and aspirations. This has been central to my writing, and maybe this is what makes my writing different from that of other writers, who see the *sharia* solely as part of society and part of culture, rather than belonging to the individual herself. It's highlighted in my work, because my characters are largely based in Britain, which is not a Muslim country, and yet they as individuals want to practise Islam.

CC: Your novels to date broadly fit into the genre of romance fiction, but there's a twist at the end of *Minaret*, at least.[19] What interests you about romance fiction as a form?

LA: I chose romance fiction because that's what I like to read and I felt comfortable with that form. Most of the novels that influenced me are from this genre; Jean Rhys's *Voyage in the Dark* was an influence on *Minaret* and *Jane Eyre* had great impact on *The Translator*. Romance is the background that I came from. I saw *The Translator* as being a Muslim *Jane Eyre*. The problem in *Jane Eyre* is that Mr Rochester can't marry both Bertha and Jane at the same time. As a Muslim I was reading it, and from an Islamic point of view there *is* no problem, because he can be married to both women at the same time. But even though I realized that,

I still got caught up in the story and I could still see things from Jane's perspective. When I wrote *The Translator*, then, I presented a specifically Muslim dilemma, that she can't marry Rae unless he converts. I was hoping that the reader, even though the reader is not a Muslim, would still get caught up in Sammar's dilemma, just as I had been engrossed by Jane's predicament. I see *Jane Eyre* as being a very Christian book, a very religious book, in that the bigamy conflict is specific to Christianity. At the end of the novel, Rochester converts after he becomes blind, and there are pages and pages of him talking about God and faith and so on.

CC: And similarly Rae gets ill at the end of *The Translator*, so like Mr Rochester he's emasculated. Are there any other romance fiction influences on your writing?
LA: Daphne Du Maurier's *Rebecca*, but that of course doesn't have the spirituality; it's quite a secular book. I like the voice of the heroine, this girl who's young and inexperienced. I can relate to that, the prefeminist woman character. The same with the characters of Jean Rhys, whose writing I love. I can relate to this stage in feminism, where the heroine is quite dependent on men, to some extent helpless, and so on. I find it easier to connect with them than with contemporary heroines. I do read some contemporary romance fiction, but I find it hard to engage with. I've even read some 'chick lit': I tried reading Helen Fielding's *Bridget Jones's Diary*, but I found it hard to relate to this attitude to romance.

CC: When discussing *Jane Eyre*, you stated that the reader of *The Translator* isn't a Muslim but nonetheless he or she can relate to this Muslim dilemma. Do you see your readership as mostly Western, then?
LA: Well, yes, in terms of numbers. My books are published here and they are marketed for the general reader, so if I count most of the people who read me, they are Western and non-Muslim. But the warmest response comes from Muslims, and over the years I'm being increasingly well received by young, second-generation

Muslims who grew up in the West. I just spoke to a girl from the University of California at Los Angeles, who's part of a Muslim girls' book group which wanted to talk to me after reading *Minaret*, and they responded very warmly to my writing. Even though I started out writing for a Western audience, the word 'Western' seems to have changed over the years, with the growing numbers of young Muslims who have grown up in the West.

CC: If your reader belonged to a women's group, do you feel you're also writing for a female audience?
LA: I think so. I mean, I'm not writing specifically for women. When writing *Minaret*, I was very conscious that it was a kind of Muslim feminist novel, and girly or womanly as well, I was aware of that. But *The Translator*, no, I wanted men to read it. The female protagonist of *Minaret* is disappointed in the men in her life: her father disappoints her, then her brother lets her down, she becomes very disillusioned with her boyfriend Anwar, and even Tamer – who is represented sympathetically because he's religious like Najwa – even he disappoints her because of his immaturity. At the end, Najwa relies on God and on her faith. That's how my logic went. And I thought that if this were a secular feminist novel, then at the end she would rely on her career and maybe her friends after her disappointment with men. In *Minaret*, on the other hand, I wanted it to be that at the end she's relying on her faith rather than a career.

CC: Are there any Muslim feminist theorists that have influenced your thinking?
LA: Well, there's Fatima Mernissi, she's written an interesting book called *Women and Islam*, and of course I also know Leila Ahmed's work, but I'm not much of a reader of high theory, to be honest.[20] Instead, I was influenced greatly in my teens by two biographies I read in Arabic, *The Wives of Prophet Muhammad* and *The Daughters of the Prophet*, by the Egyptian academic Aisha Abdelrahman who wrote under the pseudonym Bint Al-Shati (which means 'Daughter of the River Bank'). These books detailed the lives of the women who shared their life with

the Prophet Mohammed. They also focused on the domestic life of the Prophet and his role as a husband and father. I think the book on the Prophet's wives is available in English translation.[21]

CC: In *Minaret* emphasis is placed on different concepts of freedom in the Western and Muslim worlds. After her brother's imprisoned and her mother dies, Najwa comments 'this empty space was called freedom'.[22] Could you say a bit more about different concepts of freedom in the West and in the Islamic world?

LA: This is really Najwa's frustration with herself. Instead of making her do something, she's not doing anything with this freedom and it just feels like an emptiness. I have this feeling that, especially for young people in the West, freedom of choice just becomes a kind of confusion. They have a lot of choices, but it doesn't necessarily mean that they are making the right choices. Freedom then can be a negative thing, rather than a galvanizing force.

CC: Finally, hardline religious politics are absent from *Minaret*. In your depiction of the Muslims who attend Regent's Park mosque, London's most prestigious Muslim place of worship, we don't see any radical views. Did you intend to show that extremism isn't terribly prevalent?

LA: No, I just wanted to highlight the non-political part of the religion. I wasn't saying that extremism doesn't exist, but showing other aspects of Islam and demonstrating that many Muslims aren't interested in politics, and not interested in extremism. That was my concern. There *is* extremism, but I wanted to explore the lives of Muslims who aren't passionate about politics. I wanted to write about faith itself and how spiritual development is a need which is as valid and as urgent as love and career. I wanted to write about the average, devout Muslim and the dilemmas and challenges he or she faces.

5
Abdulrazak Gurnah

Abdulrazak Gurnah was born in Zanzibar in 1948, but emigrated to Britain in 1968, in part impelled by the hardships and state-sponsored terror that he and his family experienced there in the 1960s. A few months after Zanzibar peacefully achieved independence from British colonial rule in 1963, it underwent a revolution, which was inflected by African, socialist, and Muslim ideologies, and in which the country was forcibly brought together with Tanganyika to become Tanzania. In his essay 'An Idea of the Past', Gurnah writes that during the presidentship of Abeid Karume 'the category "Arab" had been used to dispossess, expel, and murder thousands of people who had had a different idea of who they were, that is, they were Zanzibaris'.[1] As a member of this group of hybrid Zanzibari Arabs,[2] Gurnah seeks to complicate any easy nostalgia for the precolonial past. In many of his eight novels to date, he examines the issue of longstanding inter-ethnic conflict and exploitation,[3] as well as intermixture and tolerance, between the myriad groups found in parts of East Africa fringing the Indian Ocean. Yet he shows the Europeans' colonial divide-and-rule tactics and continuing colour and cultural racisms to have caused greater harm to African societies than any local dispute or abuse.[4] Another of Gurnah's pressing thematic concerns is to explore themes of migration, displacement, and crossings both within East Africa, and from Zanzibar to Europe (particularly to Britain and, to a lesser extent, Germany[5]).

As well as Gurnah's eight novels to date, he has also published a two-volume study of African writing and an edited collection on Salman Rushdie's fiction,[6] which derive from his other career as a professor of postcolonial literature at the University of Kent. Gurnah's role as an academic intersects with his writing and, like Aamer Hussein's, many of his characters are either academics or teachers. Furthermore, he quite often satirizes the discipline of English – as with the narrator's girlfriend, the Austenian-named Emma Willoughby in *Admiring Silence*, who is doing an almost incomprehensible PhD in 'the semiotics of dedicated narrative';[7] the lampooning of the 'absurd vanity' of university websites in *Desertion*;[8] or the academic boyfriend of the protagonist's daughter in *The Last Gift*, who uses conferences as a cover for adultery.[9]

In 'Writing and Place', Gurnah describes how he 'stumbled into'[10] writing in his early twenties out of his experiences in the postwar Britain of 'imperialism, [...] dislocation, [...] the realities of our times'.[11] His first novel, *Memory of Departure* (1987) was circulated to various publishers, eventually being picked up by Jonathan Cape when the author was almost 40. As its title suggests, the novel scrutinizes the abandonment of the homeland, and its permanent loss in all but memory and storytelling: concerns which resonate throughout his *oeuvre*. However, the 'departure' in question, is not, as some critics assume,[12] a journey from Zanzibar to the West, but a displacement intrinsic to East Africa. The protagonist, Hassan, journeys to Nairobi from the coastal region further east, and along the way meets the charismatic, dissembling figure of Moses, who falsely claims to be a literature student and expounds on urban virtues while belittling Hassan's small town milieu. Hassan visits his rich, patronizing uncle, Ahmed, and falls in love with his daughter, Salma, which causes him to be expelled from their paradisiacal house to make the reverse journey back to respite at home with family in Zanzibar. From the start of the debut novel *Memory of Departure*, Gurnah asserts a multifarious Muslim identity through images of a violent Qur'anic school; angels recording deeds; and a tranquil mosque.[13]

The next two novels, *Pilgrim's Way* (1988) and *Dottie* (1990)[14] document racism and mixed-heritage relationships in postwar Britain characterized by immigration and fearful discourses on its impact, such as Enoch Powell's 'Rivers of Blood' speech of 1968, and the hatred promulgated by the National Front in the 1970s and 1980s. Gurnah's early work also predates Critical Race Theory in its uncompromising suggestion that British society and its institutions, in part because of their imperial past, are pervasively racist, rather than the cosier view that racism is confined to a bigoted minority.[15] Like the Critical Race Theorists, Gurnah suggests that racism operates through 'microaggressions',[16] apparent humour and insidious gibes, which are equally as psychologically damaging as more overt acts of racism. For example, at the beginning of Gurnah's fifth novel, *Admiring Silence* (1996), a White doctor makes stereotypical assumptions about Black people's health, breezily remarking that 'Afro-Caribbean people have dickey hearts'.[17] The unnamed protagonist is not Afro-Caribbean, but an 'Indian Ocean lad',[18] and the doctor thus ignores differences between various Black ethnicities in such a way as to cause what Gayatri Spivak has termed 'epistemic violence'.[19] Similarly, the narrator's father-in-law, Mr Willoughby, unwittingly insults him in almost every sentence, with self-satisfied remarks such as, 'I suppose we've given your country independence. Do you think it's too soon?'[20]

Gurnah's fourth novel, *Paradise* (1994), was shortlisted for the Booker Prize, and represents at once a rewriting of the

Qur'anic story of Yusuf/Joseph, and a pessimistic account of the colonization of East Africa in the late nineteenth century (compare this to Aamer Hussein's story, discussed on p. 75). In Gurnah's richly resonant chapter, 'A Clot of Blood',[21] the good-looking *rehani* (slave-boy), Yusuf, faces attempted seduction by the vampiric older woman, Zulekha.[22] As in Surah Yusuf, Yusuf's innocence is proven by the fact that Zulekha tore Yusuf's shirt at the back when he was running away from her, yet in this corrupt, hierarchical society, the evidence counts for little.[23] In contrast with Surah Yusuf's concluding optimism, demonstrated when the young man's steadfast faith is rewarded in his return to his family, Gurnah's Yusuf makes the cowardly, if under-standable decision to abandon Amina, the woman he loves, and despairingly joins the ruthless German colonizers he had despised.[24] As can be seen, this Surah lends itself well to discus-sions of migration, exile, slavery, and the position of women.

Gurnah frequently wrongfoots the reader, subverting his or her expectations of the narrative's likely shape. His sixth novel *By the Sea* (2001), for example, begins with an image of an asylum seeker in Britain, but ultimately deals more closely with issues relating to memory and ideas of home. Largely narrated by the elderly, unreliable Zanzibari, Saleh Omar, *By the Sea*'s plot focuses on how he comes to be seeking refuge in Britain, and his connections with Latif Mahmud, a well-established lecturer and poet at the University of London. Saleh initially finds accommo-dation in the small English seaside town of the title. His board-ing house is run by Celia, a landlady to migrants, who outlines a myth of national hospitality that she believes derives from Britain 'help[ing]' other countries during the Second World War.[25] She only lazily differentiates between a Czech Roma and a Kosovan tenant, tetchily positioning both as generic victims of 'terrible [...] bloodlust'.[26] However, Celia treats the Eastern Europeans better than Saleh because they are White, thus exposing the racism that lies behind her 'hospitality'. In con-trast to Celia's reductionism towards her tenant, the complex circumstances that have caused Latif's enmity towards Saleh are revealed via a casket of incense, *ud-al-qamari*, which was gifted him by Hussein, a scheming Persian trader who seduced Latif's mother and brother. Hussein also passed on to Saleh a loan owed him by Latif's father, which leads to Saleh taking possession of Latif's family home, a situation for which the younger man mistakenly accords Saleh full blame.

Gurnah's subsequent novel, *Desertion* (2005), similarly appears to be about Martin Pearce, a relatively non-coercive Orientalist, who falls in love with a Zanzibari shopkeeper's daughter, the deserted wife Rehana. However, the narrative leaves Martin and Rehana's mixed-race relationship hanging, and moves forward to the 1950s and 1960s to describe the thwarted love affair of Rehana's daughter Jamila with a boy, Amin, and the migration of his brother, Rashid, to England. *Desertion* is, *inter alia*, a book about books (Melville,[27] P. B. Shelley,[28] Edward Lane,[29] *qasidas*,[30] Shaaban Roberts[31] and *Othello*[32] are just some of its intertexts); colonialism's sunset; and identity (the novel centres on communitarian rather than individual identity). At various moments during the narrative, there are meditations on aspects of Islam, as in discussion of a conflict between prayer and love;[33] the socialist government's corruption driving people to the mosque;[34] and Amin being taken for a religious man after his disappointment with Jamila, when in fact he believes that '[t]here is nothing out there'.[35]

Gurnah's *The Last Gift* (2011) represents a culmination of his work so far, touching on issues relating to race and racism, migration, memory, ageing, intergenerational tensions, ill-treatment of women and children, and storytelling. The protagonist, Abbas, collapses from undiagnosed late-onset diabetes at the start of the novel, and this and his subsequent strokes necessitate a re-evaluation of his life, which he considers 'as useless as a life can be'.[36] His wife, Maryam, is a foundling who was fostered by couples of varying degrees of unkindness, until she met and ran away with the 34-year-old Abbas when she was still in her teens. Now Maryam takes a job at the local refugee centre in order to support her bed-ridden husband, which enables Gurnah to develop his exploration of the predicament of asylum seekers, first begun in *By the Sea*. The couple's son, Jamal, is also doing a PhD on asylum at Leeds University, where he falls in love with his housemate, the Italian-Irish student Lena Salvati. Jamal's older sister, Anna (born Hanna) is living with her boyfriend Nick, but she increasingly finds him and his family culturally chauvinist, and when she discovers that Nick has been having an affair, she has no compunction about leaving him. The 'last gift' of the title is a voice recording Abbas has made that is discovered after his third and fatal stroke, which recounts to the children his undisclaimed childhood in Zanzibar, and his secret first marriage to a Zanzibari woman he got pregnant and then abandoned for life as a sailor and for his later bigamous marriage to Maryam. As well as exploring many of Gurnah's signature concerns, this novel is unique in offering commentary on recent socio-political events, including 9/11, the 2003 Iraq War and associated demonstrations, and recent violence against the Palestinians. It is also strong on the internalization of racist discourse by the younger generation, the British-born children of migrants. Anna is ashamed of her 'immigrant' past, which she regards as 'pathetic and sordid',[37] whereas the more likeable Jamal reacts to his hidden past by researching the 'desperate flight' of refugees[38] and joining an Islamic Reading Group.

Following Ahdaf Soueif[39] and Tariq Mehmood,[40] Gurnah is one of the earliest anglophone writers to have charted the experiences of Muslims living in Britain and their connections elsewhere. Gurnah was discussing Muslimness, religion, race, gender, class, and their complex intersectionality[41] before Salman Rushdie controversially brought these issues under the spotlight during the furore over the publication of *The Satanic Verses* in 1988. Alongside Amitav Ghosh, Gurnah is also the pre-eminent writer of anglophone Indian Ocean literature. In Amitav Ghosh's *In an Antique Land*, medieval trade along the Indian Ocean is portrayed as a 'shared enterprise', and Ghosh arguably romanticizes the early slavery system in the Indian Ocean as being 'in some small way ennobling'.[42] Gurnah takes a more balanced approach to forms of oppression that predate European colonialism, representing, for instance, tensions between Africans and the descendants of Arab colonizers, and the fraught issue of African involvement in slavery. Especially in *Paradise* and *Desertion*, Gurnah depicts linked townships along the Indian Ocean as comprising a littoral zone of culture. In this interview he uses the word 'archipelago' to describe the shared culture of societies along the Mediterranean, Indian, and African coastlines, which is the same term used by Ghosh[43] and the scholar Janet Abu-Lughod.[44] All three writers thus indicate that cosmopolitan, interconnected cities lined the shores of the Indian Ocean, but were in many ways remote from the more monocultural rural hinterlands further inland.

CC: Could you start by talking about themes in your writing of migration and displacement?

AG: I'm very interested in the dynamic condition of being migrant. I'm not interested in it as a distant pathology; rather, as my experience and a dominant experience of the contemporary world. I think of it as living in one place, but having an imaginary as well as imaginative life somewhere else. This is also possible for people who have only moved within their own country: you could be in London and living your imaginative life in Glasgow. In *Memory of Departure*, which I wrote when I was quite young, I was trying to write about the protagonist's frustrated desire to leave, although at that time I didn't want to give too much away to the reader. I have always been interested in people's sense of being isolated even when they're at home. The distance and inaccessibility between one location and another, or between one age and another, gives the condition of migration a tragic quality. This harrowing dimension is inescapable, and has to do with loss and a regret of things incomplete, or badly done, that cannot be put right. In my writing, I find myself rummaging around in this patch of ground in order to dramatize and understand different dimensions of migrant experience.

CC: Your argument about migration, loss, and the imaginative life recalls a quotation from Salman Rushdie's *Imaginary Homelands*, 'The past is home albeit a lost home in a lost city in the mists of lost time', with which you open your recent book on Rushdie.[45] To what extent is this true for you in relation to Zanzibar?

AG: Rushdie left India at 14, whereas I left Zanzibar when I was almost 18, so his imaginary homeland would be even hazier than mine. He might not agree, but there's a big difference between going from a relatively well-off life in Bombay to an English public school aged 14, and leaving Zanzibar as an adult illegal emigrant, as I did. At that time and for a long time after, Zanzibar was a frightening place to be and, although I thought I knew how different England would be, the experience was unimaginably more intense than I anticipated. I also came at a bad time, in 1967–8, when Enoch Powell and others were stirring up craziness about 'race'. Immigration was an issue that seemed to frighten everybody. In the newspapers, Idi Amin was beginning to expel or pressurize Asian Ugandans into leaving, so to some extent the fear of hundreds of thousands of foreigners coming to England was understandable.

Given this context, it took me a long time to start thinking with any clarity. Even though I had my share of difficulties, I had to cope with the guilt associated with leaving people behind, because I knew how hard it was in Zanzibar. Once I began to think straight, I wanted to see how much I could remember and understand about Zanzibar. It wasn't a straightforward exercise, but involved complete engagement, and realizing that there were some things I couldn't remember, but would have to invent. My writing then was about lived experience, and the notion of people trying to remember is a recurring theme for me. Other issues that continue to preoccupy me include strategies for writing tragedy without alienating the reader, and, of course, methods of representing one language and culture in another. Silence has always been something that has stumped me. As such, the primary activity wasn't remembering, but issues related to method and form: how much do you tell; how much do you suppress? I wasn't thinking of any one particular reader, be it an English, Maori, or African reader, and didn't have expectations about what my reader would know: I wanted *everybody* to read what I was writing. All of these questions were, for me and I'm sure for Rushdie, what engaged me about writing, so it wasn't just about memory.

CC: Given that you mentioned Enoch Powell, could you expand on your experiences arriving in the 1960s and the early encounters with racism, which are particularly explored in the books with significant British settings, such as *Admiring Silence* and *Pilgrim's Way*?

AG: Although I was familiar with many novels and films about racism, I located it in particular places, such as South Africa and various parts of the United States. Yet, when I came to Britain, it was a shock to find racism so much a part of the experience, and to meet it in such a casual, relentless way. Racism wasn't necessarily about abusive words; often, it was something subtler, such as abusive looks. It's hard to explain just how pervasive, ordinary, and constant this kind of response was. Distance gives you an ability to refute it, but if you're a young person, and you routinely encounter people shouting at you in the street, and abuse in classrooms, jobs, public transport, it wears you down.

CC: You're using the past tense, so to what extent has racism disappeared or changed?

AG: I'm different now, so I wouldn't know. I think some of these things befall you because you don't know how to protect yourself, how to hold yourself, how or when to get angry. Perhaps today, a penniless stranger coming from a different culture and being as awkward and linguistically inept as I probably was, would still experience at least some of the racism I suffered. Racism does not necessarily mean somebody throwing things at you, grabbing your shirt, or pushing you. No one ever hit me, but I knew when there was resentment, derision, or scorn, in people's tone, words, or gestures. I don't meet this violence now, but I don't believe it's gone. It's still going on, some way or another.

CC: Returning to Rushdie, to what extent do you think the *Satanic Verses* Affair was a turning point in the way that Muslims are treated? From 1989 onwards, were religion and culture accorded greater prominence in racist discourses than colour?

AG: There's been a complete sea change. Back then, culture and religion didn't matter, it was colour. One heard offensive words like 'Pakis', but people weren't talking about 'Muslims'. I think you're right that the Rushdie Affair changed this, although it may have been just the first disturbance in the air on these issues. Now Islamophobia is pervasive as a result of the attacks on America in 2001 and the war on terror. Before the war in Afghanistan and Iraq, Muslims were 'frightening' or 'terrorists', whereas now they have become 'enemies'. This allows people to feel no guilt in viewing Muslims as dangerous and unstable. There is a steady accretion of images and news stories that inevitably, even if implicitly, portrays Muslims – radical Muslims, obviously, but that's not how it always comes across – as crazy and fanatical. This allows people to have no caution in saying things like, 'There they go again.' If you think of the way the majority of the liberal intellectual community in Britain and Europe came out in defence of *The Satanic Verses*, and the right to write a novel like that, I don't think the same people would come out in support of Islam.

CC: In an essay, you highlight 'those societies [...] which in some cases have been Muslim for a thousand years or so'[46] and there are images in all your novels of 'the House of Islam' as a highly civilized place.[47] You argue against Wole Soyinka's argument that Islam has been an oppressive force in Africa and his desire to recuperate an 'authentic' Africanness,[48] demonstrating that Islam has played an important part in East Africa for a long time. Qur'anic influences on your writing are evident, particularly in

Paradise's intertextual use of Surah Yusuf. To what extent do Islamic themes and art forms shape your writing?

AG: Well, I grew up a Muslim, so it's not much of an achievement to imagine that world: I just have to take myself back there. As you suggest, I dealt with these themes most strongly in *Paradise*, which was probably the first novel for which I did any real research. I wanted to explore the notion of a paradisiacal garden on earth, and how this was not just an expression, but almost an expectation: that a society might be able to create such a thing. I did a lot of reading, and travelled along the coasts of East Africa for several weeks just to observe simple things such as mosques and people's way of life. My interest is not only in Islam as a religion, but also in the crucial role it plays in the culture of the coast of East Africa, the terrain I'm interested in writing about. When I explore people as Muslims, I'm not necessarily insisting that they are pious, law-abiding, believing, practising Muslims, but that their culture is Muslim. To accuse them of being colonized by religion over a thousand years, as Soyinka does, is unlikely without them having possessed Islam themselves for their own uses and ends. Again and again, I disagree with Soyinka and others who argue for some kind of authentic African position which requires suppression of other ways of being African. It seems to me that this way of speaking about Islam in Africa as a foreign, colonizing influence is almost a nineteenth-century discourse. The whole debate indicates how one colonial discourse attempts to supplant another. European colonialism established itself by asserting that Muslims were simply slavers, and it's somewhat surprising to hear the same discourse being picked up now by Africans. As a writer, I'm also trying to speak about something that is not usually discussed, as with James Baldwin's books about African Americans, or V. S. Naipaul's novels about the Caribbean. For me, African writing has excluded Muslims living on the east coast of Africa. I couldn't find myself in the mirror of fiction. As such, the interest in writing about Islam is not about religion in itself; it's about representing the lives of the people that I want to write about.

CC: Your official job title at the University of Kent is 'Professor of Postcolonial Literature', so how do you feel about literary categories such as 'Muslim writing' or 'postcolonial writing'?
AG: I never think of myself as a Muslim writer any more than I think of myself as belonging to any other category. If somebody said to me, as sometimes happens, 'Are you an English writer?' I'd say, 'You must be joking, how can I possibly be one?' However, if it makes sense to people to think of me in a particular way, that's fine. I don't want to argue with any of these categories; some of them fit better than others, but I don't think of myself like that. I know writers are always saying this, and it's not for reasons of wanting not to be cramped, or some concept of artistic freedom, but I only really think of myself as Abdulrazak, who lives in England, teaches in a university, and writes books.

I also don't think of myself as a postcolonialist. There's clearly just a useful postcolonial way of thinking about how we organize the texts that we teach. We find that we can say things in common about these texts, but postcolonialism isn't a piety, or something you can believe or disbelieve in. I can't imagine somebody saying 'I'm a postcolonialist' in the way that you can say 'I'm a feminist', indicating that you hold certain positions in relation to gender and how it is represented. It seems helpful at this juncture to have a category that allows us to group certain texts together, to find shared tropes and concerns, and perhaps theorize and analyse in a certain way. It's not a part of identity, but a nice tolerant term, that is so capacious that you can put it almost anywhere these days.

CC: Images of paradise abound in your writing, most obviously in *Paradise*, in the seven layers of paradise which are explored. Kalasinga's evocation of Kashmir and Herat as heavens on earth is ironic because they are war-torn and violent places in the present day. Towards the end of the novel, Amina says, 'If there is Hell on earth, then it is here',[49] satirizing the Mughal emperor, Jehangir's, famous phrase about Kashmir as a paradise on earth,[50] so could you say

something about your sombre, almost Conradian portrayal
of paradise in that novel?

AG: Novels are often complex and there isn't a single perspective,
but one of the things I was interested in when writing *Paradise*
was the period before the First World War. I was interested in
that context, because European colonialism came very late
to East Africa and the coast, around the turn of the century.
Zanzibar became a British Protectorate in 1890, while the same
thing happened to Kenya in 1895, and I wanted to see if I could
evoke that period's experience of losing control over the running
of one's community and polity to strangers. I was interested in
how people would have understood, and coped with, what was
happening.

Another factor I tried to explore is the kind of society that
would have allowed, or been unable to prevent, colonization.
Why was it that they could not stop themselves from being
taken over, almost without violence? There had been creeping
violence for several decades, and I suppose you don't need to
send in a powerful army if you've already demonstrated how
powerful it is. Nonetheless, the fact that there wasn't a war of
resistance suggests that East Africa comprised a very fragmented
society, because people came from different places, with different languages and religions. They were constantly engaged
in negotiating ways of being together, and I believe that this
was a tolerant, even an enviable society, rather than having one
dominant group dictating what goes. However, in the novel
paradise is ironically presented, because it is overwhelmed
and defeated. Furthermore, I wanted to show that this super-
ficial paradise of good will, courtesy, and the apparent ability
to live together has ugliness below the surface, in the shape of
oppression of other groups. This particularly concerns baggage
and property: women and children, who were suppressed by
patriarchy.

CC: Especially in *Desertion*, you explore what happens when
people from different cultures mix, and how the prejudice

that arises from involvement with a member of another
ethnic group is played out in relation to women.

AG: George Wallace, who was intermittently the governor of
Alabama between 1963 and 1987, made his name because he
refused to allow African Americans to enter what used to be the
Whites-only University of Alabama. When the law changed, he
was forced to step aside, but in 1963 he actually stood at the
doors of the university to prevent a young Black woman from
coming in. He became a national figure, and ran for president
in a couple of the elections. I remember him being interviewed,
I think by David Frost, who asked him the crunch question:
'Would you allow your daughter to marry an African American?'
This question of family ties is a euphemism for saying, 'Just
how racist are you?' Women bear the brunt of racism, because
they are seen as property, to be owned by men. The woman is
also a representative of your masculinity, because your capacity to protect her reflects on your honour and virility. Inability
to ensure that your women don't do the 'disgusting' things
that they always wanted to do, reflects whether or not you are
a proper man.

CC: You deal sensitively with the loaded issue of intra-ethnic
involvement in slavery. In *Memory of Departure*, a character
is described as 'the grandson of the original slave-drivers',
which means that he is 'a man of distinction'.[51] The violence
of the European slave trade clearly surpassed any indigenous
institutions, but you also describe anti-Indian, anti-Arab, and
anti-African prejudices within different communities.

AG: Indeed, you cannot avoid that if you're trying to write with
any degree of truthfulness about East Africa. These intra-ethnic
tensions are not subjects that people like to talk about, because
we like to think of ourselves as courteous and civilized. I don't
necessarily want to offer devastating criticism, but rather to give
the complete picture of what we are. The appearance of courtesy, as with the character Aziz in *Paradise*, quite often disguises
or obscures a hard-hearted, even cruel mentality. Anybody who

writes about their community with a certain amount of honesty is bound to level criticisms at that community, and often this isn't liked. Writers expect it of themselves to have to hurt people to the degree to which they dare: this may depend on who's alive, who's dead, and who they can bear to hurt, but it has to be done.

CC: Why this interest in the Indian Ocean and the shared history of its coastal regions?

AG: The more I research it, the clearer it appears that people's understanding and the stories they told of the world were firmly linked to connections across the sea. The view of the world from East Africa, I suspect, is not astonishingly different from a view of the world from South Arabia, or from western India. It's as though the ocean creates islands of culture along a broader archipelago, which are linked together by the sea and by mercantile connections. Even when I was a child, it wasn't surprising for people to say that they were going to Bombay or Mauritius, as well as to nearby Mombasa. The coming and going between these places was not remarkable, although it was still relatively dangerous. This is important to a cultural sense of who you are: you're not just somebody from Zanzibar, but belong to this other world. You also share the stories of the Ocean: for example, I was surprised to read tales in a book of *The Arabian Nights*, because these stories were told by my mother and grandmother, and so on, and it felt as though they were our stories. It also never occurred to me to ask why we told each other stories about China, Persia, and Syria, but these places existed in our imaginary world, because the sea routes made us part of the wider world.

CC: Could you speak about islands' status along what you describe as the shared 'archipelago' of the Indian Ocean?

AG: It's an interesting feature of East Africa that almost all of the places that we recognize, both historically and in their current status, as centres of this culture, are islands. Zanzibar, Mombasa,

Kilwa, Lamu are islands, but why their centrality? It's partly because their inhabitants were terrified of mainland Africa, as this was the place where they acquired their material possessions. Slaves made up only a tiny proportion of their trade. Mostly, it was gold, hide, timber, ivory. You could almost walk, and certainly you could swim, across the channel between Mombasa Island and the mainland, because it's not very big or deep. Yet, like a ditch, this small channel still provides safety, keeping the Island an island. Zanzibar and Lamu are similarly close to the mainland. In addition, because these islands were maritime colonies, they looked out to sea and had harbours. My understanding of 'archipelago' is the sense of having an island mentality, being fearful but also ready to go out to sea, rather than the mentality of settling on land and building great cities. Anecdotally, when I was at school, the class included Indian, Arab, African, and Somali kids, and we were quite used to that, because everywhere you travelled along the coastline of the Indian Ocean, it was the same recognizable admixture of people. Not only does it reflect society's interchange, but I think its origins lie in the fact that people come from around the same seas.

CC: In an interview, you hesitate to use the word 'hybrid', as you argue that it gives the phenomenon 'a kind of energy' which obfuscates violence and oppression.[52] As such, you seem more pessimistic than Homi Bhabha about what he calls the enabling, transformative 'third space' of hybridity that 'breaks the symmetry and duality of self-other, inside/outside'.[53]

AG: What many postcolonialists didn't acknowledge in discussions of hybridity was various kinds of racism. In *Admiring Silence*, I suggest that we thought of ourselves as 'we' but really we were all locked away in our separate yards.[54] I'm talking about schoolchildren, but even among adults, certain of these communities simply did not have anything to do with others. For example, Muslims and certain other communities, such as Catholics and some Indian groups, wouldn't establish marriage or much interaction with other groups, and they also insisted on separate schools. This isn't hybridity, because they didn't mix pervasively in a way that produced something new. Divisions existed, and unless you're a scholar of the politics of 'race' and society in places like Zanzibar and along the coast, it is too complex to go into these in much detail. It isn't a clear picture, as it's not that Indians and others didn't mix with other people: they did and they didn't.

CC: A common trope in your writing is the bestowing of hospitality on a guest, and the guest being tempted to, or actually seducing the host's daughter or son. What does this suggest about hospitality, sexuality, and gender?
AG: I suppose I'm saying if you treat these issues as forms of honourability, then a mischievous inclination to offend arises straightaway. Of course, Martin Pearce, the English character in *Desertion*, wouldn't have known about these values and would not have been doing it for that reason. But that's presumably one of the reasons why someone like *By the Sea*'s Hussein chooses to seduce his host's son. Equally, if you perceive your women's behaviour as a blow to your self-esteem or reputation, it's not reflective of the thing itself, but its meaning becomes caught up in a kind of piety which is not religion, and out of that, I think, a great deal of sorrow comes. Even if hospitality is bestowed out of kindness, if it's not done in a properly thought out or truthful way, but follows conventions, the result is always, it seems to me, unkindness.

CC: I've already mentioned your intertextual references to Conrad, Rushdie, and the Qur'an, but there are also allusions to nineteenth-century figures, such as Robert Louis Stevenson (whom you invoke in the title of *Admiring Silence* and its epigraph), and Melville's 'Bartleby, the Scrivener' in *By the Sea*.[55] Please discuss your influences.
AG: Sometimes, certain writers are very important to you for a while, and then the moment passes. I read J. M. Coetzee and

V. S. Naipaul frequently, to the extent that I think I've probably finished reading Naipaul now, as I don't read his more recent works with much pleasure, and this makes even the older books harder to read. The trajectory his thinking has taken makes you sense that statements you previously took to be ironic, are actually more strongly felt than you imagined at the time. I was out of England for a while, and when I got back he'd published both *A Bend in the River* and *Among the Believers*, which I read at more or less the same time and thought they had many things in common. Because of that self-assurance that he has, he was often wrong about Africa in *A Bend in the River*, and it seems to me he also got the wrong impression about Islam, and about Iran, Pakistan, and the other Muslim countries he describes in *Among the Believers*, although I don't know those places. However, I wasn't too bothered about it, because I thought it was characteristic of how he writes: some of his shooting-off you take, and some you don't. Yet, Naipaul has become increasingly intolerant, and it makes me think maybe I was too tolerant of him. In his later text *Beyond Belief* he really meant a lot of those appalling statements, and wasn't just saying them as a way of stirring people up. When I sensed this, his writing began to seem less of an analysis, and more of a polemic or diatribe. He's got a hook in his throat about Islam at the moment, although it's not the only issue that enrages him.

I also read other less gigantic writers in terms of reputation and *oeuvre*; people who might have produced just one or two books over time. I read widely, and people influence me in different ways, if influence is the right word. When I return to Melville, which I seem to do at least every other book, it's not because I'm influenced in any way by him, it's just that I find him amusing, engaging, and sometimes wise. Sometimes, you write something and notice a familiarity although you don't know where it comes from. Perhaps eventually you'll remember a moment from Chekhov, an image of somebody looking at a mirror or something, which has crept into your writing. I wouldn't call *Paradise* a deliberate rewriting of Conrad's *Heart of Darkness*, but there are moments when one might recognize parallels. Shakespeare was a key reference point for *By the Sea*, including his ideas of what it might mean to be in love. Also, when Saleh Omar is at the airport, he wonders whether the immigration officer, Kevin Edelman, is Jewish, and the passage begins with the quotation 'That this too too solid flesh should melt, thaw and resolve itself into a dew.'[56] The references to 'flesh' and 'Jew' make the reader think of *Merchant of Venice*, but the line comes from *Hamlet*. These are deliberate intertextualities, which are part of the pleasure of reading as well as writing. It doesn't always have to signify a big connection. It's really part of that mingling of ideas. Why shouldn't Saleh Omar be deeply interested in Shakespeare, say? For whatever reason, he is, but it doesn't have to be a profound meaning as to who he is.

CC: Finally, please talk about the relationship between writing and history. In your essay 'An Idea of the Past', you discuss this issue in relation to the anger Derek Walcott feels about Caribbean slavery, but his love for the English language.[57] Do you share Walcott's belief in an 'enabling tradition'?

AG: I'm sympathetic to the idea of an enabling tradition, but it's different for Walcott, because he has no real alternative source than English to give him a sense of belonging to the world, to literature, or whatever. Even someone like me, who grew up in Zanzibar, influenced deeply by African, Indian, and certainly by Arabic/Islamic culture, can understand the feeling of not wanting to refuse something that can't be given back. In that essay, I was talking about two different ways of thinking about what you are part of, and what ideas the past gives you. On the one hand, it's a Soyinkan idea of clearing the decks, throwing out all of the accretions, and recuperating authenticity, and on the other, like Walcott, embracing everything that comes your way. I'm more sympathetic to the second idea, of not trying to purify anything, but just understanding and accepting all influences.

6
Nadeem Aslam

Nadeem Aslam is a novelist who was born in 1966 in the Punjabi city of Gujranwala, Pakistan, and went to a mediocre Urdu medium school, before moving to Huddersfield when he was 14, knowing no English. He continues to live in West Yorkshire, but now in a lakeside setting in the countryside. Given his relatively late arrival in the UK, he is neither a diasporic 'British Pakistani writer', nor a Pakistani writer, but is situated in an in-between position, complicating conceptual boundaries between East and West. He dropped out of a biochemistry degree at the University of Manchester in his third year, because he felt that if he had the safety net of qualifying as a marine biologist he would be 'dragged into worldly affairs' and never become a writer. Given that Aslam is one of the most linguistically adept and poetic of contemporary English-language writers, it is surprising to learn that he only studied for a science education because his English initially wasn't strong enough to allow him to pursue his love of literature.

Aslam comes from a large, broadly working-class, family, and has over 50 first cousins. He describes the paternal side of the family as being bohemian and artistic, whereas his mother's side is more conservative, although he stresses that his mother was not the blueprint for one of his more hardline Muslim characters, the strict but lonely Kaukab in *Maps for Lost Lovers*. His father is Mian Mohammed Aslam, who was a communist poet and film-maker and a member of the Progressive Writers Association,[1] writing under the pen-name of Wamaq Saleem. The family 'shuttled between Britain and Pakistan'[2] for many years before finally fleeing persecution by Zia-ul-Haq's regime in the 1980s. Once permanently settled in Britain, Mian was compelled to give up writing by the pressures of supporting his family as a political refugee.[3] His father's pseudonym is significant to Aslam, who created the great Urdu poet Wamaq Saleem as a homage to Mian, the fictional poet said to have done for Pakistan 'what Homer did for the Mediterranean and what the Bible did for Jerusalem'.[4] Wamaq first appears in *Season of the Rainbirds* as a luminous poet who learns Persian in order to come to a greater understanding of Urdu's nuances, and who is so widely beloved that his name is even tattooed to a police sergeant's chest.[5] In *Maps for Lost Lovers*, the character Suraya recalls Wamaq's trip to England during his enforced exile from Pakistan's military regime, and both a young girl and the Qawwali singer Nusrat Fateh Ali Khan (who makes a cameo appearance in the novel) are described singing his poetry.[6] In *The Wasted Vigil*, Wamaq appears 'visiting Afghanistan to give a recital of his poems'.[7] Finally, in his recent novella, 'Leila in the Wilderness', which opens Freeman's celebrated *Granta 112* on Pakistani writing, the male protagonist Qes's brother Wamaq is named after the socialist poet.[8]

Aslam explained to me that the brothers in 'Leila in the Wilderness' are in part a coded reference to himself and his father, because Mian wanted to call his son Qes. His mother felt this to be an insufficiently orthodox Muslim name, so they compromised on Nadeem, after the Pakistani short story writer and poet Ahmad Nadeem Qasimi, thus linking Aslam to Urdu literature from birth. Like V. S. Naipaul, Orhan Pamuk, Hanif Kureishi, and others,[9] then, Aslam has achieved writerly success where his father was unable to, in part because of Mian's exile and childcare responsibilities. As Aslam described it to me, 'sometimes the constraints are too much for one person to become a writer in one generation; you need two lifetimes to do that, so I hit the ground running after my father prepared the way'. Aslam originally envisioned his three novels to date as a triptych, with the first examining Pakistan, the second multicultural Britain, and the third Afghanistan. Astonishingly, he now has a further eight books mapped out very precisely, and Wamaq Saleem features to varying degrees in every pro- jected volume in what he describes a 'relatively unified body of work'.

His first novel, *Season of the Rainbirds*, written in 11 months when he was just 22 years old, was shortlisted for or won several awards including the Betty Trask Prize. In this novel, Aslam por- trays a member of a strict Muslim sect breaking a child relative's toy as he sees it as idolatrous, something which an uncle did to Aslam himself when he bought a mask as a boy.[10] Like Salman Rushdie's *Shame* and Rukhsana Ahmad's pathbreaking *We Sinful Women* anthology of English translations from Urdu poetry,[11] *Season of the Rainbirds* is an early text to examine the damage that Zia-ul-Haq's Islamizing regime did to Pakistan between 1977 and 1988, and continuing residues in the post-Zia era. Aslam lambasts Zia's programmes of censorship and Islamization (the latter taking the form of blasphemy laws which persecute minorities, such as the novel's Christian character, Elizabeth), and his fiercely misogynistic Hudood Ordinance. *Season of the Rainbirds* also revolves around the trope of lost letters, as a bag of post that had been lost in a train crash two decades earlier is rediscovered. The impact of this mailbag coming to light is similar to that described in Agha Shahid Ali's later poetry collection *The Country without a Post Office*, which deals with letters lost in the war zone of 1990s Kashmir.[12] Letters enable intimate and more prosaic communication across borderlines and between far-flung places. In some respects, both Aslam's and Ali's writing functions as a series of letters between an exile and his homeland.

Never one to shy from controversial or difficult topics, Aslam is unequivocal in his condemnation of superstitions associated with Islam, which harm many people, particularly women. He is an impassioned opponent of 'honour' killings, about which he writes extensively in his second novel, *Maps for Lost Lovers*, which was garlanded even further than was his debut by critics and literary prize judges (for example, it found a place on the Booker Prize longlist of 2004). He wrote *Maps for Lost Lovers* over 11 impoverished years, sleeping in friends' flats in Huddersfield, Edinburgh, Leicester, and Reading.[13] During our dialogue, he explained that in the third year of the novel's creation, he stopped working on the forward momentum of the story, and, in order to develop his characters more thoroughly, spent the next four years writing hundred-page biographies for each one. Around the same time, Jonathan Franzen was using similar methods and also spent about a decade writing *The Corrections*, although Franzen's writer's block appears to have been greater than Aslam's (the latter extensively educated himself in literature during his apparent 11-year disappearance).[14] As well as scrutinizing Aslam's sharp critique of problems in Pakistani communities, which has led to critics rightly observing that he overloads the abuses,[15] it should be noted that he is caustic about White racism. This racism (which he depicts as stemming from colour prejudice towards Pakistani migrants in Britain, rather than from Islamophobia, for example), is condemned for its aggression and ignorance. However, official Faber book club material argues that Aslam 'decided not to tread the well-trodden path of white racism'[16] in *Maps for Lost Lovers*. While this is too sweeping, certainly his inversion of the ugliness of racism is innovative. Here, for example, he describes Pakistani migrant families' responses to the violent, physical attacks prevalent in 1970s Britain:

> At night the scented geraniums were dragged to the centres of the downstairs rooms in the hope that the breeze dense with rosehips and ripening limes would get to the sleepers upstairs ahead of the white intruders who had generated it by brushing past the foliage in the dark after breaking in.[17]

Here, Aslam characteristically finds a Yeatsian 'terrible beauty'[18] in the flowers designed to raise a perfumed alarm if racists force an entry into the somnolent house.

Throughout his *oeuvre*, Aslam also demonstrates that class is at least as important an issue as race or religion in characters' interactions with each other. For example, in *Maps for Lost Lovers*, he describes a wealthy Pakistani woman who blames poor immigrants for White racism towards their better-educated compatriots, memorably denouncing them as 'sister-murdering, nose-blowing, mosque-going, cousin-marrying, veil-wearing, inbred imbeciles'.[19] Pakistan's complex class divisions are further explored when Kaukab responds, '[w]e are driven out of our countries because of people like her, the rich and the powerful. [...] And now they resent our being *here* too. Where are we supposed to go?'[20] Similarly, in 'Leila in the Wilderness', Aslam provides a searing portrayal of the suffering of the two brothers, Qes and Wamaq, who are just two of the 'millions of youths who d[o] menial work' throughout Pakistan,[21] and whom the bourgeoisie prefers to keep illiterate so that they don't get above themselves.[22]

According to Muneeza Shamsie, Aslam's Afghan paternal grandmother was very important in his childhood and continues to influence his fiction.[23] His most recent novel, *The Wasted Vigil*, recounts 30 years of war-torn Afghan history through the stories of several characters trapped together in a house, including two doctors, Marcus (now an English perfume factory owner, who has his hand amputated by the Taliban) and Qatrina (his wife of 20 years, nonetheless considered his mistress because a female cleric performed their wedding rites). The violence in Afghanistan was triggered during Zia's regime when the CIA was encouraged to pour money and weapons into Afghanistan via Pakistan in support of the *mujahideen* fighting against the Soviets. This has had a devastating impact on both nations, because the weapons and *jihadi* mindset have continued to proliferate in the subsequent Afghan civil war and America's occupation from 2001 onwards.

The style of Aslam's novel is intense and uncompromising, and yet there is more incongruous beauty in many of his images. For example, Marcus's mutilation is described elegiacally and horrifically as follows: 'the skin cup he could make with the palms of his hands is broken in half'.[24] Aslam's borrowings in this novel are extremely eclectic, ranging from Michael Ondaatje and John Berger to Aamer Hussein and Yevgeny Vinokurov. One of the novel's scenes is deliberately set in March 2001, when ancient Buddha statues were destroyed in the Bamiyan valley,[25] and a picture of the statue of a Buddha's head makes the frontispiece of both hard-back and paperback editions, so this was Aslam's refutation of the Taliban's destruction. He says of the Taliban, 'although I may not have been able to stop you in real life, in my mind and my book you won't succeed in destroying this Buddha'. On the debit side, however, *The Wasted Vigil*'s only significant Afghan character, Casa, sometimes lapses into acting as a one-dimensional mouthpiece for a violent, joyless Islamism, and the slipperiness of the narrative voice means that misleading statements such as Lara's, '[t]he religion of Islam at its core does not believe in the study of science',[26] can all too easily be mistaken for authorial diktats.[27]

Finally, the long short story 'Leila in the Wilderness' centres on a child-bride whose daughters are taken away from her and who is punished by her husband and mother-in-law for not producing boys. Her husband's family has prided itself on turning out exclusively male progeny for countless generations, so suspicion also falls on Leila that her daughters may come from an affair with another man. Although not guilty of adultery, the marriage was a forced one, and the teenaged Leila is still in love with her childhood sweetheart, Qes, the latter embarking on a quest to find her during the course of the story. As well as detailing what he argues is a prevalent antipathy towards the birth of girl-children in Pakistan, the lush novella is also inspired by the ancient Arab legend of Leila and Majnun. This is signalled, for example, in the choice of both the hero's and heroine's names, because Qes in the legend is often known as Majnun, meaning the Mad One, due to his grief at the loss of his lover, Leila. The ancient love story of Leila–Majnun is one of the central metaphorical, romantic, and mystic texts of Muslim civilization, its subject matter foreshadowing *Romeo and Juliet*. Like Shakespeare's later tale of star-crossed lovers, Leila–Majnun's influence is extensive, and other English-language writers, including Kamila Shamsie and Afghan-American Khaled Hosseini, also make reference to it.[28] The issue of female infanticide is Aslam's addition to the existing melange of forbidden love and insanity in Leila–Majnun but, despite this gloomy synopsis, 'Leila in the Wilderness' is also a love story shot through with optimism and with a fairytale happy ending.

I would like to conclude by quoting an excerpt from a breathtaking (both literally and figuratively) two-page sentence, which stopped me in my tracks (another deliberate pun) towards the end of the novella. It describes Leila's lover, Qes (now an amnesiac) telepathically sensing Leila's suffering from hundreds of miles away, and being drawn to the train station in a way that is 'almost involuntary [...] like falling, or like rising in a dream'.[29] Once there he buys a ticket, telling the official his name is Leila, just as the legendary Leila and Majnun's identities become almost interchangeable.[30] From there he travels through Pakistan to be by her side, the train going:

> past the towns and cities and villages of his immense homeland of heartbreaking beauty, containing saints and sinners and a gentle religion, kind mothers and dutiful fathers who indulged their obedient children, its crimson dawns, and its blue-smoke dusks and its unforgivable cruelty [...] its

rich for whom the poor died shallower deaths, its poor for whom only stories about hunger seemed true, its snow-blind mountains and sunburned deserts and beehives producing honey as sweet as the sound of Urdu, and its unforgivable brutality and its unforgivable dishonesty [...].[31]

The long sentence, from which I have abstracted just a fragment of its many clauses, reflects the rhythm of the train journey, in that it sometimes slows down and at other times maintains a uniform pace or speeds up, mimicking the iterative repetitiveness of the train's clacking on rails, and also indicates the great variety of sights spotted through its window. Aslam explained that being a nocturnal writer he wrote it at two in the morning. Returning from a 20-minute run, he immediately sat at his desk and, without even taking his trainers off, wrote the sentence detailing all the things he could remember about Pakistan in an intense five-minute burst. With its paradoxical blend of despair and joyful optimism, irony and stream-of-consciousness candour, this one sentence shadows forth many of Aslam's literary concerns in his work as a whole, including aestheticism, gender, religion, Urdu, sexuality, violence, and poetry.

CC: You provide a subtle portrayal of the internal life of the orthodox Muslim character Kaukab in *Maps for Lost Lovers*, so that the reader has some sympathy for her despite her frequent mistreatment of her family. However, do you worry about presenting gloomy depictions of Muslim/Pakistani culture given prevalent negative images in the media?
NA: People like Kaukab exist and therefore can be dismissed neither as incomprehensible, nor inconsequential. She is an amalgamation of my aunts and the mothers of my friends and girlfriends. Wole Soyinka said recently, 'England is a cesspit [...] the breeding ground of fundamentalist Muslims.'[32] He is entitled to his opinion. However, he went on to say that, as a result of Ayatollah Khomeini's 1989 *fatwa* against Salman Rushdie, 'the assumption of power over life and death then passed to every single inconsequential Muslim

in the world – as if someone had given them a new stature'.[33] Again, I do not have a problem with the point he is trying to make, but I am troubled by his reference to certain Muslims as 'inconsequential'. What kind of a worldview is it when people like Kaukab are relegated to an inconsequential category because, in Soyinka's view, she isn't involved in things that he considers of consequence? Soyinka is right to say that a sense of empowerment was derived from the *fatwa* against Rushdie by some people, who then used this as justification to commit acts of violence. But to say some people are inconsequential; that I don't understand.

In response to the part of your question about counter-balancing media representations, I would say that I'm not going to do PR for Islam, or Pakistan, or US imperialisms. My novel *The Wasted Vigil* has many different characters and invites contrasting readings. I did some events to promote the novel, and in New York, an American man who hadn't been on a plane since 9/11 walked out of my reading because he said I'd made him sympathize with a *jihadi* character and that I was clearly pro-Taliban. In Lahore, a woman was angry because I'd made her empathize with an American, and she circulated a pamphlet claiming that the CIA and MI5 had directed my writing of the novel. At an event in London I was criticized for writing a sympathetic portrayal of a communist Russian character. A novel is a democracy, and as a novelist I have to work hard at making the reader understand every character. You can't present three characters and explore the childhood and relationships of the first two but not the third. The reader will reject your writing if you don't make everybody human, but that's also what gets me into trouble with certain ideologues.

CC: While an understanding of the process of Casa's radicalization is arrived at in *The Wasted Vigil*, there is less sense of his internal world than there is with Kaukab in *Maps for Lost Lovers*. Was that deliberate?
NA: This novel differs from *Maps for Lost Lovers* both structurally and physically. It is shorter, yet there are more characters,

meaning a degree of allusion was necessary. The first 70 pages or so of *Maps for Lost Lovers* consists of nothing but texture, with the central plot element (Shamas's affair) not occurring until some way into the novel. With *The Wasted Vigil*, the plot begins with the first line. I don't necessarily want readers to sympathize with Casa, as many readers have told me that they do, but I want them better to understand where these people come from, and how they arrive at the point they have. This is not to encourage forgiveness, but is rather about preventing such radicalization in the future.

I've been criticized[34] for lines such as, '[t]he religion of Islam at its core does not believe in the study of science',[35] but I tried to make it clear that that thought came from Lara, not me. In the earlier pages I am at pains to make it apparent that we are in somebody else's mind, through free indirect discourse. By the stage this statement occurs, I was hoping the reader would realize we are in her mind, without me having to explicitly say, 'she thinks'. Lara is someone who earlier had thought about 'Muslim terrorists', rather than 'Islamist terrorists'. The irony is that this is a woman from Russia whose own worldview is a spiritual one based on Christianity. She may say that the Muslims are irrational, but is Gabriel coming down to Mary rational? Once she has been in the house for a couple of weeks, she begins to see the house as the ruins of Islamic civilization.

CC: All three books contain unexpected metaphors, particularly *Maps for Lost Lovers*, in which the writing is loaded with imagery.[36]
NA: The metaphors actually become less frequent with the later novels. My intention with *Maps for Lost Lovers* was to create the literary equivalent of a Persian miniature, in which there is a remarkable density of detail. I know this perhaps can't be done successfully in prose, just as a song cannot be painted, but can only be sung. At that time, I was experimenting with a language that was still relatively new to me, while at the same time going back to my Urdu roots, in particular the lush imagery of Urdu

poetry. I don't know how successful I have been in carrying this out, but on the other hand, as an artist, I don't think it is my concern to think how my work will go down in the bookshops. For me, my job ends the day I write the last full stop. Beyond that, it is the publisher who takes over.

CC: Speaking of which, you did remarkably well to be signed to André Deutsch and then Faber, so could you describe your experiences of publishing?
NA: I was very young and naïve when I wrote my first novel, *Season of the Rainbirds*, living in the provinces. Some of my favourite writers were Gore Vidal, John Updike, and V. S. Naipaul, all of whom, I learnt from looking at the copyright pages of their novels, at the time wrote for André Deutsch. So I sent my manuscript to Deutsch, not knowing to make a copy of it or to go through agents and, some time later, I got the call from them, asking, 'Could I speak to Miss Nadeem Aslam?' They thought I was a woman, because *Season of the Rainbirds* (and all my subsequent writing) explores women's issues either obliquely or directly. The publisher admitted later that she'd also assumed I was at least 45, when I was actually in my early twenties, because as a young writer I didn't feel able to take on the grief of the young – which the world often underestimates – until I'd written about older characters first. It's only now, in my forties, that I'm beginning to turn my attention to the young in a sustained way. Anyway, Deutsch called me and invited me to come to lunch to discuss the manuscript. I refused on the grounds that I had no money to pay for any lunch and they said, 'Don't worry; we'll give you money.'

Then I was picked up by Faber, which is a wonderful house, with a real 'family' feel. The editors look after you, they love the books, promote them well, and make you feel appreciated. They've published Kureishi, Pamuk, Peter Carey, and Paul Auster, these gods I was reading when I was younger, and of course their poets are peerless. As for promoting my books: on the one hand, I'd rather be with a new novel. The whole process of bringing out a book takes about a year, during which time you can't sit twiddling your thumbs, so you're working on new material. On the other, I am deeply involved with the aesthetic appearance of the books, as I have lived with them for years and know what the key images should be. With *The Wasted Vigil*, I wanted the novel to breathe, so such things as font size and layout were important. Fortunately, I am involved with the top publishing houses around the world, such as Knopf in the States and Germany's Rowohlt, and each is very cooperative.

CC: Returning to the miniature form, was Pakistani miniaturist Abdur Rahman Chughtai your main influence when producing *Maps for Lost Lovers* as a detailed, intricate work?
NA: When I first went to India in 2005, I visited the National Gallery of Modern Art in New Delhi. There was something unfathomable about the pictures there. I walked around three or four times, yet I still couldn't quite grasp what they were saying to me. The following day I returned, in order to work out what made the place special and arresting. Then, after a day and a half, I realized: every art gallery I had ever visited up to that point had been in the West, and the subjects in the paintings had been White people. For the first time, I was in a gallery where the people on the walls staring back at me were the colour of my own skin.

I had worked so hard at settling in England that I had almost forgotten who I was and where I was from. My early years in Pakistan had been erased and I thought I would never go there again, because I couldn't afford the trip. East and West at one level are complete opposites: you guys take your hats off on entering a holy place, while we [Muslims] cover our heads in a holy place. A friend visited Pakistan, and gave me a book by Chughtai containing paintings of people who looked like me; people who read the Qur'an, rather than the Bible. This was a great influence, and of course the dedication to *Maps for Lost Lovers* reads, 'for My Father, who advised me at the outset, all those years ago, to always write about love, and for Faiz Ahmed Faiz 1911–1984 and

Abdur Rahman Chughtai 1897–1975, two masters who taught me, each in his own way, what else is worth loving'.[37]

Chughtai showed me that art can be composed by people like me. This statement indicates how difficult it can be to live in another culture. It is easy to idealize cultural migration, and of course it can be a positive experience. However, more often than not, migration is terribly traumatic, particularly for those people from the Indian subcontinent who are not affluent and have lived in an enclosed environment all their lives. Personally, I think cultures should intermingle, but we mustn't romanticize the immigrant's often cruel journey. If people assume that immigration to the West brings comparable wealth and happiness, they should speak to a taxi driver. I can protect myself from the racism of certain White people, but a taxi driver can't, because they're getting into the back of his car, drunk, on a Saturday night. His idea of immigration will be totally different from mine and, as a writer, I have to keep that in mind.

CC: Please discuss the different circumstances faced by the first generation of Pakistani immigrants who came to Britain, and their sons and daughters who were born here.
NA: In many ways the children became conduits to the outside world. For example, a mother who didn't speak English would have taken the child with her to the doctor's surgery to act as an interpreter. It's been over 40 years now since the beginning of immigration, so the circumstances for the grandchildren are different again. The younger generations have to consider the question of identity, and to what extent they feel an affinity with their background.

In my own extended family, when staying with my father's relatives, people were painting, singing, the radio was on, and there were beautiful pictures on the wall. My mother's side of the family was far more austere; their walls were white – in line with Islamic law – there was no radio and we were forbidden to have toys. Although I found my mother's side difficult, it helped me understand a range of people. It is interesting to consider what being 'good' means, outside of religion: there's a lot to be said for religion enhancing the importance of such ideals. Before Christ, my moral obligation to you was as a fellow human being, but with Christ came the idea of the 'brotherhood of man': I am good towards you because you are my sister/brother. That is not to say that Buddhism and Hinduism do not preach compassion, but it is without this same sense of strangers' relationships involving filial obligation. If we were to remove Christianity from the world, would that idea go away? I don't think we need Christianity to enforce this notion, because it is part of the fabric of the world now.

CC: What did Islam add to these existing beliefs about human interaction?
NA: My understanding of Islam, from a non-believer's perspective, is that Mohammed was trying to build a state. A state needs an army, taxes, and so forth: essentially, he was a politician. What happened on 9/11 to the West was just a widescreen version of what has been happening in the Muslim world since day one. The factions began to fight as soon as Mohammed died. Through an uncle breaking my toys, I got to learn about the conflict and contradictions from a very early age. I was born into this struggle, one that until recently the wider world was ignorant of. After the Rushdie Affair, people were aware that something was going on, but it wasn't a pressing concern to mainstream society.

The West has obviously to some degree added to these tensions. For example, in the epigraph to *The Wasted Vigil*, I cite a pre-9/11 interview with Zbigniew Brzezinsky, President Carter's National Security Adviser, during which he was asked whether he regretted giving weapons and advice to future terrorists in Afghanistan. He shortsightedly replied, '[w]hat is more important to the history of the world – the Taliban or the [...] end of the Cold War?'[38] However, we mustn't romanticize. Whatever the Americans are doing to maintain their power now, Muslims, Incas, Spanish, and British colonizers would also have done. This is what empires do. I am deeply suspicious of the idea of 'empire', or that someone can be converted with love, which for me means nothing. Once you are in somebody else's country, you have already altered the balance of power one way or another. There are 1.5 billion Muslims in the world, but five billion other people, so Muslims make up only about a fifth of the world's population, and that is something that Islamists don't understand.

CC: You provide a fascinating depiction of the Taliban *madrasa*, in which Casa is indoctrinated as a child. How did you go about researching such schools?
NA: I made a research trip to Afghanistan, and in Pakistan you are never more than a few people away from someone who has direct knowledge of these things, so I asked people. For example, I got speaking to a young man while on a bus from Faisalabad to Lahore. I told him I was writing a book about a boy who grew up in a *madrasa* and went on to join a terrorist training camp. He grinned, and said that he himself had spent time in a terrorist camp in Kashmir. On another occasion, I went to see my aunt, who was a headmistress, and she was visibly shaken. I asked her what was wrong, and she told me she'd had a triumphalist call from a student whose brother had just died fighting in the Kashmir insurgency. My aunt asked to speak to her mother to pass on her condolences, but the girl refused, saying that her mother was being chastized by her father for grieving, when she should be celebrating that the boy was in heaven. So it wasn't difficult to research at all, as these things are occurring all around us. I had no direct experience of studying in a *madrasa*, because as a boy I wasn't interested in learning Arabic or studying the Qur'an. However, my city, Gujranwala, now sends more boys to terrorist training camps in Kashmir than any other town in Pakistan, and one of my old school friends also died fighting there.

CC: What has caused this level of insurrection in this part of the Pakistani Punjab?
NA: The two main contributing factors are its proximity to Kashmir and the poor standard of schooling. The school I went

to was terrible, and in no way equipped you for adult life in the modern world. When you are so poorly trained, you either have to move abroad to find work, or you fall into the hands of the *jihadis*. The last time I went over, I tried to look up some old school friends, but everybody has left due to the lack of employment. They take up menial jobs abroad: some are driving taxis in New York, others are washing dishes in Barcelona, but no young person stays in Gujranwala, if they can help it.

CC: It seems as though you've encountered a lot of despair about the future of Pakistan.
NA: While what I have said may sound quite desperate, you cannot get me to believe that Pakistan will not exist in ten years. The whole country could be on fire, and yet I would still believe everything will eventually pan out. Ultimately I feel it is a good thing that Pakistan's problems are being discussed. This is why I'm so suspicious of what is going on in India, this idea of 'India Shining'.[39] While India's middle-class population may have grown to around 100 million – an enormous number of people – there are 900 million other people whose voices are not being heard. At least we don't have a 'Pakistan Shining' campaign to obscure the social problems of the country.

CC: A central idea in *Maps for Lost Lovers* is that immigrants are involved in a new cartographical enterprise, remapping English landscapes, and translating the northern street names.
NA: One of my ideas for the cover was a map of England with all the city names in Urdu, which I thought would be a strange, powerful image. As writers we may exaggerate, but in fact, there are people from my community – particularly from the previous generation – who feel apprehensive about venturing into some areas of Huddersfield because they are straying outside the Asian neighbourhood. In these predominantly Asian areas, everything in the neighbourhood, from the post office to the doctor's surgery, is Pakistani-run. It's strange to think there are people, living in England, who can count on the fingers of

one hand the number of White people they have spoken to. In the neighbourhood I grew up in, where *Maps for Lost Lovers* is set, most of the White people moved out years ago. I have seen small children, kids of six or seven with their jaws on the floor because an elderly White lady has walked by. However, I do not feel there is any cause for despair with this younger generation. Once they get to school, or start heading into town, they will mingle with everybody. People often say my books are dark, but I will not accept that Muslims and White people are going to kill each other. Of course there will be problems, but all is not lost.

CC: There are elements of magic realism in *Maps for Lost Lovers*, which bring to my mind the following observation by Salman Rushdie: 'If one is to attempt honestly to describe reality as it is experienced by religious people, for whom God is no symbol but an everyday fact, then the conventions of what is called realism are quite inadequate. The rationalism of that form comes to seem like a judgement upon, an invalidation of, the religious faith of the characters being described. A form must be created which allows the miraculous and the mundane to co-exist at the same level.'[40]

NA: In Islam, it is written that the angel Gabriel spoke to Mohammed, so you are required to believe in the existence of a winged creature. It says in the Qur'an that God created angels out of light, humans out of earth, and the demon and *djinns* out of fire, which people absolutely believe. So if I am to talk about Kaukab seriously, then I also have to describe *djinns* in earnest, because she believes they are around her. I've heard a family anecdote in which a girl's father tried to break into her room to molest her and she screamed, so he used the smokescreen explanation in the morning that she was alarmed because she heard a *djinn* come in. Of course it's a lie, but devout people are going to believe it. Is the way I write about these issues magic realism? I don't know, but then I don't really care! I am not going to condemn magical realism just to be fashionable. If I feel I can make a point using a magical realist device, then I will. Not to do so would be like a painter deciding not to use the colour red. In 'Leila in the Wilderness', the two lovers yearn for one another so much that their hearts become magnetic: that could be considered magic realism, but it makes my point well, as do various literary devices in other situations.

CC: To what extent are you influenced by modernist techniques?

NA: I was speaking to a young writer some time ago, and he said he could not imagine a 25-year-old in our times being interested in the work of Proust. Now I remember being 25, and I was totally obsessed by Proust! Joyce was also a great influence, particularly the first story of *Dubliners*, 'The Sisters'.[41] The whole of *Season of the Rainbirds* comes out of that story; it gave me the confidence to go ahead with my first novel. Books by Camus, Hardy, Faulkner, Lawrence, Joyce, Proust, Dostoevsky, are all within an arm's-length of me when I write.

CC: How do you feel about the new category of 'Muslim writing' that is under scrutiny, or are you more comfortable being interpreted in terms of your nationality?

NA: Having lived in England for most of my life, I'm more aware of my class than my race or religion. If initiatives around the category of 'Muslim writing' are being made because British Bangladeshi and Pakistani kids are not doing well at school[42] the same will be true of poor White kids in the same area. I'm writing about human beings. While it is impossible to say all people and nationalities are the same, there are certain constants that permeate all humanity: mothers, fathers, friends, cousins, and so on. The social, economic, political, and religious categories into which we are dropped of course shape the way we act as mothers and fathers, but parenthood retains the same basic reality.

I am Pakistani, British, northern, working-class: that is my background, and you can find my books in the 'ethnic' section of bookshops, but also in the alphabetized literature section. Nation is of little importance to me as a writer, because I come from a country that came into being in the name of nationalism, ideology, religion, and politics. As a result, one million people were killed in the violence of Partition. I am deeply suspicious of this ideology of nationhood, as I know what can happen when it gets into the wrong hands. On this issue of Partition, if I were alive back in 1947, ideally I would have been against the idea that Muslims needed a country for themselves, but that belongs to a longer conversation. We have to understand what Congress were up to, and why the Muslim League made their demands. But to say now that Pakistan should not exist is to play into the hands of the Hindu fundamentalists: only in the dreams of the BJP-wallahs can Pakistan not exist. It is not part of India, but a distinct country in its own right, there are similarities, but it has its own distinct identity. While some Pakistanis love Indian people and vice versa, if our rulers do not want us to be together, we will not be together. Politicians don't give a damn what ordinary people think, and if they want war there will be war. It is a lovely idea to think we can take over, empower the people, and let the powerful know they are answerable to us. Yet in 1965 and 1971, relatively speaking there was greater cultural exchange than there is now, and there were wars. Before 1947 we lived in the same country – what more cultural exchange can you wish for than that? – yet a different country was created. In truth, cultural exchange is never going to mean anything, if the politicians aren't kept in check.

CC: Would you agree that in comparison with your serious criticisms of what Nawal El Saadawi calls 'establishment Islam',[43] you are more positive about Sufism and associated art forms, such as Qawwali music?
NA: In Lahore on a Thursday night you can go to the tomb of Sufi saint Shah Jamal and hear the former *tonga-wallah*, Pappu Sain, playing the drum. It is two o'clock in the morning, pitch black, and you see brilliant points of light as people smoke

marijuana. All the while, the Taliban are just over the horizon. Yet Sufism has its corruptions too. The last time I was at the mausoleum, I saw a six foot five transvestite – this is in a country supposedly in the grip of clerical militancy – and with him was a girl who could not have been older than 12. They sat down with another man, passing a joint between them, and the girl left with the man. In short, a deal was done and the girl was sold. So we mustn't romanticize and say how wonderful Sufism is, because there are two sides to everything.

When light travels through a prism, depending on where you are standing, you are either going to see only white light, or all the colours of the spectrum. If there is a theme in my writing, it is that I am standing on the side of the prism in which I can see that the light isn't just white.[44] I'm lucky that my family is so diverse, including communists and rightwingers, religious nuts and atheists, educated and illiterate people, poor and rich. Some of my female cousins are covered head-to-toe in *burqas* and haven't left the house since marriage, while there are feminists and one woman cousin is a flight instructor in the Pakistani army. Since a very early age I have been acutely aware of the various different ways in which one can be a Muslim. If you ask me what a 25-year-old Pakistani woman is like, I would be unable to generalize. As a novelist it is a great gift.

CC: Is the discovery of the cache of photographs of immigrants in *Maps for Lost Lovers*[45] a reference to Tony Walker's Belle Vue portrait studio in Bradford, which from 1926–75 was known for taking archaically formal photographs of the city's immigrant workers and their families?[46]

NA: That's right. I saw it on the cover of the *Independent* magazine in the 1990s when I was writing *Maps for Lost Lovers*. I will come back to those photographs, as I want to write another novel about the north. *Maps for Lost Lovers* by and large concentrates on the older generation, but I will write a novel about younger people in the same town, because my generation's story has yet to be told. It will incorporate the 7/7 bombings, because the perpetrators came from Leeds. The mosque in Dewsbury at which one of the bombers was radicalized was actually founded by my late uncle – the same uncle who used to break my toys and beat my mother when she was young.[47] In the 1960s and 70s, he used to go on preaching missions to the West, and when he moved to Dewsbury he helped found a mosque, the Markazi Masjid, which became the European headquarters of Tablighi Jamaat.[48] That is how deeply linked I am to all of this, and I'm going to discuss it in my future novel. I heard the bus explosion go off on 7/7, I was a couple of blocks away coming out my agent's office. I thought it was a car backfiring. My mother rang me in a panic, as I was due to get a train up north. I'd had no idea about 9/11 on the other hand, and didn't find out until 20 September because I was writing. My father saved all the newspapers from 12 September through to the 'liberation' of Afghanistan in November, which I am using now for a new novel.

Of course it's a good thing the Taliban are gone but, once again, one can't say this without qualification. If you read books about postwar Europe, people knew that people in certain towns had been Nazi sympathizers, but while the big leaders were taken out, the town needed order and if members of the police force had collaborated, you had to tolerate the more minor criminals and just keep an eye on them. I'm not saying that this was right, but it happened in Italy, France, and Germany. This is a phenomenon I write about in *The Wasted Vigil*. Tragically, it's all about money, and none of this is in the control of us ordinary people. We know what the Taliban have done, but the town needs to be run again, so these people are brought back in.

CC: A lot of Pakistani writers are now depicting Afghanistan, so how much of an impact have the various Afghan conflicts had on Pakistan and in particular its writers?
NA: I can only speak for myself, and I was writing about these things in my first book in 1992. All three of my books have started with a personal concern. I wanted to talk about religious fundamentalism, which I did in *Season of the Rainbirds*, and

honour killings, which I wrote about in *Maps for Lost Lovers*. In the time it took me to write those books, those concerns became everybody else's concerns, and it looks as though I chose them because they were popular topics. Yet when I started writing *Maps for Lost Lovers*, the term 'honour killings' was not known and I thought I would have to explain to people what it means. Now there have been honour killings in Spain, Canada, and Germany. Likewise with *The Wasted Vigil*, it appears that I decided to write about current events in Afghanistan, but the story is actually as old as *Maps for Lost Lovers*. Why, as a writer, would you not want to talk about that if you're from that area? In the 1980s and 90s, there were hundreds of thousands of war orphans. It just so happens that over the course of time those orphans, now militarized, have become something the whole world knows about.

CC: Could you describe why and how you set about writing 'Leila in the Wilderness'?
NA: In previous writing I'd discussed women's issues tangentially, but in the novella I wanted to come at these head-on. Some topics are so obvious that they're never discussed, and the antipathy towards female children in Pakistan is one of those. I thought about writing about this for 15 years, and kept thinking that another writer would get there first, but nobody did. For some time, I didn't have the courage to write the story, because it's upsetting to talk about people not wanting their daughters. About four years ago, I went to Pakistan, and two incidents occurred to galvanized me, which I've written about in 'Where to Begin'.[49] The first was reading about a woman who gave birth and promptly accused the hospital doctor of swapping her son for a girl baby, later admitting that she lied due to fears about her husband's reaction to having another daughter. The second came when I met an educated man at a party and, on learning that I am child-free and think of my books as my children, he advised me to view my successful novels as my boys, and my unsuccessful ones as daughters. Pakistan is

one of the few countries in the world that has more men than women, so I wrote 'Leila in the Wilderness' for all the women who should be there but are not.[50] I heard that *Granta*, one of the world's great literary magazines, with more than a century's history, was producing a Pakistan issue, so I finished the novella in two months during early 2010. I thought they might find it too long, at over 50 pages, but they immediately bought it and put it at the front of the volume.

CC: What do you think of this emerging category of 'new Pakistani writing' in English, as showcased in *Granta 112*?
NA: In his 2008 Nobel Prize lecture,[51] Jean Marie Gustave Le Clézio named some of the seminal works of our times, among which he mentions Qurratulain Hyder's novel *Ag ka Darya* [*River of Fire*].[52] To most, it would seem that this work is something of a lost classic, being relatively unknown in the West. In Lahore, however, Hyder's novel has been considered a masterpiece from the instant it was published in 1959. When I was growing up, it was one of the seminal works of Urdu literature. It is perfectly understandable that the majority of Westerners have no prior knowledge of *River of Fire*, just as I'm sure there are great Latvian novelists of whom we have not heard. Arriving in England at 14, I was very troubled by the concept of racism. Until then, if somebody disliked me, it was as a result of having spent time with me and formed an opinion based on my personality. The idea that people could decide they did not wish talk to me based on appearance alone freaked me out. My position was supposed to be one of inferiority, having come from this country of ill repute. However, I knew that some of the world's greatest writers, singers, painters, thinkers, and leaders had come from Pakistan, this so-called inferior part of the world. So my relationship to this country is different to that of my cousins who were born here. They internalize this apparent inferiority, as they don't have 14 years' worth of experience to fall back on and give them confidence that the slurs are unfounded. This relates to multiculturalism: should we not teach dark-skinned

kids in schools something about their own background, their own history and culture? You can be totally ruthless and say we want to produce competent people who contribute to society, but one way to do that is to make people feel good about themselves that they come from somewhere that is a part of the world's story.

It's complicated, because as well as a Pakistani writer, I'm also an Englishman, whether or not I, or anyone else, likes it. Within that, I'm a Yorkshireman and, even though I have a place in London, after a month there, I begin to miss my hills. As a writer, an artist, and a thinker, the only nationality I have is my desk: this is my passport. When I look at Yellowstone Park, I don't say to myself, 'This is American', and if I gazed at Lake Geneva, I wouldn't be thinking of it as a Swiss lake; I'd be thinking of the world's beauty. Nature, beauty, and art belong to everyone and are without nationality. To quote Derek Walcott, with his mixed Caribbean heritage, 'either I'm nobody or I'm a nation'.[53] So either I'm everything or nothing, and I don't really see a contradiction there. My alphabet doesn't only have 26 letters, but also the 32 of the Urdu alphabet, so I have a total of 58 letters at my disposal.

7
Tahmima Anam[*]

Credit: Roland Lamb.

Tahmima Anam was born in Dhaka, Bangladesh in 1975, but raised in New York, Paris, and Bangkok while her father worked as a media consultant for UNESCO. Although she now lives in London, she has retained close connections with Bangladesh during her years away. Her father, Mahfuz Anam, is a high-profile journalist in Bangladesh, who currently edits the largest circulating Bangladeshi English-language newspaper, *The Daily Star*. He was formerly the publisher of a Bengali daily newspaper, *Prothom Alo*,[1] which – in an incident reminiscent of the Danish cartoon controversy – in 2007 printed a cartoon that was deemed blasphemous. Many people, especially Islamic right-wing groups, protested against the publication and threatened

---

to shut *Prothom Alo* down and arrest both the cartoonist and Mahfuz, so the newspaper had to apologize and retract.[2]

Her mother, Shaheen Anam, is a feminist political activist and executive director of Manusher Jonno, an NGO campaigning for human rights and good governance.[3] Her grandfather, Abul Mansur Ahmad (1898–1979), was a satirical writer, lawyer, and politician, whose Bengali books, such as his autobiography, *Atmakatha*, achieved great renown.[4] He worked with Subhas Chandra Bose in the Congress, then joined the Bengal Muslim League, before becoming founder-secretary of Bangladesh's Awami League (he was imprisoned by Ayub Khan for his nationalist activity in the late 1950s).[5]

Anam graduated from Mount Holyoke College, Massachussetts, in 1997, and went on to Harvard University, where she was awarded a PhD in Social Anthropology in 2005. Her doctoral thesis, like *A Golden Age*, deals with the 1971 Pakistan civil war (known to Bengalis as the Bangladeshi liberation war),[6] and during the course of her research she conducted interviews in Bangladesh with hundreds of people who were involved in the war as fighters or in other ways. In 2004–5, she took a creative writing Masters at Royal Holloway, University of London, supervised by poet laureate Andrew Motion. Anam's writing has been published in *Granta, Guardian,* and *New Statesman* (she also works as a contributing editor for the latter publication). Finally, Anam acted as a consultant for the acclaimed film about the Bangladesh war, *The Clay Bird.*[7]

Her first novel, *A Golden Age*, was longlisted for the 2007 Guardian First Book Award, shortlisted for the Costa First Novel Award, and Europe/South Asia regional winner of the 2008 Commonwealth Writers' Prize for Best First Book. For the most part the novel is set in East Pakistan during the nine months of the war, and Anam's family stories inform the narrative. Perhaps most influential is the story of her grandmother, who, like the protagonist Rehana, was a widow who allowed arms to be buried in her garden during the war and defied soldiers when questioned.[8] The novel begins in epistolary fashion – 'Dear Husband, I lost our children today'[9] – as Rehana's two children, Sohail and

Maya, are taken away from her to live in West Pakistan by her brother- and sister-in-law because of her depression after the untimely death of her husband. In order to become self-sufficient and reclaim her children, Rehana builds another house on her land, Shona (meaning 'gold'),[10] which she lets out to a Hindu family, the Dasguptas. Each year, she hosts a gathering to celebrate her children's return, but her contentment is shortlived. Following the elections of 1970 (which the Awami League won by a landslide, a result the East Pakistani government of Yahya Khan overturned[11]), the Pakistani army enters Bengal and the *mukti bahini*, or Bangladeshi liberation army, also begins to mobilize. Despite his innate pacifism, Sohail (now 19), is soon so angry at the army's abuses that he joins the freedom fighters, while Maya and Rehana become increasingly involved in supporting the resistance. Shona is used as a storehouse and refuge for the fighters, and it is here that Rehana meets and falls in love with the Major, who has a serious injury to his leg.

Following the success of *A Golden Age*, a ferocious bidding war took place between four publishers over rights to Anam's further novels in her Bengal Trilogy, which Scottish publisher Canongate acquired from John Murray.[12] *The Good Muslim*, the second novel in the Trilogy, largely focuses on the 1980s, which she describes in the interview as a decade when 'both the global and local contexts of mainstream religion were becoming increasingly central to the political conversation'. The narrative shifts from *A Golden Age*'s focus on Rehana towards the two children, now in their thirties, who respond very differently to the turn taken by the young Bangladeshi state under the dictatorship of Hussain Muhammad Ershad and the growing influence of the Islamic Right. Sohail joins the Tablighi Jamaat, a proselytizing Islamic movement,[13] while Maya is loyal to the secular, Marxist-inflected nationalism that provided solidarity during the war years (an era of political idealism she looks back on with nostalgia).

Sohail is haunted by his memories of the war, in particular of one of its female victims whom he failed to help, and the reasons behind his desire to atone are made apparent through fragmentary flashbacks. Soon after peace comes, he begins to 'lean [...] towards God',[14] initially embracing pluralism, then becoming increasingly intolerant. His otherworldliness develops into an indifference towards the suffering of his six-year-old son Zaid, who is allowed to run wild, and of his ailing mother Rehana. Sohail's religious wife, Silvi, for whom he felt such love in *A Golden Age*, encourages his spiritual zeal, although romance plays a smaller part here than it did in the previous novel. In many ways *The Good Muslim* is a novel of ideas; in addition to religion and atheism, it explores war, its aftermath, and the vulnerable position of women, children, and 'tribal' peoples. The scientifically minded Maya becomes a 'lady doctor', rather than following her early aspirations towards surgery, because she wants to help women and to counter patriarchal superstitions that surround pregnancy and childbirth. She becomes caught up in complex feelings of guilt when she finds herself performing abortions for women raped by Pakistani soldiers during the war.

The novel contests the simplistic 'good Muslim/bad Muslim' binary thinking,[15] ironically figured in Anam's title. Indeed, it is not easy to identify the novel's 'good Muslim'. Maya's equation of Islam with bigotry and backwardness is shown to be as closed-minded as her brother's dogmatism, and both characters also have flashes of compassion, self-doubt, and insight. The third volume of this Trilogy, which Anam explains here will be about the devastating impact of climate change on already flood-bound Bangladesh, is eagerly awaited.

At literary events and festivals, Anam often shares a platform with Pakistani writers, such as Kamila Shamsie, Daniyal Mueenuddin, and Nadeem Aslam,[16] but she acknowledges that this collegiality between Pakistanis and Bangladeshis would have been unthinkable in the years following the 1971 war. In *A Golden Age*, Anam is unashamedly nationalistic, and she dedicates the novel to Bangladesh with 'gratitude and love',[17] while *The Good Muslim* ends with the historical writer Jahanara Imam (whom Anam discusses in this interview) demanding that war criminals make reparations and the victims are brought justice.[18] Notwithstanding this self-declared bias, both her novels are complex and thoughtful meditations on war, linguistic conflict, parenthood, sibling rivalry, and love.

CC: How did research from your PhD thesis feed into _A Golden Age_ and vice versa, and to what extent did ethical considerations constrain you in fictionalizing the history of the 1971 war?

TA: I was thinking about writing a novel when I started the PhD. The PhD provided me with the research for the novel, because while writing up all my interviews, I became convinced that stories, forming the narrative arc of the work, would lend themselves well to fiction. You can convey certain ideas through fiction in a way that can't be done through academic books, images that capture something of the spirit of the time. The stories were real and I met people who inspired my own narrative, so at first I felt compelled not to improvise on my own. However, Andrew Motion advised me not to be 'too dutiful' about my ethics,[19] because no one who had lived through the war would be able unequivocally to recognize themselves in the book. When you write a novel you have to think about which details to include and which to leave out. It's not just about describing history, but of telling a story in an interesting way. The novel has other pressures on it, of plot, form, and so on.

CC: Adib Khan's novel _Seasonal Adjustments_ was an early Bengali novel in English to deal with the 1971 war,[20] but is not very widely known. Recently, British Bangladeshi writer Manzu Islam published a novel on 1971 entitled _Song of Our Swampland_.[21] However, representations of the 1971 war by Pakistanis or Indians, such as Salman Rushdie, Kamila Shamsie, Ghazala Hameed and Durdana Soomro, Moni Mohsin, and Sorayya Khan have a higher profile.[22] How do you account for this relative lack of discussion of the civil war in Bangladeshi English-language writing?

TA: Partly it's because Bangladesh hasn't had a generation of writers in English coming to maturity, as happened 20 to 30 years ago in India, and is happening now in Pakistan. Most Bengali-language novelists who are well known in Bangladesh have written about the war, but the English-language novel has not really taken off yet. Apart from a few, most authors are writing in Bengali. Of the Bengali-language novelists, Selina Hossain has written a number of short stories that allude to the war.[23] Then there's *Maa* by Anisul Hoque, which is about 1971.[24] Many memoirs, autobiographies, and testimonials also touch on the war so there has been a wealth of literature concerning 1971, but not by Bangladeshis writing in English. I was most influenced by the first-hand accounts of the war told by Jahanara Imam, whose diaries were rewritten and then published in the 1980s in Bangladesh.[25] She tells the story of the war from the perspective of a mother, because her son was killed in 1971 and she also lost her husband. I was influenced by her style and by her thinking about war through the prism of a widow.

CC: At a recent lecture, you said that readers often interpret *A Golden Age* as history rather than fiction.[26] How do you cope with this burden of representation?
TA: There are simultaneously challenges and virtues. The challenges are that people often read the book as historical non-fiction, so they want to correct me on anything from minute facts to challenging the veracity of the basic claim about Pakistani genocide of Bengalis. I think that when people interpret fiction as non-fiction they give it the burden of being comprehensive or exclusive in some way. I'll point out that this is one story about 1971; it is not the whole story. However, the lines are blurred, so it's difficult to get that point across sometimes. The virtues include the fact that the book became in a small way an opportunity for people to have conversations about the war, whether it's Westerners who didn't know about that aspect of South Asian history, or Bengali children who had never talked to their parents about what happened in 1971. One of the wonderful things about *A Golden Age* is that readers interpret it as more than a novel, and take it to be a document or a way to talk about the past.

CC: *A Golden Age* focuses on the mother, Rehana. Could you tell us about the next novel in your Bengal Trilogy, *The Good Muslim*?

TA: *The Good Muslim* mostly centres on the relationship between Sohail and his sister Maya, and that conflict between the religious and the secular which is represented by the two characters. Debates from the 1980s about whether Bangladesh should continue to hold to its secular, Marxist-inflected nationalism, or embrace new Islamist movements are embedded in the family story. Neither of the two characters is particularly in the public sphere of that conflict, which is part of a larger debate. The third part is going to be set in the future and will be about climate change, although I'm not sure whether it will be science fiction.

CC: At the lecture mentioned earlier, you argued that anyone who writes about Muslims in the current Manichaean political climate should strive for literary balance. They should include some male characters who grow beards and some who are shaven, some female characters who wear the *burqa* and some who don't. How easy has it been to create such balance in *The Good Muslim*?

TA: I try not to think too much about imposing a top-down method in which certain characters represent particular points of view. If you do that, the writing can become stilted. But if you try to present an accurate portrayal of any Muslim society, you will find people who are more extreme and those who are less religious, especially in countries like Bangladesh, where there are people who are very secular, people who live the religious life 100 per cent, and others who use religion for political ends. It came naturally that my characters represented people along a spectrum.

CC: Religion in *A Golden Age* is understated. Rehana recites Aytul Kursi[27] and Surah Yahseen to bless people; there are details of *suhoor*, *iftar*, and fasting; dawn and *maghrib* prayers. However, you present Rehana as viewing her religion

as being based on tolerance, as compared with Silvi's traumatized Islamism.

TA: I think that for most people in most Muslim countries – though obviously I don't know them all and can't speak for them – religion is just a part of everyday life, so it's both centrally important and taken for granted. For Rehana, it's critical that she prays five times a day, and that she says Aytul Kursi when she feels she needs to. These practices are totally embedded in her life but, on the other hand, she doesn't do them because she feels pressurized or is afraid of what others think. Yet religion has become a politically charged issue within Muslim countries. In the dialogue between 'the Muslim world' and 'the non-Muslim world', a younger person like Sohail would have to show outwardly that he is religious, and would have to have the trappings of being a religious person, more than someone like Rehana, for whom it's just a part of life which doesn't have to be externalized. In *A Golden Age*, religion is an integrated part of who Rehana is, but in *The Good Muslim*, religion becomes a symbol. For Maya, Islam signifies backwardness, anti-politics, and closed-mindedness. She's narrow in how she views religion and becomes alienated from her brother because his religion goes against the Marxist politics for which they had fought during the war. Maya feels that if she budges even slightly from her secular ideals, something will be taken away from her. She doesn't realize that this means her being extremely disconnected, not only from her brother, but from the many people for whom religion is an important and inescapable part of life. In his own way, Sohail is also closed-minded, feeling that religion is the only way he can redeem the past and salvage himself, thus positioning religion as an outward and dominant part of his life.

CC: In your own upbringing, was the Marxist nationalist influence stronger than a religious worldview?

TA: Definitely. My parents were involved in the war, especially my father, who was a socialist student leader. I didn't have any religious instruction when I was growing up. I didn't realize how odd that was until I got older and all of my friends had been forced to memorize the Qur'an when they were kids and had to say their prayers, while I hadn't had any of that education. When writing this book, I read the Qur'an for the first time. It was the first time I'd ever really understood anything about Islam. I have enjoyed that, because it's always good to come to a position of knowledge rather than ignorance. I found the Qur'an interesting and illuminating, and I understood a lot of things about that world which I hadn't known before.

CC: In *A Golden Age*, Maya questions the idea of the *ummah*, which had been used as justification for keeping Pakistan together.[28] In many ways, this concept of *ummah* seems untenable, given that Pakistan was supposed to be a home to protect the religious minority of Muslims, but was followed by colonial relationship, secession, and genocide. In the post-war on terror world do you think the idea of the *ummah* has more feasibility, or do you feel that nations are still more important building blocks of world politics?

TA: As time goes on and the world become increasingly inter-connected, I think that international and transnational Muslims are rising in power, and that the nation-state is losing its power. I think it's important politically to resist the idea of a 'Muslim world', because once you categorize millions of people from different cultures, languages, and nations into one grouping, it's that much easier to stereotype them, or to identify the entire community by just a few members of that community. Bangladeshi Muslims are very different from Pakistani or Malaysian Muslims: this is a simple idea, and not new in any way. It's necessary to resist the idea of the *ummah*, the idea of a global community of Muslims, even though it's a very powerful concept for Muslims who believe in that community. Coming from the outside, I think that people want to label the Muslim community. For instance, in the UK, it gets reported that 'the Muslim community wants *sharia* law'. This is just the opinion of some people in the Muslim Council of Britain, but the Council is taken to represent the whole Muslim community. I think that's a really dangerous conflation to make. Perhaps you think about it differently according to whether you're on the inside or the outside.

CC: What do you think of the emerging category of Muslim writing and Muslim Writers Awards?
TA: I don't really know a lot about Muslim writing. I know Muslim writers and I know writers who write about Islam, but I don't really know what 'Muslim writers' means, and I've never been to any of the Muslim Writers Awards events. I think any of these categories, such as 'South Asian writing' can be useful, but should also be taken with a grain of salt. South Asia is an idea, in the same way that people try to define 'African writing'. There was a lot of debate about which countries the Man Asian Literary Prize should include. Should it include Mongolia and Turkey, for example? All of these are concepts or categories that we have which need to be questioned, but they can also be useful.

CC: *A Golden Age* is strong on the interchange and tolerance between Hindus and Muslims in East Pakistan compared with West. Yet you're alert to the fact that Hindus are victimized at times of tension and the novel contains notes of pessimism when Supriya Sengupta, rendered mute by the trauma she has suffered, refuses to return to Bangladesh.[29] In the years since the civil war, how has the position of the country's almost ten per cent Hindu population changed?
TA: The Bangladesh war was about an ethnic minority fighting against a majority. We were being oppressed, in terms of not being allowed to have Bengali as an official language, and other reasons, but after Independence, Bangladesh has had a shameful record on the treatment of minorities, and the Hindu population has really shrunk since Independence. Millions of people have fled across the border to India, where they are equally hated because Indian Bengalis are resentful of immigrants coming in from Bangladesh, so they're in a very vulnerable position. So many times during moments of political unrest in

Bangladesh, Hindus have suffered because their land has been grabbed, people have been raped and killed and sent from their land. Our treatment of the indigenous, tribal population has also been horrible.

CC: Rehana looks at people in Calcutta who seem ordinary but she can see from their facial expressions and clothes that they are refugees,[30] so could you say a bit about the status of refugees in *A Golden Age*?
TA: I think Rehana was having a kind of communal moment. The way that people in Calcutta and in West Bengal took in millions of refugees in 1971 is one of the untold stories about that time. One story is that every apartment in Calcutta had people sleeping in the corridors who were refugees. Everyone was donating food and what little money they had, and it was a great moment for Bengali unity and solidarity. Rehana was in that moment feeling the overwhelming presence of her people on the Indian side of the border.

CC: On the issue of language, Rehana is Bengali but could you explain why she speaks Urdu more fluently than Bengali?
TA: Back then, in my grandfather's generation, the way that Bengali Muslims distinguished themselves from Hindus was by speaking Urdu. They were ethnically Bengali but they identified themselves by developing a distinct mode of speech. There was a prevalent notion that Bengali Muslims were inferior, because they were from the villages and unlikely to have been urbane people from Calcutta. My maternal great-grandfather was a *zamindar*'s son from Bardhaman. Among these very wealthy, but possibly not very educated Muslim Bengalis, the way they showed themselves to be upper-class was to speak Urdu: it was about status.

CC: West Pakistanis imposed Urdu as national language on the whole country, Bengali was frowned upon, and Tagore's poetry was banned. Rehana's Urdu-speaking makes her question her own nationalism,[31] yet it is Rehana's proficiency in

Urdu that saves Maya from being raped.[32] **Please discuss how language became a battleground in the war**.

TA: Language was a huge issue, because – even though there were also many economic factors that contributed to Independence – language was the most symbolic aspect of the war. People felt that they had the right to speak Bengali and to celebrate their Bengaliness. Bengalis' cultural identity often resides in the language, as well as the music and songs of Tagore, so not being allowed to speak Bengali and being coerced to speak Urdu was a huge issue in what became Bangladesh. People known to be 'Urdu-speakers' were considered foreign, or somehow part of the enemy matrix. Rehana's an interesting character, because, as someone not totally comfortable with the language, she has an ambivalent relationship with Bengali and Bengal. Her children can tell when she speaks Bengali that she comes slightly from the outside. She's just a small example of the complexities of the language issue. One of the terrible things that happened during the War and just after Independence, was that a lot of Bengali freedom fighters killed Urdu-speaking people, because they believed they had collaborated with the Pakistan army during the war. It's true that some of them did, but most of the people who were killed were innocent. Or maybe they were innocent but had supported Pakistan in a public way throughout the war, or believed that Pakistan would win the war. Then their neighbours took revenge on them.

CC: Could you tell me about your own relationships with Urdu and Bengali?

TA: My mother tongue is Bengali; it's the language we spoke in the house. Some of my mother's relations speak Urdu, so when they get together, they talk in Urdu rather than Bengali. I can more or less understand what they're saying, but I can't really speak Urdu. I can read and write in Bengali, but not in Urdu. My parents were from the war generation, so the Urdu part of our identity was not celebrated as much as the Bengali. However, it would take me years, possibly a lifetime, to become as fluent in Bengali as I am in English. That's because English is the language in which I was educated. It's my most comfortable language, by far.

CC: As regards gender, women are liberated by the war in *A Golden Age*. **Maya says 'It's a war [...] We can do what-ever we want.'**[33] **How does the position of female national-ists in 1971 compare with current situation for Bangladeshi women? Would you describe yourself as a feminist?**
TA: I would say that war opened up a lot of possibilities for women, as it did in Britain during World War Two, when women were building bridges and driving ambulances. Then in the 1950s, these women were expected to go back home and become housewives. I was trying to hint at such parallels in the book. It's probably true of any war – such as nationalist wars of indepen-dence in the 1960s – that through economic necessity women get to play roles in society they wouldn't otherwise be allowed. Yet this trend is more documented in relation to World War Two than in other cases. Having said that, women's situation in the 1971 war laid the groundwork for what has become the modern feminist movement in Bangladesh, which is very strong. Bangladesh is a traditional society in many ways and there's still a long way to go, but the Constitution was written in a very pro-gressive way, affording equal rights to everyone, without discrim-ination on the grounds of gender, ethnicity, race, or religion. Using the Constitution as a basis, the feminist movement has made a lot of important legal strides and has always been a solid grassroots progressive movement. In fact, whenever the Jamaat-i-Islami party gets kicked out of power, they blame the femi-nists, which is a compliment to how strong and how powerful the feminist movement is. I feel part of that movement, as is my mother, and I proudly regard myself as a feminist. It's become a bit of a dirty word in our generation but I firmly dispute that negativity. Important things remain to be achieved in the strug-gle, even in developed countries. In Bangladesh, there's so much still to be fought for; we're still far from achieving equality on many levels. So it's crucial to openly acknowledge feminism.

CC: *A Golden Age* ends with a eulogy to 'beautiful and bruised' Bangladesh,[34] and elsewhere you write: '[l]ike many expatriate Bangladeshis, my *desh-prem* [love for my country] makes me believe there will come a day when I pack my bags and leave London for good. My *desh-prem* is a long-distance affair, full of passion and misunderstanding.'[35] Could you say a little more about the passion and misunderstanding inherent in being a diasporic writer?

TA: I think it's a question one could answer in different ways. It's much easier to have a relationship of nostalgia with a place if you don't have to live with all the complexities of that place and be subject to its limitations. It's easy to sit in London and say, 'We really need democracy', or come up with solutions for the country, but when I visit Bangladesh, the reality of it is much more complex than I'd thought. Sometimes, having a distance helps me to write. I just received British citizenship in summer 2010, but I still feel that my main political and emotional ties are to Bangladesh. I hope I get to live there again some day.

CC: How do you feel when critics compare you to that other Bengali-heritage writer based in Britain, Monica Ali?[36]

TA: I think that's a false comparison. She's great and I'd be happy to be in company with her, but *Brick Lane* was about Britain. I live in Britain but my novels are about Bangladesh. Maybe some day I'll write novels about Britain, but I didn't grow up here and I don't have the sensitivity, knowledge, or insider experience that I would need to write a good novel about Britain. I feel more of an affinity with writers like Kamila Shamsie, who makes Britain her home and writes about Pakistan and other nations. Another example is Chimamanda Adichie, who lives in America, writes about Nigeria, and most of her characters live and grow up in Nigeria as she did. That's not to say that people shouldn't write about things they didn't themselves experience. I didn't experience the war myself. But people have their stakes and loyalties when it comes to their fiction.

CC: There's a lot of intertextuality in *A Golden Age*, including references to the film *Mughal-e-Azam*,[37] Iqbal and Ghalib's *ghazals*,[38] the story 'Sultana's Dream' by the Bengali woman writer Rokeya Sakhawat Hossain,[39] Dylan Thomas,[40] the Beatles and Elvis,[41] Tagore,[42] Thackeray,[43] *Porgy and Bess*,[44] and various pieces of political writing. What texts do you consider to have had the greatest influence on you, and do you feel that there's a strain of cosmopolitanism in your writing?

TA: Because I didn't grow up during the war or live through the moments in history that I wrote about, I had to bring myself in. For example, I love Nina Simone, so I decided to put her in the book, not just because I thought someone like Rehana would listen to jazz, but because I like jazz. Having said that, one reason for the number of eclectic references in *A Golden Age* is because I think there was a lot of cultural magpie-picking in the 1960s. People were trying to do something beyond their own lives and felt part of a global movement. Every time some other dictator was overthrown in a far-flung country, student activists in Bangladesh felt an affinity, not least to the Vietnamese when they were fighting the Americans. We think of globalization as being post-internet, but in fact 1968 was the real moment of globalization and political ideas. I was trying to reflect the cosmopolitanism of that time, through its music, song, poetry, and literature, but it was easy for me because of my own cosmopolitanism. It was enjoyable to put in those different eclectic references.

CC: Is this eclecticism and cosmopolitanism open to the working classes and underclass?

TA: I have mostly written novels about middle-class people. I've written two books about people who are educated and have the opportunities to read and learn about the rest of the world, because that's what I felt most comfortable with. Who knows, maybe the next book will be different.

CC: How have you found researching and writing about religion, as someone so vocally opposed to the Islamic Right?
TA: I think it's important to keep politics just on the periphery of novels. I didn't write this novel as a kind of anti-fundamentalist tract. I could have, because I think the rise of the Islamic Right has been dangerous in Bangladesh. I'm totally against everything that it stands for: that anti-feminist, anti-progressive movement has nothing to recommend it. Having said that, I think every character in a novel has to be understood by the writer and can't just be portrayed as representing something bad. Even though I disagree with a lot of the things that Sohail does in *The Good Muslim*, I had to write about him from the inside. There's an explicit logic in his mind to everything he does, and that logic is very important. You can decide if you want to judge him or not. I, as a novelist, don't weigh the scales very much, because it would be doing a disservice to that particular novel, and the novel in general. One of the things the novel can do, which no other form of writing can, is to bring out the ambiguities and ambivalences in categories such as extremism. Sohail's extremism is a product of his sister's narrow-minded ideas of what religion is, but it's also a narrow and closed viewpoint in its own right. Although I have a lot of problems with the Islamic Right in Bangladesh and all over the world, this novel isn't an anti-fundamentalist polemic. I also write journalistic pieces, but I think the two worlds have to be very distinct. When I write journalism, I'm not usually in the middle of a book, so it's a good way to get my anger out about particular issues. Doing that is better than to try and channel that into a book, because novels are hurt by excessive political commentary.

8
Mohsin Hamid

Credit: Ed Kashi.

Mohsin Hamid was born in Lahore in 1971, the year the Pakistani nation watched its eastern wing secede to become Bangladesh after a nine-month civil war (see previous chapter). He was named after his great-grandfather, a lawyer who was stabbed by another Muslim during tension in Lahore in early 1947, because he was mistaken for a Hindu. Although his grandfather, a member of the Muslim League, survived and went on to help Hindus caught up in the violence later that fateful year, Hamid ironically comments, '[f]rom the start, Pakistan has been prone to turning its knife upon itself'.[1] Hamid grew up speaking Urdu and English, but describes his Punjabi as 'very poor'. He lived in the United States between the ages of three and nine (while his father was doing doctoral research in economics at Stanford University), and later went to America for his own studies at Princeton and Harvard Law.

At Princeton, Hamid was taught creative writing by such luminaries as Joyce Carol Oates and Toni Morrison, the latter overseeing the first draft of his debut novel, *Moth Smoke* (2000). This novel is set in Lahore during the late 1990s, and documents millennial Pakistan's voluptuary, ecstasy-taking social whirl, as well as more familiar scenes of violence and stark class divisions. *Moth Smoke* was regarded by critics such as Anita Desai as marking something of a watershed in subcontinental literature, as an early novel to move away from the fabular Indo-chic fashionable in the 1980s and 1990s towards grittier 'renditions' of Pakistan.[2] To some extent, parallels are indicated between Darashikoh (known as Daru, who is an ex-banker turned heroin addict) and his best friend Aurangzeb/Ozi (with whose wife, Mumtaz, Daru has an affair), as compared with the Mughal secularist Dara Shikoh and more intolerant Emperor Aurangzeb. Yet perhaps more than such religious divisions, the novel highlights the fact that for those who can afford Pajero jeeps, servants, and foreign educations, life is far more stable than those with only precarious access to these vital commodities. As the university professor Julius Superb observes, '[t]he distinction between members of these two groups is made on the basis of control of an important resource: air-conditioning', and there follows a wittily persuasive chapter about the polarization of the A/C'd and non-A/C'd classes.[3] The novel won a Betty Trask Award and reached the finals of the PEN/Hemingway Award. It also appeared on Pakistani television as the three-hour long drama, *Daira* [*Circle of Life*],[4] with the tag-line 'a vicious circle of lust, longing and Lahore'. In part because of the liberalization of the media that occurred during Musharraf's dictatorship,[5] the director, Afzar Ali, was able to do a fairly 'straight' adaptation, including the story of the couple's adultery, drug-taking, and a silhouetted embrace, which Hamid thinks 'might have been the first kiss on Pakistani television'.

As the filmmakers' tag-line indicates, *Moth Smoke* may partly be interpreted as a paean to Hamid's home city of Lahore. To date, much interdisciplinary research has been undertaken on

Indian cities, particularly Bombay/Mumbai,[6] but also Calcutta/Kolkata[7] and Delhi.[8] However, Pakistani urban environments have been relatively under-represented, with Lahore receiving only a small amount of scholarly attention,[9] not to be compared with the vast archive on Bombay. Like Bapsi Sidhwa's acclaimed Partition novel, *Ice-Candy-Man*,[10] Mohsin Hamid's *Moth Smoke* represents Lahore as an unevenly developed, international urban centre, which constantly interconnects with its Punjabi rural hinterland. For example, Dilaram, the madam of a brothel in the iconic red-light district of Heera Mandi, as a young village girl had been raped by her landlord and sent into prostitution in Lahore.[11] Formally, in *Moth Smoke*, various characters take turns to narrate the story, and sometimes the reader is addressed in the second person (an unusual technique that Hamid reworks in *The Reluctant Fundamentalist*), and positioned as the judge presiding over the central murder trial.

In 2003, Hamid wrote a story-memoir, 'The Pathos of Exile', first published by *Time* and reproduced in Sidhwa's *City of Splendour: Writings on Lahore*.[12] In this piece, he focuses on the changes that have occurred in Lahore during the 'difficult decade and a half'[13] he has been overseas. He describes increasing numbers of militant, Islamized youth as 'frown lines of disappointment on the face of the city'[14] and discusses Lahore's technological revolution, 'with Internet cafes [...] [and] billboards offering broadband connections'[15] juxtaposed with old city landmarks such as Anarkali bazaar and the Lahore Fort. Yet, he concludes that Lahore has always given him 'a sense of home to sustain me on my travels'.[16] Unsurprisingly, then, in 2009 this 'transcontinental mongrel'[17] decided to spend more time in Lahore again, becoming for the first time a full-time writer, but continuing to spend time in New York, London, and elsewhere. That same year, he had his first child, a daughter called Dina, and he writes movingly in recent articles about becoming a father, but also about his fears for her future in a Pakistan where there are snipers on the rooftops of many private childcare institutions.[18]

The greater part of Hamid's second novel, *The Reluctant Fundamentalist* (2007), was written while he was working part-time as a strategist for the London branch of brand business Wolff Olins. Thus he is familiar with the corporate world transmogrified in the novel into the ruthless valuation firm, Underwood Samson (its name implies underhandedness, undertakers, dead wood, and the biblical behemoth, Samson, who eventually loses his strength). Hamid explores the theme of post-9/11 Islamophobia through the character Changez (another pronunciation of the first name of Mongol leader, Genghis Khan), who feels compelled to return to Pakistan after changes in attitude towards him, and Pakistanis as a group, in post-9/11 New York. Changez is aware of other Pakistanis being beaten and arrested, himself experiences verbal abuse from strangers, and 'become[s] overnight a subject of whispers and stares'[19] for assuming the potent visual symbol of a beard. In conversation, Hamid described his own experiences in Pakistan and the West wearing 'different types of beard', arguing that in Pakistan he is treated as more of an 'insider' than when he is clean-shaven, whereas a beard 'repositions you in a negative way to the officials when you arrive at Heathrow airport'.

Changez is also spurred to leave the USA by his moribund relationship with his depressed girlfriend, Erica,[20] and by a Chilean publisher, Juan-Bautista, who makes him realize, 'I was a modern-day janissary, a servant of the American empire at a time when it was invading a country with a kinship to mine [Afghanistan] and was perhaps colluding to ensure that my own country faced the threat of war [with India].'[21] Once sacked from Underwood Samson and sent unceremoniously back to Lahore, Changez becomes a university lecturer and gets involved in incendiary Lahori campus politics.[22] In its portrayal of post-9/11 America, the novel has inspired H. M. Naqvi's *Home Boy*, which won the 2011 DSC Prize for South Asian Literature, and recounts the story of well-integrated Pakistani American, Shehzad ('Chuck'), and his two friends, who are arrested on terrorism charges in the toxic post-9/11 climate.[23]

In *The Reluctant Fundamentalist*, Hamid deploys an unusual narrative strategy, adapted from Camus's *The Fall*,[24] in which the narrator relates his disaffection with the US in an interrupted narrative to an unnamed American interlocutor in a café in Lahore. In an interview, Hamid has stated:

> In my novel, there is also an attempt to fundamentally implicate the reader. So if you view the world as fundamentally as [sic] a world where there is a war between civilizations, then the novel is a thriller. If you don't, it equally is a random encounter between two separate guys who go their separate ways. So if it's a thriller or not depends on the preconceptions we bring to it as readers.[25]

Here, Hamid alludes to the fact that the reader is put in the position of 'you', a burly American interrogator, and is therefore to some extent 'implicated' in US foreign policy. He also addresses the ambivalence of the novel's ending and overall structure, such that it can be interpreted as a thriller with a violent ending or, more prosaically, an account of an inconclusive meeting. Finally, Hamid's reference to a specious Huntingtonian thesis about a war between civilizations[26] demonstrates that there is much ambiguity in the novel as to whether Changez is an insurgent of some kind, or indeed whether his interlocutor is a CIA assassin. Of course, many Westerners fear that any Pakistani they meet is associated with terror, while, as Hamid and Kamila Shamsie elegantly show,[27] similar numbers of Pakistanis assume that any American in their country must be working for the intelligence agencies. However, in *The Reluctant Fundamentalist* and Shamsie's *Burnt Shadows*, each side's stereotypes of the Other contains some truth. Both Changez and his unnamed American companion appear to have support waiting in the shadows (such as the Pashtun waiter who attentively serves Changez, and the mysterious recipient of regular SMS messages from the American), and neither Changez nor the American seems to be what they purport to be. A section of the novel, 'Focus on the

Fundamentals' (the title comes from Underwood Samson's business mission statement), was first published in the *Paris Review*,[28] and the novel went on to become an international bestseller, multiple award winner, and a runner-up for the Booker Prize. It is currently being turned into a film, directed by Mira Nair and due for release later in 2011. I have been calling this text a novel, but strictly speaking it comes closer to the novella, criticized as a weird, hybrid 'platypus of a beast', but praised by Erica, who is also writing a novella, as a form that 'leaves space for your thoughts to echo'.[29]

Hamid's recent story, 'A Beheading', written for the special issue of *Granta* on Pakistan, takes up where Hanif Kureishi's short story 'Weddings and Beheadings' leaves off. Kureishi's story is written from the perspective of an aspiring film-maker in an unnamed country (probably Iraq), who is coerced into filming and posting on the internet footage of beheadings. At the end of the story, he expresses his desire to make an artistic film, 'maybe beginning with a beheading, telling the story that leads up to it'.[30] Hamid writes such a narrative from the victim's point of view, but moves the setting to Pakistan, with references to cricket and the Pashto language. Written in the present tense, the story is that of a writer who is taken from his house by *jihadis*, who drive him to a dilapidated house and film his murder. The deeply pessimistic ending describes the man witnessing his own beheading: 'Then I hear it. I hear the sound of my blood rushing out and I open my eyes to see it on the floor like ink and I watch as I end before I am empty.'[31] As well as fiction, Hamid also regularly writes journalistic pieces for such publications as *Dawn*, the *Guardian*, the *New York Times*, and *La Repubblica*. He caused controversy with his public support for General Musharraf in the 2002 referendum,[32] although he later became increasingly critical of the General in his journalism.[33]

CC: What are you working on at the moment?
MH: I'm working on my third novel, and as usual it's not easy. My first two took seven years each. After writing *Moth Smoke*, I thought I would finish *The Reluctant Fundamentalist* more quickly,

but it took exactly the same amount of time. It's now several years since the publication of my second novel, and I'm still not that far along in my third. I put this down to a mixture of laziness, travel, other work, and dislocation. For me, writing is a bit like doing a puzzle. I keep trying different approaches and figuring out what works, and I haven't yet figured out what's going to work for the third book, or really what it's about. But I think I'd like this one to be at least partly set in Britain. When I started writing *Moth Smoke*, I was just 22 and had lived in Pakistan most of my life. I'd gone to America for college when I was 18, but I was still very much a Pakistani. By the time I began to write *The Reluctant Fundamentalist* at the age of 29, I had been in America on and off for about a decade, so it made sense to locate it in America. And now I've lived mostly in the UK for nearly eight years, so it feels as though the time has come to deal with this place. My focus as far as Britain is concerned would be London (I don't know small-town or rural Britain), and possibly a couple of European cities as well. Part of me thinks I should just write a purely British or European book, but Pakistan's very much on my mind, so I'm planning to write about both, probably in a similar way to *The Reluctant Fundamentalist*'s representations of both America and Pakistan.

CC: You keep returning to Lahore in your fiction. Like Salman Rushdie with Bombay and Kamila Shamsie with Karachi, you are a remarkable chronicler of the city. In *Moth Smoke* you portray the Badshahi Mosque and 'fundos' in close proximity to the red light district of Heera Mandi, with its sex, hashish, and alcohol. In *The Reluctant Fundamentalist* you give a sense of Lahore as a frontier town, vulnerable because of its proximity to the Indian border. Could you say a bit more about your representations of this city of contrasts?

MH: I think by definition all big cities are cities of contrasts, whether we're talking about New York, London, Lahore, Delhi, or Shanghai. Once you get towards ten million people living in a place, contrasts are inevitable and, if you're relatively familiar with the city and able to wander around, you see them. I don't know whether Lahore is more of a city of contrasts than other cities. Often, people who are not from a place impose a kind of flatness on it and assume that the people there are all similar and interact within a small, defined zone of behaviour and conduct. This is invariably wrong, so people might come to Lahore with certain stereotypes, and realize, 'Wow, it's very diverse; there's a lot more stuff going on than I thought.' Similarly, Pakistanis that I know have come to London, and been shocked that there are parts of London where people dress and behave more conservatively than people in Lahore would be expected to.

As for the other part of your question, Lahore only feels like a frontier town when Pakistan and India are coming close to war, which happens about every five or ten years. In recent years, there was a stand-off between India and Pakistan after the Kargil conflict of 1999; it happened again after the 2001 Delhi parliament and 2008 Mumbai attacks. When India and Pakistan prepare for war, Lahore is right in the flight path: you see aircraft and helicopters flying overhead, soldiers fortifying positions outside the city, and it does feel like a frontier town then. But otherwise its frontier status is different, because Lahore is the last major city as you head westward out of the Indian subcontinent, before you get to Central Asia. Peshawar is further west, but is in many ways a Central Asian city. Lahore, Delhi, and several other cities further east, share many similarities that make you feel as though you're in part of a continuous zone. Pakistan is in that sense a frontier country, between South Asia and Afghanistan/Central Asia. Lahore is a symbolic frontier for South Asian-style liberalism and coexistence, even inside Pakistan, which is why it is now being particularly targeted.

CC: You discuss east–west divisions within Pakistan in your essay 'Divided We Fall', in which you describe going to Balochistan, and seeing the army and security agents antagonizing the local population.[34]
MH: The Pakistani state still functions reasonably well in much of the Punjab and Karachi. And parts of Balochistan and the

Northwest Frontier are properly governed, but much of those provinces is effectively stateless and lawless, run by local tribes, with the state as the enforcer in an armed capacity. The tribal areas are now much more than just areas for particular peoples; they are outside of state control. Thus, there is a west–east division in Pakistan.

Karachiite friends often tell me that Karachi is the most liberal city in Pakistan, and maybe it is; it's hard to generalize about cities. But the sense I get it is that there is a lot of conservatism in Karachi because of the existence of different groups, each mostly cut off from the place where they come from, living as immigrants in Karachi; not just the *muhajirs*, but people from other parts of Pakistan. Diversity can be frightening for people, so many cling to their ethnic group, religion, and various types of social conservatism, in a way that Lahoris don't so much, because Lahore is a more homogeneous city and less threatened by modernity. There have been attempts to radicalize parts of Punjab, and *jihadist* organizations from the Punjab have a footprint in Lahore. Until recently, these groups have been looking outside Pakistan, towards Kashmir and Afghanistan, so Lahore hasn't felt their virulence. However, now it too is on the receiving end, which is a huge and shocking change.

CC: Please could you discuss your representations of the relationship between Punjab's rural hinterland and the metropolis?
MH: There are other writers who deal with that more than I do. I don't spend enough time in rural Punjab to deal with it in a substantive way in my writing. Again, it's hard to generalize, because there are very affluent parts and extremely poor parts of rural Punjab; relatively stable and comparatively violent areas; religiously conservative and much more liberal regions of rural Punjab. The Pakistani part of Punjab has the same size population as Germany (about 81 million people), so it's huge. We think of it as a province, but anywhere else it would be a large country. However, I think the rural/urban split is blurring, because all along

Pakistan's many major roads, there's an urbanization taking place. If you drive around the GT Road, or any other large road in Punjab, little towns and shops have grown up around it. People live along those roads, have electricity, televisions, satellite dishes, and mobile phone coverage, and they watch the cars passing through. They are traders, selling things in their shops, and paying for services. They are not like the farmers. This network cuts across all of Punjab now, so it isn't as though there's an urban core and then periphery, but a tracery of urbanization that penetrates the periphery. Obviously, the further away from Lahore, Rawalpindi, Islamabad, and other big cities you get, the smaller its influence is. However, it is transforming Punjab and a majority of Punjabis now live either in cities or these semi-urban roads, and don't have the traditional farming life that was the original Punjabi way. I imagine this trend will only increase, because the population is growing and there are only so many people needed for farming, so others will sell, trade, and work in service industries.

CC: *Moth Smoke* **is set in the late 1990s, when India and Pakistan were testing their nuclear bombs and you portray jubilation among people of all political persuasions when Pakistan detonated its own nuclear explosions in response to Indian tests.[35] Why do you think there was an outpouring of joy in Pakistan at the military posturing?**
MH: When you're the smaller, weaker party in a conflict, the idea of going out and buying a gun is more attractive than if you're the bigger, stronger one. If you're the stronger party, like India, then it's easy to moralize that guns are bad, but if you're the weaker one, like Pakistan, then weapons can seem like an equalizer. That said, the nuclear tests sparked enormous popular pride in India too, not just the pacifism and protests against the nuclear testing expressed by such writers as Arundhati Roy.[36] Aside from the issue of whether or not there should be nuclear weapons, many Indians probably rightly wondered what these weapons would deter. They're unlikely

to prevent terrorism or insurgency in places like Kashmir. India is not at risk from war with China, so there's no real deterrence there. Pakistan's unlikely to invade them, so what is the supposed nuclear deterrence for? In contrast, Pakistan's case is very clear: India could invade, so having a bomb will deter that invasion. The difference between Iraq and Pakistan is that Pakistan happens to have nuclear weapons, otherwise who knows what would have happened after 9/11? That can explain part of the difference in intellectuals' reactions to the tests in India and Pakistan. However, the popular reaction in both countries was one of real support and excitement, and in both countries there's a collective sense of having underperformed for centuries, so nuclear testing was read as a statement of strength and achievement. It's understandable that people would be excited about it.

CC: America has long defined itself in exceptionalist terms, but in *The Reluctant Fundamentalist*, you controversially define American foreign policy and globalization as 'empire'.[37] In his role as a business valuer, Changez is compared to a janissary, one of the Christian slaves taken as children to fight for the Ottoman Empire. Guns are mistaken for money-belts and business card holders, or vice versa, showing the intimate relationship between capitalism and violence. How have Americans reacted to this unflattering depiction of their empire?
MH: I'm not an anti-capitalist; it's not that I think that business is wrong. However, it's certainly the case that the system of money and the protection of property necessitate violence. I don't know that one could dismantle and replace it with anything better, so I'm not suggesting any complete overhaul, although much tinkering would probably be a good idea. But ultimately, the way it works is that you can buy shares in your pension fund here in London, and those shares might be in companies that do manufacturing in Indonesia, so if your pension goes up, then the profit that you make is perhaps equal to the labour of several salaried people in an Indonesian factory.

Effectively, you have allocated yourself the profits of those people's work. Your property rights are protected, so nobody can get away with stealing your money or implementing a different system, because your system is backed by the militarily strongest people and your domestic police force. This is why people who don't have money don't simply come and take the money from people who do have money.

The idea that there is violence behind a system of capital can't be denied, but capitalism allows us to act as though we're not violent. I can have a million pounds in my pension fund and retire on an income of 60,000 pounds a year, and I haven't directly done anything violent. Yet the system that allows me to benefit from my million-pound pension fund depends on at least the threat of violence to protect what I have. I'm not the first person to observe that big business is a modern distancing mechanism that separates us from the more primal marauding armies that conquer, rape, pillage, and steal money. I'm not saying big business and the Mongol hordes are the same and, for most people, probably the encounter with big business is better than getting your head chopped off by raiding armies, so we have progressed a little. However, there are interesting affinities in how the two operate, and to some extent the Mongols created a very meritocratic civilization. The best warriors rose up, and the strongest brother became king. The corporate world can be similarly meritocratic, and Changez begins to become aware of this and wonders whose empire he's actually serving.

As for how Americans reacted to the novel, it's difficult to generalize about their 300 million different points of view. I've experienced very negative reactions to *The Reluctant Fundamentalist*, but also warm, positive responses. To give you an example of a positive reaction, a young guy with blond dreadlocks and piercings came up to me after a reading in Washington DC, and he announced, 'This book is about me.' I was surprised, but he explained that he'd gone to Dartmouth, and worked for a year at an investment bank after college, but he couldn't stand it, so he quit and became a yoga instructor in DC. I hadn't thought of Changez's story as reflecting such a situation, but of course, as much as anything else, it's about a young college graduate who's an idealist and walks away from corporate life. In that sense it's a very American story, or certainly it reflects counter-culture America.

CC: I was struck that both your novels centre on someone getting the sack and having a breakdown.
MH: There are certain recurring themes in my fiction: work and loss of work; what it takes to acquire money; the loss of privilege that accompanies losing money; and a sense of alienation from the whole system. I'm not sure why I'm so preoccupied by these issues or whether I will always write about them, but at the moment they keep resurfacing in different ways. Work and what it does to people, and reactions to other people's work and financial situations, strike me as interesting. I suppose it's timely with so many people losing their jobs in the current recession, but I think everybody loses their jobs at least once in every generation. I have felt acutely the conflicts that come with work: the conflict between time for my writing and time to work, between my political commitments and working in a corporate world, between being Pakistani and working in the West. I'm interested in exploring these fissures, and I'll probably examine them again in my third book. In the early twenty-first century, when many people have begun to feel as though they can find self-fulfilment through work, and others believe work to be a complete betrayal, this great conflict seems like a rich topic to explore. In the twentieth century, there was the ideological debate between communism and capitalism, but now I think it tends to be an ongoing personal crisis in the individual.

CC: There is also great affection for America, especially New York, in *The Reluctant Fundamentalist*. You discuss the city's 'cosmopolitanism'[38] and Erica opens a door for Changez into an exciting elite New York world, of gallery openings, picnics, and literary agents, but the city turns

against Changez after 9/11. Could you discuss your double-edged relationship with the nation/city?

MH: Well I've lived in America for almost half my life, and they've been good years for the most part, with close friends and fond memories. I think much of my worldview comes from my American education. I feel an affinity towards Utopian American ideals, and am less ready to accept European explanations that seem to be based on the way things are. When I was growing up and being educated there, immigration seemed like a very American phenomenon. Currently America is recoiling from immigration, but my early experiences conditioned my attitude towards immigration, which is that countries should not have the right to control or demand things from immigrants. Immigration is a human right, and what we are doing in our various attempts to control, moderate, and change it, is something that goes against that right. If I'm having a gigantic meal and someone in Sudan or Somalia is starving to death, there's no right by which I can say that person should starve to death and I shouldn't. Similarly there's no right by which we can say that this immigrant shouldn't be here.

Once here, the idea that there should be any difference in how the immigrant is treated because he or she is brown or Muslim or whatever, seems very odd to me. It seems bizarre that Britain has a monarchy, and Europe as a whole still feels tribal. The French are so French, the Germans so German, and everything's about narrow nationalism, as opposed to reaching out for a common humanity. This viewpoint is shaped by my American experience, and I subscribe to many of the ideals that American civilization is supposedly built on. However, I often have serious problems with the way those ideals are put into practice, and I'm very favourably inclined to the European welfare state, for example, even if I'm not inclined towards European attitudes towards immigration, race relations, nationalism, or tribal identity. If I'm honest, a big chunk of me is American, just as a large part of me is Pakistani, and a small but probably growing portion of me is British or European. I have a lot of affection for New York, in particular, because in some ways that is America at its best. In other ways, though, it's America at its most economically stratified, with unrestrained free-market capitalism, in a way that disturbs me.

CC: *The Reluctant Fundamentalist* is an interesting title, particularly because although Changez grows a beard and gets involved in radical politics, he shows little, if any, interest in Islam. Indeed, there is a marked absence of religious thought or ideology in the novel. However, you highlight another sort of 'fundamentalism': that of global capital. The employees of Underwood Samson are repeatedly urged to 'focus on the fundamentals',[39] by which you show that the West has its own forms of extremism, such as the ruthlessness of big business. Changez grows reluctant to remain a representative of globalization and its values and thus ostensibly becomes a 'fundamentalist'. How do you view these two forms of 'fundamentalism' in the world?
MH: You're absolutely right that Changez isn't religious. He's the reluctant fundamentalist in the sense that valuing companies on the basis of their economic fundamentals is something that he comes to do very unwillingly. The idea that he is a Muslim fundamentalist is also something that he resists, and so it works in both of those directions. But what I find very interesting is that, by calling the book *The Reluctant Fundamentalist* and giving the guy a beard, it tends to be assumed that he is spiritually or philosophically a Muslim. There's no evidence for that whatsoever in the novel. Changez isn't actually a violent person, but leaving that on one side, what you have in Changez is a secular, humanist rationalist. He has a tribal identity which is Muslim, but it would be the same if he were Afro-Caribbean, or anything else. This identity only involves belonging to a group, and he doesn't describe the world in specifically Muslim terms, or even begin to wonder what such terms might be. While the novel is often interpreted as being about the radicalization of a Muslim youth, if you strip religion completely out of it, it still works. It's possible to recast this entire conflict in non-religious terms and find the

conflict unchanged, except in our understanding of it. And that for me is very interesting.

CC: Robin Yassin-Kassab points out that the fundamentalists aren't bombing the bikini beaches of Brazil, for example.[40] Is Islamism less about moralizing on the West's sexuality or decadence, and more of a political movement?
MH: It *is* a political faction, and one that's confused. For example, in 2009 Islamists in Lahore attacked the Sri Lankan cricket team, which isn't even anti-Muslim. The fundamentalists are now trying to destroy cricket, which means eviscerating the one visible symbol of national pride. Terrorism is a form of communication and marketing for particular political ideologies. Read as that, it isn't religious in any sense. Fundamentalists behave in certain way or display particular symbols to appeal to some co-religionists. To signal that you're being true, you'll blow up Buddha statues, for example [see p. 137]. However, to accept that these acts are religiously motivated is to accept that a new religion has been born with these people, because nobody previously blew up these Buddhas during the last couple of thousand years of their existence. Terrorism doesn't have anything to do with their religion. People use religion as a way of differentiating themselves from other groups and asserting power over other people. If I can justify my view as being religious, it means that your non-religious outlook is not equal to mine, and therefore I have righteous justification to impose my view on you. Such a system appeals to people who have had other views forced on them, with equal lack of concern for their views and with even less reason, in the name of empire, capitalism, the nation-state, whatever. If the landlord, the company, the colonizer, or the nation-state tells me and my family to do something, how is that different from another idiot telling me I should do it because of Islam? All these political movements amount to the same thing: a dictatorship based on an appeal to an authority that I may or may not accept.

Religion tries to answer fundamental questions for people. What is a good life? How do you deal with the fact that you're going to die? How do you accept a universe which is beyond your control? How do you accept that you love someone but can't direct what happens? If anything is a sign of religious crisis, it's that we now live in a world where people feel insecure and frightened about these questions. Religion isn't doing its job, but all that we're offering people in its place is a secularism that so far isn't addressing these emotional, spiritual concerns, and only focuses on material things. I don't think you need God to talk about these issues, and I think it would be perfectly possible for secularism to tackle them, but it hasn't yet tapped into this market. What's needed is a belief system that cuts across these issues and is inclusive. This is how the major religions originally worked: by including people from different tribes, beliefs, social backgrounds, within a system. A secularism or atheism that accepts Muslims, Christians, and Jews as equal members, doesn't exist, or hasn't been properly articulated, so there is a political and spiritual crisis. As part of the spiritual crisis, symbols that were previously associated with spirituality and religion are being deployed in political terms. What we're left with is a gaping hole where spirituality used to be – which is growing by the second and is going to be a source of major problems – and a new politics that's calling itself religion. I don't subscribe to aggressive atheism on the one hand, or to the hijacking of religion by politicians with no spiritual integrity on the other. For most people, the idea that they will die for their religion and therefore go to heaven, is at best a very partial answer to the spiritual questions that they face. That's why Islam had so many other components to its answers, and that's why there are so many different versions of Islam being practised, because each of these evolved in different ways.

9
Robin Yassin-Kassab

British Syrian novelist Robin Yassin-Kassab was born in London, and grew up in Merseyside and Scotland, spending another year in England's capital before studying at the University of Oxford. After university, he worked abroad in Pakistan, France, Saudi Arabia, Oman, Morocco, Turkey, and Syria, mostly teaching English to adults, but in 1994–5, he again lived in West London. In 2008, he moved with his Syrian wife and their two children from Oman, where he had taught for five years, to the Scottish Borders where his mother lives,[1] but he remains fascinated by London, to which city he has a sense of belonging which he says 'isn't logical'. His first novel, *The Road From Damascus* (2008), was taken up by Simon Prosser (the publishing director who gave Zadie Smith her break), published by Hamish Hamilton and Penguin, and translated as *Il Traditore* [*The Traitor*] by Saggiatore publisher in Italy. He is marketed as a writer of 'postcolonial London',[2] and the hardback dustjacket to *The Road from Damascus* features a drawing of Harrow Road in West London, replete with the migrant-run fried chicken restaurants humorously discussed in the novel.[3]

Yet the novel provides more than just a glimpse into the lives of Arabs in London (a topic already explored in Hanan al-Shaykh's Arabic-language novel, *Only in London*,[4] *inter alia*), addressing issues relating to migration, faith, identity, love, and politics. As well as writing occasional book reviews for the *Guardian* and other publications, Yassin-Kassab is a co-editor and regular contributor to *PULSE*, a collaborative web-based magazine which can be found at pulsemedia.org. He is currently working on his second novel. In a textbook example of what Peter Morey and Amina Yaqin call the 'framing' of Muslims,[5] in 2010 Yassin-Kassab's comments to a *Scottish Mail on Sunday* reporter were isolated and taken out of context in such a way as to present him as a supporter of 9/11 and suicide bombing,[6] which, as my interview makes clear, is a distortion of his gradated, yet radical politics. The *Daily Express* picked up the story and ran with the headline 'Fury at traitor who backs our enemies',[7] bringing great anxiety to Yassin-Kassab and his family. It seems likely he was targeted in this way because of the sentiments expressed on his blog, qunfuz.com (so named because *qunfuz* in Arabic means 'porcupine', and the blog is certainly spiky, especially in relation to the occupation of Palestine). The issue of blogging is discussed in this interview, which was conducted before the *Mail/Express* smear.

The Road from Damascus opens in early 2001 with the protagonist, Sami, visiting relatives who live, unsurprisingly, in the suburbs of Damascus. Sami has been trying for over a decade to write his doctorate on Arabic poetry, following in the footsteps of his late father, Mustafa, a secular, pan-Arabist intellectual, who made his academic name in Britain. Sami hopes that this trip to Syria will help him to find the central idea for his thesis which he badly needs and, with this in mind, he intends to interview his aunt and cousins, to find out 'the responses of [...] ordinary Syrian Arabs, to [his] poetic enquiries'.[8] But early into the conversation, Sami hears a noise from an adjacent room, and discovers a 'loonish relative'[9] there, counting prayer beads. His aunt leads him to understand that this is his mother's brother, Uncle Faris, and that he was imprisoned and tortured by the secularist dictator government for 22 years, for being a card-carrying though inactive member of the Islamist group, the Muslim Brotherhood. In conversation, Yassin-Kassab explained that this idea was the novel's starting point and was based on his Syrian wife's uncle, who like Faris was imprisoned for nominal Muslim Brotherhood activity and tortured for most of his 20-year sentence. In the novel, when a cousin wonders aloud who informed on Faris to the *mukhabarat*, or Syrian secret police, Sami notices frostiness on the part of his relatives, who say point-edly that only *family* had been aware that Faris was a Muslim Brother.

Back in London, Sami returns to his long-suffering wife, the Iraqi-born teacher, Muntaha, with whom arguments soon ensue, because her increasing religiousness has led her to start praying and covering her head, and Sami, like his father before him, sees this as a 'step backwards'.[10] The breakdown in their relationship culminates when Sami, distraught after a meeting with his super-visor in which he is persuaded to give up his PhD, goes on a two-day drink and drugs binge, is unfaithful to Muntaha, and endures a brief stint in prison for possession of cannabis. However, perhaps Sami's worst breach of trust during his 'lost weekend' is that he misses the death of Muntaha's father, Marwan, and his *ta'ziya*, or condolence ceremony. This leads Muntaha to expel Sami from their house, and to take solace in her friendship with a colleague, the Hungarian-Russian Jew, Gabor, who soon shows signs of being in love with her.

With 'guilt to appease',[11] Sami rekindles a friendship with Muntaha's younger brother, the hip-hop enthusiast turned Islamist, Ammar. Disgusted at his former indulgences, Sami cuts his hair short, grows a beard, and gives up drugs and alcohol. He even begins attending Ammar's 'underground mosque',[12] despite his earlier contempt for religion. Here he hears millennial talk of Signs of the Hour (Muslim beliefs about the world's end); anti-Semitic, anti-Shia, and anti-American diatribes; and much political discussion of the state of the Arab world.

In the meantime, after a summer of getting closer as friends, Gabor plans to seduce Muntaha by impressing her with pictures he has painted which blend Muslim concepts, such as *tawheed* or unity, with art. However, his efforts prove fruitless, as Muntaha reminds him that although she and Sami are currently separated, she still considers herself married. Sami is briefly arrested soon after 11 September. His estranged mother picks him up from the police station, and Sami confronts her about his Uncle Faris in Damascus. She confirms the half-knowledge that he has been repressing: his beloved father, the secular-nationalist, Mustafa, was the one who informed on Faris to the *mukhabarat*. The novel ends with the reconciled Sami and Muntaha holidaying in Scotland and Sami thinking about cultivating a flexible faith.[13] To some extent, in the Syrian/Iraqi sections of the novel, Yassin-Kassab presents a face-off between secular humanism and reinvented religious traditions. At one point, secularism is termed 'a late 19th-century hiccup'.[14] The epigraphs to the novel, Ahmad Yasavi's 'unbelief itself is a religion with its own form of belief' and Pascal's 'Atheism indicates strength of mind, but only up to a certain point',[15] suggest that atheism has its own types of extremism, an issue that we discuss in this interview.

CC: How do you feel about people categorizing you as a British Muslim writer?

R Y-K: I don't mind, as long as it doesn't get taken too seriously. I was rather disappointed that *The Road from Damascus* was reviewed as a Muslim book, but then it is [laughs], so I can't complain. I just wanted to write a book; ultimately I want to be a writer, not a Muslim, Arab, or British writer. But I'm not concerned, so long as people aren't using it to reinforce stereotypes. Nowadays, people tend to make assumptions about what you think, as a Muslim, before you even open your mouth.

CC: You write, 'Always, with Sami, issues returned to hijabs and beards',[16] so why are you interested in these visible symbols of Islam?

R Y-K: Because the world is, unfortunately. Not just Muslims, everybody is holding on to signs. You wave your football shirt in Scotland, or your flag if you're a nationalist. People all over the world are reducing issues to signs and judging other people according to those signs in order to make themselves feel comfortable. This is part of the general collapse of analysis and ideology and thought. The *hijab* is something that most people annoy me on, whether it's people who think that if your wife's in a *hijab* and you've got a beard that makes you morally upright, or people who assume that because a woman's wearing the *hijab*, she's oppressed and uneducated.

In most parts of the Arab world, you can't draw lines between religion, politics, and identity. My wife didn't wear a *hijab* when we met and now she does;[17] and my father wasn't very happy when my sisters started wearing *hijab*s but they do. In Damascus ten years ago, at least 50 per cent of women didn't wear the *hijab*, but now, if you subtract the Christians and the Alawi people, more or less everybody does. Syria hasn't become more conservative; nor has it become more spiritual – it's becoming less spiritual and much more global-capitalist – but it's to do with identity and politics, and a great sense of disappointment that other systems have failed, so let's hold on to Islam.

I'm not an Islamist of any stripe, but Islamism is diverse, and I admire a few Islamist organizations. Some Islamist groups, like the Saudis, Wahhabi groups, and the Taliban, are very right-wing and oppressive, but Hizbullah, for example, doesn't try to enforce anything on anybody. They believe that women should wear the *hijab*, but in South Beirut or the Bekaa, girls in miniskirts and make-up rub shoulders with girls in *hijab*s, and people have their alcohol shops open, and nobody bothers them. In many ways, Hizbullah is about a historically oppressed community valuing itself and working together, so it's close to an Arab socialism. Ultimately race is also about class. In today's world,

African Americans of a certain class can be successful, such as Condoleezza Rice, Colin Powell, or Barack Obama, and similarly the imperial ruling classes working with the US in countries such as Saudi Arabia are Arabs by birth, but they're oppressing their own people. I wish Islamist discourse showed greater awareness of the class dimension.

CC: You've got a blog in which you write about political events, particularly Palestine. How does your journalism and blogging inform your novel-writing?
R Y-K: One of the conscious reasons I started the blog was so that politics didn't infect my fiction too much, although it still does. In the novel, Sami comes back from Paris at the start of the *intifada*, and he wants to write his PhD about Mahmoud Darwish and the poet's sense of engagement, but finds that he's just rewriting the day's body count.[18] If I write about an issue that's burning me up and put it on the blog, then I can forget about it. One of the reasons I like the novel is that it's a very holistic form: you can write about relationships, psychology, politics, sex, and religion within the same space, and in real life these things aren't in separate categories. Now that we're all supposedly postmodern, there's a tendency to dismiss writing that's in any way ideological or contains grand narratives. I'm not a postmodernist, because I like big ideas. One reviewer of *The Road from Damascus* wrote that the characters speak the same unmediated, earnest stuff that you can find on the author's blog.[19] I don't have enough distance on it to say whether that's true or not, but I object to the word 'earnest', because it's like saying, 'Why do you give a damn about things?' I *am* earnest, enthusiastic, and emotional about certain political issues, and I'm not ashamed of it. By all means criticize my horrific, Arabist point of view: that's all right, because you're taking on what I'm saying.

CC: You write that *sharia* only works if men are noble,[20] but Muntaha defends it and talks about it as being 'flexible',[21] with

a balance between 'mercy and wrath, severity and lenience'.[22] What's your own view of *sharia*?

R Y-K: Very similar to Muntaha's. Whenever I hear about people – not the British Archbishop of Canterbury[23] – but people in Pakistan or Egypt talking about wanting to bring in *sharia* law, then it's probably a bad idea, because they want to bring in a fossilized interpretation of it. *Sharia* means 'the way', it's the same word for 'road' in Arabic, and so it's simply a set of guiding principles. The actual punishments that we hear so much about are called *hudood* – in Pakistan they were known as the Hudood Ordinance – and *hudood* is an Arabic word meaning 'border', so it's the furthest limits to which you could go. It doesn't mean you're supposed to go to that limit. When I was teaching in Saudi Arabia, I'd discuss capital punishment with my students and when they heard that I opposed it they'd argue that in Islam you have to execute people. I think they're wrong, because I researched religious texts, and if you kill me and I have ten brothers, out of whom one doesn't want you to be executed, then the judge has to abide by the wishes of that one brother. In the Prophet's day, there wasn't a complex bureaucratic and legal system, so siding with the one brother is a way of ensuring mercy in the system. *Sharia* is a flexible system and, as Muntaha suggests, it prescribes extreme punishment, but makes the conditions on which it can be implemented almost impossible. People would come to the Prophet, admit they'd committed adultery and ask for punishment, and he'd tell them that because they'd repented, it was forgiven. How you get from that to Zia-ul-Haq executing rape victims in Pakistan, I don't know.

CC: I was interested in the portrayal of Rashid Iqbal, your novel's Salman Rushdie figure. What's your own opinion of Rushdie?

R Y-K: I don't like him, but to an extent I may only be reacting with embarrassment to a writer who was once important to me (I wrote a long essay on him at university). If a large

portion of the world was baying for my blood, I would probably behave foolishly as well, so I can't really blame him, and
I wish that he hadn't been built up and terrorized by the *fatwa*.
That said, almost everything that he's said since the *fatwa* about
Muslims and Arabs has been simplistic. In *The Satanic Verses*,
he uses the term 'brown uncle Tom',[24] but he plays this role
well himself. Stylistically I find his novels to involve pyrotech-
nics and showing off. On my old copy of *Midnight's Children*,
the blurb reads, 'It sounds like a continent finding its voice.'[25]
Salman Rushdie is not the first articulate brown person. Part of
the problem is the way he's been marketed, but he's played up
to that because he could have vetoed the blurb. Martin Amis
is similarly weak in his political thinking: he's a good comic
writer, but a clueless commentator. When *The Satanic Verses*
fuss was going on, Rushdie said, 'I'm glad I've upset people and
I wrote it because I wanted to start a dialogue with the Muslim
community', but that's rubbish. *The Satanic Verses* was written
as a cosmopolitan, postmodern novel, and his readership is not
the people in Pakistan, for example, who got so angry about the
novel, or the people in communities here who felt victimized by
it. If he'd wanted to engage those people he could have written
a pamphlet in Urdu. He was using myths and stereotypes that
have existed in Christendom for centuries: using the insulting
name for the Prophet, 'Mahound'; portraying him as an epi-
leptic bawd; and his wives as whores. Before Islam was seen as
a puritan religion, it was regarded as libertine, so the stereotypes
went from one extreme to the other, and the novel plays on
these Orientalist slurs. To be fair, he was portraying somebody
who's losing his mind, and is between worlds, and how he
internalizes stereotypes about his own religion. However, that
wasn't really signalled to the reader, and 90 per cent of readers
wouldn't realize it's a mad person having hallucinations.

**CC: In the blog you talk about 'the delicate issue of a writ-
er's responsibility in an Islamophobic climate'.[26] The BNP
behave atrociously at the Rashid Iqbal talk, but the police**

beat only the Muslim protesters.[27] At the end of the novel Sami is arrested because of his newly grown beard, and the police ask him to become an informer on his own community.[28] What's your position on Islamophobia?

R Y-K: Islamophobia is scary and it's getting worse all the time. Discourses of hatred about Muslims, Jews, Arabs, Blacks, women, gays all exist, and they sometimes seem to be disappearing, but if the political circumstances change, they return. Politically, Islamophobia has been very useful for the powers-that-be. At the time of the invasion of Iraq, many British people were asking, 'Why are we violently involved in the Muslim world?' That question may still exist somewhere, but now the main question is, 'What's wrong with Muslims?' That's been cleverly done, but prejudice exists underneath, and it ignites when you light a spark. Similarly, Jack Straw's remarks about the *niqab* were politically generated. Few women wear the *niqab*, and making a media circus about it only makes *niqab*-wearers feel uncomfortable and feeds usefully into Islamophobia. Straw's argument goes that if people take their *niqabs* off, then the West and the East can communicate better, but they would understand each other better if the non-Muslims stopped dropping bombs on Muslims. I hate the *niqab* myself, because you communicate with your face, and covering it up is a withdrawal of communication. Islamically it's also unnecessary, but that's not really my business because we live in a society in which people have different ideas.

Islamophobia is less about race than cultural prejudice these days. In London at least, I pass for White, but once people know where you're from, they have a set of assumptions about who you are and what you think. It's a way of not engaging with the reality of the Other, and that, combined with the police-state laws that are coming in, is frightening. People are being imprisoned for thought crime, as in the Atif Siddique case in Scotland.[29] He was downloading material in Arabic that he couldn't read from al-Qa'ida-type websites, and seems to have confused, malicious politics. The authorities should keep an eye on him, and punish him if he steps over the line into organizing violence. However, sending him to maximum security prison for eight years for playing on the internet, while BNP people are actually building bombs and don't get such sentences, is just going to marginalize bitter people even more. Samina Malik, the 'lyrical terrorist' from Southall, is in her early twenties and many people write angry poetry in their youth, and there are gangsta rap CDs on sale with those kinds of sentiment in it, but she was convicted of storing materials for terrorist purposes, even if the conviction was later quashed.[30] In the last few weeks it's become illegal to support the military wing of Hizbullah in this country, or even to glorify them. I argue that the military wing of Hizbullah is a wonderful organization, the best organization the modern Arab world has produced, and that criminalizes me. Yet British people can and do go and fight for the Israel Defense Forces and half the commentariat every day praises the Israeli armed forces who commit far more crimes than Hizbullah ever has.

CC: In the novel, Sami's reaction to 9/11 is, 'If it was Arabs who did it, it is all anyone is going to talk to him about. Ever again.'[31] At the risk of pigeonholing you in that way, what was your reaction to 9/11?
R Y-K: On 9/11, we'd left Saudi Arabia, and were staying in Damascus before moving to Oman. My wife told me about the attacks over the phone and I didn't believe her, but then I saw a TV screen, and noticed a strange and initially somewhat joyful atmosphere in the streets. It was hard to process the reality of it, and what it would mean. The Americans cast it as an unparalleled crime, but crimes on that scale happen in the Third World all the time. 11 September is the anniversary of the 1973 Chilean coup that removed Pinochet.[32] During 'Black September' of 1970, there was a series of massacres of Palestinians in Jordan,[33] but cataclysmic events in the Third World are not remembered.

9/11 shouldn't have been a turning point for international affairs, but it has been, for good and bad reasons. America, the First World in general, and especially the Empire, didn't expect to be hit in its heart like that, and it was a shock. It should have provoked a re-examination, but the Empire is so ideologically blinkered that in most sections of society it hasn't. The whole thing is very suspicious. I don't go along with the blatant conspiracy theorists, but I feel certain that Osama bin Laden – wittingly or unwittingly, perhaps just out of stupidity – is working for America, because al-Qa'ida has saved the Empire's skin on three occasions that I can think of.

CC: What were those three occasions?
R Y-K: Firstly, the Project for a New American Century wrote a report well before 11 September, and they argued that dominance of the Middle East and Central Asia was achievable, but that the American people didn't have the appetite for a string of wars in the Middle East, unless 'some catastrophic and catalyzing event – like a new Pearl Harbor' – occurred.[34] They got it, and by 12 September they had their plans for Iraq on the table. The second is that when I lived in Saudi Arabia in the run-up to the invasion of Iraq, there was a strong sense that the Saudi regime was going to fall. Taliban types hated Saudi Arabia's pro-Western policies and the presence of foreigners, and Western-educated kids wanted to go to nightclubs and hated the religious police. Revolution was in the air, but after we'd left, around the time of the invasion of Iraq, there was a series of al-Qa'ida atrocities on residential compounds in which foreigners lived, which killed some Lebanese Muslim children and nice Americans who'd been quietly working there for 20 years. When the Saudi people saw that, they thought, 'If that's the alternative, let's stick with the devil we know.' Al-Qa'ida saved the skin of the Saudi regime at that point, and the latter has some more intelligent policies now, because it recognizes the regime came close to the brink. The third instance is in Iraq. Despite all the fractures which do exist in this damaged society, there would have been a unified national resistance against the Americans, but this didn't happen because of al-Qa'ida bomb attacks on Shia civilians, which led to Shia

retaliations, and turned into a civil war. It may be three coincidences, but I find it hard to believe, especially as Osama bin Laden was the CIA contact man in Peshawar for years. When you compare bin Laden with real revolutionary Islamists like Hizbullah and Hamas, who've been formed in conflict, he's just a multimillionaire playboy.

CC: Tom Field in the novel argues that it doesn't matter who's responsible for 9/11, '[i]t's how they'll exploit it that's the point'.[35] **Aren't conspiracy theories less interesting than some of the appalling things that we know to have happened?**
R Y-K: Buying into conspiracy theories can discredit your other political ideas, because you can't prove anything, and you're probably wrong. What I am certain about 11 September, as I am with every other political event, is that the official version is not accurate. What really happened, I don't know. You have to be naïve to think that the world is not run by conspiracies, but the problem with conspiracy theorists is that they try to fit everything into a total theory.

CC: You describe different religions prophesying the end of the world, particularly Christian and Muslim groups. As well as 9/11, discourses around the Apocalypse and climate change are figured in the novel. Please discuss the novel's representations of millenarian ideas.
R Y-K: These ideas are very prevalent at the moment. In Iraq, for example, followers of Moqtada al Sadr are called the Mahdi Army, because they're preparing for the return of the expected one, so there's an immediate millenarianism.[36] Almost every discourse is converged on apocalypse at the moment: leftwing, environmentalist green, Sunni Islamic, Shia Islamic, and evangelical Christians are all talking about the end times. These ideas don't go away when religion goes away, but they come back in different forms. Throughout history there have been periods like now when millenarian thought is dominant, and it doesn't

necessarily mean it is the end (although global warming might mean that it is), but it's worth exploring.

I feel sympathetic towards environmental activists, but in Britain or the West, people are not very good at protesting or political action, and ultimately it's because they're comfortable and ideologically lulled. They also confuse non-violence, which is a perfectly valid political strategy, with non-confrontation. A good politicized non-violence can be very confrontational indeed, and can involve different varieties of direct action. It's like the big demonstration before the Iraq War in 2003, which everyone was so happy about, seeing it as a defining moment in British history. One to two million people attended,[37] many of them people who hadn't been on demonstrations before, and with that number of people, they could have closed down London, the way they do in protests in Argentina or South Korea. But they didn't, and the war happened anyway.

CC: In response to these frightening portents, some characters seek nihilist solutions including Wahhabism and hedonist consumption. What compensations does a nihilist approach offer people who feel lost?
R Y-K: The problems that we're facing are so great that it's natural to deny them. Nihilism is the ultimate denial, and it's also saying that it doesn't matter and everything's meaningless. Consumerism is an addiction, because you're not a connoisseur of anything, and the objects in themselves are meaningless, but you consume more and more, like cigarettes. Violent Wahhabi rightwingers argue that if a suicide bomb kills Muslim women and children, then if they're good Muslims they'll go straight to paradise, and if they're *kuffar* then they deserve to be dead. That's another way of saying nothing matters; there's no weight to it at all.

CC: The novel contains what you've called a 'backstory in Syria and Iraq',[38] with portrayals of the Ba'ath party and secular intellectuals like the young Marwan and Mustafa.

What did you hope to achieve in the Middle East sections of the book?
R Y-K: The West has been the only game going in the Arab world for many years, and even Ba'athism and almost all Islamism are Western projects, because they are based around notions of a state and central control. In the nineteenth and twentieth centuries there was a collapse of religion internationally. Other dreams have been tried, and religious energy has been channelled into other things, but in the Muslim world – particularly the Arab world – those initiatives haven't worked, and people are poorer and more economically controlled and culturally confused than ever before. As a result, people are trying to hold on to new forms of identity, such as modernist versions of Islam. Muntaha's father, Marwan, directs his religious passions towards socialist-nationalism, but his dream ends when his wife is killed and he's arrested. He needs to look for some other pattern, and a version of Islam is what he finds.

CC: Marwan has a passion for poetry, but it's through photo-copying radical poems that he gets his wife killed, so he can't be interested in poetry again. To what extent can literature provide an alternative to the 'god-shaped hole' left by religion?
R Y-K: I don't see the two as mutually exclusive. A fundamental reason for the spread and success of Islam is that the Qur'an is the most beautiful and interesting text. It doesn't quite seem to hang together, but if you analyse it mathematically, it fits to a ridiculous extent. There are many stories of famous early converts: one of them was 'Umar ibn al Khattab, who was angrily on his way to kill his sister, because he'd heard that she'd been converted to Islam. When he arrived at her door and heard the chanting of the Qur'an, he began weeping and, on finding out it was the Qur'an, he dropped his sword and said the *shahadah*. To religious Muslims, the music and poetry of the Qur'an is proof that it's the word of God. In the novel, I'm using religion in a wide sense of the word. There's a simplistic discourse that the

religious people in the world are Muslim, and they're causing political trouble because they're religious, and then there are societies based on reason. That's not true; no one society in the world is more or less rational than another one, because irrationality is and always has been an important part of being human. But people in the West are often not aware of their own belief structures. New Atheists like Richard Dawkins and Christopher Hitchens are simplistic, because atheists' beliefs are also belief.[39] I suspect that part of the reason these figures are so controversial is to sell books.

CC: **This is a highly intertextual novel, with references to hip-hop lyrics, *Gilgamesh*, Arab poetry, Gabor's scientific art, *Anna Karenina*, and Linton Kwesi Johnson. Could you say something about these references?**
R Y-K: People have talked about mine as a didactic novel, and it probably is didactic in that I wanted to show people Arabic poetry. I was motivated by the desire to show that not everyone who wears the *hijab* is an idiot, that beautiful Arabic poetry exists, and that there's been a raging debate within the Arab world about secularism and religion. Take *The Epic of Gilgamesh* which (in the form that we now have it) is from the seventh century BCE, but is actually much older.[40] Everyone should read *Gilgamesh*, the same way they read the Bible, because it's a constant source. It's about the relationship with the mother and escaping that relationship; the wild man, and the taming of the wild. It's Jungian psychology from thousands of years ago. There's a Noah story in there, and there's so much else in Sumerian civilization that you find again in the Bible and the Qur'an. Mesopotamia was the first literate society, so *Gilgamesh* is where literature begins, but it suggests that those stories in different forms go further back, to the hunter-gatherer past.

Arabs quote poetry much more readily than British people do. This isn't a class-bound phenomenon either, because working-class people have as much access to poetry as the higher-class people. In the Middle East, poets like Darwish become towering nationalist figures, in a way that's almost unheard-of for poets in the West. Qabbani was also representative of a certain kind of idea of what Arab modernity was going to be about. But inter-textuality was just something that I enjoyed doing. You mentioned *Anna Karenina* and Linton Kwesi Johnson, but there's also Dostoevsky in there. I have a chapter called 'Devils',[41] and Dostoevsky wrote a novel, which tends to be translated with the same title. In it, a big party has been organized, and it's subverted by nihilists.[42] There's a long, dramatic scene in which everything goes wrong, much like that chapter when the Iqbal Rashid character gives his speech and there's almost a riot. My novel should have been called *Bread, Hashish, and Moon*, with reference to the Qabbani poem: that's a much better title, but Qabbani's estate wouldn't let me. I enjoyed writing the hip-hop chapter, with Linton Kwesi Johnson and the hip-hop references.

CC: Talking of hip-hop, I was intrigued by the character of Ammar, with his hip-hop Islamism.

R Y-K: It's based on the hip-hop *niqab* posse, haven't you met them in the East End? They have an assertive identity, bringing together different cultural aspects from East and West that they grew up with, in a way that makes sense to them. It creates people like Ammar, although he is somewhat satirized. They're all around us; not just people like Ammar, but all sorts of strange combinations. Mujahid, the Irish Muslim convert in the novel, is based on a real person, who'd been a Catholic involved in Sinn Fein, then he was a smack addict, and he got off that with the help of an evangelical church, which later excommunicated him for having blasphemous, non-doctrinal ideas, and then he became a Wahhabi Muslim. I met him in Saudi Arabia, and he was the most extreme Muslim I've ever met, with a strange mixture of influences.

10
Kamila Shamsie

Kamila Shamsie is a Pakistani novelist who led an itinerant life for 15 years during the 1990s and 2000s, moving between Karachi, the United States, and Britain, but has now chosen London as her main residence. Born in Karachi in 1973, she is from an elite *muhajir* family, her mother's relatives being *taluqdar* feudals from Lucknow in India, and the Shamsies belonging to an eminent family of Syeds from Delhi. Her mother is the well-known Pakistani literary critic, Muneeza Shamsie, and her great-aunt was Attia Hosain (1913–98), the author of two seminal works about vanishing Muslim culture in India and also Partition.[1] Three generations of her talented, literary family have been published by Oxford University Press. Kamila's grandmother, Jahanara Habibullah, was 84 when her first book, *Remembrance of Days Past* appeared;[2] Muneeza is the editor of the ground-breaking 1990s anthology of anglophone Pakistani writing, *A Dragonfly in the Sun*, among other works;[3] while her older sister, Saman, is a children's author;[4] and Kamila herself distributed two of her novels with the publisher in Pakistan.[5]

Shamsie was awarded a BA in Creative Writing from Hamilton College, before joining the MFA Program for Poets and Writers at the University of Massachusetts, Amherst. In the words of V. S. Naipaul's famous blurb, she has 'followed no other profession' than writing.[6] At Hamilton College, Kamila was taught by the late, great Kashmiri poet, Agha Shahid Ali, whom she followed to Amherst and describes as 'all laughter and dramatic utterances', despite the 'increasing virtuosity' of his poetry.[7] She writes, 'in many of my best moments as a writer I reveal Shahid's influence on my work'.[8] This influence is particularly evident in her first novel, *In the City by the Sea* (1998), the first draft of which was written as the thesis for her MFA, and in which Shamsie briefly discusses the issue of nostalgia also explored in Ali's *The Nostalgist's Map of America*.[9] The father character, Aba, traces the etymology of the word 'nostalgia', posing the question, 'is nostalgia about return or about standing still and watching someone else return?'[10] To some extent, Shamsie solves this riddle in her third novel, *Kartography* (2002), in which nostalgia is experienced both by Karim, a Karachiite who moves away from his city in his teens, and Raheen, a girl who for the most part stays in the city, but whose view of it is tinged by memories of the friend who left Karachi. In 'Agha Shahid Ali, Teacher', Shamsie describes how Ali helped her restructure *Kartography* over five years, by 'prod[ding]' her to develop the image of a spinning globe which she originally wrote for a short story.[11]

Her five novels to date have garnered increasing recognition, with the latest, the epic family novel, *Burnt Shadows*, being reviewed especially positively[12] and shortlisted for the Orange Prize, as well as winning the USA's Anisfield Wolf Award, the ALOA award in Denmark, the Muslim Writers Award for Published Fiction, and Italy's Nord-Sud and Boccaccio Literary Prizes. In 1999, Shamsie received the Prime Minister's Award for Literature, and in 2004 and 2006 the Patras Bokhari Award, both from the Pakistan Academy of Letters. In 2010, she was named one of Britain's '20 best novelists under 40' by the *Daily Telegraph*.[13] Written in her early twenties, Shamsie's first novel, *In the City by the Sea* (1998) is promising and mature. Its protagonist, the pre-pubescent Hasan, witnesses a boy of a similar age fatally fall from a rooftop while flying a kite and, shortly afterwards, his favourite uncle, Salman Mamoo, is arrested for treason. Hasan's coping mechanism is to escape through his imagination, effervescent word-play (a signature of Shamsie's early work), and humour shared with his educated and lively family.

Salt and Saffron (2000) is a Rushdiean novel, in which 'not-quite-twins', Mariam, and her younger second cousin, the America-returned protagonist, Aliya, transgress feudal and class codes by falling in love with men deemed to be of a lower class than their affluent family, the House of Dard-e-Dil (translated in the text as 'aching heart'[14]). The family has been divided by Partition, and the novel dramatizes the near-impossibility of dialogue between Indian and Pakistani Muslims in tense family arguments about Partition:[15] as Aliya remarks, 'One person's lament can be someone else's elegy.'[16] Irreconcilable differences are also explored in *Kartography*'s portrayal of discord between West and East Pakistanis before and during the civil war of 1971, and between Sindhis and *muhajirs* in violent, ethnically divided Karachi of the 1990s. As well as the characters Raheen and Karim mentioned earlier, the novel also focuses on their parents (Zafar and Yasmin, and Maheen and Ali, respectively), whose partner swap and lies about their past recall Ford Madox Ford's *The Good Soldier*, with its 'minuet de la cour'[17] between two couples.

Broken Verses (2005) is perhaps Shamsie's most Muslim novel to date, raising as it does issues of justice, compassion, and women's rights. Set against the backdrop of Zia-ul-Haq's Islamizing regime (1977–88), the novel contains unequivocal rejection of Zia's hegemonic version of Islam, stridently anti-women Hudood Ordinance, and brutal suppression of the freedom of speech of such figures as the novel's Poet. That said, in *Broken Verses* Shamsie refers extensively to, and often celebrates, the Qur'an, Sufi philosophy, Ramadan fasting[18] and prayer.[19] Early on there is an evocation of

Surah Rahman, the Beneficent, with its famous refrain, 'Which of your Lord's blessings would you deny?'[20] Shamsie examines this line, providing the Arabic calligraphy to illustrate 'its variedness and its balance',[21] but also discusses the Surah's wider implications (its celebration of creation; promises of *houris* in heaven, but fearsome warnings about hell) and poetic language use (for example, its description of the sky 'redden[ing] like a rose or stainèd leather'[22]). The feminist activist, Samina, half-playfully exhorts her daughter, the protagonist Aasmani, to translate the Qur'an into English and Urdu, in order to create 'versions free from patriarchal interpretations'.[23] In contrast, Samina's lover, an indomitable Marxist poet reminiscent of such bards as Faiz Ahmed Faiz and Habib Jalib, addresses the aesthetic merit of Surah Rahman's imagery.

Broken Verses also examines the secular Arab legend of Laila and Majnun, explored too in Aslam's 'Leila in the Wilderness' (see pp. 137–8). The same month he marries Samina, Shamsie's Poet writes his own version of the legend, in which he emphasizes the increasingly blurred identities of the lovers, Laila and Qais.[24] Laila realizes that through impersonating Qais, 'she has finally succeeded in becoming her Beloved',[25] a phrase that echoes the Sufi's longing to be unified with God, the object of desire, in such a way that his or her identity is effaced.[26] The issue of mental illness is explored in Aasmani's almost psychotic denial of her mother's depression and suicide, and the Poet's murder. The reader is drawn into believing her wild conspiracy theories concerning her mother's survival, because Sameena was such a strong character before the Poet's death that it is difficult to accept that grief would reduce her to near-catatonia, but, as her friend Shahnaz comments, her illness meant that '[s]he stepped out of her character'.[27] Finally, Islamophobia is discussed when the sophisticated New York-resident Mir Adnan Akbar Khan (nicknamed Ed by his friends) is sacked from his job and questioned by the FBI in the suspicious atmosphere following the 2001 attacks. Returning to Pakistan, Ed cites a depressingly familiar list of post-war on terror outrages: 'the INS. Guantanamo Bay. The unrandom random security checks.'[28]

Broken Verses also begins with an image of Guantanamo: this time that of a prisoner stripping and being dressed in its iconic orange jumpsuit.[29] To answer the prisoner's anguished query, *'How did it come to this'*,[30] Shamsie moves backwards in history to the atomic bomb's detonation on Nagasaki in 1945, the bloodshed of Partition two years later, culminating in discussion of the Afghan conflict of the last three decades, 9/11, and the war on terror. *Burnt Shadows'* searing critique of Anglo-American involvement in these flashpoints makes it somewhat surprising that New Labour wife Sarah Brown described the novel as 'a book that transformed [her] life'.[31] *Burnt Shadows* represents a change of direction for Shamsie, given that she eschews the first-person narrator used in her previous three novels in favour of free indirect discourse and multiple perspectives, widening her scope from upper-class Karachi to encompass Japan, India, Afghanistan, and America as well as Pakistan. The interconnected nature of nations is also deftly evoked, as unexpected but telling parallels are drawn between the fear and zeal of kamikaze pilots in 1940s Japan and that of Afghanistan's *mujahideen* of the 1980s and 1990s, and the suffering of victims of the Japanese bombs, of Partition genocide, and of the New York attacks and ensuing 'war on terror'. The Japanese protagonist Hiroko Tanaka feels compelled to leave Pakistan after the nuclear tests, because the situation brings too many painful memories of being a *hibakusha* (bomb survivor) in Nagasaki.

This global picture is continued in Shamsie's most recent book, and her first foray into book-length non-fiction, *Offence: The Muslim Case* (2009). The slim volume traces the history of the creation of an image of the 'Violently Offended Muslim',[32] through discussion of the furores surrounding the publication of *The Satanic Verses* and the Danish cartoons. However, the book focuses specifically on the Pakistani nation as a case study and, in this approach, Shamsie signals a robust challenge to what she terms the 'illusion of a united *ummah*',[33] or global Islamic community. She argues that it is important not to speak of a 'Muslim Monolith',[34] but rather to recognize the fissures and inequalities that exist within and between different Muslim nations. Shamsie highlights the 1971 civil war, in which Bangladesh came into existence after seceding from the Pakistani union,[35] and the Ahmadi community's scapegoating over many years by various Pakistani parties,[36] as examples of the oppression of Muslims by other Muslims. She also suggests that visible symbols of Islam, such as beards, *hijabs*, or marks on the forehead denoting excessive prayer, gained assent over private devotion from Zia's Islamizing regime onwards.[37] That said, Shamsie flags up history that often gets forgotten in stereotypes of Pakistan as a hotbed of Islamist radicals. In the 60 years since independence, she argues, the Pakistani populace has repeatedly and decisively voted out the religious parties, such as the Jamaat-i-Islami (except in the 2002 elections, in which there was a short-lived surge in support for right-wing religious parties because of the American invasion of Afghanistan).[38] Shamsie emphasizes the many and varied dissenting voices that speak out against the religious hardliners in Pakistan. She pays greatest attention to the women's movement (WAF, or the Women's Action Forum),[39] and political poets,[40] arguing that these two groups came closest to putting a brake on Zia-ul-Haq's Islamization programme in the 1980s. Consideration of the diversity of hardline, conservative, radical, and left-wing groups that exist in Pakistan, she indicates, counters 'this world where the "Clash of Civilizations" is becoming a self-fulfilling prophecy'.[41] Shamsie continues this non-fictional trend in her deceptively light essay 'Pop Idols' in *Granta 112*, in which she uses the rise of popular culture in 1980s and 1990s Pakistan as a launchpad for discussing the nation's tumultuous recent history.[42]

CC: In what ways does your most recent novel, *Burnt Shadows*, mark a departure from your first four novels?
KS: *Burnt Shadows* is more international and less focused on one character than the first four, so it is a departure and I can't go

back to writing the sort of books I wrote before. It's simultaneously liberating and terrifying because, having written about the
bomb falling in Nagasaki, there's now nothing that I need to consider off-limits. I've always been interested in using novels to talk
about Pakistan's history, which is interconnected with the histories of India, America, and Afghanistan. Japan was the nation
that came out of left-field. The central idea is still common to
my other books: to use characters and stories to move through
history. The characters come first for me: I want to explore how
history impacts on their lives, rather than using them as a vehicle
to talk about history. I wrote in free indirect discourse because
this time I wanted to create a tapestry, rather than a novel with
one central character like my others. It's also a reaction to the
previous novel, *Broken Verses*, which was written from Aasmani's
point of view. To stay in one person's head, while as the author
hinting at the many things that she, an intelligent person, is
nonetheless unaware of, was challenging. While struggling with
these issues, having the freedom to move from one person's
head to the other seemed invigorating rather than difficult. At
the beginning of writing *Burnt Shadows* I had to restrain myself
in order to maintain some continuity, because I was constantly
tempted to move between different people's thoughts.

**CC: Compared to your earlier work, which largely focuses
on an elite Karachi of gated communities, private members'
clubs, and exclusive beaches, in *Burnt Shadows* you examine
other cities such as Nagasaki, Delhi, and New York. Karachi
is still a central presence in the new novel, but this time you
focus on the Karachi of Afghan migrants and refugees,[43] the
fish market,[44] and the middle-class neighbourhood[45] where
Hiroko and her family live. How did you write about this
unfamiliar world?**
KS: In order to write about the fish market, for example, I did
a bit of research, wrote a draft, and only then did I go there.
I went for a visit to Karachi and persuaded a friend to go with
me. It was great, because I realized that the research had been

good enough, even though I'd only looked at four photographs and an article on the fish market. Having gone there I saw details I could add in, but only about five sentences. Similarly, I had been to Delhi, but never to the Civil Lines, where the Burtons live, or Haus Khas, where they have a picnic.[46] When I visited, again nothing was inaccurate; I could just fill in certain details, rather than deleting anything I'd already written.

CC: In your early work, Rushdie is your most obvious influence, as in _Salt and Saffron_ with the 'not-quite-twins' and linguistic playfulness. However, in the last two books, there are intertextual allusions to Faiz, Shakespeare, soap operas, high and low culture, Urdu and folk tales, David Mitchell, and Michael Ondaatje. Please could you discuss your influences?

KS: I have trouble with the word 'influences', because I know the things that I've loved, but have no idea who my influences are most of the time. Certainly I'm aware that Rushdie lurked behind the early books, and _Salt and Saffron_'s divided family was a metaphor for India–Pakistan division. Maya Jaggi argues that _The English Patient_ is a guiding light for _Burnt Shadows_[47] and that's interesting, because it's my favourite novel. I wouldn't presume to say that you can see Michael Ondaatje's influence in my work, but I've learnt certain things from him. For example, there's a scene just after Hiroko and Sajad's wedding, when James and Ilsa are arguing, while the newly-weds are having a conversation,[48] and the writing cuts between the two couples almost cinematically, in a technique I draw from Ondaatje. The end of his _The English Patient_ cuts between Kip and Hana,[49] and that novel, like mine, also depicts people of different nations affected by war. David Mitchell has also been helpful; firstly because he sent me a wonderful email about Japan, providing references to the kind of books a writer knows that another writer needs in order to visualize period detail and the interiors of homes. Secondly, when I read his debut novel, _Ghostwritten_, I was struck by the fact that every major chapter takes place in a different country. At that time, I was still writing books that were entirely set in Karachi, and I was amazed that someone could write with equal confidence about Tokyo, London, and Ulan Bator. That gave me the first inkling of a technique that eventually I would try my hand at. Of course Agha Shahid Ali influences me poetically, because he was my first teacher, so attention to language and the rhythms of speech comes from him.

CC: You're interested in anagrams, backwards writing, acronyms, and puns, but in *Burnt Shadows* you've moved away from this play with language.
KS: People believe that the anagrams and all come from Rushdie, but I've done anagrams and backwards reading since childhood. I've always loved what you can do with language, but this book is less playful; it's about people who know several languages, and what that does to their ability to move between different worlds and worldviews. This is why the split character of Harry interests me, because on the one hand he does awful things and is involved in a shady world, but on the other, he has genuine love for the subcontinent, and dies interacting in Urdu with Pakistani men, whom his American colleagues have nothing to do with. Harry's immoral but not a racist, and his relationship with Raza is fascinating to me because it doesn't involve an evil imperialist and his victim. Harry is genuinely concerned about Raza, but the only way he knows how to look out for him is to say, 'Come and work with me for a private military company.' Harry at least has ideals about his country and winning the Cold War but Raza is completely amoral: for him it's just a nice job.

CC: Do these departures represent a natural process of maturing, or a conscious decision to highlight connections between apparently discrete nations?
KS: My first four novels were written in quick succession and there's overlap between the first three. After *Broken Verses*, I took 18 months off, during which I noticed certain writerly habits I had developed. For instance, I often portrayed a young person

looking back at the previous generation, and either unravelling a mystery or discovering a secret. I decided not to do that any more, so I had to structure the new novel very differently. I also thought that if I was departing from what went before, then I needed to move away from Karachi as well, because that had defined my early writing. It was a small set of interlinked decisions, rather than an abstract idea about the national versus the global novel. Nadeem Aslam was the first person I told I was writing about Nagasaki, and he said 'Oh, will this be your 9/11 book?' I remember being annoyed and wondering why this necessitated writing about 9/11: I had no idea until very late that the book would examine that event.

CC: Your new book, *Offence: The Muslim Case*, is non-fiction and you are also a journalist and cultural commentator. As a writer, how do you view your role in talking about politics?
KS: I started writing for newspapers just after 9/11, and my flippant line is that I was in the wrong religion at the right time. In 2001, people began talking about Afghanistan and Pakistan, often making misinformed claims, because many didn't know the area. I at least know a little more, and am very interested in politics. In the early 2000s, there weren't many Pakistanis whom journalists knew and could ring. Now and then, they asked me to write something, so I fell into journalism. Then I was asked to write on 'Islam and Offence' for a Seagull publishing series,[50] and I dislike people making generalizations about the 'Islamic world', so I wrote about what I know: Pakistan.

CC: I'm interested in your decision, in *Offence*, to privilege the nation-state as a unit, when Pakistan, as you've acknowledged, has shared history with Afghanistan, India, and Bangladesh, among other nations.
KS: I was uneasy about pulling the strand of Muslim history out of the history of the Indian subcontinent. However, as sceptical as I am about the nation in various ways, I believe that the Pakistani government, armed forces, intelligence agencies, and

political parties have played a significant role in the rise of extremism. Of course, I acknowledge that the relationships with Afghanistan, India, and America also contribute. As dubious as the idea of nation is, it exists, and central governments still have great influence. In 11 years, Zia-ul-Haq warped the fabric of the nation, but he didn't come out of a vacuum. I wanted to make this case for the importance of nations because, in relation to Muslims, people aren't discussing national politics, but a mythical 'Muslim world'. They discuss what is written in the Qur'an, as if there's one interpretation of what it means. When I look at events in Pakistan, the context of national government and politics helps me understand what's going on far more than I understand anything that's happening in Palestine, Chechnya, or elsewhere in the so-called Muslim world.

CC: Could you expand on *Offence*'s depiction of the *Satanic Verses* Affair and your incomprehension, as a teenager in Pakistan, at people in Bradford burning the book.[51]
KS: When people ask me about British Muslims, I point out that just because I grew up in Pakistan doesn't mean I know anything about people from Dewsbury, a place I've never been. Any understanding I have comes from *Maps for Lost Lovers*, because that describes the Huddersfield of mosques and associated factions that Nadeem Aslam grew up in. That's my entry point, not experience, and there are also class dimensions. I live in London, and almost all the Muslims I know are ex-pat Pakistanis, from affluent families, who carry class privilege with them to Britian. Most British-born Muslims are from a more working-class background and often have stronger religious feelings than my ex-pat friends. The notion that I understand their world is predicated on a false idea of Muslim community, or *ummah*. In Pakistan, it's easy to spot British Muslims who have come to visit, from clothing, the way they walk, the language. There's a Pakistani connection, but to talk about people who've been born and bred in Yorkshire as being Pakistani, rather than British Pakistani, is silly.

217

CC: You argue that there was offence at *The Satanic Verses* in Pakistan, but that it was exploited for political gain. What was your own response to the novel's controversial passages?

KS: When I read *The Satanic Verses*, long after the controversy, I found the insults I had been told were in the book weren't there. My reaction was that the protesters hadn't read the book. I remember reading *Midnight's Children* and feeling that the top of my head had blown off. It made a lot of us realize that it was possible to write about our world, without having to explain it, or worry about outsiders understanding it. I thought *Shame* was a very sharp satire on Pakistan's politics, and *The Satanic Verses* is fascinating on the migrant condition.

CC: You argue that Pakistan was created as a secular state to safeguard the rights of India's minority Muslim population, but that the focus on a religious minority led to religion being privileged over all other components of identity, and oppression of minority groups.[52] Please discuss the creation of Pakistan and its aftermath.

KS: Well, there were various reasons for Pakistan's creation, but yes, I do argue that it was possible to have a founding myth based around the idea of minority rights. But to a large extent we Pakistanis don't fully understand what our history is. We often lived under censorship and military rule, particularly in Zia's 1980s, when we had no idea about events, even as they unfolded before us. If you don't even understand contemporary history, how can you know your earlier history? We should be saying that anything that happened in the geographical territory is Pakistan's history, including rich Buddhist and Hindu pasts from Taxila, Harappa, and the Indus Valley civilization, but post-Partition rhetoric about Muslimness and Islam makes this hard to do.

CC: Where do post-Partition migrants from India fit into the historiography of Pakistan? In your early writing, you focus on *muhajirs* in Karachi and the violence of the 1980s and 1990s.

KS: Karachi is the city with strongest *muhajir* influences. In 1947 many of the *muhajirs* who came were economically and politically powerful, disproportionate to their numbers, and to exacerbate things they had a sense of superiority, believing that Lucknow and Delhi were seats of culture, and that Sindh and Punjab were culturally inferior. That caused great resentment, and of course in such extensive migration there are always clashes between indigenous peoples and newcomers. Karachi is the capital and main commercial centre of Sindh, and it has a very different ethnic make-up to the rest of the province. Karachi feels that it is generating income but isn't getting a fair amount back, and the rest of Sindh feels that it is underdeveloped because economic and political power are concentrated in Karachi. Such wrangling gets played out in ethnic terms. Of the communities within Karachi there are also clashes over economic and political power, and that can spill into violence – as happened between Pashtuns and *muhajirs* in the 1980s and 90s (and continuing today).

CC: What's your own perspective on Partition?

KS: Unlike some historians, I emphasize that not all those who moved to Pakistan hated Hindus or were feudals concerned with their own welfare. Many of those who chose to come to Pakistan saw it as protecting minority groups, although undoubtedly some had vile, pernicious reasons. I'm not interested in speculating about what the region would look like if 1947 hadn't happened, and whether Muslims would have been better or worse off in a united, Congress-ruled India. While many Pakistanis look at rightwing Hindu groups, and say that it was right to leave, plenty of Indian Muslims say that these groups only acquired power because of Partition. We're here now, and India and Pakistan should resolve differences by refusing to demonize each other's viewpoints on Partition, dealing only with the present.

CC: What do you make of the current widespread emphasis on outward markers of Islam, such as beards and veils,
which you argue have taken over from private devotion in
Pakistan and elsewhere?

KS: In Zia's Pakistan, religion became politicized, not just about
what you believe at home. Laws caught people out for not
being Islamic enough, and the police would ask lone couples
for their wedding certificates. Such aggression created the desire
to display piety in order not to arouse suspicion. You can't
see into someone's heart or mind for their views on religion,
but you can see the length of their beard and how covered up
they are. And the influx of Saudi money meant Wahhabi Islam
gained ground in Pakistan. Globally, Jewish, Christian, Hindu,
and Muslim fundamentalist groups have been getting stronger
in the last two decades. I don't know whether that's a response
to the 1970s when many people moved away from religion,
and leftwing secular ideologies gained ground. When those
ideologies were deemed to have failed, there was a movement
in the other direction, towards dogmatic religious positions.

CC: You suggest that Huntington's clash of civilizations thesis
is being made a reality because of one-sided reporting, particularly in the West. As someone who moves between the West and
Pakistan, how do you negotiate binary rhetorical positions?

KS: Manichaean reporting exists on both sides, but it's not an
equivalent situation because of the cultural power that America
wields. The reporting in the Pakistani press about America is
often negative, and you find people in many parts of Pakistan
frothing at the mouth about America, but wanting to emigrate
there. America's politics are loathed and its cultural and economic aspects desired, whereas Pakistan isn't able to counter
negative reporting via cultural exports, so people in America
don't get beyond the single narrative of a terrible place. I don't
deny that the worst of Pakistan is horrendous, but it's important to also note many Pakistanis have been fighting against
extremism for a long time, largely unrecognized by the rest

of the world. I don't buy into the clash of civilizations thesis, and to its proponents I'd point out that in Pakistan there is an ongoing fight between the extremists, who want Talibanization, and the majority of the population, who don't. It's not 'Islam vs. the West' so much as 'Extremists vs. Everyone Else'.

CC: As part of your representation of secularist currents within Pakistan, you depict the women's movement of the 1980s in *Broken Verses*. What's your attitude towards feminism and its impact on Pakistan?

KS: *Broken Verses* deals with generational differences, because many from Aasmani's and my generation felt that the activism of the 1980s has done no good, and that women's position is worse than ever. But I've always been interested in those often unnoticed people who keep fighting the good fight. It's ridiculous to argue that feminism hasn't achieved much; the women's movement has changed a great many things for the better. I'd certainly call myself a feminist, as are most women I know. However, often they don't use the term because of its manipulation by people who hate it. You'll say to a woman, 'Are you a feminist?', and she'll say 'No', 'But do you agree with equal pay, for instance?' 'Yes.' 'Then how are you not a feminist? 'Well, I like men.' I say, 'It's not about men, it's about women.' I've written an article about the women in my family.[53] My great-grandmother was a politician and writer, so for four generations in my family it's been the norm for the women to fight against patriarchy, refusing to accept submissive or traditional roles. The battles that still need to be fought and won in Pakistan are depressing. Instead of equal pay and maternity leave we still have to argue the case as to why girls should be allowed to go to school, or why women are not property. Pakistan contains some of the most radical feminists in the world, because reacting to misogynism as hideous as that which can be found there creates a powerful opposite trajectory. Yet there's also heterogeneity: there are secular feminists like me, and thinkers who want to produce valuable feminist reinterpretations of the Qur'an. They play on the religious parties' terms, but challenge their arguments about what Islam dictates for women with their own counterclaims about Islam. For example, Riffat Hassan is a Pakistani American, who is looking at the Qur'an from a feminist perspective. In many people's daily lives – in which religion plays an important part – it's natural for them to discuss feminism, along with many other issues, from within the tradition of Islam.

CC: Please talk about your representations of Karachi, with which city you're very much associated.
KS: Karachi is my hometown, so I'm biased, but to me it's one of the world's great, fascinating cities. I can't think of any other city which has had such extensive growth and population exchange. In 1940, Karachi had a population of about 100,000, almost 50 per cent of which was Hindu. In 1947, nearly all the Hindus left, and twice their number of Muslims came, and today the population is around 15 million. I can't think of any other city which has lost half its population and yet grown by such an unimaginable proportion. Karachi is the only really cosmopolitan place, I would argue, in Pakistan, inasmuch as every single ethnic and religious group of Pakistan is present – you have people from all the provinces, plus *muhajirs*, Afghans of various ethnicities, Bengali Muslims, Parsis, Hindus, Christians, and of course *makranis*, the original inhabitants of Karachi who are largely fisherfolk. It can be a terrible city because of the violence and ethnic conflict, but at its best groups interact and rely on each other; this is of course in large part a commercial necessity.

CC: Could you discuss your remappings of the city from different perspectives and perhaps also the colonial history of maps.[54] In *Kartography*, you juxtapose the insider's view: '[G]o towards the beach, and when you come to the turtle sign take a right',[55] against the tourist's perspective of the Lonely Planet map.
KS: Until two years ago, I was living half in Karachi and half elsewhere, so I knew both sides of the insider/outsider

dichotomy. I was never away from it long enough to become an outsider, but when I was writing *Kartography*, I thought of friends who'd left Karachi to go to university overseas and only came back for a few weeks in the winter, so they had a distant view of the place. Because I've lived abroad I know of sitting somewhere else hearing shocking stories about the situation there, and having to force myself to remember that these newspaper items are not the whole picture. These experiences made that insider–outsider issue familiar to write about. Belonging to Karachi doesn't negate being interested in the world, because the city is made up of so many different groups and has connections to various places and histories, leading to many Karachiites thinking in a cosmopolitan way, outside narrow groupings and ethnicities. Maps have an imperial aspect, because historically they've assisted in invasions, territorial acquisition, and trade. I was excited during the research for *Kartography* when I discovered that originally maps were considered to belong more to the world of literature than geography or science, because they are used to illustrate stories. I hope through my novels to create different story-maps on Karachi. Even within *Kartography*, the Lonely Planet map is brilliantly wrong about so much, and then the hand-drawn map is intimate but also exclusionary, because it is only for people who know what Raheen's talking about.

CC: You also describe an interactive internet map where people can click on links which take them to pictures, sound-files, and narratives[56] so what's your attitude to these new technologies and their possibilities for storytelling?

KS: I would love it if someone actually created such a map, and once met someone who said they were working along those lines. This map would be inclusive, allowing people to present underlying stories through hyperlinks and photographs. Even looking at Karachi on Google Maps and Google Earth is interesting, because, among the great monuments, people have mapped their own houses. A map that isn't necessarily drawn up by whoever is in authority allows people to negotiate their way around, making an unfamiliar place familiar. As for hyper-textual writing, as a writer I think that kind of thing might be fun to do as a one-off, but I can't see myself writing seriously in this way, because what I love about the novel is just the words creating images, rather than having hyperlinks where you get images.

CC: *Burnt Shadows* is an attempt to look beyond the con-strained world of that private map of the elite world that you problematize in *Kartography*, so are you suggesting that it's impossible to look at the world in isolation since 9/11?
KS: 9/11 wasn't the turning point; it was the war on terror. It's important to make that distinction. 9/11 happened and it was horrible: I was wondering whether my friends in New York were alive. However, the fallout wasn't inevitable, and the turning point was America's invasion of Afghanistan in October 2001. That's when the war on terror came to Pakistan. In 2002, Pakistan's religious parties became serious players in the govern-ment for the first time, and at that moment I thought the world had changed. Of course, the word 'Muslim' has become more contentious, but it's a fallacy to think that before 9/11 it wasn't. Remember Huntington gave his clash of civilizations lecture some years before, in 1992.[57] By the time I was at university in America in the 90s, I was aware that a certain demonization was already under way. In 1993, *Time* had a cover headline 'Hitting Back at Terrorists' and several articles basically argued that Islam was the new enemy.[58] In Britain, *The Satanic Verses* was probably an earlier turning point.

CC: Could you talk about your portrayal of Muslims who are believed to be terrorists, which overlaps productively with Mohsin Hamid's ambivalence as to whether the extrem-ist in *The Reluctant Fundamentalist* is the Pakistani or the American?
KS: Nadeem Aslam's *The Wasted Vigil* is a wonderful portrayal of extremism, focusing on Casa, a *jihadi* boy who's trained as a

suicide bomber. Nadeem had started writing his previous novel, *Maps for Lost Lovers*, well before 9/11. It wasn't published until 2004, and my mother, Muneeza, read the novel the following year and told me then that she regarded it as a description of the world out of which the next suicide bombers were going to come. Three months later the London bombings occurred, carried out by extremists most of whom came from a similar part of West Yorkshire. Nadeem is a writer who's been engaging with these issues for a long time, just as Mohsin Hamid was talking to me about *The Reluctant Fundamentalist* on 9 September 2001. In *Burnt Shadows*, I didn't want to add to the debate about why Muslims become terrorists, but to examine what happens to peaceful Muslims when they live in a world where many people view them as potential terrorists. Steve assumes Raza killed Harry, and Kim, who is largely a wonderful person, can't look at Abdullah without wondering about his background. *Burnt Shadows* is a consequence of what I have been seeing, feeling, and thinking for several years.

CC: Rushdie, in many of his works,[59] and to some extent Aslam, posit literature, storytelling, and love as alternatives to religion. In contrast, your writing mixes literary with religious stories, showing that the sacred and secular constantly interpenetrate. Your portrayals of Ramadan not only illustrate its spiritual aspect, but also heightened appreciation of food and the feasting of Eid.[60] Some of your characters are observant, while others secretly read books during prayer. What's your view about literature's relationship with religion?
KS: The Islam I grew up among didn't make distinctions between the sacred and secular, and intermingling of traditions makes it hard to separate religion from culture. Pakistani Islam is quite haphazard and capacious: for example, weddings are cultural events, in which the religious component is three seconds long. Pakistan is at least 98 per cent Muslim, and at its best there's a relaxed atmosphere about religion, but at its worst – and this worst is gaining ground rapidly – people try

to stuff extremist ideology down your throat. It's also a great storytelling country, not so much in written literature, because of course there are high rates of illiteracy, but through the oral tradition. And, of course, there are strong Sufi currents in Punjab and Sindh. The older Sufi tradition relies on poetry and music, and the cultural sphere works its way into the fabric of life. Pakistan generally has no interest in the word 'secular', because that's seen by many to denote absence. The real argument against extremist Islam in Pakistan comes from the more welcoming tradition of Sufism. However, even that's becoming problematic: I travelled around parts of Punjab recently, visiting various Sufi shrines, and one shrine didn't let women come in.

CC: We've touched on class already, but I wanted to ask you about representations of the Progressive Writers Association, and leftwing politics more broadly, in your fiction. The Poet in *Broken Verses* is a fervent Marxist, and some of *Kartography*'s characters are simultaneously Marxists and feudal landlords. Have Pakistan's successive governments failed to alleviate the sufferings of the poor?
KS: In the early twentieth century you did have members of the elite who lived lives of privilege and yet were attracted by elements of Marxism. There's one character in *Kartography* who is a feudal and, as a young man, he identifies as Marxist, so I'm poking a bit of fun at him there. The veneer of Marxism very quickly fades away. Any feudal who was really Marxist would give his land away, end of story.

Faiz Ahmed Faiz, and many feminist poets of Pakistan, come out of, or are linked to, the Marxist tradition. I came to the Progressive Writers from an odd angle, not through growing up in Pakistan, where I had an Anglicized education and didn't know very much about Urdu poetry at all, because of a disparaging attitude towards Urdu among the English-language elite. My school had a strange colonial hangover – 40 years after Independence lessons were in English, with just one half-hour Urdu lesson four times a week, and we would be told off for speaking Urdu in the playground. I do remember the headlines the day Faiz died, and my mother sitting in her study saying, 'This is a disaster, one of the great losses.' I actually learnt about these writers' mixture of the political and the aesthetic from Agha Shahid Ali, whom I met at Hamilton College in the US. Shahid had translated Faiz, and he said that Faiz taught him how to write about the politics of Kashmir, while also being a committed aesthete, conscious of every word and every syllable.

CC: To what extent was the Poet from _Broken Verses_ based on Faiz?
KS: The Poet's personality and biography weren't based on him, but when I imagined his poetry and national stature, I thought of Faiz. I'm always interested in Pakistan's alternative narratives, rather than stories of the military and extremists. Faiz was greatly loved and, even though this is a largely illiterate country, his poems were made into songs, which are known by everyone. Tariq Ali writes about rallies in Pakistan where the biggest draw was the poet Habib Jalib in 1968[61] – there was a genuine popular uprising against Ayub Khan's government, and everyone was singing his songs and reciting his poetry. Many of the great poets of Pakistan have had their verses set to music and sung by the most popular singers. It's as though Seamus Heaney's poems were sung by George Michael or in another era if Ella Fitzgerald had been singing the poetry of Robert Frost. Singers, like the towering figure of Noor Jehan, sang Faiz's poetry. It deserves to be acknowledged that poetry is an utterly populist and simultaneously politically crucial art in the subcontinent, in a way that prose fiction can't be, because it has to be read.

11
Hanif Kureishi

Hanif Kureishi was born in Bromley, Kent, in 1954, the son of a White working-class mother, Audrey, and an Indian Muslim father called Rafiushan. His father's affluent, educated family moved to Pakistan from Bombay on Partition,[1] at which point Rafiushan emigrated to Britain and began a downwardly mobile existence working as a clerk at the Pakistan Embassy. Rafiushan was one of 11 children, and his brother, Kureishi's Uncle Omar was a cricket commentator in Pakistan, whom Kureishi describes as a 'celebrity [whose] name [...] was known by everyone'.[2] Rafiushan's elder sister, Maki Kureishi, was a much-loved lecturer at Karachi University and a poet about whom Muneeza Shamsie writes, 'she opened out a new path for Pakistani English writers and remains an important influence',[3] and whose daughter is the poet Shireen Z. Haroun. Maki makes an appearance in the literary family in Karachi that is presented in Kureishi's most recent and, in places, semi-autobiographical novel, *Something to Tell You*:

> Dad insisted I go to meet his older sister, a poet and university lecturer. [...] She taught English literature: Shakespeare, Austen, the Romantics. However, the place had been attacked frequently by radical Islamists, and no one had returned to classes.[4]

The fictional aunt, like Maki Kureishi, has arthritis, and is keen on Derek Walcott, who is described as 'her light'.[5] The trip to Pakistan in which Kureishi's narrator, Jamal, meets his aunt appears to be a version of Kureishi's own sojourn in Karachi in 1984 that he depicts as hospitable and warm in his important essay 'The Rainbow Sign'.[6]

Kureishi studied philosophy at King's College, London, and his first play, *Soaking Up the Heat*, was staged in 1976 at the Royal Court Theatre,[7] where he would work as Writer in Residence in 1982 and still later would comment on the directors' aristocratic backgrounds: '[t]he most radical of them still had the accents of colonels, though they attempted to identify with the proletariat'.[8] His play *The King and Me* was performed at Soho Theatre in 1980, and Kureishi was subsequently awarded the Thames TV Playwright Award for his script *The Mother Country* (1980), and the George Devine Award for *Outskirts* (1981).[9] However, perhaps the most important of his theatrical outputs is *Borderline*, which in 1981 was the first play by an Asian writer to be performed on the main stage of the Royal Court, and explores the lives of Asian working-class residents of London's 'Little India' suburb, Southall. Re-reading the play two decades on, Kureishi writes of being struck by 'how little talk of religion there was among the characters. The unifying ideology of that time and place was socialism, with feminist groups [...] also contributing to the debate.'[10] Kureishi was to chart the turn away from ideology towards religious identity politics in his mid-career work. After quite a break from theatre, in 1999,

Kureishi's *Sleep With Me* was produced at the National Theatre,[11] followed by *When the Night Begins* at the Hampstead Theatre in 2004.[12]

As a screenwriter, Kureishi's *My Beautiful Laundrette* (1985)[13] earned him Best Screenplay nominations from the Academy Awards and BAFTA, as well as plaudits from such high-profile postcolonial figures as Salman Rushdie and Gayatri Spivak.[14] This was followed by *Sammy and Rosie Get Laid* (1988) and *London Kills Me* (1991),[15] which Kureishi wrote and directed. In 1997, *My Son the Fanatic* – adapted from his short story of the same title – was shown at the Cannes Film Festival, and received three nominations from the inaugural British Independent Film Awards, including Best Screenplay.[16] In recent years, Kureishi and Roger Michell (the director of *The Buddha of Suburbia* BBC television series) have collaborated on two further film projects. *The Mother* (2003), once more premiered at Cannes, featured a cameo from Kureishi's twin sons, Carlo and Sachin, but his sister, Yasmin Kureishi, criticizes his portrait of the daughter as a thinly veiled and 'spiteful' caricature of her.[17] His next film, *Venus* (2006), earned Kureishi a Best Screenplay nomination from BIFA.

Kureishi completed his first, unpublished novel, *Run Hard Black Man*, at the age of 14[18] and later went on to write pornography under the pen name Antonia French,[19] but it was with *The Buddha of Suburbia* in 1990 that he achieved critical acclaim, winning the Whitbread Award for Best First Novel. *The Buddha of Suburbia* has been described as 'the first novel to supposedly herald diversity and create the possibility of imagining a different kind of mixed-race Englishman',[20] while Zadie Smith describes the excitement of passing around a 'contraband' copy of the novel at her West London school and seeing for the first time people 'like me' reflected in fiction's mirror.[21] References to popular culture, particularly music, are frequently found in Kureishi's work.[22] David Bowie, who attended the same high school as Kureishi, wrote the soundtrack to the BBC adaptation of *The Buddha of Suburbia*. Kureishi's second novel, *The Black Album* (1995), took its name from the controversial Prince record released a year earlier, which in its turn inverted the Beatles' *White Album* title. The novel was also staged at the National Theatre and West Yorkshire Playhouse in 2009. Kureishi is successful in showing how alienation due to their experiences of racism might cause young Muslims to turn to religion, but his portrayal in *The Black Album* and the film *My Son the Fanatic* of a restrictive group of fanatics contains little to indicate what features of Islamism might hold their interest. In 1995 Kureishi also co-edited *The Faber Book of Pop* with music journalist Jon Savage, in which he writes 'Literature had too often been used as a boot stamped in the face of the young [...] It was rejected. [...] [P]op is a form crying out not to be written about. It is physical, sensual, of the body rather than the mind, and in some ways it is anti-intellectual.'[23] Kureishi relishes the challenge of writing about topics that resist rational discussion, such as pop, sex, the unconscious mind, and ageing bodies.

Kureishi's third novel, *Intimacy* (1998), was heavily criticized for its unflinching, semi-autobiographical portrayal of a man leaving his wife and two young sons. Kureishi, who had recently separated from his partner and Faber editor Tracey Scoffield, was accused of 'an absolute abdication of responsibility' in basing his novel upon their situation.[24] For most of the late 1990s and 2000s, however, Kureishi concentrated on short stories and novellas, releasing *Love in a Blue Time* in 1997, *Midnight All Day* (1999), the short novel, *Gabriel's Gift* (2001), and *The Body and Other Stories* (2002). A number of non-fiction titles were also written during this period, including *Dreaming and Scheming: Reflections on Writing and Politics* (2002), and *The Word and the Bomb* (2005), which collects his pathbreaking writing on 'race, immigration, identity, Islam'.[25] 2004 saw the publication of Kureishi's *My Ear at His Heart: Reading My Father*, a contemplative memoir. Most critics interpreted this text as centring on his relationship with his father, but neglected the subtitle,[26] which indicates that reading (and writing) constitute an equally important part of the narrative. Kureishi reads his father's incomplete manuscript after the latter's death in 1991, and ponders what it tells him about family relations, his own active reading habits, and writerly responsibility.

In 2008, Kureishi returned to lengthy fiction with the novel *Something to Tell You*, which describes the attempts of the mixed-race character Jamal to prevent the coming to light of a violent act of his youth in the mid-1970s, when he unintentionally killed the abusive father of his affluent Ugandan-Indian girlfriend, Ajita.[27] By the early 2000s, Jamal is a successful psychoanalyst and writer with a pre-teenage son, Rafi, from a failed marriage. He is invited to a hedonistic weekend party at the extravagant country house of Mustaq, the son of the man he killed, which is attended by such intertextual celebrities as the actor Karim Amir and punk idol Charlie Hero (both characters from Kureishi's first novel *The Buddha of Suburbia*), and the Muslim peer Lord Omar Ali (from *My Beautiful Laundrette*). Jamal also meets his host's sister and his ex-girlfriend, Ajita, for the first time since the murder, and they re-embark upon an emotional but this time curiously asexual relationship. The novel concludes in shell-shocked post-7/7 London when Jamal admits to the remarkably forgiving Ajita what happened to her father. The novel shows religion becoming a central marker of identity in post-7/7 Britain, and growing currents of Islamophobia. Perhaps most memorable, however, is Kureishi's depiction of London as 'one of the great Muslim cities', evident in a description of Shepherd's Bush Market, in which Morocco, the Middle East, and Europe coalesce in the pursuit of commerce.[28]

His *Collected Stories* was published in 2010, and Aamer Hussein astutely identifies a pattern of stories 'told from the perspective of a man in early middle age, embroiled in a less than satisfactory, if often sexually exciting, relationship', usually involving intense male friendship, a Thatcherite or neo-Thatcherite backdrop, incomprehensible children, and ageing parents.[29] Yet psychology, desire, and the unconscious are also important themes in his work, particularly the films. Desire to Kureishi seems best represented through the metaphor of awakening. As Kristyn Gorton has observed, 'one of the most potent metaphors of desire used within film and television is desire as an awakening, as a force or movement that draws the subject from her position and trans-forms her life',[30] and we see this transformative potential at play in films like *Venus*, *The Mother*, and *My Beautiful Laundrette*. While Kureishi is often regarded as a comic novelist, he also discusses the metamorphosing capacity of mental illness, and knowledg-ably represents such conditions as depression, anxiety, and psy-chosis. He has just brought out his *Collected Essays*.[31] In 2007, Hanif Kureishi received a CBE for services to literature and drama, the same year his tale 'Weddings and Beheadings'[32] (see p. 177) won the National Short Story Prize. In 2010, he was awarded the PEN/Pinter prize for 'courageously and irreverently speak[ing] the truth about life in our multicultural world'.[33]

CC: It's often said that there's little commercial appeal in short stories,[34] but you've been very successful in that genre. What eventually attracted you to the form, having first written plays, films, and novels?
HK: I like writing stories, although not all of them are short. 'The Body' is really a novella,[35] which is a flexible form. I'm now working on something that will probably be 10,000 words, so it's neither a novella nor a short story, but each story has its own natural length. Working on a novel requires such patience. You have to stay with the same characters and ideas, usually for between three and five years, so the idea that I can write a story in a week is liberating. I'm trying to make a living at writing, which is very difficult, and stories don't pay, so I write movies and do some hustling, because I've got three children to support. You try to find a path between making a living and doing pro-jects that you like, and I've mostly enjoyed my work.

CC: Your youngest son, Kier, is here as well, and you've written a lot recently about father–son relationships. In *My Ear at His Heart*, you talk about father figures, gurus, and authority figures, and these issues seem to preoccupy you.[36]
HK: Fathers and sons have always interested me. My father had 11 siblings, all men apart from two sisters. I spent much of my

childhood with these Pakistani men, who sat around talking about books and politics, telling jokes, entertaining each other, arguing, fighting, in the way brothers do. They were incredibly exciting, impressive people to be with when I was a young boy. That's when I fell in love with books, because books were something that you could exchange words about. My father's brothers all read, and talked seriously about books. But I'm not only interested in men and men: the subject for me, and for any writer, is love. Love concerns people's interest in one another; what they want from one another; what they can do; and how they inspire each other. However, at the other ends of relationships, there are also catastrophes. As I've got older, I've become more interested in losses, but also subsequent renewals. I write from different points of view.

CC: In 'The Body', the narrator looks back on his younger self, and meditates on the topic of race.[37] As in Stephen Frears's film, *Dirty Pretty Things*, you present the idea of young, ethnically Other bodies being used as resources for the West.

HK: I hadn't thought about 'The Body' in relation to *Dirty Pretty Things*,[38] but there are parallels. As you get older, you get more interested in decay, illness, and death as part of life, not the end of life. Ageing is as much a part of life as sexuality or childhood; it's part of the natural process. I'm interested in everything. That might seem an absurd thing to say, but as a writer, you can put anything into a book. The more open your mind is, the richer your work will be, particularly if you have a long career, which I hope to have.

CC: Psychologists and therapists increasingly crop up in your writing, as in the character of Jamal in *Something to Tell You*, who works as a psychoanalyst. Deedee Osgood, from *The Black Album*, features in later fictional works, and she makes a career move, from lecturer to psychiatrist.[39]

HK: Deedee's a great woman. Since *The Buddha of Suburbia*, I've been interested in what healing is, and the idea of madness as a form of isolation. I was greatly struck by the comment that D. W. Winnicott made, when a vicar asked him how he could tell the difference between people who are just distressed, and those who are mad; Winnicott made the fascinating reply, 'People flee from the mad. They're not in the system.' Literature, as well as speech, is part of the symbolic system. Freud thought that literature was a form of therapy. It isn't possible for everybody to have psychoanalysis, but literature, particularly Russian literature, is where extreme states of minds are symbolized. My most recent piece of writing is about drugs, both illegal and legal. These days drugs, such as ritalin and its derivatives, are given to children in order to control them. They're giving speed to kids and, when you're on speed, you can put up with any crap. I also think that attacks on illegal drugs function as a mask to enable drug companies to exploit people's vulnerabilities. If I go to my doctor and describe myself as being depressed, he'll write a prescription for antidepressants that I could stay on for years. I want to write about the fact that I could say to a medic, 'I feel sad', and I'd be done for. I'm also interested in the decline of psychoanalysis. It's as though everybody now thinks they know what depression is, and that depression manifests itself in the same way in everyone, which is a pre-psychoanalytical idea. Psychoanalysis was the idea that your mental distress could only make sense in the context of your whole life, so you explored that. I think the decline of psychoanalysis is a decline in the desire to engage with other people.

CC: You were one of the pioneers to discuss issues relating to Muslims and Islam, years before other people, although now of course such discussions are topical. Several of the essays in *The Word and the Bomb* explore attitudes towards Muslims in post-7/7 London.[40] Does this subject still interest you?
HK: Things stop interesting me when everybody else is interested in them. People are always asking for comments on, say, the position of the Muslim in London today, and I think, 'I don't know anything about it and no longer have anything new to say.'

I was interested in these issues because I come from a Muslim family. That said, we never thought of ourselves as Muslim; we thought of ourselves as being Indian or Pakistani. You look at the derivation of the concept of the 'Muslim', and this was a word that was never used. We were immigrants, or Asians, or even, at one time, we were Black. The Muslim thing never really emerged until around the time of the *fatwa*. If you were from the subcontinent, whether you were Sikh, Shia, or whatever; on the whole, you were Indian. Naipaul is probably the person who wrote about it best, particularly in *Among the Believers*.[41]

CC: *Among the Believers* made many critics' hackles rise, and in *My Ear at His Heart* you explore the resentment in Pakistan at Naipaul's portrayal of the country.[42]
HK: Well, look at the country, how can you be surprised? There can't be any bad PR about Pakistan. It's a madness and chaos there, and I know, because my family still lives there. My women cousins are like Chekhov's female characters, hanging around in Karachi with nothing to do. They're bored out of their minds, sitting in those big houses with no work, the kids all gone.

CC: Going back to what you said about the changing terms used to describe 'Blacks', 'Asians', and now 'Muslims'. You trace this lexical evolution in *Something to Tell You*,[43] but what's your opinion of the turn towards identity?
HK: I've turned against it all now. In the last few weeks, I've got sick of identity politics, and have decided to become a Marxist. Tariq Ali will be pleased: finally, I've joined! I'm tired of niche marketing for minorities. There was a time when it was useful and politically potent to define oneself as Lesbian, gay, Black, Asian, Muslim, Hindu, transsexual. All those definitions came out of the 1970s, were refined in the 1980s, and really developed under Blair. It seems that now we need wider identifications, in terms, probably, of class, or other identifications that we haven't thought of yet. The important identifications are of the people who need jobs, or housing. Their demands are not to

do with their ethnicity, but their position as regards the financial crash. A poor Muslim, a poor gay, and so on, would have more in common with each other in terms of wanting education, resources, or work. New creative forms of alliances are needed.

It seems to me that class – where you stand in terms of your positioning with power – is increasingly important. In the light of the recent financial collapse, you can see that class really is present and always has been. This was a subject that John Osborne and other people were portraying in the 1950s, but by the mid-1970s, we were sick of it. New groups were emerging around that time, which you see in *My Beautiful Laundrette*. We need new ways of seeing now. How do we reinvigorate people's thinking, in terms of the new economic climate? That's what interests me. I don't actually think we should return to some sort of Marxist picture. We need new depictions, and I can't yet say what they will be like, but they will emerge from people's conversations.

CC: In your recent story, 'The Decline of the West',[44] people recklessly accrue debt, and then watch helplessly as their world crumbles around them. Will you continue to write about the current recession?
HK: I am fascinated by debt. I grew up in the 1950s in a family where being in debt was anathema. Then in the 1980s, everyone was in debt, and still is. The financial companies and banks themselves are in debt. There isn't anybody who isn't in debt. Apart from my mum! And perhaps other people's mums. I thought about that a lot, and then I started to consider debt as a psychological subject, about what you owe other people, and what you can never pay back. The recession is a sort of punishment, and it's one that in many ways people welcomed. Once you get over the hardship, there are opportunities for new forms of politics, of thriftier living. I hold News Corporation's Rupert Murdoch responsible for a lot of the problems. This media mogul has had more influence on my time and on our country than most politicians, particularly in terms of consumerism and celebrity. We've got Murdoch's Sky TV at home, so we can

watch the football, but broadly I agree with Dennis Potter, who just before he died fulminated against Murdoch and his degradation of the culture.[45]

Then in the 1980s, partly because of Rushdie, postmodernism became popular. I rather liked all that, because I like low culture and vulgarity, but it would be hateful if that were all that existed. What we call postmodernism was invented by very intellectual people, but what we call high culture is still crucial. If you think, for instance, of psychoanalytical therapy as being high culture, and giving people drugs or electroconvulsive therapy as popular culture, then high culture has a lot to recommend it. It's profoundly humanistic, and comes out of Plato, Milton, the philosophical, literary, psychological tradition of the West, in which many intelligent people have been involved.

CC: What's your attitude to Cultural Studies and studying pop culture, which you to some extent satirize in Deedee's pick 'n' mix curriculum in *The Black Album*?
HK: I'm a big fan of all that. It's like taking a bit of a dream, or a throwaway remark that somebody's said: these things may be a point of departure. If you think of a dream as a way into the psyche and having profound meaning, then the part of the dream that leads you into the centre of the psyche is important. Similarly, taking the history of Coca-Cola could tell you a lot about corporate America, capitalism, advertising, consumption, sugar, and so on. You can take these kinds of subjects and make them brilliantly interesting. It would be silly to say people should be reading Shakespeare and not studying Coca-Cola: it just depends on how good the teaching is.

CC: How much of a turning point have 7/7 and the war on terror been? You might like to consider this in relation to the way ideas about security have changed, which you explore in recent work.
HK: 'Security's' the big word, and whenever you hear it, you feel more frightened. Paranoia tends to come from American

culture, and you don't have so much of it over here, but Blair tried to create it. He attempted to make us all believe that within 45 minutes, Saddam Hussein could be attacking us here, in Shepherd's Bush. London is so cosmopolitan, and it is a Muslim city, but the Muslims don't all live together. People in London don't really live in communities, because there's too much movement all the time. You live in Leeds, and presumably up there, people have lived in the same streets with their families for years, so there's a big difference between the British capital and the provinces. Most Muslims I know are really interested in getting their kids into good schools, getting jobs, and getting by. They don't want to live under *sharia* law and send their kids to Muslim schools, although they'll send them to Arabic classes. Most Muslims, although not all, are working-class. It seems to me that they need some sort of alliance with other groups – Afro-Caribbeans, Palestinians, the White working class – in order to have any political force. The current discourse about creating exclusive community centres and mosques seems increasingly irrelevant to me. Joining the so-called mainstream is not a cultural choice, but a political and economic necessity. You need to work with power in order to have *access* to power. However, power has to be used properly by Muslim groups: not in banning books, for instance, but in sustaining futures for young people.

CC: You discussed faith schools in 'The Carnival of Culture',[46] but could you expand on your attitude to New Labour's policy on this issue?

HK: I'm absolutely against faith schools, because I'm a big fan of secularism. I really don't feel that children's futures should be determined by their parents' religious views until the children are of an age where they can choose: 16, I'd guess. We should ensure that every child has a wide knowledge of all religions. I'm interested in the militant atheism that's arisen recently. I don't mean crude attacks on religion, but seeing atheism as an important force in the West since the Enlightenment, which I don't think we'd fully recognized before. It was a big deal to have achieved secularity, particularly in being able to criticize religion. Religions refuse to see themselves as being like any other institutions. For example, if the Catholic Church had been a corporation or a scientific body, the child-abusing clerics would have been kicked out years ago. Somehow, these institutions like to believe that they are not accountable, or that they're accountable only to their own consciences and to God, not to other people or to democracy. That's partly why I think we need a good dose of atheism into the curriculum, as a critical perspective.

CC: Doesn't secularism have its own share of fundamentalism? In Ba'athist Syria and Iraq, for example, people with the most tenuous links to the Muslim Brotherhood were hideously oppressed, and tens of thousands of people were killed.[47] In your own writing you dramatize this, as when the secular father Parvez beats up his religious son, Ali, at the end of 'My Son the Fanatic', the latter declaring, 'So who's the fanatic now?'[48]

HK: That's what happens: any liberalism, any system or process of thought, ultimately has to be based on force. An analogy would be the father with his child: he's nice to the child and persuasive, but in the end he says, 'Look mate, you've got to go to school. Those are the rules, pal.' Liberalism on a secular basis has had, and will have to, assert itself. Yet secularism is the only possible basis for a multiplicity of faiths. It doesn't follow that that necessarily leads to the murder of a Muslim Brotherhood member, although it seems to me that the mass murder of the Muslim Brotherhood probably wouldn't have been such a bad idea. Secular liberalism seems to me the only hope, and I'd argue that liberalisms and fundamentalisms generate each other. These apparently polarized forms are actually linked; one is usually the unconscious of the other. It is also my view that the prevalent desire in the 1960s and 70s to turn away from religion and push it out, makes it ironic that it returned at the end of the 1980s and through the 90s with radical Islam. Who could have predicted it, and who can't laugh at that? The 'clash of civilizations' idea is banal, and not interesting to me at all, as these things are deeply knitted together. As you rightly observe, at the end of *My Son the Fanatic*, they tend to end up at the same place – with force.

CC: **Then you're ultimately on the side of *The Black Album*'s Deedee Osgood, and share her secular liberalism. However, when Deedee's Muslim students get angry about the book that clearly represents *The Satanic Verses*, she shouts them down. Even though she's anti-authoritarian, she calls the police in to tackle their book burning,[49] so there is much complexity in the novel. As well as containing implicit criticism of the Islamist group for directing people's anger about racism into the wrong channels, the novel suggests that there are problems with liberalism and secularism too.**
HK: Yeah, I don't think my final position on this is necessarily as interesting as staging an argument and keeping it going. This is what a play, a film, and a novel can do: having the argument, and sharing it in the most sophisticated ways possible through the characters. It's the debate, the argument, and the failure of the argument that interest me, and I personalize this in 'My Son the Fanatic'. My job is to explore character in relation to ideology. I don't write, 'I believe so and so'; I write stories, because writers' personal positions are banal.

CC: **As regards the Rushdie Affair, you've told Kenan Malik there was a similar but much smaller protest about *My Beautiful Laundrette* in America.[50]**
HK: In 1985 there was a cinema on 72nd Street in Manhattan where *My Beautiful Laundrette* was shown with another gay film, whose title I forget, and every Sunday, there were demonstrations by the Pakistani Action Committee, marching up and down with placards. They weren't complaining that the film was anti-Islamic, but that it was gay. They threatened to blow up the cinema. I've got photographs of me walking amongst the demonstrators, rather enjoying the attention. That was long before the

fatwa. They didn't manage to stop the film being shown. They just wanted to shout, and I was rather sympathetic. If there aren't any films about Pakistanis, and then a film comes out at the centre of which is a gay Pakistani, I can see how they'd think 'Fuck! This was my chance to be shown as a nice fellow.' However, the protesters were really in denial about homosexuality. One guy said to me, 'I don't know why you're saying this, because there aren't any homosexuals in Pakistan, and those that are there are quite rightly in jail.' In Pakistan, where I stayed for a while in 1984, people were already having the kinds of debates that took place in Britain years later around *The Satanic Verses*. In the early 1980s, Muslims had taken over the colleges and schools, and my family was supporting Reagan and Thatcher, much to my surprise.

CC: Talking of *The Satanic Verses*, are you still in touch with Salman Rushdie?
HK: Yes. Kier's a friend of his boy.

CC: Are you?
Kier: Yeah.
HK: You won't get through to Kier when he's playing games on his iPod Touch. It's like trying to communicate with the Chinese government via email.

CC: In *Something to Tell You*, you describe Jamal getting funny looks when he wears a rucksack on the Underground after 7/7,[51] and Ajita receives 'some curiosity and many hostile looks' as well as a verbal insult for wearing a *burqa*.[52] Do you think that racism is taking a cultural turn?
HK: All the young Asian actors in the play version of *The Black Album* talked about their anxieties around that. They said whenever they got on the tube, they'd always got a few seats to sit on, so they could spread out, particularly if they said *Allahu Akbar* as they sat down. However, on the whole I think racism is different in London. London's such a bubble, because it's still relatively

affluent, and people haven't lost their jobs the way they have outside London, in Luton, and further north. I knew the economy was getting bad when all the Poles left. Our area was more or less entirely Polish. We had our house decorated by Poles three or four times; everybody did, because they were great workers. Then suddenly, they started packing up their things and fucking off home. This was a few months before the crash, and they must have realized the game was up. Our lives now are more or less entirely run by Brazilians, and Kier wants to learn Portuguese in order to communicate with the underclass. Brazilians have made a much longer journey than European immigrants, and they can't speak English, so they're more akin to old-fashioned immigrants than the Poles are. It's become like the nineteenth century again. My friends tend to be people who became wealthy since the growth of the media in the 1980s and 90s, and all of their nannies and cleaners are Brazilian, Ecuadorian, Venezuelan. That's what *Dirty Pretty Things* is partly about.

CC: Some critics describe your depictions of women as having misogynist tendencies, and you said you were influenced by all these men in your family …
HK: Liking men doesn't mean that you hate women.

CC: Sure, but you have reservations about radical feminists, using words like 'absurdities' and 'mad ugliness' to describe currents within feminism.[53]
HK: True, but I was a big fan of feminism, too, as that was the period I grew up in. Feminism was a big deal, and I remember Britain before the movement, and it was awful. I would absolutely support feminism, particularly in the Muslim world, where it's a huge struggle. There are a great number of Muslim feminists, who need to be supported by feminists in the West. I do read some women writers, and admire Muriel Spark, Jean Rhys, Mavis Gallant, Flannery O'Connor. Melanie Klein and the therapists that came out of the Kleinian school, and the Lacanians, all had a huge influence on me. I mean, we've all had mothers.

243

How could you not hate women? Having a mother is a night-mare, as anyone must know. The mother is the ultimate unreli-able object. But in a way, our relationship with the mother is the most profound that any of us will have. The mother who isn't always present when you want her to be will infuriate you for the rest of your life. The father comes into the picture much later. Yet feminism has had a few losses as well as many gains, and there isn't a single mother I know who doesn't feel guilty when she's at work and, when she's with the kids, wishes she was having an adult conversation. I don't feel torn, because I get on with my work, and I look after my kids.

Kier: Only just.

HK: Only just. I don't feel guilty when I'm doing something else, because I'm a writer, and it's my job to write. But if you're a woman, I guess, you feel it's your destiny to look after your children all the time. Nadine Gordimer writes about this; the sound of them scratching at the door to come in when she was writing, and how terrible she felt, keeping the door closed, so I've never closed my door.

Kier: You do, you closed it this morning! You had the door closed.

HK: I did, yes, because you were being very annoying this morning.

Kier: And then you closed the door.

HK: But on the whole I make the choice to keep the door open.

Kier: No you don't, me and Mum are always complaining about you shutting the door. I can't believe you're lying on the recorder!

CC: At least we've got your voice explaining what it's really like!

HK: The counter voice.

Kier: The *truth* voice.

HK: To be fair, I try not to shut myself off too much, and I work at home, so I'm around. The kids come and go. It's harder for women. But then they have the consolation of having more time with the children.

12
Ahdaf Soueif

Credit: Eamom McCabe of the *Guardian.*

Born in Cairo in 1950, Ahdaf Soueif is a high-profile cultural commentator and political activist, as well as the author of several works of fiction and journalism. She is Founding Chair of the Palestine Festival of Literature (a touring literary festival, the first and only to be held in Palestine's occupied territories), and much of her recent work has focused on the Israeli–Palestinian conflict. Soueif's groundbreaking English-language fiction represents an early and penetrating attempt to describe interactions between British and Arab characters.[1]

Soueif spent the majority of her childhood in Egypt, but has divided her time between Egypt and Britain since 1984.[2] However, even in her childhood, she had two extended sojourns in England: one a happy experience as a primary school child in Stockwell, south London, while her mother completed her doctorate, and a further sorrowful few months in Putney aged 13, when she was plagued by racist questions about her identity.[3] She gained degrees from Cairo University and the American University in Cairo, before studying, again unhappily, for a PhD in Linguistics at Lancaster University. The trauma of having chosen the wrong PhD, a dry, quasi-scientific attempt to classify metaphors; her dislike of a nameless northern English town that resembles Lancaster; and the breakdown of her first marriage to an Egyptian man are discussed in her semi-autobiographical debut novel, *In the Eye of the Sun*.[4] With her mother and father both holding academic positions in Egypt, Soueif's career seemed predestined. However, after completing her doctorate in 1978, a period of unpaid leave from a teaching position at Cairo University prompted her to pursue her ambition to become a creative writer,[5] and in 1983 her collection of interlinked short stories, *Aisha*,[6] was shortlisted for the *Guardian* Fiction Prize. This promising collection created a great deal of excitement,[7] although she has been criticized for the class politics in this and other works,[8] because she is regarded as being ultimately too shaped by her upper-middle-class background, despite recognizing the great gap between the Western-educated elite and the *fellaheen*.

In 1981, Soueif married poet and critic Ian Hamilton, and the two appear to have had a productive writing relationship, although she separated from him before his death from cancer in 2001. In 1984 she gave birth to their first son, Omar Robert, and devoted the next three years to motherhood,[9] although she was patronized for this role as a homemaker, which she argues is better recognized and rewarded in the Arab world.[10] During her two-year tenure at King Saud University, Riyadh (1987–9), Soueif began writing her first novel, and also had their second child, Ismail Richard, before returning to London. Set against the backdrop of the 1967 Six-Day War between Egypt and Israel and later turbulent events in the region, *In the Eye of the Sun* recalls the nineteenth-century triple-decker novels that Soueif loves, particularly George Eliot's *Middlemarch*, which provides the novel's epigraph and inspires its reflections on sexual and intellectual frustration. It was followed four years later by a further collection of short stories entitled *Sandpiper*,[11] which was named Best Collection of Short Stories by the Cairo International Book Fair. In 1999, her second novel, *The Map of Love*,[12] made the Booker Prize shortlist, losing out to J. M. Coetzee's *Disgrace*.[13] The novel contains representations of travel and travel writing by Westerners to Egypt and Egyptians to the West. Lady Anna's diaries find echoes with real colonial women's travel writing by such figures as Lady Lucie Duff Gordon and Lady Anne Blunt,[14] but also with fictional characters such as Forster's Adela Quested. Yet Anna goes further than Adela's patronizing desire to see the 'real India'[15] by taking the frowned-upon step of 'going native' and entering an Egyptian harem, where she becomes in many ways more independent and intellectually adventurous than she was able to be in Britain.

Much of Soueif's work, including *The Map of Love*, was translated into Arabic by her mother, Fatma Moussa, while Soueif herself has provided English translations of *In Deepest Night* (1998), performed by the al-Warsha Theatre Group in Washington,[16] and the award-winning memoir *I Saw Ramallah* (2000), by Palestinian author Mourid Barghouti.[17] Soueif's practical, theoretical, and political understanding of translation is most wittily explored in Asya's *bravura* explanation of protest singer Sheikh Imam's 'Sharraft ya Nixon Baba', which satirizes Nixon's 1974 visit to Cairo.[18] Here, and elsewhere in her work, Soueif makes translation seem like an almost impossible task of pinpointing meaning from within a vast constellation of connotations. Poor Asya dislikes the task of translating the song that is thrust upon her by her unappealing boyfriend Gerald, because every line needs reams of explanation for its multiple meanings, making the song 'seem ponderous and convoluted while in fact it's totally direct'.[19] Like Walter Benjamin, Soueif appears uninterested in rendering the original Arabic meaning smoothly into English, but seeks to 'powerfully affect' the English language by its contact with Arabic.[20] We observe this again in *The Map of Love*, in which the

Egyptian protagonist, Amal, teaches Arabic to an American visitor, Isabel Parkman, who is trying to translate the Arabic documents of her great-grandmother, Anna. Amal shows Isabel that the Arabic root q-l-b denotes a range of meanings, including 'heart', 'inversion', and 'coup'. She articulates the seditious opinion that this demonstrates to Arabic-speakers 'at the heart of things is the germ of their overthrow; the closer you are to the heart, the closer to the reversal'.[21] Several critics have noticed that Soueif's use of English is like a translation in the sense of forcibly moulding the dominant language to reflect the cadences of Arabic.[22]

Soueif is also a fine essayist, described in the *London Review of Books* as 'a political analyst and commentator of the best kind'.[23] *Mezzaterra* is a collection of her political essays, book reviews, and cultural reflections, written between 1981 and 2004. In it, she writes about such issues as 9/11 and its legacies, identity politics, and Palestine. She famously describes the 'alienation' of Arab- and Muslim-heritage people in the West, 'doing daily double-takes when faced with their reflection in a Western mirror'.[24] Soueif is understandably reluctant to talk about the much-discussed signifier of the *hijab*, but in one essay in the collection, she pertinently critiques the Western preoccupation with this signifier.[25] In both this essay and *In the Eye of the Sun*, she also traces the way in which Egyptian women went from taking off the *hijab* as a sign of feminist liberation to '[c]overing the hair [...] as a woman's act of political protest and a symbol of a search for a liberal, non-Westernised identity'.[26] Asya (and perhaps the young Soueif) seems unconscious of her own class prejudices in assuming that the *muhajaba* girls at her university campus wear the veil as part of a misguided attempt to 'h[o]ld on to their privacy',[27] rather than as a political, identitarian act. Yet *The Map of Love*'s Lady Anna, although a foreigner, realizes there can be liberatory qualities in Muslim coverage, in that it provides a cloak of anonymity to allow the nineteenth-century wearer greater freedom of movement and association.[28] Emma Tarlo's research emphasizes the fashionable, as well as political and faith-based aspects of veiling, describing 'the emergence of a variety of hybrid styles that blend concerns with religion, modesty, politics, and identity with an engagement with both Western and Eastern fashion'.[29]

As a journalist Soueif has written extensively in both English and Arabic, most notably her first-hand account of the Palestinian occupied territories entitled 'Under the Gun: A Palestinian Journey'.[30] Aside from a selection of short stories taken from her first two collections, *I Think of You* (2007), Soueif has continued in this vein of reportage and commentary. An explanation of the absence of fiction from Soueif's post-*Map of Love* work is given in the preface to *Mezzaterra*. While she sees herself primarily as a writer of fiction, its production 'follows its own rhythms; it cannot be forced'. She argues that today's fiction 'will not be born out of today's events', while journalism offers the opportunity for more immediate engagement, and 'responds to the day's most pressing concerns, tries, even, to nudge them on to a different track'.[31]

Soueif's longstanding commitment to Palestine was exemplified in 2008 when she founded the Palestine Festival of Literature. Inspired by cultural theorist and close friend Edward Said's manifesto to 'reaffirm the power of culture over the culture of power',[32] the inaugural festival spanned four days and involved 16 authors of various nationalities. Despite continuing opposition from Israeli authorities,[33] PalFest has flourished, and the fourth annual event was held in April 2011. In 2010, Soueif received the first Mahmoud Darwish Award for her written work, alongside South African poet, Breyton Bretenbach. Soueif's film, *Maydoum*, co-written with her son Omar Robert, premiered at the Dubai International Film Festival in December 2010.[34] Soueif recently took part in the protests against Mubarak in Cairo's Tahrir Square, which she describes as having become 'the civil space that we all longed for', as the Egyptian people rediscovered themselves and threw off the yoke of autocratic rule.[35]

This interview is unique in the volume, as Soueif chose for it to be conducted by email, and the rather short answers make it somewhat anomalous in style compared to the others. Soueif emailed me the following explanation:

> I'm really sorry to have kept you waiting so long; I had to have several goes at this. I did my best – but it's really not my kind of thing; I don't think it's my job to comment on my own writing. In any case, I hope you find something here of use.

To me, this apology is itself interesting, because Soueif (a reviewer, literary critic, and linguistics expert herself) resists analysing her own fiction. The interview sheds light on her unease that her political work is not allowing her to devote enough time to her creative writing, and on her opposition to academic interpretations of her work, which perhaps remind her of her postgraduate past.

CC: Your heroines, Aisha, Asya, Amal, and Anna share certain preoccupations and have similar passionate temperaments. To what extent does the choice of these names beginning with 'A'; the overspilling of characters across several texts (with Deena, Aisha, and Asya reappearing as minor characters in other novels and stories); the fictionalized version of a friend like Edward Said in *The Map of Love*'s 'Omar; and your characters' recurring political and literary interests indicate what Amin Malak calls a 'quasi-autobiographical slant'[36] to your writing?
AS: I feel free to use any of the material that life throws at me – from history, from my own life or other people's; anything can go into the pot. I had not noticed that all my heroines' names begin with 'A'.

CC: How do you negotiate your alertness to the problems of women (both Arab and Western) with your resistance to Orientalist pressures to stereotype the Middle East Muslim? In 'Melody',[37] you describe cultural chauvinism in the Western feminist narrator's patronizing assumptions about her Turkish neighbour and yet her blindness to patriarchal oppression in her own life. Additionally, you've written '[o]ne finds oneself

constantly in a situation now of defending Islam'.[38] Does that word 'now' indicate that the urge to defend Islam is a new development, and came after the publication of your outspoken and intensely personal collection *Aisha* in 1983?

AS: Yes. And I think I wrote in the preface to *Mezzaterra* that the first stories, like the first articles, were written in a free space in which I was as yet innocent of any knowledge of the politics of reception.[39] In other words I hadn't realized that we still needed defending!

CC: Please could you discuss your use of intertextuality, including references to Western novelists such as Eliot, Lorca, Tolstoy, and Alcott and to Arabic writing by such authors as Tayeb Salih and Naguib Mafouz.

AS: Other texts are as much part of my world/reality as other people, so see my first answer.

CC: To some extent your own writing is marketed as enjoyable and middlebrow, even popular fiction, notwithstanding the political and interpretational demands you place on your reader. *In the Eye of the Sun* and *The Map of Love* both have dustjackets that emphasize the 'postcolonial exotic' aspects, and the latter has emblazoned on the front cover a quotation from the *Daily Telegraph*: 'A page-turning holiday read'. How do you feel about the marketing of your fiction?

AS: I stopped worrying about that long ago. What matters to me is that my readers have found me and I've found them.

CC: You have spoken of your discomfort with your early stories being consumed 'by aficionados of the *Arabian Nights*',[40] who look for images of 'odalisques and slave markets and drug dealers'[41] in Arab writing, and I think you've refused to re-anthologize early stories such as 'The Wedding of Zeina' and 'The Nativity',[42] which deal with such issues as virgin deflowering and rape. Does an awareness of the politics of reception indicate that in the current Manichaean political climate one has to measure the impact of every word?

AS: I think so – although I regret the necessity.

CC: You have also written 'the mask of the image can be used to manipulate reality to sinister ends',[43] so please also discuss the politics of representation, particularly in relation to Arabs and Muslims.

AS: That's been discussed ad infinitum in *The Map of Love* and *Mezzaterra*. I've nothing extra to say.

CC: In *Mezzaterra* you discuss Muslims' and Arabs' non-recognition of the 'reflection' of their societies and cultures 'in a Western mirror'.[44] How do you combat such distorting images?

AS: At this stage my personal leaning is towards getting on with my life and producing what I want to produce without being overly concerned with this issue. Sometimes it seems as if every Arab and every Muslim is living with an eye on their image in the West, and that is hampering. Maybe we should just forget about this and get on with our lives without reference to this at all.

CC: Do you think it's possible for modern-day Orientalists or area studies specialists to follow the models of John Frederick Lewis and Lady Anna and provide accounts of Muslim or Arab culture that are knowledgeable, nuanced, and non-coercive?

AS: Yes, indeed, I believe it's possible and necessary. And it should be much easier now that we've been through the postcolonial phase and everybody is or should be far more politically aware. Actually, there's absolutely no excuse now for not being 'knowledgeable, nuanced, and non-coercive'.

CC: How do you balance the demands of fiction with your activism on the issue of Palestine?

AS: I've not managed to balance them; since I've become actively engaged with Palestine and other political issues, I've not produced any fiction.

CC: How much of a turning point was 1967 and the Six-Day War for you?

AS: As much as it was for my whole generation. Massive. The life we have lived has been a direct result of 1967.

CC: You have argued that 'Palestine is constantly at the heart of our relationship with the West, that whatever happens, we see it against the background of what has been done and continues to be done in Palestine.'[45] Have the 2009 massacres in Gaza and the West's responses to these made any difference to this picture?

AS: They've just made it more true and brought it more into focus. But what is happening now is that more and more people in the West are waking up to what's happening and are taking action. We might say that the divisions are re-forming as between 'peoples' and 'regimes' rather than between East and West.

CC: Could you tell me more about your experiences at the most recent PalFest, and about the festival's aims more broadly?

AS: Readers can access the PalFest 2010 report online.[46] This is our mission statement:

> PalFest aims to bring world class cultural events to Palestinian cities; to give Palestinian students access to some of the finest authors writing today, and to create a forum for the exchange of ideas and stories between international and Palestinian writers, readers and students.

> PalFest uses the power of culture against the culture of power.[47]

There's also www.palfest.org. I would just say that it's achieving its aims faster and more comprehensively than I would have dared to hope.

CC: At one point in *The Map of Love*, Omar argues that he thinks of himself as Egyptian, American, and Palestinian, exclaiming, 'I have no problem with identity.'[48] If we replace

'American' with 'British', and emphasize the cultural and political (rather than familial) aspects of Palestinian identity, does this statement also hold for your own identity?
AS: No. I don't know what 'British' feels like. The closest I could come to that would be to say that I'm a Londoner as much as I'm a Cairene.

CC: Staying with *The Map of Love*, to what extent does Anna depart from being a travel writer and become an Egyptian nationalist writer, who casts a searching, outsider's eye on both East and West?
AS: Totally.

CC: You have worked as a translator to bring Mourid Barghouti's *I Saw Ramallah* to a Western readership, and in partnership with your mother to translate *The Map of Love* into Arabic. How would you compare the difficulties of practical translation, on the one hand, and representing Arabic to a Western audience in anglophone fiction, on the other?
AS: They're the same.

CC: To what extent are the representations of migrants and migration from Egypt to Britain in *Aisha* and *In the Eye of the Sun* pessimistic? I'm thinking, for example, of Asya's misery in Lancaster when faced with what Naipaul calls 'the enigma of arrival',[49] and various fictional and autobiographical representations of your unhappy teenage stay at a London state school, which you eventually refused to attend. Do you regard your view of migration from the West to Egypt as being more positive in *Sandpiper* and *The Map of Love*?
AS: It's all to do with people, really, and with love. Anna finds love in Egypt so Egypt is benign and becomes her home. The protagonist of *Sandpiper* loses love in Egypt and so Egypt for her is desolate.

CC: Could you discuss what we might term 'hybridity' in your writing? I take this hybridity as referring to your representations of Egypt's mixed Coptic Christian and Muslim culture; fictional characters rubbing shoulders with historical figures such as Nasser, Sadat, Lord Cromer, and Qasim Amin; the admixture of English and Arabic vocabulary and idioms; Pharaonic and Islamic influences (perhaps best exemplified in Anna's tapestry triptych); and a mosaic-like juxtaposition of different texts, such as diary entries, letters, and newspaper accounts (particularly evident in *The Map of Love*).

AS: See my answer to the first question.

CC: You are well known as a frank chronicler of sexual mores, such as homosexuality in *Aisha*, fear of penetration juxtaposed with 'sexual imperialis[m]' in *In the Eye of the Sun*,[50] and heterosexual bliss contrasted with divorce and possible incest in *The Map of Love*, so could you analyse depictions of desire and sexuality in your *oeuvre*?

AS: How can I possibly do that? My job is to write, not to analyse my writing.

CC: What does it mean to you to be a Muslim post-9/11? How much has changed since the colonialism and stereotyping of the nineteenth century, about which Sharif says, 'the Foreign Office [...] will read "camels" and "God is generous" [...] and they will say "fanatical Arabs" and send the troops'.[51]

AS: As it turns out, everything is still the same. Edward Said's *Covering Islam*,[52] even though published in 1981 is totally brilliant on the subject.

CC: Although you're an outspoken critic of abuses and accretions that attach to Islam, there's also great respect and love for the religion in your work, evinced for example in Chrissie and Asya taking half each of a Surah of the Qur'an because they know the pieces are destined to come together again. Ultimately, are you arguing for *ijtihad* or reasoning to formulate context-specific protocols, as when Amal discusses the prohibition against sculpture and historicizes it as coming out of 'the days of idolatory'?[53]

AS: I think that the principles of Usul al-Fiqh – using *ijtihad* to work out how to realize the basic principles of Islam in different ages and contexts – are a brilliant mechanism to ensure its creative development and continued relevance. We need to remember that Islam started as a revolutionary, dissident, progressive, egalitarian, and global idea and movement, and it continues to hold all these potentials within it.

CC: Could you discuss the spectres of Islamism, terrorism, and the more moderate Muslim Brotherhood, which exist in the margins of *In the Eye of the Sun* but are foregrounded more overtly in *The Map of Love*? Amal understands the desperation 'about the sale of the national industries, about the deals and the corruption and the hopelessness and brutality' that causes some young men to become terrorists, and she deplores the caging of one suspect 'like an animal', but ultimately rejects their solutions as representing attempts to 'bomb their way into a long-gone past'.[54] Is this a position you share?

AS: I'd have to write a book right here to even attempt to deal with this.

CC: You evince a strong interest in material culture, especially of women and migrants, and I'm wondering why you're keen to explore this. Material culture in your novels includes, but is not limited to, clothes, food and drink, interior design, gardens, weaving, art works, and artefacts. Despite your unflinching descriptions of political injustices, there is humour and an almost voluptuary pleasure in 'the good life' in your writing – would you agree?

AS: Yes. I enjoy life, and I think that's probably a good thing. It's all we have.

CC: If you'd like to talk about it, I'd be interested in learning more about the novel you are currently writing.

AS: Probably best if I actually write it …

13
Zahid Hussain

British Pakistani novelist, poet, community worker, and blogger, Zahid Hussain, was born in Darwen, Lancashire, in 1972. He now lives and works in Manchester, but grew up in Blackburn (where the town's MP, Jack Straw, made his infamous remarks about *niqabs* in 2006[1] and recently described young men of Pakistani heritage as 'fizzing and popping with testosterone'[2]). Hussain's father is from Pakistani-administered Kashmir and speaks Mirpuri, while his mother is a Pashto-speaker from Pakistan's Khyber Pakhtunkhwa province, but he grew up trilingual in Urdu, Punjabi, and English. Because Blackburn's Muslim communities are predominantly either Pakistani or Indian-Gujarati,[3] as a child, Hussain attended Indian-majority mosques, and his eldest brother became a *hafiz* (someone who has memorized the Qur'an) in an Indian mosque. He describes this dual attendance at Indian and Pakistani mosques as being fortuitous because 'I experienced two worlds.' This early experience also gifted Hussain with further exposure to languages, as Gujarati and Arabic were used as well as Urdu in mosque services, and he went on to learn French, Spanish, and Turkish. He is newly married, and he and his wife had their first child in early 2011.

As a teenager, Hussain began a degree in IT at the University of Salford, but transferred to Sheffield Hallam for the second year, to study a European version of the IT degree that he was doing. This gave him over a year in France, after which he did a European MBA programme, again conducted in part in France and Spain. Then he returned to England to run a Social Enterprise Development Initiative in Cheetham Hill, Manchester, and work as an IT consultant for IBM Global Services in Europe. In 2001, he left the private sector and, as well as increasing his community work, began seriously to write. His family had moved from Blackburn to Manchester in 1990, at which time he joined Commonword's Identity Writers' Group. It was led by Lemn Sissay, who taught Hussain before moving to London to work as a high-profile poet, playwright, and media figure. Hussain points out that many good writers came out of 'that cradle of Identity', including British Asian poet John Siddique, and describes it as acting as a conduit to many events and activities. Hussain teaches creative writing and keeps a blog, *Writeopia: One Writer's Way*,[4] through which he replies to aspiring writers' emails and offers advice on publishing. He says modestly, 'I'm no expert, I can only share my experience', going on to argue that the most important attribute for a writer is confidence.

Hussain is a former regional Poetry Slam champion and has performed widely as a poet. His debut novel, *The Curry Mile*, is set in Manchester, and describes the intergenerational rivalry between Sorayah and her father Ajmal as they compete for a National Curry Award in the close-knit Rusholme restaurant trade. Ziauddin Sardar named *The Curry Mile* one of his Books of the Year for 2006.[5] Religious studies scholar Philip Lewis observes that '[o]ne of the strengths of Hussain's novel [...] is Ajmal's dawning realization that discrete Pakistani and English social and cultural worlds – "ours" (*apne*) and "theirs" (*goray*) – no longer exist for their children'.[6] Indeed, if *The Curry Mile* has a moral it is that Sorayah wants to maintain a good relationship with her father and follow him into the restaurant trade. Eventually she becomes a success in the business world, as her father was hoping would happen for a child of his, and she does this without breaking the family and notwithstanding her gender, which Ajmal sees as a handicap. In *The Curry Mile*, Hussain also takes on issues that are commonly associated with Islam – even if they are cultural rather than religious – such as arranged or forced marriage, which is powerfully evoked in Sorayah's friend Yasmeen, who attempts suicide rather than accepting her father, Jafar's, choice of husband.[7] Additionally, he presents a *pir* character in the novel, a powerful and corrupt Sufi teacher, whom Ajmal sees as a living saint and who greatly influences him.[8] Some *pirs* are politicians and their devotees are zealous about them, so they can manipulate them and accrue money as Ajmal's *pir* does, while others are worthy and reputable figures.[9]

As mentioned in this book's introduction and discussed in the interview, Hussain runs the writers' group Manchester Muslim Writers, which is affiliated with the Muslim Writers Awards. Recently, he has also become Chief Executive Officer for MiST, a medical charity that brings together surgeons and other health-care professionals to respond to disasters worldwide.[10] He leads the Manchester Division of Mosaic, Prince Charles's charity that aims to create opportunities for young people, through organizing mentorship and speaking engagements by Muslims. Hussain now also works as the Co-ordinator for the Manchester Council of Muslims. There are around 15 mosques in Manchester and his role is to act an impartial gatekeeper (not representing any particular mosque) and liaison officer, if people need to speak to their council. Chapter 6 of *The Curry Mile* is set in a mosque,[11] and in it Ajmal's greatest rival, Jafar, wins a psychological victory when the Imam of the mosque humiliates Ajmal, by exposing the fact that he has not donated as much money to the mosque as his foe. As a further blow to Ajmal's pride, his son Basharat has a fight after the prayers. Hussain explained that some people have been critical of this scene, but points out that he is not commenting on the mosque, but observing the symbiotic relationship between mosques as social spaces and businessmen's connections. He explores the religious world, which is also very social, encapsulating family tensions and one-upmanship as well as faith. He is currently working on his second novel.

CC: Could you tell readers about the Muslim Writers Awards and the writing group you founded, Manchester Muslim Writers?
ZH: The Muslim Writers Awards began in 2006 as a Birmingham-based project, but it's grown quickly and become a national phenomenon. It's quite unusual in the world of literature in that, firstly, it's about writing that is somehow connected with the Muslim world and Muslim heritage. Secondly, it deals with both published and unpublished writers. Most awards and celebrations tend either just to deal with published writing, or they are writing competitions for unpublished work, but the Muslim Writers Awards tries to cover everything. I think there is growing interest in writing by Muslims or writing that has echoes of Muslim heritage. The experience of British Muslims and British Asians post-9/11 is a world people are captivated by. To hear the same story, but narrated from a different angle, gives it new life.

Manchester Muslim Writers was set up in May 2009 as a collective of writers of Muslim origin. It aims to bring writers together to support other writers. Whether one writes poetry, fiction, drama, blogs, or academic texts, it doesn't matter. We have Muslim and non-Muslim members and the writers have different levels of ability. The range of ethnicities is quite wide and members travel from Leeds, Preston, Rochdale, and further afield. Many of our members, particularly women, are writing autobiographies, and for them, what they're doing is almost therapeutic.

There are two aspects of the writing craft and of art in general. One is conjuring original ideas: that isn't something one can give another writer. That initial magic has to come from the individual. I truly believe that every individual has that spark, especially if they start thinking about their memories and the people they know. Manchester Muslim Writers can certainly help with the second aspect of the writing craft which is the technical side. Anybody can be taught or learn technique.

CC: What techniques do you find successful when you're teaching aspiring writers?
ZH: I use a range of techniques. Sometimes, I will go into a class and say, 'Do you watch *CSI*?' Most of them do, so I say, 'Why don't we do a BSI, a Book Scene Investigation?' We take a famous book that they've read, and pin up character profiles on walls, just as they have criminal profiles on the walls in *CSI*. We create the locations and plot, and work out the motives. It's a different way of looking at books, and it feeds into their understanding of the world.

Sometimes I begin sessions by teaching children how to read a book. They tend to be shocked when I lift up a book, and say, 'Never open it straight away and start reading. That's wasting your time.' I advise them first to look at the cover, the back, and the spine, and they can find out things about the book without even opening it. These are basic skills. There are strategies you can use, not to make it cool, but to make young people understand that reading has value.

CC: *The Curry Mile* is largely told from Sorayah's perspective, although her father, Ajmal's, perspective also features. Was it difficult, as a male author, writing about a female protagonist?
ZH: Until it was brought to my attention, I didn't know there was a problem associated with my being male and writing from a female perspective. The published book is actually the fourth draft of the original manuscript. Draft one of *The Curry Mile* was set during 24 hours in Manchester, and every chapter was conveyed through the eyes of a different character, around ten in all. A female agent in London told me she liked the parts of the novel narrated from a female perspective, and she wanted

more of that, so I went away and rewrote it. They may have felt that it was fresh that an Asian male was writing from a female Asian perspective. I drafted and redrafted, and in the end Suitcase Books in Manchester published it.

CC: Have you had much criticism from people in the Muslim communities where you work for the fact that Sorayah lives with her Hindu boyfriend and has an abortion?
ZH: In general, the reception has been very warm. My novel is not trying to judge; it juxtaposes a father and daughter, who are similar in many ways, but are received differently by society. I think that many White people assume that Asian men are not necessarily religious, but that they are usually very patriarchal. Every single reviewer jumped to the conclusion that I was female, including Qaisra Shahraz,[12] who reviewed the novel to write a blurb and thought my name had been misspelt. To me, the book is neither female nor male. However, I have older sisters, I've listened in to their conversations, and because I speak many languages, I sense that the way women speak about the world is different from men. Even now, people write to me and say that they love Sorayah, which is great. The only negative reaction was a minor argument that erupted in my family. Some people were asking why I chose certain names that also belonged to relatives, and they felt I was being dishonourable. My reply was that these were just names, and were not based on anyone's family. A stranger wrote that I should not be discussing issues such as a Muslim girl living with her Hindu boyfriend. However, my role as a writer is like that of a journalist: I'm just describing events that occur. I don't want to criticize Sorayah, because she's somebody who is very much in love. If she is committing a sin, then juxtapose that with her father's behaviour. Who is the greatest sinner? That's for you to decide, it's not for me.

CC: Would you describe yourself as a religious person?
ZH: Since around 2001, I have become much more of a practising Muslim. I pray regularly, work closely with Muslim

communities, and carry out a lot of inter-faith work. As a teenager, I was less devout and more interested in travelling and seeing the world, but I've always had at least some involvement in Islamic work. My family is quite devout, so I've always had an interest in faith, and my experience has been such that I wanted to give something back to the community. Serving society is something which I think all faiths prioritize.

CC: What sort of writing do you enjoy to read?
ZH: I'm impatient with writers who expound rather than telling a good story. I sometimes wonder whether they are failed poets, because something in the over-use of metaphorical language suggests poetry. For example, E. Annie Proulx's *The Shipping News* is drenched in confused metaphors, although it also contains some dazzling gems. I must come from the school of George Orwell, or even Dostoevsky, because for me the story is essential: not plot, so much as characterization.

I write poetry and love it for its timelessness and stubborn images. In poetry each word is there to take your breath away, and even the pauses are important. Prose is more relaxed and you can flesh things out. In prose, metaphors are an acquired taste; you can't enjoy too much of a rich dish, so it's better to be sparing with imagery in fiction. Margaret Atwood is an outstanding writer, because she writes both poetry and prose so well. I'm a great fan of Maupassant and Carver, two very different writers, but both were great psychologists, as writers should be. I'm also influenced by *One Thousand and One Nights*, which I know more as an oral rather than a literary text. That kind of narrative, a story-within-a-story, still works to this day.

CC: The world in Manchester that you present is quite middle-class, with many characters who have been to university and become doctors, lawyers, or entrepreneurs. Was this a deliberate decision to distance yourself from

representations of British Muslims which tend to focus on the working classes?

ZH: In a way, *The Curry Mile* is the child of the original version, which was called *Abrasion*. 'BrAsian' is a sociological term for British Asian. So the title conveyed 'A British Asian', but also 'abrasion' in the wearing away of the characters' identities. In the first version, many of the characters were working-class and uneducated. The draft opened with a mother, performing *fajr* (morning) prayer. Although in *The Curry Mile* we still get glimpses of working-class people, they are less visible as the focus is on father and daughter. The father is working-class and remains so, but has become a successful entrepreneur, and Sorayah is a middle-class character because of her education and her family's prosperity, but she retains working-class characteristics.

CC: **The term '*halal* fiction' has been used to describe Leila Aboulela's writing, but implicitly this could lead to other fiction being described as '*haram*'. Do you think such categories as '*halal* novelist' could promote (self-)censorship?**

ZH: I believe writing is fundamentally about intention. I told my mother, who doesn't speak English, what *The Curry Mile* was about, and the reactions it could potentially generate. She astounded me by the accuracy of her response, pointing out that if you were to assess each story strand of TV and film dramas from the Indian subcontinent, you'd have to conclude that they are all immoral. There's lying, bickering, cheating, killing, so why is that an acceptable norm? However, if somebody in Britain writes about these topics, it becomes *haram* and people judge it. One close friend of mine, who is not a writer, even referred to my book as 'pornography'. He said it tongue-in-cheek, but he is from a very austere background. Such reactions are not from any one school of thought. When you have a community under siege, or which has the perception that it's under siege, and a novel like *The Curry Mile* is published, people are suspicious of its representations of the Muslim community.

CC: You provide an insider's view of Manchester, so can you say something about the city in your writing?

ZH: My sense of it is that there's a certain pragmatic realism, something visceral and gritty about Manchester. If you come to a place like Manchester and you're Irish, Polish, Jewish, Black, or Pakistani, there has historically been a place for you. Manchester has fewer Muslims than, say, Bradford, but ethnically, we're more diverse, with Somali and Arab communities. In the 1970s and 1980s, the Muslim population was mainly Pakistani, but in recent years, that has changed enormously, and the different mosques around the city reflect the many Muslim communities. Bradford is, strangely, more monocultural, with mostly Kashmiri and Mirpuri communities. Yet I haven't read many novels which reflect the diversity or give a sense of the ethnic communities of Manchester. Manchester's usually a backdrop for thrillers, about police, detectives, and criminals, but not the Manchester of ordinary people. This is surprising, given that this is a labouring, broadly working-class city. I wanted to give a sense of the working class and the Muslim communities that become part of that class structure. Spatially, Manchester is a huge part of my inspiration. I couldn't write if I didn't have a sense of space.

CC: In *The Curry Mile*, which is set in the 1990s, there are many references to text messages, Walkmans, and so on. Why this interest in popular culture and new technologies?

ZH: I think I was trying to capture the zeitgeist, because that's the world we live in. I also wanted to suggest that the so-called social networks that we talk about today are just extensions of the social networks that used to exist in communities anyway. It seems to me that, particularly in the West, individualism has developed to such an extent that people almost need social networks to fill a gap. Other communities, however, use technology in a slightly different way. On Facebook, for example – which I'm not a big fan of – but with many Asian people I know, half of their Facebook friends are family.

They post family pictures on their profiles and use social networking as an extension of family communication. In contrast, young Western people mainly use Facebook to connect with friends.

CC: How do you feel about any attempts to categorize you as a British Muslim writer?

ZH: I'm quite pragmatic about it. This category has to emerge so that certain voices can be heard, but I think that for most confident writers, it's really irrelevant whether they're Muslim, Christian, or whatever. I'm comfortable with or without categorization, because we are all many things. For example, I'm a literary poet, a performance poet, short story writer, and novelist. In the context we live in, it's probably important for Muslim writers to feel that there is a special space for them right now. Many people feel besieged and under threat. For me, the term 'Muslim writers' is just a doorway into a huge house, which has little to do with Muslims *per se*, but is about providing access to agents and literary festivals, and so on. Many writers wouldn't be introduced into this house if they didn't come in through the initial doorway.

CC: Does the prejudice towards Muslims stem from Islamophobia?

ZH: As a writer, terms are important to me, and I think 'Islamophobia' doesn't hit the mark. I sometimes use the term 'neo anti-Semitism', because we're not so far away from the way the Jews were treated in the mid-twentieth century. People have scoffed when I've said this at conferences, but it has been argued that there were eight steps to the Holocaust and other genocides,[13] which include, for example, creating special laws for a particular community, as is happening with Muslims today. I'm perfectly happy to say that the Muslim faith is a Semitic faith. Arabs, not Jews, make up the largest Semitic population in the world. If anybody claims Muslims are anti-Semitic, I'd point out Islam is an Arab, Semitic faith.

CC: Have you noticed prejudice getting worse since 9/11 and 7/7?
ZH: Yes. During the European elections, when the BNP came in, I was racially abused and called 'Paki' one afternoon in Manchester city centre. In 2010 in Manchester's Southern Cemetery, Muslim graves were desecrated three times in a row within the space of a few weeks. If those had been Jewish graves, the police would have rightly worked around the clock to ensure it didn't happen again.

CC: How much of an impact did the Rushdie Affair have on you?
ZH: It was probably *the* turning-point. I was about 16 and attending school in Blackburn. At that time there were only a few Muslims in the school, and we were totally ostracized because of the Affair. When I look back, the things teachers said to us were just racist. They'd make snide comments about our 'culture', which teachers used to get away with, although they don't so much now. The ill-treatment pushed us few Muslims together, and the Rushdie Affair was the first time we had a prayer meeting at school. Our generation started the ball rolling for Muslims, although the current schoolkids don't realize that. That period marked the rise of the Young Muslims and the Islamic Society of Britain, so it was a time of emergence.

CC: Did you read *The Satanic Verses* at the time?
ZH: No, I've never read it in its entirety. I find much of Salman Rushdie's work stodgy, although I enjoy his essays, which are incredibly clear and well-written. As for his fiction – even *Midnight's Children* which everybody loves – I don't know who he's writing to. To me, he's in the same bracket as Anthony Burgess. I think they're too self-conscious as writers, as if they always have to make erudite references to other texts. In real life, we hate people like that; they're know-it-alls! To some extent I think Rushdie encouraged the controversy as part of marketing or 'spin' that got out of hand, but I also think

The Satanic Verses, like many of Rushdie's books, is designed to hurt and offend. It makes me think of a Judo master who in combat can pick on his opponent's weakest points.

CC: What did Muslim communities find most upsetting about the novel?
ZH: He used certain words such as *Jahilia*, *hijab*, and so on. The symbolism was very powerful, and you wouldn't use it in that way unless you were trying to make a cruel point. If he was doing it as a storyteller, well, where was the story? If he was aiming these references at Western people who don't know Islam or the terms, what was he trying to say? Muslims understood exactly what he was trying to say and the fact he was pitching to a non-Muslim audience made it worse. Rushdie should have realized that if you write a book, it has consequences, because it goes out into the world, but he's always been in a bubble. The Muslim community overreacted, because the best thing would have been to hush, and *The Satanic Verses* would have been just another book on a shelf. In a way, though, we in the Muslim world made him a household name and hero of freedom of speech, and taxpayers paid millions to protect him. What happened, happened, and we've learnt from it.

CC: You're obviously concerned about issues in contemporary politics, and you've spoken eloquently about neo anti-Semitism. On an international scale, do the conflicts in Kashmir, Afghanistan, Iraq, or Palestine preoccupy you?
ZH: I feel that we in the West are at the end of our empire. We seem to think that everything lasts forever, but empires fail and everything dies. The British Empire didn't exactly die; the baton was passed to America. If you look at history, no declining empire recovers. This new century belongs to China and India. One day Europe will start to call itself Northwest Asia as the balance of power shifts to the East. I feel quite strongly about the inane policies and short-term and materialistic thinking that has caused the conflicts around the world and yet I have a sense that

this status quo will change. There was a time when the Persians, the Romans, the British Empire had everyone living in fear of them. They were the superpowers of their age, yet they butchered animals, destroyed nations, and treated women like scum.

CC: We've talked about Islamophobia and oppressive treatment of Muslims, but in your community work do you come across young people who are seeking nihilistic solutions?
ZH: Is there growing frustration? Yes. Is there a growing sense of unease and injustice? Yes. As for where it's going, as I said, this is the end of an empire and America is declining. We're left with a mythos and are experiencing the breakdown of our society. Our children are uneducated. Every year, several thousand people die on the roads; there are countless deaths through drink and drug-related crime. Knife crime accounts for only a few hundred deaths, but two people die on a street corner, and it becomes sensationalized. The media takes the exception and makes it appear the norm. We have become cowed by the media, and are now more interested in Lady Gaga than real news. People come to this country and wonder how it was possible that Britain ruled a huge part of the world. Britain built its empire on the slave trade, pillage, and rape. It educated its children that 'home is lovely and ordered, but outside is threatening and lawless'. Yet rather than civilization, Britain has the illusion of civilization.

As for this idea that young people are being 'radicalized': well, in every corner of the world, at every time, there have been young people who have learnt to hate others. In the same way that the term 'radical' is applied to Muslims now, it could have been used in relation to the 1940s in Korea, or in the early twentieth century leading to the Bolshevik Revolution. This term 'radical Muslim' has come to mean so much, yet in a generation, it will mean nothing again. I do come across young people – and older ones – who are seeking to find an outlet that hints at the extreme, yet there is little we can do to staunch the tide. If we cannot affect media or society how do we change the way people perceive the world? Well, we keep trying.

Conclusion

I would like to conclude by emphasizing again the heterogeneity of the writers under study, in terms of age, gender, nationality, political, and religious positions, and also their writing styles, choice of genre, publication histories, and critical reception. Despite this emphasis, there are still problems inherent in the singling out of this religious group. Because I am interested in texts by writers of Muslim heritage, there is an attendant danger of abstracting Muslims from the historical record (when often writers are not practising or not very interested in Islam), and separating them from both other ethnic minority groups and White Britons with whom they have had a shared immigration history or other connections. On the other hand, there are also advantages to this approach, such as the fact that it brings writers together from Muslim communities with heritage in the Middle East, Africa, and Asia whose works may elucidate each other, while also highlighting divergences.

Muslims in Britain have of course been placed at the very centre of media attention and political concern in recent years. In my view, it is important to look at this group, but without pigeonholing individuals or according greater importance than is warranted to the religious or civilizational aspects of their Muslim identity. Furthermore, it would be erroneous to suggest that Islam itself is a monolithic entity. Dutch literary critic Mieke Bal, whose book *Loving Yusuf* centres on (re-)tellings of the Joseph story, from the Bible and Qur'an through to Rembrandt's etchings and Thomas Mann's *Joseph and his Brothers*, writes:

> Not only is my culture – say, Western Europe – composed of an enormous number of different traditions, including religious ones, but it is also constantly being reshuffled into categories whose importance shifts with issues and situations. Sometimes age is more important than gender; sometimes class overrules

all other groupings. At the present moment, religion, always politically inflected, is gaining renewed prominence as a tool for group formation. But never, in no situation, is that culture homogeneous.[1]

There are vast differences in the religious practices of Islam's two main branches, Sunni and Shia, as well as other groups such as the devotional Sufis and esoteric Ismailis. As has been seen, there are also great variations between the worldviews of people originally from different nations and regions. Even within a particular ethnic group, there are distinctions between 'rural and urban, rich and poor, educated and illiterate'.[2] Many of the interviewees unpack the huge category of 'Muslim' in public debate and begin to engage with the specificities. In the academy, women, social classes, various ethnicities, and so on, are commonly discussed, despite the variation that clearly exists within each grouping. Analysis of the category of people of Muslim background is also necessary and important, so long as the diversity within that is not elided.

Identity itself is, as Stuart Hall recognizes, a protean thing that is constantly being (re-)fashioned and, as the interviews show, one's religious affiliations as a Muslim intersect with other signifiers – such as gender, socio-economic status, and national origins – which assume various degrees of importance in different situations. That said, there is nonetheless a need to examine the religious components of identity, especially because as Amin Malak observes, 'many Muslims regard religion as a key component of their identity that could rival, if not supersede, their class, race, gender, or ethnic affiliation'.[3] Furthermore, I am influenced by Tariq Modood's recent book, *Multiculturalism*, in which he argues that Wittgenstein's concept of 'family resemblance' allows us to recognize distinct ethnic and religious groups, although these groups alter in different times and space, and are internally heterogeneous. Modood's contention that we can identify Muslims as a group despite all their myriad differences, just as we can detect members of the same family despite great variations in their eye colour, physique, posture, personality, and so on, is helpful when thinking about writers as British Muslims. While the writers I have interviewed, as I have outlined, exhibit very different features, styles, and affiliations, I would argue that we can usefully speak of them as a loosely connected and often discordant family. Nonetheless, they also have many connections with non-Muslims, such as like-minded political activists and other intellectuals, so this volume attempts to correct misconceptions about Muslims in Britain as strangers and Other.

My belief in the existence of close interconnections between writers of Muslim heritage does not come out of a naïve belief in a transcendental *ummah*, and nor do I mean to ignore the very real tensions between different Muslim groups within an in any case divided Britain. But I do think that the writing of this group of authors of Muslim heritage shares certain preoccupations (relating to gender, class, the war on terror, Muslim Spain, the Rushdie Affair, and a cosmopolitan outlook), and is some of the most interesting fiction in the UK today. Recognition that their work forms a unique generic category is growing, as is testified by Peter Morey and Amina Yaqin in their Framing Muslims research project,[4] and the new literary prize the Muslim Writers Awards, discussed in the Introduction. Although largely being produced by the numerically dominant South Asian community, writers of Arab and African Muslim descent are also gaining prominence.

Speaking briefly of my own feelings after conducting these interviews, I have learnt a great deal not only about the lives of Muslims in the West today, but also about the writer's craft and his or her political role in society. The writers who left the strongest impressions on me from the interview situations were often the most politically assertive, as in the eloquent but often damning indictments of life in Britain by Tariq Ali, Fadia Faqir, Robin Yassin-Kassab, and Zahid Hussain. Yet authors such as Tahmima Anam, Kamila Shamsie, and Aamer Hussein also in their different ways made quietly compelling points. Several of them indicated that the 2000s have both been marked by, and have given further impetus to, a rise in Islamophobia and violence towards Muslims. As I was putting the finishing touches to this book, a wave of revolutions swept the Middle East, in what is being termed the Arab Spring. These political convulsions surprised many commentators in the West, accustomed as they are to Orientalist discourse about Arabs and Muslims as backward and prone to authoritarianism. Yet the interviews reveal an entirely divergent image of Muslims as progressive, politically informed, and independent minded. As Soueif wrote to me (nearly a year before the Egyptian revolution and fall of Mubarak) in a comment that is startlingly resonant today, 'Islam started as a revolutionary, dissident, progressive, egalitarian, and global idea and movement, and it continues to hold all these potentials within it.'

I hope that this book has illustrated that these writers, who identify themselves as being of Muslim heritage, are writing vibrant, iconoclastic, and astute texts. It has been a privilege to work with them, learn from their creative works, in conversation with them, and to bring certain of them into classrooms to work with young people, some of whom may be the writers of the next generation.

Notes

Introduction

1. Although the first book deals exclusively with English-language writers, the later monograph will make an important mediation between English-language texts and other language writing, examining landmark texts by such writers as Tayib Salih (Arabic) and Abdullah Hussein (Urdu) through the lens of translation theory.
2. Susheila Nasta (ed.) (2004) *Writing Across Worlds: Contemporary Writers Talk* (Abingdon: Routledge).
3. Philip Tew, Fiona Tolan, and Leigh Wilson (eds) (2008) *Writers Talk: Conversations with Contemporary British Novelists* (London: Continuum).
4. Sunil Sethi (2011) *The Big Bookshelf: Sunil Sethi in Conversation with Thirty Famous Authors* (Delhi: Penguin/NDTV).
5. Philip Lewis (2007) *Young, British and Muslim* (London: Continuum) and Anshuman A. Mondal (2008) *Young British Muslim Voices* (Oxford: Greenwood).
6. Mondal, *Voices*, 183.
7. Claire Chambers (2003) 'The Relationship Between Knowledge and Power in the Work of Amitav Ghosh' (Leeds: University of Leeds, Unpublished PhD Thesis).
8. Nigel Williams (1993) *East of Wimbledon* (London: Faber), 3.
9. Afshan Malik (2003 [1996]) 'Safar', in Jeff Teare (ed.) *New Welsh Drama* (Cardiff: Parthian), 15–74; Imtiaz Dharker (2009) 'Vale of Clwyd' (unpublished poem emailed to the author); and Sara Suleri Goodyear (2003) *Boys Will be Boys: A Daughter's Elegy* (Chicago: University of Chicago Press), 11, 26, 69, 87, 108, 106.
10. Claire Chambers (2011) 'Poets of Muslim Heritage'. *Exiled Ink* 14 (Winter) (forthcoming).
11. Muslims are said to comprise up to 4,000 of Northern Ireland's population: Belfast Islamic Centre (2011) 'Introduction' (4 January), http://www.belfastislamiccentre.org.uk/about_us/new_mosque_project.htm

274

12. Colin Bateman (2001) *Mohammed Maguire* (London: HarperCollins). There is also Marsha Mehran (2006) *Pomegranate Soup* (London: Arrow), about Iranian migrants to the fictional village of Ballinacroagh in the Republic of Ireland.

13. James Procter (2003) *Dwelling Places: Postwar Black British Writing* (Manchester: Manchester University Press), 2–3.

14. Zahid Hussain (2010) 'Great Muslim Writers', Unpublished Manchester Muslim Writers Powerpoint Presentation (Manchester: Manchester University Press), n.p.

15. Robert Gleave (2010) 'Should we Teach Islam as a Religion or as a Civilisation?', unpublished paper, Islamic Studies Network: Perspectives on Islamic Studies in Higher Education, Aston University (25–26 May), http://www.heacademy.ac.uk/assets/York/multimedia/audio/islamic_studies/Professor_Ron_Geaves.mp3

16. Timothy Fitzgerald (2009) *Discourse of Civility and Barbarity: A Critical History of Religion and Related Categories* (Oxford: Oxford University Press), 6.

17. Amin Malak (2005) *Muslim Narratives and the Discourse of English* (Albany: State University of New York Press), 5.

18. The Community Religions Project was founded at Leeds University in 1976, and conducts empirical research on religions 'near at hand' in Britain. See University of Leeds (2010) 'Community Religions Project' (9 November), http://www.leeds.ac.uk/trs/irpl/crp.htm

19. Joe Moran (2002) *Interdisciplinarity* (London: Routledge), 16.

20. Ibid.

21. Salman Rushdie (1988) *The Satanic Verses* (London: Viking), 91–125.

22. Tabish Khair (2008) *Muslim Modernities* (Delhi: Vitasta), 54.

23. Salman Rushdie (1991) *Imaginary Homelands* (London: Granta), 405; emphasis in original.

24. See Anouar Abdalla (1994) *For Rushdie: Essays by Arab and Muslim Writers in Defense of Free Speech* (New York: George Braziller).

25. For representative examples, see Fay Weldon (1989) *Sacred Cows: A Portrait of Britain, Post-Rushdie, Pre-Utopia* (London: Chatto & Windus); Malise Ruthven (1990) *A Satanic Affair: Salman Rushdie and the Rage of Islam* (London: Chatto & Windus); Kenan Malik (2010) *From Fatwa to Jihad: The Rushdie Affair and its Legacy* (London: Atlantic Books).

26. See, for example, Shabbir Akhtar (1989) *Be Careful with Muhammad! The Salman Rushdie Affair* (London: Bellew Publishing); Talal Asad

(1990) 'Ethnography, Literature, and Politics: Some Readings and Uses of Salman Rushdie's *The Satanic Verses'*, *Cultural Anthropology* 5(3): 239–69; Edward W. Said (1995 [1978]) *Orientalism: Western Conceptions of the Orient* (Harmondsworth: Penguin), 367–77; Anshuman A. Mondal (2009) 'The Rushdie Fatwa: The *Satanic Verses* Affair was a Clash, Not Between Islam and the West, But Between Religious and Secular Sensibilities', guardian.co.uk (16 February), http://www.guardian.co.uk/commentisfree/2009/feb/10/religion-islam-fatwa-rushdie

27. Malak, *Narratives*, 4.

28. Mai Ghoussoub (2008) *Selected Writings* (London: Saqi), 13–14.

29. Salman Rushdie (1988) 'Minority Literatures in a Multi-cultural Society', in Kirsten Holst Petersen and Anna Rutherford (eds) *Displaced Persons* (Sydney: Dangaroo), 33–42, 39; Ana Maria Sánchez-Arce (2007) '"Authenticism", or the Authority of Authenticity', *Mosaic* 40(3): 139–55, 139.

30. Monica Ali (2006) *Alentejo Blue* (London: Black Swan). For an exemplary poor review, see Natasha Walter (2006) 'Continental Drift', *Guardian Review* (20 May), 16.

31. Hossein Pirnajmuddin (2008) 'Milton's "Dark Divan" in *Paradise Lost'*, *The Explicator* 66(2): 68–71; Jeffrey Einboden (2009) 'A Qur'ānic Milton: From Paradise to al-Firdaws', *Milton Quarterly* 43(3): 183–94.

32. Martin Amis (2008) *The Second Plane* (London: Jonathan Cape); Ian McEwan (2005) *Saturday* (London: Jonathan Cape); Sebastian Faulks (2009) *A Week in December* (London: Hutchinson).

33. See Said, *Orientalism*, viii.

34. The Other that Said examines in *Orientalism* is largely Muslim and Arab (*Orientalism*, 59–72). However, he does pay attention to other Others, notably Indian and, to a lesser extent, Chinese.

35. Ibid., 70.

36. See John McLeod (2000) *Beginning Postcolonialism* (Manchester: Manchester University Press), 33.

37. Malak, *Narratives*, 2.

38. Samuel P. Huntington (1993) 'The Clash of Civilizations', *Foreign Affairs* 72(3): 22–49 and Samuel P. Huntington (2002 [1996]) *The Clash of Civilizations and the Remaking of World Order* (London: Free Press).

39. Tariq Modood (2005) *Multicultural Politics: Racism, Ethnicity and Muslims in Britain* (Edinburgh: Edinburgh University Press), 80.

40. Islamophobia is analysed by, among others, Runnymede Trust (1997) *Islamophobia: A Challenge for us All* (London: Runnymede),

and Robin Richardson (2008) 'Islamophobia and Anti-Muslim Racism: Concepts and Terms, and Implications for Education'. *Race, Equality, Teaching* 27(1): 11–16.

41. These events mark a flashpoint for a specific generation, as did the Iranian revolution and hostage crisis for the late 1970s and early 1980s, and as the Rushdie Affair of 1989 onwards manufactured concerns about the reified figure of the Muslim.

42. Derald Wing Sue, A. I. Lin, G. C. Torino, C. M. Capodilupo, and D. P. Rivera (2009) 'Racial Microaggressions and Difficult Dialogues on Race in the Classroom', *Cultural Diversity and Ethnic Minority Psychology* 15(2): 183–90, 183.

43. Paul Auster (2010) *Sunset Park* (London: Faber), 271.

44. Roland Barthes (1977) 'The Death of the Author', in *Image, Music Text*, trans. Stephen Heath (London: Fontana), 146–7.

45. Michel Foucault (1977) 'What is an Author?', in Donald F. Bouchard (ed. and intro) *Language, Counter-memory, Practice: Selected Essays and Interviews*, trans. Donald F. Bouchard and Sherry Simon (Ithaca, NY: Cornell University Press), 113–38.

46. Seán Burke (2008) *The Death and Return of the Author: Criticism and Subjectivity in Barthes, Foucault, and Derrida* (Edinburgh: Edinburgh University Press); Liz Stanley (1992) *The Auto/biographical I: The Theory and Practice of Feminist Auto/biography* (Manchester: Manchester University Press), 16–17; Reina Lewis (1992) 'The Death of the Author and the Resurrection of the Dyke', in Sally Munt (ed.) *New Lesbian Criticism: Literary and Cultural Readings* (Hemel Hempstead: Harvester Wheatsheaf), 17–32.

47. Foucault, 'Author', 125–38.

48. Stanley, *Auto/biographical*, 16.

49. Here I appropriate Anshuman Mondal's description of his misgivings in taking on an interviews project: 'I am more accustomed to working in a library than racing around the country; professionally speaking, I was used to conversing with books rather than people.' Mondal, *Voices*, xiii.

50. For more information on literary prizes, particularly from the perspective of racial and postcolonial politics, see Pierre Bourdieu (1993) *The Field of Cultural Production: Essays on Art and Literature* (New York: Columbia University Press); Graham Huggan (2001) 'Prizing Otherness: A Short History of the Booker', in *The Postcolonial Exotic: Marketing the Margins* (London: Routlege), 105–24; James F. English

(2005) *The Economy of Prestige: Prizes, Awards, and the Circulation of Cultural Value* (Cambridge, MA: Harvard University Press); Claire Squires (2007) *Marketing Literature* (Basingstoke: Palgrave Macmillan), 97–101, 161–71, Sarah Brouillette (2007) *Postcolonial Writers in the Global Literary Marketplace* (Basingstoke: Palgrave Macmillan), 122–3.

51. See, for example, Britta Zangen (2003) 'Women as Readers, Writers, and Judges: The Controversy about the Orange Prize for Fiction', *Women's Studies: An Inter-disciplinary Journal* 32(3): 281–99; Merritt Moseley (2001) 'Britain's Women-Only Orange Prize for Fiction Magazine Article', *World and I* (16 July), http://www.worldandi.com/specialreport/2001/july/Sa21348.htm, and Marianne Macdonald (1996) 'Sexism Storm as Women-only Book Prize Launches' *Independent* (26 January), http://www.independent.co.uk/news/sexism-storm-as-womenonly-book-prize-launches-1325778.html

52. Brouillette, *Marketplace*, 71–2; Robin Yassin-Kassab and Claire Chambers (2010) 'Ghoshwood's Mendacity', *Pulse* (11 May), http://pulsemedia.org/2010/05/11/ghoshwoods-mendacity/

53. See Modood, *Politics*, 3–7.

54. Gail Low and Marion Wynne-Davies (2006) *A Black British Canon?* (Basingstoke: Palgrave Macmillan), 4.

55. See Muslim Writers Awards (2009) 'Unpublished Categories', http://muslimwritersawards.org.uk/submit-work/unpublished-categories

56. See, for example, the *Guardian*'s story about Max Malik, whose 2008 novel *The Butterfly Hunter* was allegedly withdrawn from the Awards because of its 'unpalatable' subject matter, a charge that MWA Director, Irfan Akram, robustly denies. Alison Flood (2008) 'Writers Awards Deny Censorship of "Unpalatable" Novel', guardian.co.uk (13 August) http://www.guardian.co.uk/books/2008/aug/13/muslim.awards.malik

57. Manchester Muslim Writers (2009) 'Home', http://www.muslimwriters.org.uk/ Since accessing this blurb in 2009, the copy has been changed from 'writers in the widest sense' to 'writers of Muslim origin'.

58. Claire Chambers and Fadia Faqir (2010) 'Keynote: Interview', unpublished paper, Postcolonialism and Islam (16–17 April), University of Sunderland. See also Fadia Faqir (2010) 'Dr Claire Chambers interviews Fadia Faqir I', http://www.youtube.com/watch?v=NiaxMdApHXg

59. See Maya Jaggi (2003) 'Colour Bind', *Guardian* (7 February), http://www.guardian.co.uk/books/2003/feb/07/fiction.race

60. Yasmin Crowther (2006) *The Saffron Kitchen* (London: Little, Brown).

61. Nadifa Mohamed (2010) *Black Mamba Boy* (London: HarperCollins).

62. Mirza Waheed (2011) *The Collaborator* (London: Viking).

63. Geoffrey Nash (2007) *The Anglo-Arab Encounter: Fiction and Auto-biography by Arab Writers in English* (Bern: Peter Lang), 87–112.

64. On media representations, see Edward W. Said (1997 [1981]) *Covering Islam: How the Media and the Experts Determine How we see the Rest of the World* (London: Vintage); Elizabeth Poole (2002) *Reporting Islam: Media Representations of British Muslims* (London: I. B. Tauris); John E. Richardson (2004) *(Mis-)Representing Islam: The Racism and Rhetoric of British Broadsheet Newspapers* (Amsterdam: John Benjamin); and Sara Ahmed (2008) *Evaluating the Framing of Islam and Muslims Pre- and Post-9/11: A Contextual Analysis of Articles Published by the New York Times* (Saarbrücken: VDM Verlag).

65. See Jane Hiddleston (2005) 'Shapes and Shadows: (Un)Veiling the Immigrant in Monica Ali's *Brick Lane*', *Journal of Commonwealth Literature* 40(1): 57–72 for background on the novel and Ali's 'burden of representation', and Arifa Akbar (2006) 'Brick Lane Rises up Against Filming of Ali's Novel', *Independent* (22 July), http://www.independent.co.uk/news/uk/this-britain/brick-lane-rises-up-against-filming-of-alis-novel-408885.html for specific information about the demonstrations.

66. V. S. Naipaul (1981) *Among the Believers* (London: Deutsch), 201.

67. Ibid., 11.

68. V. S. Naipaul (1999 [1998]) *Beyond Belief: Islamic Excursions Among the Converted Peoples* (London: Abacus), 1.

69. Abdulrazak Gurnah (2006 [2005]) *Desertion* (London: Bloomsbury), 217.

70. Benedicte Page (2010) 'V. S. Naipaul Withdraws from Turkish Event after Row over Islam Comments', *Guardian* (25 November), 11.

71. Faizfx (2010) 'Halal: Is it Meat you're Looking for' (28 September), http://www.youtube.com/watch?v=9W9s6rzxZ7c

72. John Erickson (1998) *Islam and Postcolonial Narrative* (Cambridge: Cambridge University Press); John C. Hawley (ed.) (1998) *The Postcolonial Crescent: Islam's Impact on Contemporary Literature* (New York: Peter Lang); Malak, *Narratives*; and Peter Morey and Amina Yaqin (2011) *Framing Muslims: Stereotyping and Representation After 9/11* (Cambridge, MA: Harvard University Press).

73. Astri Suhrke (1995) 'Refugees and Asylum in the Muslim World', in Robin Cohen (ed.) *The Cambridge Survey of World Migration*

(Cambridge: Cambridge University Press), 457–60; Rana Kabbani (1992) 'Why Muslims Fear the Future', *Guardian* (21 August), 20.

74. Lorna Bradbury (2010) 'Are These Britain's Best 20 Novelists Under 40?' *Daily Telegraph* (18 June), http://www.telegraph.co.uk/culture/books/7835258/Are-these-Britains-best-20-novelists-under-40.html and Catherine Nielan (2010) 'Canongate Wins Auction for Anam', *The Bookseller* (2 July), http://www.thebookseller.com/news/122493-canongate-wins-auction-for-anam.html

75. Mondal, *Voices*, 106.

76. Said, *Covering*, l.

77. Robin Yassin-Kassab (2009) 'Muslim Writer', *Qunfuz Blog* (21 May), http://qunfuz.blogspot.com/2009/05/muslim-writer.html

78. Sherry Jones (2008) *The Jewel of Medina* (New York: Beaufort). On the attack on Jones's publisher and suspension of the book's UK publication, see Alison Flood (2008) 'Publication of Controversial Muhammad Novel *The Jewel of Medina* Delayed', guardian.co.uk (10 October), http://www.guardian.co.uk/books/2008/oct/10/jewel-of-medina-sherry-jones-aisha

79. Salman Rushdie (1996) *The Moor's Last Sigh* (London: Vintage); Tariq Ali (1993) *Shadows of the Pomegranate Tree* (London: Verso); Mahmoud Darwish and Agha Shahid Ali (2003) 'Eleven Stars Over Andalusia', in Agha Shahid Ali (2003) *Rooms Are Never Finished: Poems* (New York: Norton), 79–93; Ali Sethi (2009) *The Wish Maker* (London: Hamish Hamilton), 258–74; Allama Iqbal (2006) 'The Mosque of Cordoba', in K. C. Kanda (ed.) *Allama Iqbal, Selected Poetry: Text, Translation and Transliteration* (Elgin, IL: New Dawn), 299; Imtiaz Dharker (2006) 'Remember Andalus', in *The Terrorist at My Table* (Newcastle: Bloodaxe), 63–82; Sitara Khan (2000) 'The Fool's Observation', in Debjani Chatterjee (ed.) *The Redbeck Anthology of British South Asian Poetry* (Bradford: Redbeck), 75–6; and Shadab Zeest Hashmi (2010) *Baker of Tarifa* (Madera, CA: Poetic Matrix). My thanks to Muneeza Shamsie for alerting me to some of these examples.

80. See, for example, Mondal, *Voices*, 74–5.

81. Kamila Shamsie (2009) *Burnt Shadows* (London: Bloomsbury); Nadeem Aslam (2008) *The Wasted Vigil* (London: Faber); Feryal Ali Gauhar (2007) *No Space for Further Burials* (Delhi: Women Unlimited).

82. On Aamer Hussein's representations of the conflicts in Iraq, see p. 78 of this volume. Uzma Aslam Khan (2003) *Trespassing* (London: Harper Perennial).

83. See Suman Gupta (2011) *Imagining Iraq: Literature in English and the Iraq Invasion* (Basingstoke: Palgrave Macmillan), 142.

84. Tariq Ali (2005 [1987]) *Street Fighting Years* (London: Verso), 19.

85. Peter G. Mandaville (2001) *Traditional Muslim Politics: Reimagining the Umma* (London: Routledge), xi.

86. Ahdaf Soueif (2004) *Mezzaterra: Fragments from the Common Ground* (London: Bloomsbury), 4.

87. Fadia Faqir (1991) 'Stories from the House of Songs', in Fadia Faqir (ed.) (1998) *In the House of Silence: Autobiographical Essays by Arab Women Writers* (Reading: Garnet), 59.

88. Charles Taylor (1997 [1994]) 'The Politics of Recognition', in Ajay Heble, Donna Palmateer Pennee, and J. R. Tim Struthers (eds) *New Contexts of Canadian Criticism* (Peterborough, ON: Broadview), 98–131, 98.

89. John Siddique (2011) 'John Siddique: Poet and Author', http://www.johnsiddique.co.uk/

90. Zahid Hussain (2011) 'Zahid Hussain: Website', http://www.zahidhussain.com/

91. Office of National Statistics (2001) 'Population Size', http://www.statistics.gov.uk/cci/nugget.asp?id=455

92. Peter Hopkins and Richard Gale (eds) (2009) *Muslims in Britain: Race, Place and Identities* (Edinburgh: Edinburgh University Press), 4–5.

93. See, for example, Lewis, *Young*, 26.

94. H. Connor, C. Tyers, S. Davis, N. D. Tackey, and T. Modood (2003) 'Minority Ethnic Students in Higher Education: Interim Report', *Research Report RR448*, Department for Education and Skills http://www.employment-studies.co.uk/pubs/summary.php?id=rr448

1   Tariq Ali

1. Tariq Ali (2009) *Protocols of the Elders of Sodom and Other Essays* (London: Verso), 38.

2. Ali, *Fighting*, 85–92.

3. Ibid., 103–7, 113–16.

4. Reproduced in ibid., 361–81.

5. Written shortly before he died in 1967, Deutscher's essay 'On the Israeli-Arab War' is reprinted as an appendix to Tariq Ali (2002) *The Clash of Fundamentalisms: Crusades, Jihads and Modernity*

(London: Verso), 314–32. As a 'non-Jewish Jew', who had lost many relatives in the Holocaust and had some optimism on the creation of Israel, Deutscher's essay is remarkable as an early indictment of Israel's neocolonial military-industrial complex.

6. Tariq Ali (2009) *The Idea of Communism* (Calcutta: Seagull), 4.

7. Tariq Ali (2010) *Night of the Golden Butterfly* (London: Verso), 37–8. In addition, Ali writes of his father that 'Moscow became his Mecca', *Clash*, 17, and he provides a tongue-in-cheek comparison of Trotskyism and Wahhabism, *Clash*, 72, footnote 14.

8. See, for example, Tariq Ali (2008) *Pirates of the Caribbean: Axis of Hope* (London: Verso) and Tariq Ali (2010) 'Oliver Stone and Tariq Ali: Brothers in Arms', *Guardian G2* (27 July), 19.

9. Tariq Ali and Howard Brenton (1989) *Iranian Nights* (Royal Court Theatre) (London: Nick Hern); Tariq Ali and Howard Brenton (1990) *Moscow Gold* (London: Nick Hern); Tariq Ali and Howard Brenton (1998) *Ugly Rumours* (Instant Playscript) (London: Nick Hern); Tariq Ali (2003) *The Illustrious Corpse* (Oberon Modern Plays) (London: Absolute Classics).

10. Ali, *Fighting*, 21–8.

11. Ali, *Clash*, 125.

12. Tariq Ali (1970) *Pakistan: Military Rule or People's Power* (New York: Morrow); Tariq Ali (1983) *Can Pakistan Survive? The Death of a State* (Harmondsworth: Penguin); and (2008) *The Duel: Pakistan on the Flight Path of American Power* (London: Simon & Schuster).

13. Tariq Ali (2010) *The Obama Syndrome: Surrender at Home, War Abroad* (London: Verso).

14. Ali, *Butterfly*, 268.

15. Ali, *Clash*, 15–30.

16. Ibid., 4.

17. Ibid., 24, 61–2.

18. Ali, *Duel*, 263.

19. Ali, *Butterfly*, 220. Ali depicts Neelam's faith as a productive response to bereavement.

20. Ibid., 191.

21. Ali, *Duel*, 165.

22. See, for example, Ali, *Butterfly*, 218.

23. Ali's *oeuvre* includes over 30 published texts, and these have already been surveyed in Muneeza Shamsie's excellent (2003) 'Tariq Ali',

Literary Encyclopedia (20 June), http://www.litencyc.com/php/
speople.php?rec=true&UID=4964

24. Ali, *Butterfly*, 111.
25. Madeline Clements (2010) 'Peaceable Kingdoms', *Times Literary Supplement* (28 May), 21.
26. Ali, *Pomegranate*, 140.
27. Ibid., 239.
28. Shamsie, 'Ali', n.p.
29. Tariq Ali (2000) *The Stone Woman* (London: Verso), 89.
30. Ibid., 270–1.
31. Mark R. Cohen (1994) *Under Crescent and Cross* (Princeton: Princeton University Press), 3–4.
32. Tariq Ali (2005) *A Sultan in Palermo* (London: Verso), 41.
33. Edward W. Said (1975) *Beginnings: Intention and Method* (New York: Basic).
34. Ali, *Palermo*, 52–3.
35. This cruel practice which still persists in parts of Sindh and the southern Punjab has already been explored in fiction in Qaisra Shahraz (2001) *The Holy Woman* (London: Black Amber), which Ali references in *Duel*, 291.
36. 'Auratpasand' translates from Urdu as 'like woman'. 'Yasmine' is probably a reference to Yasmina Khadra, the female pseudonym of Algerian writer Mohammed Moulessehoul, whose secular fundamentalist novels mostly fail to recognize France's partial responsibility for Algeria's social collapse of the 1990s, and who speaks of 'Islamofascisme', which Ali critiques as an inappropriate term in *Clash*, 284–6.
37. Ali, *Butterfly*, 188–9, 226.
38. Clements, 'Peaceable', 21.
39. Ali, *Butterfly*, 270.
40. Ibid., 32, and *Fighting*, 62.
41. Compare this with Kureishi's strikingly different view of the Muslim Brotherhood in his interview, p. 238 of this book.
42. Gabriel García Márquez (1983) *Chronicle of a Death Foretold* (London: Pan).
43. Tariq Ali (2010) 'Islamophobia Exposed'. *Socialist Worker* 2209 (10 July), http://www.socialistworker.co.uk/art.php?id=21715
44. He develops this argument in Tariq Ramadan (2005) 'An International Call for Moratorium on Corporal Punishment, Stoning and the Death

Penalty in the Islamic World' (5 April), http://www.tariqramadan.com/An-International-call-for.html

45. Ali, *Fighting*, 19.
46. Ali, *Butterfly*, 209.
47. Ayaan Hirsi Ali (2010) *Nomad: A Personal Journey Through the Clash of Civilizations* (London: Simon and Schuster), 246–51.
48. Ali, *Protocols*, 101–5, 104.
49. Ginny Dougary (2006) 'The Voice of Experience', *Times Online* (9 September), http://www.ginnydougary.co.uk/2006/09/17/the-voice-of-experience/
50. Sahir Ludhianvi (2000) 'Taj Mahal', in *Selected Poems of Sahir Ludhianvi*, trans. Khwaja Tariq Mahmood (Delhi: Star).
51. Tariq Ali (1985) *The Nehrus and the Gandhis: An Indian Dynasty* (London: Picador); Ali, *Obama*.
52. Ali, *Butterfly*, 79.
53. Tariq Ali (1998) *The Book of Saladin* (London: Verso), 7.
54. Ali, *Butterfly*, 231–4.
55. Tariq Ali (2005) *Rough Music: Blair, Bombs, Baghdad, London, Terror* (London: Verso), 83.
56. David Goodhart (2010) 'Labour Must Become the Anti-Immigration Party', *Labour Uncut* (18 May), http://labour-uncut.co.uk/2010/05/18/labour-must-become-the-anti-immigration-party-david-goodhart/
57. Radwa Ashour (2003) *Granada: A Novel* (Middle East Literature in Translation) (Syracuse, NY: Syracuse University Press).
58. Guiseppe Tomasi di Lampedusa (2007) *The Leopard: Revised and with New Material* (London: Vintage) and Leonardo Sciascia (2001) *Sicilian Uncles*, trans. N. S. Thompson (London: Granta).
59. James Joyce (1939) *Finnegans Wake* (London: Faber).
60. David G. Atwill (2006) *The Chinese Sultanate: Islam, Ethnicity, and the Panthay Rebellion in Southwest China, 1856–1873* (Palo Alto, CA: Stanford University Press).

2 Fadia Faqir

1. The dedication to Fadia Faqir (1996) *Pillars of Salt* (London: Quartet Books), v, makes mention of Bradbury and Carter, while the Acknowledgements to Fadia Faqir (2007) *My Name is Salma* (London: Doubleday), 287, include the statement, 'I had guiding

spirits [...]: Angela Carter, Malcolm Bradbury and Lorna Sage, now dead but their souls will always soar above my head.'

2. Faqir, 'House', 61. Soueif, *Mezzaterra*, 4.
3. Faqir, 'House', 59.
4. See, for example, Fadia Faqir (1997) 'Engendering Democracy and Islam', *Third World Quarterly* 18(1): 165–74; Fadia Faqir (2000) 'Arab Democracy Minus Women: Gender, Democracy and Citizenship in Jordan', *Asian Women* 11: 61–89; Fadia Faqir (2001) 'Intrafamily Femicide in Defence of Honour: The Case of Jordan', *Third World Quarterly* 22(1): 65–82.
5. Lindsey Moore (2008) *Arab, Muslim, Woman: Voice and Vision in Postcolonial Literature and Film* (Abingdon: Routledge), 105.
6. Fadia Faqir (2007) *The Cry of the Dove* (New York: Grove Press/Black Cat).
7. Faqir, *Pillars*, 201.
8. Faqir, *Salma*, 140.
9. Faqir, *Pillars*, 86.
10. Fadia Faqir (1987) *Nisanit* (Salcombe: Aidan Ellis), 44–8.
11. Faqir, *Pillars*, 19–21, 40–3, 51–4, 76–7, 111, 116–18, 222–3, 236–7.
12. Faqir, *Salma*, 50, 54–63, 75, 102, 134–6, 141–2, 145, 238.
13. Ibid., 37.
14. Ibid., 253.
15. This is particularly apparent in *Pillars of Salt*, in which Um Saad's description of her life in Amman indicates that Bedouin Maha actually has greater freedom of movement than the city-dweller.
16. Faqir, *Salma*, 8–9, 20–1, 250, 252.
17. Fadia Faqir (2009) 'Spinning a Self in the Language of the Other', unpublished paper, Arab Women Writers in Diaspora: Horizons of Dialogue, University of Manchester (10 December), n.p.
18. Alice Walker (1984 [1983]) *In Search of our Mother's Garden: Womanist Prose* (London: Women's Press), especially xi–xii; Aoi Mori (2000) *Toni Morrison and Womanist Discourse* (New York: Peter Lang); Sugiyama Naoko (2007) '"Blessed Malelessness" as Womanist Critique: Toni Morrison's Representation of Goddess in *Paradise*', *Nanzan Review of American Studies* 29: 177–85.
19. Faqir, *Salma*, 25.
20. Faqir, 'House', 53.
21. Guy Debord (1997) *Comments on the Society of the Spectacle*, trans. Malcolm Imrie (London: Verso).

22. Nash, *Anglo-Arab*, 113.
23. Faqir, *Nisanit*, 149.
24. Ibid., 206.
25. Rushdie argues that 'human beings do not perceive things whole; we are not gods but wounded creatures, cracked lenses, capable only of fractured perceptions'. Rushdie, *Homelands*, 12. Walcott also defends the fragments of postcolonial societies by championing a fractured epistemological or artistic approach: 'Break a vase, and the love that reassembles the fragments is stronger than that love which took its symmetry for granted when it was whole.' Derek Walcott (1993) *The Antilles: Fragments of Epic Memory* (New York: Farrar, Straus & Giroux), n.p.
26. Fadia Faqir (2011) 'A Dalek in a Burqa', *Qantara* (21 April), http://en.qantara.de/A-Dalek-in-a-Burqa/15936c16127i1p169/index.html
27. As is well known, Al-Qa'ida's second-in-command, Ayman al Zawahiri, is an Egyptian surgeon. Dr Fadl, the most important religious scholar of Egyptian Islamic Jihad, has also worked as a medical doctor (Brynjar Lia (2008) *Architect of Global Jihad: The Life of al-Qaida Strategist Abu Mus'ab al-Suri* (New York: Columbia University Press), 88–9). Dr Abul-Harith al Liby, who worked with the Afghan mujahideen, was a Libyan medical doctor (Evan Kohlmann (2004) *Al-Qaida's Jihad in Europe: The Afghan–Bosnian Network* (Oxford: Berg), 80). Finally, in Fadia Faqir's unpublished interview with 'Abu-Jihad', an ex Arab-Afghani fighter, in Amman, May 2010, he stated that many Arab Afghanis were medics.
28. Darwish and Ali, 'Eleven', 82.

3   Aamer Hussein

1. Aamer Hussein (1993) 'Last Companions', in *Mirror to the Sun* (London: Mantra), 118–33.
2. Aamer Hussein (2005) 'The Blue Direction', in *This Other Salt* (London: Saqi), 154–87.
3. Aamer Hussein (2007) 'The Angelic Disposition', in *Insomnia* (London: Saqi), 81–106.
4. Texts by Shahrukh Husain include (2006) *The Wit and Wisdom of Mulla Nasruddin* (Delhi: Rupa); Shahrukh Husain (2006) *The Virago Book of Erotic Myths and Legends* (London: Virago); Shahrukh

Husain (2005) 'Rubies for a Dog: A Fable', in Muneeza Shamsie (ed.) *And the World Changed: Contemporary Stories by Pakistani Women* (Delhi: Women Unlimited), 1–13; Shahrukh Husain and Anita Desai (1997) the screenplay to *In Custody*, dir. Ismael Merchant. Actors: Shashi Kapoor, Shabana Azmi, Om Puri, Sushma Seth, and Neena Gupta (London: BBC).

5. Christopher Shackle, Shahrukh Husain, and David J. Matthews (2003) *Urdu Literature* (Karachi: Alhamra).

6. Aamer Hussein (2002) 'Living in London: A Memoir', *Wasafiri* 17(36): 36–9, 37.

7. Aamer Hussein (2009) *Another Gulmohar Tree* (London: Telegram), 57.

8. For discussion of London as a postcolonial city, see John McLeod (2004) *Postcolonial London* (Abingdon: Routledge) and Sukhdev Sandhu (2003) *London Calling: How Black and Asian Writers Imagined a City* (London: HarperCollins).

9. Hussein, *Gulmohar*, 56.

10. Email correspondence with the author.

11. Aamer Hussein (2007) 'Hibiscus Days: A Story Found in a Drawer', in *Insomnia*, 53–72, 58, 66.

12. Hussein, *Mirror*.

13. Hussein, *Other Salt*.

14. Aamer Hussein (1999) 'The Lost Cantos of the Silken Tiger', in *Other Salt*, 79–102, 89.

15. Ibid., 90–6. For discussion of the postcolonial concept of 'writing back', see Bill Ashcroft, Gareth Griffiths, and Helen Tiffin (2002 [1989]) *The Empire Writes Back: The Theory and Practice of Post-Colonial Literatures* (London: Routledge), 33. Hussein's *Another Gulmohar Tree* acts as a companion piece to 'The Lost Cantos of the Silken Tiger', because in the novella the interpolated story is positioned at the beginning of the narrative.

16. Aamer Hussein (2002) *Turquoise* (London: Saqi); Aamer Hussein (2003) *Cactus Town: Selected Stories* (Karachi: Sama).

17. Hussein, *Insomnia* (London: Saqi) and Hussein (2007) *Insomnia* (Karachi: Oxford University Press).

18. Hussein, *Gulmohar*, n.p.

19. Aamer Hussein (2009) *I Giorni dell'Ibisco* (Rome: La Lepre Edizioni), and Aamer Hussein (2010) *Il Nuvolo Messaggero* (Rome: Caravan Edizioni).

20. Khan, *Trespassing*.

21. See, for example, Shamsie, *Burnt*; Aslam, *Vigil*; Gauhar, *Burials*.

22. Aamer Hussein (1993) 'Your Children', in *Mirror*, 38–60.
23. Aamer Hussein (2007) 'The Book of Maryam', in *Insomnia*, 73–9.
24. Ibid., 77.
25. Hussein, 'Children', 49.
26. Ghulam Abbas (1965) *Chand Tara*, illus. Zainab Abbas (Karachi: Guild Ishā'at Ghar).
27. Aamer Hussein (1999) *Hoops of Fire: Fifty Years of Fiction by Pakistani Women* (London: Saqi); Aamer Hussein (2005) *Kahani: Short Stories by Pakistani Women* (London: Saqi).
28. Aamer Hussein (2011) *The Cloud Messenger* (London: Telegram), 194.
29. Both the fictional 'Lady L' and the historical Ann Lambton are seen as spies and *'éminences grises'* in Iran and return to the north in their later years, becoming increasingly outspoken in their Christian faith. Obituaries (2008) 'Persian professor, Ann Lambton', *Times* (23 July), http://www.timesonline.co.uk/tol/comment/obituaries/article4379464.ece?token=null&offset=0&page=1
30. Hussein, *Cloud*, 166–7.
31. Ibid., 194.
32. Ibid., 127.
33. Hussein, *Gulmohar*, 55.
34. Aamer Hussein (2007) 'The Lark', in *Insomnia*, 123–33, 123–4.
35. Huggan, *Postcolonial Exotic*, 13.
36. Hussein, *Cloud*, 19.
37. Hussein, *Gulmohar*, 53.
38. Ibid., 51.
39. For examples of Indian critique of secularist discourse, see Rajeev Bhargava (2010) *The Promise of India's Secular Democracy* (Delhi: Oxford University Press); Priya Kumar (2008) *Limiting Secularism: The Ethics of Coexistence in Indian Literature and Film* (Minneapolis, MN: University of Minnesota Press); Neelam Srivastava (2008) *Secularism in the Postcolonial Indian Novel: National and Cosmopolitan Narratives in English* (Abingdon: Routledge).
40. For more on this socialist literary movement, which began in India in the 1930s, but continued to exert great influence on art being produced in post-Partition India and Pakistan, see Priyamvada Gopal (2005) *Literary Radicalism in India: Gender, Nation and the Transition to Independence* (London: Routledge).
41. Aamer Hussein (2005) 'Sweet Rice', in *Other Salt*, 31–40.
42. Aamer Hussein (2005) 'This Other Salt', in *Other Salt*, 7–30, 29–30.

43. Hussein, *Gulmohar*, 60.
44. Hussein 'Lark', 123.
45. Aamer Hussein (2002) 'What Do You Call Those Birds?', in *Turquoise*, 61–84, 80–1; Hussein, *Gulmohar*, 104.
46. Mohammad Marmaduke Pickthall (2000) *The Meaning of the Glorious Qur'an: An Explanatory Translation* (London: Albirr Foundation), 468–71.
47. See Christopher Andreae (2007) *Mary Fedden: Enigmas and Variations* (Aldershot: Lund Humphries).
48. Lynn Knight (1990) 'Introduction', in E. H. Young, *Celia* (London: Virago [1937]), i–vi.
49. Lara Pawson (2009) 'Aamer Hussen's *Another Gulmohar Tree'*, *Times Literary Supplement* (29 May), 19.
50. Marie-Louise von Franz (1996 [1987]) *The Interpretation of Fairy Tales* (Boston, MA: Shambhala).
51. Doris Lessing (1982) 'Introduction', in Widad El Sakkakini, *First Among Sufis: The Life and Thought of Rabia al-Adawiyya, the Woman Saint of Basra*, trans. Nabil Safwat (London: Octagon Press), 1–6. Lessing writes of Rabia that, 'there survives in the terse accounts of the authentic traditions about her, some of no more than a few words, a dry wit, an originality, something salty and simple'; 'Introduction', 5.
52. Mir Amman (2006) *A Tale of Four Dervishes*, trans. Mohammed Zakir (Harmondsworth: Penguin); Widad El Sakkakini (1982) *First Among Sufis: The Life and Thought of Rabia al-Adawiyya, the Woman Saint of Basra*, trans. Nabil Safwat (London: Octagon Press); Shah Waliullah (1982) *The Sacred Knowledge of the Higher Functions of the Mind: The Altaf al-Quds of Shah Waliullah*, trans. G. N. Jalbani and David Pendlebury (London: Octagon).
53. Attia Hosain (1961) *Sunlight on a Broken Column* (London: Chatto & Windus); Attia Hosain (1988 [1953]) *Phoenix Fled* (London: Virago).
54. John Freeman (ed.) (2010) *Granta 112: Pakistan* (London: Granta).
55. For example, Aamer Hussein (1997) 'The Lost Cantos of the Silken Tiger', in Muneeza Shamsie (ed.) (1997) *A Dragonfly in the Sun: An Anthology of Pakistani Writing in English* (Oxford: Oxford University Press), 454–76.
56. Cesare Pavese (1952 [1950]) *The Moon and the Bonfire*, trans. Louise Sinclair (London: Peter Owen).
57. Gustave Flaubert (2009 [1877]) *A Simple Heart*, trans. Charlotte Mandell (Brooklyn, NY: Melville House).

4 Leila Aboulela

1. According to one online resource, her mother was 'Sudan's first ever female demographer'. English PEN (2008) 'Leila Aboulela', http://penatlas.org/online/index.php?option=com_content&task=view&id=109&Itemid=16

2. Anita Fabos (2008) *'Brothers' or Others? Gender and Propriety for Muslim Arab Sudanese in Egypt* (Oxford: Berghahn).

3. Edgar O'Ballance (2000) *Sudan, Civil War and Terrorism, 1956–99* (Basingstoke: Macmillan), vii–viii.

4. Ibid., 123, 205; Julie Flint and Alex de Waal (2005) *Darfur: A Short History of a Long War* (London: Zed), 126–34; Robert O. Collins (2006) 'Disaster in Darfur: Historical Overview', in Samuel Totten and Eric Markusen (eds) *Genocide in Darfur: Investigating the Atrocities in the Sudan* (London: Routledge), 3–24, 16.

5. Leila Aboulela (2002) 'Moving Away from Accuracy', *Alif: Journal of Comparative Poetics* 22: 198–207, 204.

6. Leila Aboulela (2000) 'And my Fate was Scotland', in Kevin MacNeil and Alec Finlay (eds) *Wish I Was Here: A Scottish Multicultural Anthology* (Edinburgh: Polygon), 175–92, 189.

7. See McLeod, *Postcolonial*; Sandhu, *Calling*.

8. Leila Aboulela (2001) *Coloured Lights* (Edinburgh: Polygon), 132.

9. Leila Aboulela (1999) *The Translator* (Oxford: Heinemann Educational), 166–7.

10. Leila Aboulela (2005) *Minaret* (London: Bloomsbury), 81.

11. Ibid., 100.

12. Claire Chambers (2009) 'An Interview with Leila Aboulela', *Contemporary Women's Writing* 3(1): 86–102.

13. For more on Hassan Awad Aboulela, see Lee Randall (2010) 'Interview: Leila Aboulela' (4 December), http://living.scotsman.com/books/Interview-Leila-Aboulela-author.6649588.jp

14. See David Steele (1998) 'Lord Salisbury, the "False Religion" of Islam, and the Reconquest of the Sudan', in Edward M. Spiers (ed.) *Sudan: The Reconquest Reappraised* (London: Frank Cass), 11–33.

15. *Minaret* book blurb, quoting *The Muslim News*.

16. Aboulela, *Minaret*, 186.

17. Jack Straw (2006) 'I Felt Uneasy Talking to Someone I Couldn't See' (full text of Straw's article originally in the *Lancashire Telegraph*), *Guardian* (6 October), 1.

18. See, for example, Faiza Guène (2006) *Just Like Tomorrow*, trans. Sarah Adams (London: Chatto & Windus); Faiza Guène (2006) *Dreams from the Endz*, trans. Sarah Ardizzone (London: Chatto & Windus); Khaled Hosseini (2004) *The Kite Runner* (London: Bloomsbury); Khaled Hosseini (2007) *A Thousand Splendid Suns* (London: Bloomsbury); Rajaa AlSanea (2008) *Girls of Riyadh*, trans. Marilyn Booth (London: Penguin); Alaa Al Aswany (2002) *The Yacoubian Building*, trans. Humphrey Davis (London: HarperCollins); Alaa Al Aswany (2008) *Chicago* (London: Fourth Estate).

19. Over the budding romance between her and Tamer, Najwa chooses the religious pilgrimage of Hajj. See Aboulela, *Minaret*, 209.

20. Leila Ahmed is the author of, amongst other works (1992) *Women and Gender in Islam: Historical Roots of a Modern Debate* (New Haven, CT: Yale University Press).

21. Al-Shatie (2006) *The Wives of Prophet Muhammad* (Piscataway, NJ: Gorgias Press).

22. Aboulela, *Minaret*, 175.

5   Abdulrazak Gurnah

1. Abdulrazak Gurnah (2002) 'An Idea of the Past', *Moving Worlds* 2(2): 6–17, 12.

2. See Malak, *Narratives*, 57.

3. Gurnah documents racist discourse including anti-Indian, anti-African, and anti-Arab sentiment (Abdulrazak Gurnah (1987) *Memory of Departure* (London: Jonathan Cape), 72, 76, 107; Gurnah, 'Idea', 12).

4. Gurnah, *Memory*, 114. The brutality of both the Germans and the British is documented in Abdulrazak Gurnah (2004 [1994]) *Paradise* (London: Bloomsbury), 115, 119.

5. In Abdulrazak Gurnah (2002 [2001]) *By the Sea* (London: Bloomsbury), for example, Latif spends time in East Germany before coming to Britain, 104–39.

6. Abdulrazak Gurnah (1993, 1995) *Essays on African Writing: A Re-Evaluation: 1 and 2* (London Heinemann); Abdulrazak Gurnah (ed.) (2007) *The Cambridge Companion to Salman Rushdie* (Cambridge: Cambridge University Press).

7. Abdulrazak Gurnah (1997 [1996]) *Admiring Silence* (Harmondsworth: Penguin), 75.

8. Gurnah, *Desertion*, 257.

9. Abdulrazak Gurnah (2011) *The Last Gift* (London: Bloomsbury), 166–7, 230–4.

10. Abdulrazak Gurnah (2004) 'Writing and Place', *World Literature Today* (May–August), 26–8, 26.

11. Ibid., 28.

12. For example, Luca Prono (2005) 'Abdulrazak Gurnah: Biography', http://www.contemporarywriters.com/authors/?p=auth46, argues that *Memory of Departure* 'document[s] the immigrant experience in contemporary Britain' (n.p.).

13. Gurnah, *Memory*, 7, 15, 19–23.

14. Abdulrazak Gurnah (1988) *Pilgrim's Way* (London: Jonathan Cape); Abdulrazak Gurnah (1990) *Dottie* (London: Jonathan Cape).

15. See Dorothy A. Brown (2003) *Critical Race Theory: Cases, Materials and Problems* (Eagan, MN: West Group), 3.

16. Sue *et al.*, 'Racial Microaggressions', 183.

17. Gurnah, *Admiring*, 9.

18. Ibid., 10.

19. Gayatri Chakravorty Spivak (1988) 'Can the Subaltern Speak?', in Cary Nelson and Lawrence Grossberg (eds) (1988) *Marxism and the Interpretation of Culture* (Basingstoke: Macmillan Education), 271–313, 280–3 and Gayatri Chakravorty Spivak (1999) *A Critique of Postcolonial Reason: Toward a History of the Vanishing Present* (Cambridge, MA: Harvard University Press), 266–9.

20. Gurnah, *Admiring*, 21.

21. In the Qur'an, this is one of the ingredients out of which Allah made man.

22. Probably because phonetic representations of Arabic words vary according to the writer's mother tongue, subcontinental writers tend to spell the name 'Zuleikha', whereas Gurnah consistently writes 'Zulekha'.

23. Gurnah, *Paradise*, 238–9.

24. Ibid., 247.

25. Gurnah, *Sea*, 51.

26. Ibid., 50.

27. Gurnah, *Desertion*, 87, 200.

28. Ibid., 97–8.

29. Ibid., 113.

30. Ibid., 146–7.

31. Ibid., 232.

32. Ibid., 257–8.

33. Ibid., 202–3.

34. Ibid., 249.

35. Ibid., 254.

36. Gurnah, *Gift*, 9.

37. Ibid., 196.

38. Ibid., 73.

39. Ahdaf Soueif (1996 [1983]) *Aisha* (London: Bloomsbury).

40. Tariq Mehmood (1983) *Hand on the Sun* (Harmondsworth: Penguin).

41. See Avtar Brah (1996) *Cartographies of Diaspora: Contesting Identities* (London: Routledge); Emily Grabham, Davina Cooper, Jane Krishnadas, and Didi Herman (eds) (2009) *Intersectionality and Beyond: Law, Power and the Politics of Location* (Abingdon: Routledge-Cavendish).

42. Amitav Ghosh (1992) *In an Antique Land* (London: Granta), 80–1, 263.

43. Ghosh only uses the term 'archipelago of towns' once to describe Cairo as a city that has evolved out of a number of different villages (Ghosh, *Antique*, 33). However, elsewhere in *In an Antique Land*, he also suggests the existence of a conglomerate of urban satellites lining the Indian Ocean, whose economy largely excludes the rural areas.

44. Abu-Lughod, following Fernand Braudel, also portrays medieval Mediterranean society as an 'archipelago of towns', which term, she argues, 'capture[s] the fact that, within the same general region, a variety of social formations coexisted'. Janet L. Abu-Lughod (1989) *Before European Hegemony: The World System, A.D. 1250–1350* (New York: Oxford University Press), 13.

45. Rushdie, *Imaginary*, 9; quoted in Gurnah, *Rushdie*, 1.

46. Gurnah, 'Idea', 12.

47. Ibid., 14.

48. Ibid., 10–13, citing Wole Soyinka (1976) *Myth, Literature and the African World* (Cambridge: Cambridge University Press).

49. Gurnah, *Paradise*, 229.

50. Ali, *Clash*, 222–3.

51. Gurnah, *Memory*, 39.

52. Nisha Jones (2005) 'Abdulrazak Gurnah in Conversation', *Wasafiri* (Winter): 37–42, 39.

53. Homi K. Bhabha (1994) *The Location of Culture* (London: Routledge), 116.

54. Gurnah, *Admiring*, 66–7.

55. Gurnah, *Sea*, 65. Here Saleh Omar cites the famous formulation 'I preferred not to' from Herman Melville (1981 [1853]) 'Bartleby', in *Billy Budd, Sailor and Other Stories* (New York: Bantam), 95–130, 103. This passage from Gurnah's novel is analysed virtuosically in David Farrier (2008) 'Terms of Hospitality: Abdulrazak Gurnah's *By the Sea*', *Journal of Commonwealth Literature* 43(3): 121–39, 132–3.

56. Gurnah, *Sea*, 12.

57. Gurnah, 'Idea', 6–10.

6 Nadeem Aslam

1. See Gopal, *Radicalism*.

2. Muneeza Shamsie (2007) 'Nadeem Aslam', *Literary Encyclopedia* (2 March), http://www.litencyc.com/php/speople.php?rec=true&UID=11771

3. Ibid.

4. Nadeem Aslam (2004) *Maps for Lost Lovers* (London: Bloomsbury), 155.

5. Nadeem Aslam (1993) *Season of the Rainbirds* (London: Bloomsbury), 170–2.

6. Aslam, *Maps*, 155, 200, 212.

7. Aslam, *Vigil*, 208.

8. Nadeem Aslam (2010) 'Leila in the Wilderness', in John Freeman (ed.) *Granta 112: Pakistan* (London: Granta), 9–53, 21.

9. V. S. Naipaul (2009 [1999]) *Letters Between a Father and Son* (London: Picador), especially 391–449; Orhan Pamuk (2006) 'My Father's Suitcase' (lecture on accepting the Nobel Prize), http://nobelprize.org/nobel_prizes/literature/laureates/2006/pamuk-lecture_en.html; Hanif Kureishi (2004) *My Ear at His Heart: Reading My Father* (London: Faber).

10. Nadeem Aslam (1993) 'God and Me', *Granta 93*, http://www.granta.com/Online-Only/Nadeem-Aslam

11. Salman Rushdie (1983) *Shame* (London: Picador); Rukhsana Ahmad (ed.) (1991) *We Sinful Women: Contemporary Urdu Feminist Poetry* (London: Women's Press).

12. Agha Shahid Ali (1997) *The Country without a Post Office* (New York: Norton), especially 43.

13. Marianne Brace (2004) 'Nadeem Aslam: A Question of Honour', *Independent* (11 June), http://enjoyment.independent.co.uk/books/features/article42260.ece

14. Jonathan Franzen (2010) 'On Writing *The Corrections*', *Guardian Review* (30 October), 6.

15. Robin Yassin-Kassab (2008) 'Two Reviews', *Qunfuz Blog* (22 September), http://qunfuz.com/2008/09/23/two-reviews/, and Lindsey Moore (2009) 'British Muslim Identities and Spectres of Terror in Nadeem Aslam's *Maps for Lost Lovers*', *Postcolonial Text* 5(2): 1–19, 9.

16. Nadeem Aslam (n.d.) '*Maps for Lost Lovers* by Nadeem Aslam: Reading Guide', http://www.faber.co.uk/site-media/reading-guides/maps-for-lost-lovers_reading-guide.pdf

17. Aslam, *Maps*, 11.

18. W. B. Yeats (2000 [1916]) 'Easter 1916', in *Selected Poems*, ed. and intro. Timothy Walsh (London: Penguin), 119–21, 121.

19. Aslam, *Maps*, 312.

20. Ibid., 312.

21. Aslam, 'Leila', 20.

22. Ibid., 23.

23. Shamsie, 'Aslam', n.p.

24. Aslam, *Vigil*, 6.

25. See Ahmed Rashid (2001 [2000]) *Taliban: The Story of the Afghan Warlords* (London: Pan Macmillan), 68, 76.

26. Aslam, *Vigil*, 112.

27. See Yassin-Kassab, 'Two Reviews', n.p. and James Buchan (2008) 'Between Two Worlds', *Guardian Review* (20 September), 10.

28. Kamila Shamsie (2005) *Broken Verses* (London: Bloomsbury), 49–51, 327–9, and Hosseini, *Suns*, 240.

29. Aslam, 'Wilderness', 47.

30. K. Shamsie, *Broken*, 49.

31. Aslam, 'Leila', 48.

32. Tunku Varadarajan (2010) 'Wole Soyinka's British Problem', *The Daily Beast* (31 January), http://www.thedailybeast.com/blogs-and-stories/2010-01-31/wole-soyinkas-british-problem/?cid=hp:mainpromo5

33. Ibid., n.p.

34. See Yassin-Kassab, 'Two Reviews', n.p. and Buchan 'Worlds', 10.

35. Aslam, *Vigil*, 112.

36. Aslam, *Maps*, 122 contains some particularly good examples.

37. Ibid., n.p.
38. Aslam, *Vigil*, n.p.
39. For more on the Bharatiya Janata Party (BJP) slogan about India's 'shining' economy, see Andrew Wyatt (2005) 'Building the Temples of Postmodern India: Economic Construction of National Identity', *Contemporary South Asia* 14(4): 465–80.
40. Rushdie (1991) 'In God We Trust', in *Imaginary*, 376–92, 376.
41. James Joyce (1989 [1914]) 'The Sisters', in *Dubliners* (London: Grafton), 7–17.
42. See the discussion of British Muslim children's under-attainment as compared with that of non-Muslim children, pp. 31–2.
43. Nawal El Saadawi (1997) *The Nawal El Saadawi Reader* (London: Zed), 43.
44. He has written up this metaphor in a recent essay, Nadeem Aslam (2010) 'Where to Begin', *Granta Online* (29 September), http://www.granta.com/Online-Only/Where-to-Begin
45. Aslam, *Maps*, 319–20.
46. See Bradford Museums, Galleries and Heritage. 'Bradford Heritage and Recording Unit [BHRU]'s Belle Vue Archive', http://www.bradfordmuseums.org/bradfordmuseum/index.php?a=wordsearch&s=gallery&w=belle+vue&go=go
47. Aslam 'God and Me'.
48. The Tablighi Jamaat, or Society for the Propagation of Religion, is a proselytizing, apparently non-political Deobandi sect, based around six foundational Islamic principles. It was founded by an Indian Muslim, Muhammad Ilyas, in the mid-1920s, and spread around the world from the late 1950s onwards, having particular influence among inhabitants of, and migrants from, the Indian subcontinent and Maghrebi North Africa. See Philip Lewis (1994) *Islamic Britain: Religion, Politics and Identity Among British Muslims* (London: I. B. Tauris), 36, 39, 47, 185; John King (1997) 'Tablighi Jamaat and the Deobandi Mosques in Britain', in Steven Vertovec and Ceri Peach (eds) *Islam in Europe: The Politics of Religion and Community* (Basingstoke: Macmillan), 129–46; and Jocelyne Cesari (2004) *Where Islam and Democracy Meet: Muslims in Europe and the United States* (Basingstoke: Palgrave Macmillan), 93–5, 103–4. However, in recent years and especially because Mohammed Sidique Khan and Shehzad Tanweer were said to have worshipped at the Markazi mosque in Dewsbury before leading the 7/7 attacks, the Tablighi movement has incurred scrutiny as a possible locus of

terrorism. For a summary of this background, see Nicholas Howenstein (2007) 'Islamist Networks: The Case of Tablighi Jamaat', *United States Institute of Peace*, http://www.usip.org/publications/islamist-networks-case-tablighi-jamaat

49. Aslam, 'Begin'.

50. Aslam is correct that Pakistan is one of the countries with an inverse sex ratio, but it should be noted that India's men to women ratio is worse, with particularly high rates of young boys compared with girls, probably due to female infanticide. Neighbouring Afghanistan, on the other hand, has a lower rate of young boys to girls as compared with the world average. See Wikipedia (n.d.) 'List of Countries by Sex Ratio', http://en.wikipedia.org/wiki/List_of_countries_by_sex_ratio. Readers should be very wary about drawing any inference that female infanticide is connected to Islam, as the practice seems also to be tangled up in Hinduism, culure, and other factors.

51. Jean-Marie Gustave Le Clézio (2008) 'In the Forest of Paradoxes', *Nobel Lecture* (7 December), http://nobelprize.org/nobel_prizes/literature/laureates/2008/clezio-lecture_en.html

52. Qurratulain Hyder (2003 [1959]) *River of Fire* [*Ag ka Dariya*] (New York: New Directions).

53. Derek Walcott (1992 [1979]) 'The Schooner *Flight*', in *Collected Poems* (London: Faber), 345–61, 346.

7 Tahmima Anam

1. Karin Bergquist (2003) 'Outspoken Editor from Bangladesh: Mahfuz Anam' (14 July), http://www.culturebase.net/artist.php?1271

2. BBC (2007) 'Violence over Bangladesh Cartoon' (21 September), http://news.bbc.co.uk/1/hi/world/south_asia/7006528.stm

3. See Pipl (2011) 'Shaheen Anam', http://pipl.com/directory/people/Shaheen/Anam and Shaheen Anam (1999) 'Women Coping with Floods', in Imtiaz Ahmed (ed.) *Living With Floods: An Exercise in Alternatives* (Dhaka: University Press), 29–31.

4. Abul Mansur Ahmad (1978) *Atmakatha* (Dhaka: Khosaroja Kitaba Mahala).

5. Rana Razzaq (2007) 'Abul Mansur Ahmad', *Banglapedia*, http://www.banglapedia.org/httpdocs/HT/A_0107.HTM

6. Tahmima Anam (2005) 'Fixing the Past: War, Violence, and the Habitations of Memory in Post-Independence Bangladesh' (Cambridge, MA: University of Harvard Unpublished PhD Thesis).

7. Tareque Masud and Catherine Masud (2002) *The Clay Bird*, dir. Tareque Masud. Actors: Nurul Islam Bablu, Russell Farazi, Jayanto Chattopadhyay, Rokeya Prachy, and Soaeb Islam (New York: Oscilloscope).

8. Catherine Nielan (2006) 'Tahmima Anam: Golden Girl', *The Bookseller* (12 December), http://www.thebookseller.com/control/?p=1&msg Code=2. BBC (2007) 'The Family Story in Bangladesh's War' (23 April), http://news.bbc.co.uk/1/hi/world/south_asia/6434479.stm; Tahmima Anam (2007) *A Golden Age* (London: John Murray), 259–65.

9. Anam, *Golden*, 3.

10. Ibid., 16.

11. Christophe Jaffrelot (2004) *A History of Pakistan and its Origins* (London: Anthem), 73–6.

12. Nielan, 'Canongate'.

13. For discussion of the Tablighi Jamaat, see pp. 296–7, note 48.

14. Tahmima Anam (2011) *The Good Muslim* (Edinburgh: Canongate), 14.

15. See, for example, Mahmood Mamdani (2004) *Good Muslim, Bad Muslim: America, the Cold War, and the Roots of Terror* (New York: Pantheon).

16. Tahmima Anam (moderator) (2009) 'Politics and Place in Fiction: Kamila Shamsie, Daniyal Mueenuddin, Nadeem Aslam', unpublished panel, London: Asia House (18 May).

17. Anam, *Golden*, 276.

18. Anam *Good*, 294–6.

19. Motion's words are quoted in Vanessa Thorpe and Mahtab Haider (2006) 'New Fiction Star Taps Bangladeshi Roots' *Observer* (26 November), 22.

20. Adib Khan (1994) *Seasonal Adjustments* (St Leonards, NSW: Allen & Unwin).

21. Manzu Islam (2010) *Song of Our Swampland* (Leeds: Peepal Tree).

22. Salman Rushdie (1981) *Midnight's Children* (London: Jonathan Cape); Kamila Shamsie (2003 [2002]) *Kartography* (London: Bloomsbury); Ghazala Hameed and Durdana Soomro (2006) *Bengal Raag* (Dhaka: Writers Ink); Moni Mohsin (2006) *The End of Innocence* (London: Fig Tree); Sorayya Khan (2006) *Noor* (Wilmington, NC: Publishing Laboratory).

23. Selina Hossain (2007) *Selected Short Stories* (Dhaka: Bangla Academy).
24. Anisul Hoque (2003) *Maa* [*Mother*], available as untranslated ebook: http://www.somoy.com/pdf/maa_emb.pdf
25. Jahanara Imam (1989) *Of Blood and Fire: The Untold Story of Bangladesh's War of Independence* (Delhi: Stirling).
26. Tahmima Anam and Kamila Shamsie (2009) 'History and the Storyteller: A Dialogue' (Leeds: University of Leeds Unpublished Arthur Ravenscroft Lecture).
27. Thought by many to be the Qur'an's most excellent verse, Rehana regularly recites Aytul Kursi (the Throne Verse). Anam, *Golden*, 113, 136, 253.
28. Ibid., 248.
29. Ibid., 237.
30. Ibid., 227.
31. Ibid., 118–20, 141.
32. Ibid., 260–1.
33. Ibid., 216.
34. Ibid., 276.
35. Tahmima Anam (2007) 'Bangladesh: Give me Back my Country', *New Statesman* (22 January), http://www.newstatesman.com/asia/2007/01/bangladesh-bnp-election-vote
36. See, for example, Thorpe and Haider, 'New', 22; and Alison Roberts (2007) 'Is Tahmima the new Monica Ali?' *Evening Standard* (9 March), http://www.thefreelibrary.com/Is+Tahmima+the+new+Monica+Ali%3B+She%27s+been+hailed+as+a+major+talent,...-a0160375694
37. Anam, *Golden*, 145–7.
38. Ibid., 84, 255.
39. Ibid., 37.
40. Ibid., 84.
41. Ibid., 142.
42. Ibid., 143, 253, 255.
43. Ibid., 138.
44. Ibid., 143.

8 Mohsin Hamid

1. Mohsin Hamid (2007) 'After 60 Years, Will Pakistan Be Reborn?' *The New York Times* (15 August), http://www.mohsinhamid.com/pakistan60years.html

2. Anita Desai (2000) 'Passion in Lahore', *New York Review of Books* (21 December), http://www.nybooks.com/articles/archives/2000/dec/21/passion-in-lahore/
3. Mohsin Hamid (2000) *Moth Smoke* (London: Granta), 101–10.
4. Afzar Ali, dir. (2002) *Daira* [*Circle of Life*]. Actors: Adnan Siddiqui, Ayeshah Alam, Aijaz Aslam, Shahzad Nawaz, and Amir Abbas (Karachi: Halofly Entertainment Consortium).
5. Mohsin Hamid (2007) 'General Pervez Musharraf: Pakistan's Big Beast Unleashed', *Independent* (11 February), http://www.mohsinhamid.com/bigbeastunleashed.html
6. See, for example, Sujata Patel and Alice Thorner (eds) (1995) *Bombay: Mosaic of Modern Culture* (Bombay: Oxford University Press); Thomas Blom Hansen (2001) *Wages of Violence: Naming and Identity in Postcolonial Bombay* (Princeton: Princeton University Press); Suketu Mehta (2005) *Maximum City: Bombay Lost and Found* (London: Headline Review); Gyan Prakash (2010) *Mumbai Fables* (Princeton: Princeton University Press).
7. Sukanta Chaudhuri (ed.) (1990, 1995) *Calcutta: The Living City: Volumes 1 and 2* (Delhi: Oxford University Press); Anita Desai and Krishna Dutta (2008) *Calcutta: A Cultural and Literary History* (Oxford: Signal); Nilanjana Gupta, Sipra Mukherjee, and Himadri Banerjee (eds) (2009) *Calcutta Mosaic: Essays and Interviews on the Minority Communities of Calcutta* (Delhi: Anthem).
8. William Dalrymple (1994) *City of Djinns: A Year in Delhi* (London: Flamingo); H. K. Kaul (ed.) (1997) *Historic Delhi: An Anthology* (Delhi: Oxford University Press); Jyoti Hosagrahar (2005) *Indigenous Modernities: Negotiating Architecture, Urbanism, and Colonialism in Delhi* (Abingdon: Routledge).
9. Perhaps the most important exception is William J. Glover (2008) *Making Lahore Modern: Constructing and Imagining a Colonial City* (Minneapolis, MN: University of Minnesota Press).
10. Bapsi Sidhwa (1988) *Ice-Candy Man* (London: Heinemann); later published in the US as (1991) *Cracking India* (Minneapolis, MN: Milkweed).
11. Hamid, *Moth*, 50.
12. Mohsin Hamid (2005 [2003]) 'The Pathos of Exile', in Bapsi Sidhwa (ed.) *City of Sin and Splendour: Writings on Lahore* (Delhi: Oxford University Press), 243–50, 245.
13. Ibid., 247.

14. Ibid.
15. Ibid., 247–8.
16. Ibid., 250.
17. Ibid., 245.
18. Mohsin Hamid (2010) 'On Fatherhood', *Paper Magazine*, http://www.mohsinhamid.com/onfatherhood.html and Mohsin Hamid (2010) 'The Real Problem in the Afghan War is India, Pakistan and Kashmir', *Washington Post* (8 August), http://www. washingtonpost.com/wp-dyn/content/article/2010/08/06/AR2010080602658.html
19. Mohsin Hamid (2007) *The Reluctant Fundamentalist* (London: Hamish Hamilton), 130.
20. Erica's institutionalization in a psychiatric hospital, her writerly ambitions, and fragile beauty recall Esther's experiences in Sylvia Plath (1963) *The Bell Jar* (London: Heinemann). As Muneeza Shamsie observes, Erica's name denotes three syllables of 'America': Muneeza Shamsie (2009) '*The Reluctant Fundamentalist*', *Literary Encyclopedia* (21 May), http://www.litencyc.com/php/sworks. php?rec=true&UID=23135
21. Hamid, *Reluctant*, 152.
22. Ibid., 179.
23. H. M. Naqvi (2009) *Home Boy* (New York: Shaye Areheart).
24. Albert Camus (2006 [1956]) *The Fall*, trans. Robin Buss (London: Penguin).
25. NBCC (2007) 'Critical Outakes: Mohsin Hamid on Camus, Immigration and Love' *Critical Mass* (30 March), http://bookcritics. org/blog/archive/critical_outakes_mohsin_hamid_on_camus_immigration_and_love/
26. Huntington, 'Clash', and *Clash*.
27. Changez argues, 'you should not imagine that we Pakistanis are all potential terrorists, just as we should not imagine that you Americans are all undercover assassins' (Hamid, *Reluctant*, 183), while a rickshaw driver in Shamsie's *Burnt Shadows* indirectly tells Harry, 'If I don't overcharge an American, everyone will know I work with the CIA' (Shamsie, *Burnt*, 151).
28. Mohsin Hamid (2006) 'Focus on the Fundamentals', *Paris Review* 178 (Fall), http://www.theparisreview.org/fiction/5645/focus-on-the-fundamentals-mohsin-hamid
29. Hamid, *Reluctant*, 87, 51.

30. Hanif Kureishi (2010) 'Weddings and Beheadings', in *Collected Stories* (London: Faber), 611–13, 613.

31. Mohsin Hamid (2010) 'A Beheading', in John Freeman (ed.) *Granta 112* (London: Granta), 193–5, 195.

32. Mohsin Hamid (2007) 'Pakistan's Silent Majority is Not to be Feared', *New York Times* (27 March), http://www.nytimes.com/2007/03/27/opinion/27mohsin.html. Hamid is criticized for his political stance in Bruce King's rather reactionary (2007) 'The Image of the United States in Three Pakistani Novels', *Totalitarian Movements and Political Religions* 8(3–4): 683–8.

33. See Mohsin Hamid (2006) 'Divided We Fall', *Time Asia* (4 September), http://www.mohsinhamid.com/dividedwefall.html

34. Ibid.

35. Hamid, *Moth*, 121–2. See also Bhumitra Chakma (2009) *Pakistan's Nuclear Weapons* (Abingdon: Oxford).

36. Arundhati Roy (1998) 'The End of Imagination', *Guardian* (1 August), http://www.ratical.org/ratville/nukes/endOfImagine.html.

37. Hamid, *Reluctant*, 152. See also Michael Hardt and Antonio Negri (2001) *Empire* (Cambridge, MA: Harvard University Press).

38. Hamid, *Reluctant*, 48.

39. Ibid., 98.

40. Robin Yassin-Kassab (2007) 'Review of *The Reluctant Fundamentalist*', *Qunfuz* (1 December) http://qunfuz.com/2007/12/01/the-reluctant-fundamentalist/

9 Robin Yassin-Kassab

1. Robin Yassin-Kassab (2008) 'Leaving Oman', *Qunfuz Blog* (30 June), http://qunfuz.com/2008/06/30/leaving-oman/

2. See Sandhu, *Calling* and McLeod, *Postcolonial*.

3. Robin Yassin-Kassab (2008) *The Road from Damascus* (London: Hamish Hamilton), 28–9.

4. Hanan al-Shaykh (2002 [2001]) *Only in London*, trans. Catherine Cobham (London: Bloomsbury).

5. Morey and Yaqin, *Framing*.

6. See Robin Yassin-Kassab (2010) 'Defamation and Binary Idiocy', *Qunfuz Blog* (22 February), http://qunfuz.com/2010/02/22/defamation-and-binary-idiocy-2/

7. Rod Mills (2010) 'Fury at Traitor who Backs our Enemies', *Daily Express* (22 February), http://www.express.co.uk/posts/view/159749/Fury-at-traitor-who-backs-our-enemies

8. Yassin-Kassab, *Road*, 4.

9. Ibid., 5.

10. Ibid., 100.

11. Ibid., 204.

12. Ibid.

13. Ibid., 344–9.

14. Ibid., 245.

15. Ibid., vii.

16. Ibid., 116.

17. Robin Yassin-Kassab (2008) 'My Wife Wears the Hijab. I Wish she Didn't', *Observer Woman* (2 November), 38.

18. Yassin-Kassab, *Road*, 37–8.

19. Sameer Rahim (2008) 'In Search of an Authentic Arab Self', *Telegraph* (26 July), http://www.telegraph.co.uk/culture/books/fictionreviews/3557254/In-search-of-an-authentic-Arab-self.html. The word used is actually 'sincere'.

20. Yassin-Kassab, *Road*, 233.

21. Ibid., 240.

22. Ibid., 241.

23. Rowan Williams (2008) 'Civil and Religious Law in England: A Religious Perspective', guardian.co.uk (7 February), http://www.guardian.co.uk/uk/2008/feb/07/religion.world2

24. Rushdie, *Verses*, 267.

25. Blurb from Rushdie, *Midnight's Children*. The phrase originally appeared in Clark Blaise (1981) 'A Novel of India's Coming of Age', *New York Times* (19 April), http://www.nytimes.com/books/99/04/18/specials/rushdie-midnight.html

26. Robin Yassin-Kassab (2008) *'Maps for Lost Lovers* and Writerly Responsibility', *Qunfuz Blog* (6 February), http://qunfuz.com/2008/02/06/%E2%80%9Cmaps-for-lost-lovers%E2%80%9D-and-writerly-responsibility/#more-63

27. Yassin-Kassab, *Road*, 304–5.

28. Ibid., 335–6.

29. See Sam Jones (2007) 'Jury Convicts Aspiring Suicide Bomber of Terror Offences, *Guardian* (18 September), 7. Yassin-Kassab discusses Atif Siddique's and Samina Malik's cases in (2008) 'Flooding the

Swamp', *Qunfuz Blog* (27 April), http://qunfuz.com/2008/04/27/flooding-the-swamp/

30. Paul Lewis (2008) '"Lyrical Terrorist" has Conviction Quashed', *Guardian* (18 June), 11.

31. Yassin-Kassab, *Road*, 319.

32. See Reed Brody and Michael Ratner (2000) *The Pinochet Papers: The Case of Augusto Pinochet in Spain and Britain* (Leiden: Brill), 260.

33. Mark Ensalaco (2007) *Middle Eastern Terrorism: From Black September to September 11* (Philadelphia, PA: University of Pennsylvania Press), 29–32.

34. Project for the New American Century (2000) *Rebuilding America's Defenses: Strategies, Forces, and Resources for a New Century* (Washington, DC: Project for the New American Century), http://www.webcitation.org/5e3est5lT

35. Yassin-Kassab, *Road*, 325.

36. Lawrence Pipella (2007) *The Mahdi: The Expected One* (Bloomington, IN: Authorhouse).

37. Estimates vary, and Tariq Ali cites a compromise figure of 'a million and a half', but what is indisputable is Ali's claim that, internationally, opposition demonstrations against the Iraq war 'broke all records'. Tariq Ali (2003) *Bush in Babylon: The Recolonisation of Iraq* (London: Verso), 144.

38. Yassin-Kassab, 'Writerly', n.p.

39. For further discussion of these thinkers, see Arthur Bradley and Andrew Tate (2010) *The New Atheist Novel: Philosophy, Fiction and Polemic After 9/11* (London: Continuum), 1–10; Robin Yassin-Kassab (2008) 'Dawkins or McIntosh?', *Qunfuz Blog* (21 August), http://qunfuz.com/2008/08/21/dawkins-or-mcintosh/#more-86

40. N. K. Sandars, ed. and trans. (1987 [1960]) *The Epic of Gilgamesh* (Harmondsworth: Penguin).

41. Yassin-Kassab, *Road*, 294–305.

42. Fyodor Dostoevsky (1999 [1871]) *Devils*, ed. and trans. Michael R. Katz (Oxford: Oxford University Press), 49–50.

10 Kamila Shamsie

1. Hosain, *Sunlight* and *Phoenix Fled*. These family connections are discussed in Muneeza Shamsie (2009) 'Sunlight and Salt: The Literary

Landscapes of a Divided Family', *Journal of Commonwealth Literature* 44(1): 135–53.

2. Jahanara Habibullah (2001) *Remembrance of Days Past: Glimpses of a Princely State During the Raj* (Karachi: Oxford University Press).

3. Muneeza Shamsie (ed.) (1997) *A Dragonfly in the Sun: An Anthology of Pakistani Writing in English* (Oxford: Oxford University Press).

4. Saman Shamsie (2010) *The Adventures of Slothful Slough-off* (Karachi: Oxford University Press).

5. Kamila Shamsie (2000) *Salt and Saffron* (Karachi: Oxford University Press) and Shamsie, *Kartography*.

6. See, for example, the blurb to V. S. Naipaul (1969 [1967]) *The Mimic Men* (London: Penguin), 1.

7. Kamila Shamsie (n.d.) 'With the Ear of a Poet', http://www.kashmiri.info/index2.php?option=com_content&do_pdf=1&id=23

8. Kamila Shamsie (2002) 'Agha Shahid Ali, Teacher', *Urdu Studies* 17: 23–7, 26.

9. Agha Shahid Ali (1992) *The Nostalgist's Map of America* (New York: Norton); Kamila Shamsie (1998) *In the City by the Sea* (London: Bloomsbury), 17–18. Shamsie also discusses the issue of nostalgia in her later essay on Ali's influence, Shamsie, 'Ear', n.p. See also Dennis Walder (2011) *Postcolonial Nostalgias: Writing, Representation and Memory* (Abingdon: Routledge).

10. Shamsie, *City*, 19.

11. Shamsie, 'Teacher', 25–6, 26. For the image itself, see Shamsie, *Kartography*, 1.

12. For examples of positive reviews of *Burnt Shadows*, see Maya Jaggi (2009) 'When Worlds Collide', *Guardian Review* (7 March), 11 and Madeline Clements (2009) 'Hot and Cold Places', *Times Literary Supplement* (13 March), 20.

13. Bradbury, '20', n.p.

14. Kamila Shamsie (2001 [2000]) *Salt and Saffron* (London: Bloomsbury), 97.

15. Ibid., 36–43. These quarrels are almost certainly based on real disagreements among Shamsie's older relatives about the desirability or otherwise of the creation of Pakistan. M. Shamsie, 'Sunlight', 137–8.

16. Shamsie, *Salt*, 37.

17. Ford Madox Ford (1982 [1914]) *The Good Soldier* (Harmondsworth: Penguin), 13.

18. Shamsie, *Broken*, 131–3.
19. Ibid., 2, 144.
20. N. J. Dawood (2006 [1956]) *The Koran* (London: Penguin), 376–8.
21. Shamsie, *Broken*, 5.
22. Ibid.
23. Ibid.
24. As with Chapter 5, note 22, there are disparities in spellings of the names Leila/Laila/Layla and Qes/Qais/Qays in the Laila and Majnun myth.
25. Shamsie, *Broken*, 49.
26. See Ahmet T. Karamustafa (2007) *Sufism: The Formative Period* (Edinburgh: Edinburgh University Press), 15–16.
27. Shamsie, *Broken*, 297.
28. Ibid., 46.
29. Shamsie, *Burnt*, 1.
30. Ibid., 1.
31. Sarah Brown (2009) '*Burnt Shadows*', in Claire Sacre (ed.) 'Books that have Transformed Their Lives', *Elle* (July), 101.
32. Kamila Shamsie (2009) *Offence: The Muslim Case* (Kolkata: Seagull), 5, 13.
33. Ibid., 15. The similar phrase 'unity of the *ummah*' is also used in *Broken Verses* by a hardline *maulana* arguing in a televisual debate against Samina's Muslim feminism. Shamsie, *Broken*, 285.
34. Shamsie, *Offence*, 75.
35. Ibid., 41.
36. Ibid., 35–6, 43–6, 65.
37. Ibid., 56–7.
38. Ibid., 39, 58, 69–72.
39. Ibid., 49–51.
40. Ibid., 51–2.
41. Ibid., 15. The words 'Clash of Civilizations' refer to Huntington, 'Clash' and *Clash*.
42. Kamila Shamsie (2010) 'Pop Idols', in Freeman (ed.) *Granta 112*, 197–214.
43. The predominantly Pashtun district of Sohrab Goth is depicted in Shamsie, *Burnt*, 165, 195–201.
44. Ibid., 158–62.
45. Nazimabad, a suburb of Karachi constructed to house *muhajirs* is now multicultural and middle-class (ibid., 136, 139, 151).

46. Ibid., 78–85.
47. Jaggi, 'Collide', 11.
48. Shamsie, *Burnt*, 119–20.
49. Michael Ondaatje (1993 [1992]) *The English Patient* (London: Picador), 321–4.
50. Shamsie, *Offence*.
51. Ibid., 8–9.
52. Ibid., 29–35.
53. Kamila Shamsie (2009) 'A Long, Loving Literary Line', *Guardian G2* (1 May), 16.
54. For discussion of this issue, see J. Edward Mallot (2007) '"A Land Outside Space, An Expanse Without Distances": Amitav Ghosh, Kamila Shamsie and the Maps of Memory', *LIT: Literature, Interpretation, Theory* 18: 261–84.
55. Shamsie, *Kartography*, 25.
56. Ibid., 337.
57. Eliot A. Cohen (2009) 'Samuel P. Huntington, 1927–2008', American Enterprise Institute for Public Policy Research (January), http://www.aei.org/docLib/20090114_0223822OTIHuntington_g.pdf
58. Bruce W. Nelan *et al.* (1993) *Time Magazine* (5 July).
59. See, for example, Salman Rushdie (1991) 'Is Nothing Sacred?', *Imaginary*, 415–29.
60. Shamsie, *Salt*, 74–5.
61. Ali, *Duel*, 68.

11 Hanif Kureishi

1. Hanif Kureishi (1986) 'The Rainbow Sign', in *My Beautiful Laundrette and The Rainbow Sign* (London: Faber), 9–38, 9.
2. Kureishi, *Ear*, 109.
3. Muneeza Shamsie (2002) 'Maki Kureishi', *Literary Encyclopedia* (20 June), http://www.litencyc.com/php/speople.php?rec=true&UID=4995
4. Hanif Kureishi (2008) *Something to Tell You* (London: Faber), 131.
5. Ibid., 132.
6. Kureishi, 'Rainbow', 34.
7. See Maria Antonietta Saracino (2004) 'Hanif Kureishi: Biography', in Alba Amoia and Bettina L. Knapp (eds) *Multicultural Writers Since 1945: An A–Z Guide* (Westport, CT: Greenwood), 305–8, 305.
8. Kureishi, *Ear*, 159–60.

9. For some of these early plays, see Hanif Kureishi (1999) *Plays Volume 1: 'King and Me', 'Outskirts', 'Borderline', 'Birds of Passage'* (London: Faber).
10. Hanif Kureishi (2006) 'Fear and Paranoia: Hanif Kureishi on the Relevance of Borderline', *Guardian* (22 April), http://www.guardian.co.uk/stage/2006/apr/22/theatre.hanifkureishi
11. Hanif Kureishi (1999) *Sleep With Me* (London: Faber).
12. Hanif Kureishi (2004) *When the Night Begins* (London: Faber).
13. Hanif Kureishi (1985) *My Beautiful Laundrette*, dir. Stephen Frears. Actors: Saeed Jaffrey, Roshan Seth, Daniel Day-Lewis, Gordon Warnecke, and Derrick Branche (London: Cinema Club); Hanif Kureishi (2002) *Collected Screenplays Volume 1: 'My Beautiful Laundrette', 'Sammy and Rosie Get Laid', 'London Kills Me', 'My Son the Fanatic'* (London: Faber).
14. Rushdie 'Minority', 40–1; Gayatri Chakravorty Spivak (1989) 'In Praise of Sammy and Rosie Get Laid', *Critical Quarterly* 31(2) (Summer): 80–8.
15. Kureishi, *Screenplays*, 46–93, 208–64.
16. Moët British Independent Film Awards (1998) '1998 Nominations' (21 November), http://bifa.org.uk/nominations/1998; Hanif Kureishi (1997) *My Son the Fanatic*, dir. Udayan Prasad. Actors: Om Puri, Rachel Griffiths, Akbar Kurtha, Stellan Skarsgård, and Gopi Desai (London: BBC); Hanif Kureishi (1997) 'My Son the Fanatic' (short story), in *Love in a Blue Time* (London: Faber), 119–31.
17. Hanif Kureishi (2003) *The Mother*, dir. Roger Mitchell. Actors: Anne Reid, Daniel Craig, Steven Mackintosh, Cathryn Bradshaw, and Peter Vaughan (London: Momentum). See also Kureishi, *Ear*, 34–5. Yasmin Kureishi (2008) '"Keep me out of your Novels": Hanif Kureishi's Sister has had Enough', *Independent* (4 March), http://www.independent.co.uk/arts-entertainment/books/features/keep-me-out-of-your-novels-hanif-kureishis-sister-has-had-enough-790839.html
18. Mick Brown (2008) 'Hanif Kureishi: A Life Laid Bare', *Telegraph* (20 November), http://www.telegraph.co.uk/culture/books/3671392/Hanif-Kureishi-A-life-laid-bare.html
19. Hanif Kureishi (2008) 'Biography', guardian.co.uk (22 July), http://www.guardian.co.uk/books/2008/jun/13/hanif.kureishi
20. Nasta, *Writing*, 4.
21. Rachel Donadio (2008) 'My Beautiful London', *New York Times* (8 August), http://www.nytimes.com/2008/08/10/magazine/10kureishi-t.html?pagewanted=3&_r=1

22. For further discussion of Kureishi's use of pop culture, see Bart Moore-Gilbert (2001) *Contemporary World Writers: Hanif Kureishi* (Manchester and New York: Manchester University Press), 115–20.

23. Hanif Kureishi (1995) 'That's How Good it Was', in Hanif Kureishi and Jon Savage (eds) *The Faber Book of Pop* (London: Faber), xvii–xx, xviii–xix.

24. Brown, 'Bare', n.p.

25. Hanif Kureishi (2005) *The Word and the Bomb* (London: Faber), 3.

26. A good example is Michiko Kakutani (2010) 'A Writer Recalls His Mentor, Critic and Father, All in One Complex Man', *New York Times* (22 March), http://www.nytimes.com/2010/03/23/books/23book.html

27. Kureishi, *Something*, 31.

28. Ibid., 10.

29. Aamer Hussein (2010) 'Hanif Kureishi *Collected Stories*', *Wasafiri* (24 October), http://www.wasafiri.org/pages/content/index.asp?PageID=221

30. Kristyn Gorton (2007) *Theorising Desire: From Freud to Feminism to Film* (Basingstoke: Palgrave Macmillan), 1.

31. Hanif Kureishi (2011) *Collected Essays* (London: Faber).

32. Kureishi, 'Beheadings', 611–13.

33. Antonia Fraser (2010) 'PEN/Pinter Prize' (24 November), http://www.englishpen.org/prizes/penpinterprize/

34. Mary Louise Pratt (1981) 'The Short Story: The Long AND the Short of It', *Poetics* 10: 175–94.

35. Hanif Kureishi (2002) 'The Body', in *The Body and Seven Stories* (London: Faber), 3–126.

36. Exemplary representations of father–son relationships include Kureishi, *Buddha*; *Ear*; 'Hullaballoo in the Tree', *Body*, 131–9; and 'Remember this Moment, Remember Us', *Body*, 223–31.

37. Kureishi, 'Body', 46–7.

38. Steven Knight (2002) *Dirty Pretty Things*, dir. Stephen Frears. Actors: Audrey Tautou, Chiwetel Ejiofor, Sophie Okonedo, Sergi López, and Zlatko Buric (London: Disney Home Entertainment).

39. Kureishi, 'Body', 58; Hanif Kureishi (2001) *Gabriel's Gift* (London: Faber), 107.

40. Hanif Kureishi (2005) 'The Word and the Bomb', 'The Arduous Conversation Will Continue' and 'The Carnival of Culture', in *Bomb*, 3–11, 91–3, 97–100.

41. Naipaul, *Believers*.

42. Kureishi, *Ear*, 68–9.

43. Kureishi, *Something*, 320.
44. Hanif Kureishi, 'The Decline of the West', in *Collected Stories*, 651–9.
45. Dennis Potter and Melvyn Bragg (2007) 'Great Interviews of the 20th Century: Dennis Potter Interviewed by Melvyn Bragg', *Guardian* (12 September), http://www.guardian.co.uk/theguardian/2007/sep/12/greatinterviews
46. Kureishi, 'Carnival', 99–100.
47. Steve Bruce (2003) *Politics and Religion* (London: Polity), 61–2.
48. Kureishi, 'Fanatic', 131.
49. Kureishi, *Black*, 186–9.
50. Malik, *Fatwa*, 199–200.
51. Kureishi, *Something*, 315.
52. Ibid., 320.
53. Kureishi, *Stories*, 16; 425.

12   Ahdaf Soueif

1. For analysis, see Nash, *Anglo-Arab*, 65–86.
2. Soueif, *Mezzaterra*, 1.
3. She has described this experience in both fiction and non-fiction: Ahdaf Soueif (1995) '1964', in *Aisha*, 23–39 and Soueif, 'Preface', in *Mezzaterra*, 1–23, 4.
4. Ahdaf Soueif (1999 [1992]) *In the Eye of the Sun* (London: Bloomsbury).
5. Pascale Ghazaleh (2001) 'Ahdaf Soueif: Different Readings', *Al-Ahram Weekly Online*, 559 (8–14 December), http://weekly.ahram.org.eg/2001/559/profile.htm
6. Soueif, *Aisha*.
7. See Soueif Official Web Site (2010) '*Aisha*', http://www.ahdafsoueif.com/Books/aisha.htm and Hechmi Travelsi (2003) 'Transcultural Writing: Ahdaf Soueif's *Aisha* as a Case Study', *Jouvert* 7(2), http://english.chass.ncsu.edu/jouvert/v7i2/trabel.htm
8. Linda Maloul (2010) 'The Oriental Tale in Ahdaf Soueif's *Aisha*', unpublished paper, Arab Women Writers in Diaspora: Horizons of Dialogue, University of Manchester (10 December), n.p. and Hala Halim (1999) 'Translating Egypt' (review of *The Map of Love*), *Al Ahram* (13 August), http://weekly.ahram.org.eg/1999/442/bk1_442.htm
9. Aida Edemariam (2005) 'Mapping the Divide', *Guardian Review* (11 June), 20.

10. Ahdaf Soueif (2002) 'Egyptian Memories', *Open Democracy*, http://www.opendemocracy.net/faith-europe_islam/article_403.jsp

11. Ahdaf Soueif (1996) *Sandpiper* (London: Bloomsbury).

12. Ahdaf Soueif (1999) *The Map of Love* (London: Bloomsbury).

13. Man Booker Prize (1999) 'Prize Archive', http://www.themanbookerprize.com/prize/archive/32

14. Lady Duff Gordon (1866) *Letters from Egypt* (London: Macmillan) and Lady Anne Blunt (1881) *A Pilgrimage to Nejd* (London: Murray).

15. E. M. Forster (1980 [1924]) *A Passage to India* (Harmondsworth: Penguin), 46–8.

16. See Soueif Official Web Site (2010) 'Information', http://www.ahdaf-soueif.com/about.htm

17. Mourid Barghouti (2000) *I Saw Ramallah*, intro. Edward W. Said, trans. Ahdaf Soueif (London: Bloomsbury).

18. Soueif, *Eye*, 495–9.

19. Ibid., 497.

20. Walter Benjamin (1973 [1970]). *Illuminations*, ed. and intro. Hannah Arendt, trans. Harry Zohn (London: Collins-Fontana), 81.

21. Soueif, *Map*, 82.

22. See, for example, Ahdaf Soueif and Joseph Massad (1999) 'The Politics of Desire in the Writings of Ahdaf Soueif', *Journal of Palestine Studies* 28(4):74–90, 82.

23. Gabriele Annan (1999) 'Forbidden to Grow Up' (review of *The Map of Love*), *London Review of Books* 21(14) (15 July): 28.

24. Soueif, *Mezzaterra*, 4.

25. Ahdaf Soueif (2004) 'The Language of the Veil', *Mezzaterra*, 266–74.

26. Ibid., 272.

27. Soueif, *Eye*, 753.

28. Soueif, *Map*, 158.

29. Annelies Moors and Emma Tarlo (2007) 'Introduction', *Fashion Theory* 11(2/3): 133–42, 138. See also Emma Tarlo (2010) *Visibly Muslim: Fashion, Politics, Faith* (Oxford: Berg).

30. Ahdaf Soueif (2000) 'Under the Gun: A Palestinian Journey' *Guardian G2* (18 December), 2, and http://www.guardian.co.uk/world/2000/dec/18/israel.politicsphilosophyandsociety Reprinted in Soueif, *Mezzaterra*, 29–62.

31. Soueif, *Mezzaterra*, 1.

32. PalFest (2009) 'English Press Release', http://www.palfest.org/Palfest_English_Press_Kit.pdf

33. See Matthew Rothschild (2009) 'Israel Sends Soldiers to Try to Shut Down Literature Festival', *The Progressive* (25 May), http://www.progressive.org/wx052509.html, and PalFest Closing Night Press Release (28 May), http://www.palfest.org/Closing%20Night%20Press% 20Release.pdf

34. Soueif Official Web Site (13 December), 'Home', http://www.ahdafsoueif.com/

35. Ahdaf Soueif, speaking on Riz Khan (2011) 'The Political Power of Literature', *Al-Jazeera* (23 February), http://english.aljazeera.net/programmes/rizkhan/2011/02/201122374815992508.html

36. Malak, *Narratives*, 141.

37. Ahdaf Soueif (1996) 'Melody', *Sandpiper*, 3–19.

38. Soueif, 'Egyptian', n.p.

39. Soueif, *Mezzaterra*, 2.

40. Soueif and Massad, 'Desire', 86.

41. Ahdaf Soueif (2008) 'Visions of the Harem: John Frederick Lewis', *Guardian Review* (5 July), 16.

42. Ahdaf Soueif (1992) 'The Wedding of Zeina' and 'The Nativity', in *Aisha*, 85–92, 137–84.

43. Soueif, 'Harem', 16.

44. Soueif, *Mezzaterra*, 4.

45. Soueif and Massad, 'Desire', 90.

46. PalFest (2010) 'Report', http://www.palfest.org/downloads/PalFest%202010%20Report.pdf

47. Engaged Events (2010) 'Mission Statement', http://new.thebiggive. org.uk/charity/view/6862?search=8a439092-afa1-493b-bd7f-40024b1c78ff

48. Soueif, *Map* 50.

49. V. S. Naipaul (1987) *The Enigma of Arrival* (Harmondsworth: Penguin).

50. Soueif, *Eye*, 723.

51. Soueif, *Map*, 419.

52. Said, *Covering*.

53. Soueif, *Map*, 364.

54. Soueif, *Eye* 298.

13 Zahid Hussain

1. Straw, 'Uneasy', 1.

2. David Batty (2011) 'White Girls Seen as "Easy Meat" by Pakistani Rapists, Says Jack Straw', guardian.co.uk (8 January), http://www.guardian.co.uk/world/2011/jan/08/jack-straw-white-girls-easy-meat

3. According to the 2001 Census, there are 14,654 Indians and 12,020 Pakistanis in the city, http://www.statistics.gov.uk/census2001/profiles/00ex.asp

4. Zahid Hussain (2010) 'Writetopia: A Creative Writing Toolkit', http://zahidhussainwrites.blogspot.com/

5. Ziauddin Sardar (2006) 'Books of the Year', *New Statesman* (27 November), http://www.newstatesman.com/200611270051

6. Lewis, *Young*, 149.

7. Zahid Hussain (2006) *The Curry Mile* (Manchester: Suitcase), 133–7.

8. Ibid., 185–9.

9. Pnina Werbner (2006) 'Seekers on the Path: Different Ways of Being a Sufi in Britain', in Jamal Malik and John Hinnells (eds) *Sufism in the West* (Abingdon: Routledge), 127–41.

10. http://mistngo.org/mist-team

11. Hussain, *Curry*, 81–97.

12. Qaisra Shahraz is a Pakistani writer who lives in Manchester and works as a schools inspector. As well as *The Holy Woman*, she is the author of Qaisra Shahraz (2003) *Typhoon* (London: Black Amber).

13. Gregory Stanton (1996) 'The 8 Stages of Genocide', *Genocide Watch*, http://www.genocidewatch.org/aboutgenocide/8stagesofgenocide.html. The eight stages are classification, symbolization, dehumanization, organization, polarization, preparation, extermination, and denial.

Conclusion

1. Mieke Bal (2008) *Loving Yusuf: Conceptual Travels from Present to Past* (Chicago: University of Chicago University), 15.

2. Humayan Ansari (2004) *'The Infidel Within': Muslims in Britain Since 1800* (London: Hurst), 2–3.

3. Malak, *Narratives*, 3.

4. See Framing Muslims (2011) 'Home', www.framingmuslims.org, and Morey and Yaqin, *Framing*.

Bibliography

Abbas, Ghulam (1965) *Chand Tara* [*Moon and Star*], illus. Zainab Abbas (Karachi: Guild Ishā'at Ghar).

Abdalla, Anouar (1994) *For Rushdie: Essays by Arab and Muslim Writers in Defense of Free Speech* (New York: George Braziller).

Aboulela, Leila (1999) *The Translator* (Oxford: Heinemann Educational).

—— (2000) 'And my Fate was Scotland', in Kevin MacNeil and Alec Finlay (eds) *Wish I Was Here: A Scottish Multicultural Anthology* (Edinburgh: Polygon), 175–92.

—— (2001) *Coloured Lights* (Edinburgh: Polygon).

—— (2002) 'Moving Away from Accuracy', *Alif: Journal of Comparative Poetics* 22: 198–207.

—— (2005) *Minaret* (London: Bloomsbury).

Abu-Lughod, Janet L. (1989) *Before European Hegemony: The World System, A.D. 1250–1350* (New York: Oxford University Press).

Ahmad, Abul Mansur (1978) *Atmakatha* (Dhaka: Khosaroja Kitaba Mahala).

Ahmad, Rukhsana (ed.) (1991) *We Sinful Women: Contemporary Urdu Feminist Poetry* (London: Women's Press).

Ahmed, Leila (1992) *Women and Gender in Islam: Historical Roots of a Modern Debate* (New Haven, CT: Yale University Press).

Ahmed, Sara (2008) *Evaluating the Framing of Islam and Muslims Pre- and Post-9/11: A Contextual Analysis of Articles Published by the New York Times* (Saarbrücken: VDM Verlag).

Akbar, Arifa (2006) 'Brick Lane Rises up Against Filming of Ali's Novel', *Independent* (22 July), http://www.independent.co.uk/news/uk/this-britain/brick-lane-rises-up-against-filming-of-alis-novel-408885.html

Akhtar, Shabbir (1989) *Be Careful with Muhammad! The Salman Rushdie Affair* (London: Bellew Publishing).

Al Aswany, Alaa (2002) *The Yacoubian Building*, trans. Humphrey Davis (London: HarperCollins).

—— (2008) *Chicago* (London: Fourth Estate).

Ali, Afzar, dir. (2002) *Daira* [*Circle of Life*], Actors: Adnan Siddiqui, Ayeshah Alam, Aijaz Aslam, Shahzad Nawaz, and Amir Abbas (Karachi: Halofly Entertainment Consortium).

314

Ali, Agha Shahid (1992) *The Nostalgist's Map of America* (New York: Norton).

—— (1997) *The Country without a Post Office* (New York: Norton).

Ali, Ayaan Hirsi (2010) *Nomad: A Personal Journey Through the Clash of Civilizations* (London: Simon and Schuster).

Ali, Monica (2003) *Brick Lane* (London: Transworld).

—— (2006) *Alentejo Blue* (London: Black Swan).

Ali, Tariq (1970) *Pakistan: Military Rule or People's Power* (New York: Morrow).

—— (1983) *Can Pakistan Survive? The Death of a State* (Harmondsworth: Penguin).

—— (1985) *The Nehrus and the Gandhis: An Indian Dynasty* (London: Picador).

—— (1993) *Shadows of the Pomegranate Tree* (London: Verso).

—— (1998) *The Book of Saladin* (London: Verso).

—— (2000) *The Stone Woman* (London: Verso).

—— (2002) *The Clash of Fundamentalisms: Crusades, Jihads and Modernity* (London: Verso).

—— (2003) *Bush in Babylon: The Recolonisation of Iraq* (London: Verso).

—— (2003) *The Illustrious Corpse* (Oberon Modern Plays) (London: Absolute Classics).

—— (2005) *Rough Music: Blair, Bombs, Baghdad, London, Terror* (London: Verso).

—— (2005 [1987]) *Street Fighting Years* (London: Verso).

—— (2005) *A Sultan in Palermo* (London: Verso).

—— (2008) *The Duel: Pakistan on the Flight Path of American Power* (London: Simon & Schuster).

—— (2008) *Pirates of the Caribbean: Axis of Hope* (London: Verso).

—— (2009) *The Idea of Communism* (Calcutta: Seagull).

—— (2009) *Protocols of the Elders of Sodom and Other Essays* (London: Verso).

—— (2010) 'Islamophobia Exposed', *Socialist Worker* 2209 (10 July), http://www.socialistworker.co.uk/art.php?id=21715

—— (2010) *Night of the Golden Butterfly* (London: Verso).

—— (2010) *The Obama Syndrome: Surrender at Home, War Abroad* (London: Verso).

—— (2010) 'Oliver Stone and Tariq Ali: Brothers in Arms', *Guardian G2* (27 July).

Ali, Tariq and Howard Brenton (1989) *Iranian Nights* (Royal Court Theatre) (London: Nick Hern).

—— (1990) *Moscow Gold* (London: Nick Hern).

—— (1998) *Ugly Rumours* (Instant Playscript) (London: Nick Hern).

AlSanea, Rajaa (2008) *Girls of Riyadh*, trans. Marilyn Booth (London: Penguin).

Al-Shatie, Bint (2006) *The Wives of Prophet Muhammad* (Piscataway, NJ: Gorgias Press).

Al-Shaykh, Hanan (2002 [2001]) *Only in London*, trans. Catherine Cobham (London: Bloomsbury).

Amis, Martin (2008) *The Second Plane* (London: Jonathan Cape).

Amman, Mir (2006) *A Tale of Four Dervishes*, trans. Mohammed Zakir (Harmondsworth: Penguin).

Anam, Shaheen (1999) 'Women Coping with Floods', in Imtiaz Ahmed (ed.) *Living With Floods: An Exercise in Alternatives* (Dhaka: University Press), 29–31.

Anam, Tahmima (2005) 'Fixing the Past: War, Violence, and the Habitations of Memory in Post-independence Bangladesh' (Cambridge, MA: University of Harvard Unpublished PhD Thesis).

—— (2007) 'Bangladesh: Give me Back my Country' *New Statesman* (22 January), http://www.newstatesman.com/asia/2007/01/bangladesh-bnp-election-vote

—— (2007) *A Golden Age* (London: John Murray).

—— (moderator) (2009) 'Politics and Place in Fiction: Kamila Shamsie, Daniyal Mueenuddin, Nadeem Aslam', unpublished panel, London: Asia House (18 May).

—— (2011) *The Good Muslim* (Edinburgh: Canongate).

Anam, Tahmima and Kamila Shamsie (2009) 'History and the Storyteller: A Dialogue' (Leeds: University of Leeds Unpublished Arthur Ravenscroft Lecture).

Andreae, Christopher (2007) *Mary Fedden: Enigmas and Variations* (Aldershot: Lund Humphries).

Annan, Gabriele (1999) 'Forbidden to Grow Up' (review of *The Map of Love*), *London Review of Books* 21(14) (15 July), 28.

Ansari, Humayan (2004) *'The Infidel Within': Muslims in Britain Since 1800* (London: Hurst).

Asad, Talal (1990) 'Ethnography, Literature, and Politics: Some Readings and Uses of Salman Rushdie's *The Satanic Verses*', *Cultural Anthropology* 5(3): 239–69.

Ashcroft, Bill, Gareth Griffiths, and Helen Tiffin (2002 [1989]) *The Empire Writes Back: The Theory and Practice of Post-Colonial Literatures* (London: Routledge).

Ashour, Radwa (2003) *Granada: A Novel* (Middle East Literature in Translation) (Syracuse, NY: Syracuse University Press).

Aslam, Nadeem (1993) 'God and Me', *Granta 93*, http://www.granta.com/Online-Only/Nadeem-Aslam

—— (1993) *Season of the Rainbirds* (London: Bloomsbury).

—— (2004) *Maps for Lost Lovers* (London: Bloomsbury).

—— (2008) *The Wasted Vigil* (London: Faber).

—— (2010) 'Leila in the Wilderness', in John Freeman (ed.) *Granta 112: Pakistan* (London: Granta), 9–53.

—— (2010) 'Where to Begin', *Granta Online* (29 September), http://www. granta.com/Online-Only/Where-to-Begin

—— (n.d.) '*Maps for Lost Lovers* by Nadeem Aslam: Reading Guide', http://www.faber.co.uk/site-media/reading-guides/maps-for-lost-lovers_reading-guide.pdf

Atwill, David G. (2006) *The Chinese Sultanate: Islam, Ethnicity, and the Panthay Rebellion in Southwest China, 1856–1873* (Palo Alto, CA: Stanford University Press).

Auster, Paul (2010) *Sunset Park* (London: Faber).

Bal, Mieke (2008) *Loving Yusuf: Conceptual Travels from Present to Past* (Chicago: University of Chicago Press).

Barghouti, Mourid (2000) *I Saw Ramallah*, intro. Edward W. Said, trans. Ahdaf Soueif (London: Bloomsbury).

Barthes, Roland (1977) 'The Death of the Author', in *Image, Music Text*, trans. Stephen Heath (London: Fontana), 146–7.

Bateman, Colin (2001) *Mohammed Maguire* (London: HarperCollins).

Batty, David (2011) 'White Girls Seen as "Easy Meat" by Pakistani Rapists, Says Jack Straw', guardian.co.uk (8 January), http://www. guardian.co.uk/world/2011/jan/08/jack-straw-white-girls-easy-meat

BBC (2007) 'The Family Story in Bangladesh's War' (23 April), http:// news.bbc.co.uk/1/hi/world/south_asia/6434479.stm

—— (2007) 'Violence over Bangladesh Cartoon' (21 September), http:// news.bbc.co.uk/1/hi/world/south_asia/7006528.stm

Belfast Islamic Centre (2011) 'Introduction' (4 January), http://www. belfastislamiccentre.org.uk/about_us/new_mosque_project.htm

Benjamin, Walter (1973 [1970]). *Illuminations*, ed. and intro. Hannah Arendt, trans. Harry Zohn (London: Collins-Fontana).

Bergquist, Karin (2003) 'Outspoken Editor from Bangladesh: Mahfuz Anam' (14 July), http://www.culturebase.net/artist.php?1271

Bhabha, Homi K. (1994) *The Location of Culture* (London: Routledge).

Bhargava, Rajeev (2010) *The Promise of India's Secular Democracy* (Delhi: Oxford University Press).

Blaise, Clark (1981) 'A Novel of India's Coming of Age', *New York Times* (19 April), http://www.nytimes.com/books/99/04/18/specials/rushdie-midnight.html

Blunt, Lady Anne (1881) *A Pilgrimage to Nejd* (London: John Murray).

Bourdieu, Pierre (1993) *The Field of Cultural Production: Essays on Art and Literature* (New York: Columbia University Press).

Brace, Marianne (2004) 'Nadeem Aslam: A Question of Honour', *Independent* (11 June), http://enjoyment.independent.co.uk/books/features/article42260.ece

Bradbury, Lorna (2010) 'Are These Britain's Best 20 Novelists Under 40?', *Daily Telegraph* (18 June), http://www.telegraph.co.uk/culture/books/ 7835258/Are-these-Britains-best-20-novelists-under-40.html

Bradford Museums, Galleries and Heritage (n.d.) 'Bradford Heritage and Recording Unit [BHRU]'s Belle Vue Archive', http://www.bradfordmuseums.org/bradfordmuseum/index.php?a=wordsearch&s=gallery&w= belle+vue&go=go

Bradley, Arthur and Andrew Tate (2010) *The New Atheist Novel: Philosophy, Fiction and Polemic After 9/11* (London: Continuum).

Brah, Avtar (1996) *Cartographies of Diaspora: Contesting Identities* (London: Routledge).

Brody, Reed and Michael Ratner (2000) *The Pinochet Papers: The Case of Augusto Pinochet in Spain and Britain* (Leiden: Brill).

Brouillette, Sarah (2007) *Postcolonial Writers in the Global Literary Marketplace* (Basingstoke: Palgrave Macmillan).

Brown, Dorothy A. (2003) *Critical Race Theory: Cases, Materials and Problems* (Eagan, MN: West Group).

Brown, Mick (2008) 'Hanif Kureishi: A Life Laid Bare', *Telegraph* (20 November), http://www.telegraph.co.uk/culture/books/3671392/Hanif-Kureishi-A-life-laid-bare.html

Brown, Sarah (2009) '*Burnt Shadows*', in Claire Sacre (ed.) 'Books that have Transformed Their Lives', *Elle* (July), 101.

Bruce, Steve (2003) *Politics and Religion* (London: Polity).

Buchan, James (2008) 'Between Two Worlds', *Guardian Review* (20 September), 10.

Burke, Seán (2008) *The Death and Return of the Author: Criticism and Subjectivity in Barthes, Foucault, and Derrida* (Edinburgh: Edinburgh University Press).

Camus, Albert (2006 [1956]) *The Fall*, trans. Robin Buss (London: Penguin).

Census (2001) 'Blackburn with Darwen UA', http://www.statistics.gov.uk/census2001/profiles/00ex.asp

Cesari, Jocelyne (2004) *Where Islam and Democracy Meet: Muslims in Europe and the United States* (Basingstoke: Palgrave Macmillan).

Chakma, Bhumitra (2009) *Pakistan's Nuclear Weapons* (Abingdon: Routledge).

Chambers, Claire (2003) 'The Relationship Between Knowledge and Power in the Work of Amitav Ghosh' (Leeds: University of Leeds Unpublished PhD Thesis).

—— (2009) 'An Interview with Leila Aboulela', *Contemporary Women's Writing* 3(1): 86–102.

—— (2011) 'Poets of Muslim Heritage'. *Exiled Ink* 14 (Winter): 13–14.

Chambers, Claire and Fadia Faqir (2010) 'Keynote: Interview', unpublished paper, Postcolonialism and Islam (16–17 April), University of Sunderland.

Chaudhuri, Sukanta (ed.) (1990, 1995) *Calcutta: The Living City: Volumes 1 and 2* (Delhi: Oxford University Press).

Clements, Madeline (2009) 'Hot and Cold Places', *Times Literary Supplement* (March 13), 20.

—— (2010) 'Peaceable Kingdoms', *Times Literary Supplement* (28 May), 21.

Cohen, Eliot A. (2009) 'Samuel P. Huntington, 1927–2008', American Enterprise Institute for Public Policy Research (January), http://www.aei.org/docLib/20090114_0223822OTIHuntington_g.pdf

Cohen, Mark R. (1994) *Under Crescent and Cross* (Princeton: Princeton University Press).

Collins, Robert O. (2006) 'Disaster in Darfur: Historical Overview', in Samuel Totten and Eric Markusen (eds) *Genocide in Darfur: Investigating the Atrocities in the Sudan* (London: Routledge), 3–24.

Connor, H., C. Tyers, S. Davis, N. D. Tackey and T. Modood (2003) 'Minority Ethnic Students in Higher Education: Interim Report', *Research Report RR448*, Department for Education and Skills, http://www.employment-studies.co.uk/pubs/summary.php?id=rr448

Crowther, Yasmin (2006) *The Saffron Kitchen* (London: Little, Brown).

Dalrymple, William (1994) *City of Djinns: A Year in Delhi* (London: Flamingo).

Darwish, Mahmoud and Agha Shahid Ali (2003) 'Eleven Stars Over Andalusia', in Agha Shahid Ali, *Rooms Are Never Finished: Poems* (New York: Norton), 79–93.

Dawood, N. J. (2006 [1956]) *The Koran* (London: Penguin).

Desai, Anita (2000) 'Passion in Lahore', *New York Review of Books* (21 December), http://www.nybooks.com/articles/archives/2000/dec/21/passion-in-lahore/

Desai, Anita and Krishna Dutta (2008) *Calcutta: A Cultural and Literary History* (Oxford: Signal).

Deutscher, Isaac (2002) 'On the Israeli-Arab War', in Tariq Ali, *The Clash of Fundamentalisms: Crusades, Jihads and Modernity* (London: Verso), 314–32.

Dharker, Imtiaz (2006) 'Remember Andalus', in *The Terrorist at My Table* (Newcastle: Bloodaxe), 63–82.

—— (2009) 'Vale of Clwyd', unpublished poem emailed to the author.

Di Lampedusa, Guiseppe Tomasi (2007) *The Leopard: Revised and with New Material* (London: Vintage).

Donadio, Rachel (2008) 'My Beautiful London', *New York Times* (8 August), http://www.nytimes.com/2008/08/10/magazine/10kureishi-t.html?pagewanted=3&_r=1

Dostoevsky, Fyodor (1999 [1871]) *Devils*, ed. and trans. Michael R. Katz (Oxford: Oxford University Press).

Dougary, Ginny (2006) 'The Voice of Experience', *Times Online* (9 September), http://www.ginnydougary.co.uk/2006/09/17/the-voice-of-experience/

Edemariam, Aida (2005) 'Mapping the Divide', *Guardian Review* (11 June), 20.

Einboden, Jeffrey (2009) 'A Qur'ānic Milton: From Paradise to al-Firdaws', *Milton Quarterly* 43(3): 183–94.

El Saadawi, Nawal (1997) *The Nawal El Saadawi Reader* (London: Zed).

El Sakkakini, Widad (1982) *First Among Sufis: The Life and Thought of Rabia al-Adawiyya, the Woman Saint of Basra*, trans. Nabil Safwat (London: Octagon Press).

Engaged Events (2010) 'Mission Statement', http://new.thebiggive.org.uk/charity/view/6862?search=8a439092-afa1-493b-bd7f-40024b1c78ff

English, James F. (2005) *The Economy of Prestige: Prizes, Awards, and the Circulation of Cultural Value* (Cambridge, MA: Harvard University Press).

English PEN (2008) 'Leila Aboulela', http://penatlas.org/online/index.php?option=com_content&task=view &id=109&Itemid=16

Ensalaco, Mark (2007) *Middle Eastern Terrorism: From Black September to September 11* (Philadelphia, PA: University of Pennsylvania Press).

Erickson, John (1998) *Islam and Postcolonial Narrative* (Cambridge: Cambridge University Press).

Fabos, Anita (2008) *'Brothers' or Others? Gender and Propriety for Muslim Arab Sudanese in Egypt* (Oxford: Berghahn).

Faizfx (2010) 'Halal: Is it Meat you're Looking for?' (28 September), http://www.youtube.com/watch?v=9W9s6rzxZ7c

Faqir, Fadia (1987) *Nisanit* (Salcombe: Aidan Ellis).

—— (1996) *Pillars of Salt* (London: Quartet Books).

—— (1997) 'Engendering Democracy and Islam', *Third World Quarterly* 18(1): 165–74.

—— (1998 [1991]) 'Stories from the House of Songs', in Fadia Faqir (ed.) *In the House of Silence: Autobiographical Essays by Arab Women Writers* (Reading: Garnet), 61.

—— (2000) 'Arab Democracy Minus Women: Gender, Democracy and Citizenship in Jordan', *Asian Women* 11: 61–89.

—— (2001) 'Intrafamily Femicide in Defence of Honour: The Case of Jordan', *Third World Quarterly* 22(1): 65–82.

—— (2007) 'As Soon as the Fresh Air Touched my Hair I Began to Cry', *Guardian G2* (22 October), 16.

—— (2007) *The Cry of the Dove* (New York: Grove Press/Black Cat).

—— (2007) *My Name is Salma* (London: Doubleday).

—— (2009) 'Spinning a Self in the Language of the Other', unpublished paper, Arab Women Writers in Diaspora: Horizons of Dialogue, University of Manchester (10 December).

—— (2010) 'Dr Claire Chambers interviews Fadia Faqir I', http://www.youtube.com/watch?v=NiaxMdApHXg

Farrier, David (2008) 'Terms of Hospitality: Abdulrazak Gurnah's *By the Sea*', *Journal of Commonwealth Literature* 43(3): 121–39.

Faulks, Sebastian (2009) *A Week in December* (London: Hutchinson).

Ferguson, Niall (2003) *Empire: How Britain Made the Modern World* (London: Penguin).

Fitzgerald, Timothy (2009) *Discourse of Civility and Barbarity: A Critical History of Religion and Related Categories* (Oxford: Oxford University Press).

Flaubert, Gustave (2009 [1877]) *A Simple Heart*, trans. Charlotte Mandell (Brooklyn, NY: Melville House).

Flint, Julie and Alex de Waal (2005) *Darfur: A Short History of a Long War* (London: Zed).

Flood, Alison (2008) 'Publication of Controversial Muhammad Novel *The Jewel of Medina* Delayed', guardian.co.uk (10 October), http://www.guardian.co.uk/books/2008/oct/10/jewel-of-medina-sherry-jones-aisha

—— (2008) 'Writers Awards Deny Censorship of "Unpalatable" Novel', guardian.co.uk (13 August), http://www.guardian.co.uk/books/2008/aug/13/muslim.awards.malik

Ford, Ford Madox (1982 [1914]) *The Good Soldier* (Harmondsworth: Penguin).

Forster, E. M. (1980 [1924]) *A Passage to India* (Harmondsworth: Penguin).

Foucault, Michel (1977) 'What is an Author?', in Michel Foucault, *Language, Counter-memory, Practice: Selected Essays and Interviews*, ed. and intro. Donald F. Bouchard, trans. Donald F. Bouchard and Sherry Simon (Ithaca, NY: Cornell University Press), 113–38.

Framing Muslims (2011) 'Home', www.framingmuslims.org

Franzen, Jonathan (2010) 'On Writing *The Corrections*', *Guardian Review* (30 October), 6.

Fraser, Antonia (2010) 'PEN/Pinter Prize' (24 November), http://www.englishpen.org/prizes/penpinterprize/

Freeman, John (ed.) (2010) *Granta 112: Pakistan* (London: Granta).

Gauhar, Feryal Ali (2007) *No Space for Further Burials* (Delhi: Women Unlimited).

Ghazaleh, Pascale (2001) 'Ahdaf Soueif: Different Readings', *Al-Ahram Weekly Online* 559 (8–14 December), http://weekly.ahram.org.eg/2001/559/profile.htm

Ghosh, Amitav (1992) *In an Antique Land* (London: Granta).

Ghoussoub, Mai (2008) *Selected Writings* (London: Saqi).

Gleave, Robert (2010) 'Should we Teach Islam as a Religion or as a Civilisation?', unpublished paper, Islamic Studies Network: Perspectives on Islamic Studies in Higher Education, Aston University (25–26 May),

http://www.heacademy.ac.uk/assets/York/multimedia/audio/islamic_
studies/Professor_Ron_Geaves.mp3

Glover, William J. (2008) *Making Lahore Modern: Constructing and Imagining a Colonial City* (Minneapolis, MN: University of Minnesota Press).

Goodhart, David (2010) 'Labour Must Become the Anti-Immigration Party', *Labour Uncut* (18 May), http://labour-uncut.co.uk/2010/05/18/labour-must-become-the-anti-immigration-party-david-goodhart/

Goodyear, Sara Suleri (2003) *Boys Will be Boys: A Daughter's Elegy* (Chicago: University of Chicago Press).

Gopal, Priyamvada (2005) *Literary Radicalism in India: Gender, Nation and the Transition to Independence* (London: Routledge).

Gordon, Lady Duff (1866) *Letters from Egypt* (London: Macmillan).

Gorton, Kristyn (2007) *Theorising Desire: From Freud to Feminism to Film* (Basingstoke: Palgrave Macmillan).

Grabham, Emily, Davina Cooper, Jane Krishnadas, and Didi Herman (eds) (2009) *Intersectionality and Beyond: Law, Power and the Politics of Location* (Abingdon: Routledge-Cavendish).

Guène, Faiza (2006) *Dreams from the Endz*, trans. Sarah Ardizzone (London: Chatto & Windus).

—— (2006) *Just Like Tomorrow*, trans. Sarah Adams (London: Chatto & Windus).

Gupta, Nilanjana, Sipra Mukherjee, and Himadri Banerjee (eds) (2009) *Calcutta Mosaic: Essays and Interviews on the Minority Communities of Calcutta* (Delhi: Anthem).

Gupta, Suman (2011) *Imagining Iraq: Literature in English and the Iraq Invasion* (Basingstoke: Palgrave Macmillan).

Gurnah, Abdulrazak (1987) *Memory of Departure* (London: Jonathan Cape).

—— (1988) *Pilgrim's Way* (London: Jonathan Cape).

—— (1990) *Dottie* (London: Jonathan Cape).

—— (1993, 1995) *Essays on African Writing: A Re-Evaluation: 1 and 2* (London Heinemann).

—— (1997 [1996]) *Admiring Silence* (Harmondsworth: Penguin).

—— (2002) 'An Idea of the Past', *Moving Worlds* 2(2): 6–17.

—— (2002 [2001]) *By the Sea* (London: Bloomsbury).

—— (2004 [1994]) *Paradise* (London: Bloomsbury).

—— (2004) 'Writing and Place', *World Literature Today* (May–August), 26–8.

—— (2006 [2005]) *Desertion* (London: Bloomsbury).

—— (ed.) (2007) *The Cambridge Companion to Salman Rushdie* (Cambridge: Cambridge University Press).

—— (2011) *The Last Gift* (London: Bloomsbury).

Habibullah, Jahanara (2001) *Remembrance of Days Past: Glimpses of a Princely State During the Raj* (Karachi: Oxford University Press).

Halim, Hala (1999) 'Translating Egypt' (review of *The Map of Love*), *Al-Ahram* (13 August), http://weekly.ahram.org.eg/1999/442/bk1_442. htm

Hameed, Ghazala and Durdana Soomro (2006) *Bengal Raag* (Dhaka: Writers Ink).

Hamid, Mohsin (2000) *Moth Smoke* (London Granta).

—— (2005 [2003]) 'The Pathos of Exile', in Bapsi Sidhwa (ed.) *City of Sin and Splendour: Writings on Lahore* (Delhi: Oxford University Press), 243–50.

—— (2006) 'Divided We Fall', *Time Asia* (4 September), http://www.mohsinhamid.com/dividedwefall.html

—— (2006) 'Focus on the Fundamentals', *Paris Review* 178 (Fall), http://www.theparisreview.org/fiction/5645/focus-on-the-fundamentals-mohsin-hamid

—— (2007) 'After 60 Years, Will Pakistan Be Reborn?' *The New York Times* (15 August), http://www.mohsinhamid.com/pakistan60years.html

—— (2007) 'General Pervez Musharraf: Pakistan's Big Beast Unleashed', *Independent* (11 February), http://www.mohsinhamid.com/bigbeastunleashed.html

—— (2007) 'Pakistan's Silent Majority is Not to Be Feared', *New York Times* (27 March), http://www.nytimes.com/2007/03/27/opinion/27mohsin. html

—— (2007) *The Reluctant Fundamentalist* (London: Hamish Hamilton).

—— (2010) 'A Beheading', in John Freeman (ed.) *Granta 112: Pakistan* (London: Granta), 193–5.

—— (2010) 'On Fatherhood', *Paper Magazine*, http://www.mohsinhamid.com/onfatherhood.html

—— (2010) 'The Real Problem in the Afghan War is India, Pakistan and Kashmir', *Washington Post* (8 August), http://www.washingtonpost.com/wp-dyn/content/article/2010/08/06/AR2010080602658.html

Hansen, Thomas Blom (2001) *Wages of Violence: Naming and Identity in Postcolonial Bombay* (Princeton: Princeton University Press).

Hardt, Michael and Antonio Negri (2001) *Empire* (Cambridge, MA: Harvard University Press).

Hashmi, Shadab Zeest (2010) *Baker of Tarifa* (Madera, CA: Poetic Matrix).

Hawley, John C. (ed.) (1998) *The Postcolonial Crescent: Islam's Impact on Contemporary Literature* (New York: Peter Lang).

Hiddleston, Jane (2005) 'Shapes and Shadows: (Un)Veiling the Immigrant in Monica Ali's *Brick Lane*', *Journal of Commonwealth Literature* 40(1): 57–72.

Hopkins, Peter and Richard Gale (eds) (2009) *Muslims in Britain: Race, Place and Identities* (Edinburgh: Edinburgh University Press).

Hoque, Anisul (2003) *Maa* [*Mother*], available as an untranslated ebook: http://www.somoy.com/pdf/maa_emb.pdf

Hosagrahar, Jyoti (2005) *Indigenous Modernities: Negotiating Architecture, Urbanism, and Colonialism in Delhi* (Abingdon: Routledge).

Hosain, Attia (1961) *Sunlight on a Broken Column* (London: Chatto & Windus).

—— (1988 [1953]) *Phoenix Fled* (London: Virago).

Hossain, Selina (2007) *Selected Short Stories* (Dhaka: Bangla Academy).

Hosseini, Khaled (2004) *The Kite Runner* (London: Bloomsbury).

—— (2007) *A Thousand Splendid Suns* (London: Bloomsbury).

Howenstein, Nicholas (2007) 'Islamist Networks: The Case of Tablighi Jamaat', *United States Institute of Peace*, http://www.usip.org/publications/islamist-networks-case-tablighi-jamaat

Huggan, Graham (2001) *The Postcolonial Exotic: Marketing the Margins* (London: Routledge).

Huntington, Samuel P. (1993) 'The Clash of Civilizations', *Foreign Affairs* 72(3): 22–49.

—— (2002 [1996]) *The Clash of Civilizations and the Remaking of World Order* (London: Free Press).

Husain, Shahrukh (2005) 'Rubies for a Dog: A Fable', in Muneeza Shamsie (ed.) *And the World Changed: Contemporary Stories by Pakistani Women* (Delhi: Women Unlimited), 1–13.

—— (2006) *The Virago Book of Erotic Myths and Legends* (London: Virago).

—— (2006) *The Wit and Wisdom of Mulla Nasruddin* (Delhi: Rupa).

Husain, Shahrukh and Anita Desai (1997) *In Custody*, dir. Ismael Merchant. Actors: Shashi Kapoor, Shabana Azmi, Om Puri, Sushma Seth, and Neena Gupta (London: BBC).

Hussain, Zahid (2006) *The Curry Mile* (Manchester: Suitcase).

—— (2010) 'Great Muslim Writers', Unpublished Manchester Muslim Writers Powerpoint Presentation (Manchester: Manchester Muslim Writers).

—— (2010) 'Writetopia: A Creative Writing Toolkit', http://zahid hussainwrites.blogspot.com/

—— (2011) 'Zahid Hussain: Website', http://www.zahidhussain.com/

Hussein, Aamer (1993) *Mirror to the Sun* (London: Mantra).

—— (1997) 'The Lost Cantos of the Silken Tiger', in Muneeza Shamsie (ed.) *A Dragonfly in the Sun: An Anthology of Pakistani Writing in English* (Oxford: Oxford University Press), 454–76.

—— (1999) *Hoops of Fire: Fifty Years of Fiction by Pakistani Women* (London: Saqi).

—— (2002) 'Living in London: A Memoir', *Wasafiri* 17(36): 36–9.

—— (2002) *Turquoise* (London: Saqi).

—— (2003) *Cactus Town: Selected Stories* (Karachi: Sama).

—— (2005) *Kahani: Short Stories by Pakistani Women* (London: Saqi).

—— (2005 [1999]) *This Other Salt* (London: Saqi).

—— (2007) *Insomnia* (London: Saqi).

—— (2009) *Another Gulmohar Tree* (London: Telegram).

—— (2009) *I Giorni dell'Ibisco* (Rome: La Lepre Edizioni).

—— (2010) 'Hanif Kureishi *Collected Stories*', *Wasafiri* (24 October), http://www.wasafiri.org/pages/content/index.asp?PageID=221

—— (2010) *Il Nuvolo Messaggero* (Rome: Caravan Edizioni).

—— (2011) *The Cloud Messenger* (London: Telegram).

Hussein, Abdullah (1987) 'The Journey Back', in Muhammad Umar Memon (ed. and trans.), *Downfall by Degrees* (Toronto: Tsar), 63–127.

Hyder, Qurratulain (2003 [1959]) *River of Fire [Ag ka Dariya]* (New York: New Directions).

Imam, Jahanara (1989) *Of Blood and Fire: The Untold Story of Bangladesh's War of Independence* (Delhi: Stirling).

Iqbal, Allama (2006) 'The Mosque of Cordoba', in K. C. Kanda (ed.) *Allama Iqbal, Selected Poetry: Text, Translation and Transliteration* (Elgin, IL: New Dawn).

Islam, Manzu (2010) *Song of Our Swampland* (Leeds: Peepal Tree).

Jaffrelot, Christophe (2004) *A History of Pakistan and its Origins* (London: Anthem).

Jaggi, Maya (2003) 'Colour Bind', guardian.co.uk (7 February), http://www.guardian.co.uk/books/2003/feb/07/fiction.race

—— (2009) 'When Worlds Collide', *Guardian Review* (7 March), 11.

Jones, Nisha (2005) 'Abdulrazak Gurnah in Conversation', *Wasafiri* (Winter): 37–42.

Jones, Sam (2007) 'Jury Convicts Aspiring Suicide Bomber of Terror Offences, *Guardian* (18 September), 7.

Jones, Sherry (2008) *The Jewel of Medina* (New York: Beaufort).

Joyce, James (1939) *Finnegans Wake* (London: Faber).

—— (1989 [1914]) 'The Sisters', in *Dubliners* (London: Grafton), 7–17.

Kabbani, Rana (1992) 'Why Muslims Fear the Future', *Guardian* (21 August), 20.

Kakutani, Michiko (2010) 'A Writer Recalls His Mentor, Critic and Father, All in One Complex Man' (22 March), http://www.nytimes.com/2010/03/23/books/23book.html

Karamustafa, Ahmet T. (2007) *Sufism: The Formative Period* (Berkeley, CA: University of California Press).

Kaul, H. K. (ed.) (1997) *Historic Delhi: An Anthology* (Delhi: Oxford University Press).

Khair, Tabish (2008) *Muslim Modernities* (Delhi: Vitasta).

Khan, Adib (1994) *Seasonal Adjustments* (St Leonards, NSW: Allen & Unwin).

Khan, Sitara (2000) 'The Fool's Observation', in Debjani Chatterjee (ed.) *The Redbeck Anthology of British South Asian Poetry* (Bradford: Redbeck), 75–6.

Khan, Sorayya (2006) *Noor* (Wilmington, NC: Publishing Laboratory).

Khan, Uzma Aslam (2003) *Trespassing* (London: Harper Perennial).

King, Bruce (2007) 'The Image of the United States in Three Pakistani Novels', *Totalitarian Movements and Political Religions* 8(3–4): 683–8.

King, John (1997) 'Tablighi Jamaat and the Deobandi Mosques in Britain', in Steven Vertovec and Ceri Peach (eds) *Islam in Europe: The Politics of Religion and Community* (Basingstoke: Macmillan), 129–46.

Knight, Lynn (1990) 'Introduction', in E. H. Young, *Celia* (London: Virago [1937]), i–vi.

Knight, Steven (2002) *Dirty Pretty Things*, dir. Stephen Frears. Actors: Audrey Tautou, Chiwetel Ejiofor, Sophie Okonedo, Sergi López, and Zlatko Buric (London: Disney Home Entertainment).

Kohlmann, Evan (2004) *Al-Qaida's Jihad in Europe: The Afghan–Bosnian Network* (Oxford: Berg).

Kumar, Priya (2008) *Limiting Secularism: The Ethics of Coexistence in Indian Literature and Film* (Minneapolis, MN: University of Minnesota Press).

Kureishi, Hanif (1985) *My Beautiful Laundrette*, dir. Stephen Frears. Actors: Saeed Jaffrey, Roshan Seth, Daniel Day-Lewis, Gordon Warnecke, and Derrick Branche (London: Cinema Club).

—— (1986) 'The Rainbow Sign', in *My Beautiful Laundrette and The Rainbow Sign* (London: Faber), 9–38.

—— (1995) 'That's How Good it Was', in Hanif Kureishi and Jon Savage (eds) *The Faber Book of Pop* (London: Faber), xvii–xx.

—— (1997) *Love in a Blue Time* (London: Faber).

—— (1997) *My Son the Fanatic*, dir. Udayan Prasad. Actors: Om Puri, Rachel Griffiths, Akbar Kurtha, Stellan Skarsgård, and Gopi Desai (London: BBC).

—— (1999) *Plays Volume 1: 'King and Me', 'Outskirts', 'Borderline', 'Birds of Passage'* (London: Faber).

—— (1999) *Sleep With Me* (London: Faber).

—— (2001) *Gabriel's Gift* (London: Faber).

—— (2002) *The Body and Seven Stories* (London: Faber).

—— (2002) *Collected Screenplays Volume 1: 'My Beautiful Laundrette', 'Sammy and Rosie Get Laid', 'London Kills Me', 'My Son the Fanatic'* (London: Faber).

—— (2003) *The Mother*, dir. Roger Mitchell. Actors: Anne Reid, Daniel Craig, Steven Mackintosh, Cathryn Bradshaw, and Peter Vaughan (London: Momentum).

—— (2004) *My Ear at His Heart: Reading My Father* (London: Faber).

—— (2004) *When the Night Begins* (London: Faber).

—— (2005) *The Word and the Bomb* (London: Faber).

—— (2006) 'Fear and Paranoia: Hanif Kureishi on the Relevance of Borderline', *Guardian* (22 April), http://www.guardian.co.uk/stage/2006/apr/22/theatre.hanifkureishi

—— (2008) 'Biography', guardian.co.uk, (22 July), http://www.guardian.co.uk/books/2008/jun/13/hanif.kureishi

—— (2008) *Something to Tell You* (London: Faber).

—— (2010) *Collected Stories* (London: Faber).

—— (2011) *Collected Essays* (London: Faber).

Kureishi, Yasmin (2008) '"Keep me out of your Novels": Hanif Kureishi's Sister has had Enough', *Independent* (4 March), http://www.independent.co.uk/arts-entertainment/books/features/keep-me-out-of-your-novels-hanif-kureishis-sister-has-had-enough-790839.html

Le Clézio, Jean-Marie Gustave (2008) 'In the Forest of Paradoxes', *Nobel Lecture* (7 December) http://nobelprize.org/nobel_prizes/literature/laureates/2008/clezio-lecture_en.html

Lessing, Doris (1982) 'Introduction', in Widad El Sakkakini, *First Among Sufis: The Life and Thought of Rabia al-Adawiyya, the Woman Saint of Basra*, trans. Nabil Safwat (London: Octagon Press), 1–6.

Lewis, Paul (2008) '"Lyrical Terrorist" has Conviction Quashed', *Guardian* (18 June), 11.

Lewis, Philip (1994) *Islamic Britain: Religion, Politics and Identity Among British Muslims* (London: I. B. Tauris).

—— (2007) *Young, British and Muslim* (London: Continuum).

Lewis, Reina (1992) 'The Death of the Author and the Resurrection of the Dyke', in Sally Munt (ed.) *New Lesbian Criticism: Literary and Cultural Readings* (Hemel Hempstead: Harvester Wheatsheaf), 17–32.

Lia, Brynjar (2008) *Architect of Global Jihad: The Life of al-Qaida Strategist Abu Mus'ab al-Suri* (New York: Columbia University Press).

Low, Gail and Marion Wynne-Davies (2006) *A Black British Canon?* (Basingstoke: Palgrave Macmillan).

Ludhianvi, Sahir (2000) 'Taj Mahal', in *Selected Poems of Sahir Ludhianvi*, trans. Khwaja Tariq Mahmood (Delhi: Star).

Macdonald, Marianne (1996) 'Sexism Storm as Women-only Book Prize Launches', *Independent* (26 January), http://www.independent.co.uk/news/sexism-storm-as-womenonly-book-prize-launches-1325778.html

Malak, Amin (2005) *Muslim Narratives and the Discourse of English* (Albany: State University of New York Press).

Malik, Afshan (2003 [1996]) 'Safar', in Jeff Teare (ed.) *New Welsh Drama* (Cardiff: Parthian), 15–74.

Malik, Kenan (2010) *From Fatwa to Jihad: The Rushdie Affair and its Legacy* (London: Atlantic Books).

Mallot, J. Edward (2007) '"A Land Outside Space, An Expanse Without Distances": Amitav Ghosh, Kamila Shamsie and the Maps of Memory', *LIT: Literature, Interpretation, Theory* 18: 261–84.

Maloul, Linda (2010) 'The Oriental Tale in Ahdaf Soueif's *Aisha*', unpublished paper, Arab Women Writers in Diaspora: Horizons of Dialogue, University of Manchester (10 December).

Mamdani, Mahmood (2004) *Good Muslim, Bad Muslim: America, the Cold War, and the Roots of Terror* (New York: Pantheon).

Man Booker Prize (1999) 'Prize Archive', http://www.themanbooker prize.com/prize/archive/32

Manchester Muslim Writers (2009) 'Home', http://www.muslimwriters. org.uk/

Mandaville, Peter G. (2001) *Traditional Muslim Politics: Reimagining the Umma* (London: Routledge).

Márquez, Gabriel García (1983) *Chronicle of a Death Foretold* (London: Pan).

Masud, Tareque and Catherine Masud (2002) *The Clay Bird*, dir. Tareque Masud. Actors: Nurul Islam Bablu, Russell Farazi, Jayanto Chattopadhyay, Rokeya Prachy, and Soaeb Islam (New York: Oscilloscope).

McDermott, Anthony (1988) *Egypt from Nasser to Mubarak: A Flawed Revolution* (London: Routledge).

McEwan, Ian (2005) *Saturday* (London: Jonathan Cape).

McLeod, John (2000) *Beginning Postcolonialism* (Manchester: Manchester University Press).

—— (2004) *Postcolonial London* (Abingdon: Routledge).

Mehmood, Tariq (1983) *Hand on the Sun* (Harmondsworth: Penguin).

Mehran, Marsha (2006) *Pomegranate Soup* (London: Arrow).

Mehta, Suketu (2005) *Maximum City: Bombay Lost and Found* (London: Headline Review).

Meijer, Roel (2005) *Egypt: A Modern History* (London: I. B. Tauris).

Melville, Herman (1981 [1853]) 'Bartleby', in *Billy Budd, Sailor and Other Stories* (New York: Bantam), 95–130.

Mills, Rod (2010) 'Fury at Traitor who Backs our Enemies', *Daily Express* (22 February), http://www.express.co.uk/posts/view/159749/Fury-at-traitor-who-backs-our-enemies

MiST (2010) 'The MiST Team', http://mistngo.org/mist-team

Modood, Tariq (2005) *Multicultural Politics: Racism, Ethnicity and Muslims in Britain* (Edinburgh: Edinburgh University Press).

Moët British Independent Film Awards (1998) '1998 Nominations' (21 November), http://bifa.org.uk/nominations/1998

Mohamed, Nadifa (2010) *Black Mamba Boy* (London: HarperCollins).

Mohsin, Moni (2006) *The End of Innocence* (London: Fig Tree).

Mondal, Anshuman A. (2008) *Young British Muslim Voices* (Oxford: Greenwood).

—— (2009) 'The Rushdie Fatwa: The *Satanic Verses* Affair was a Clash, Not Between Islam and the West, But Between Religious and Secular Sensibilities', *Guardian* (16 February), http://www.guardian.co.uk/commentisfree/2009/feb/10/religion-islam-fatwa-rushdie

Moore, Lindsey (2008) *Arab, Muslim, Woman: Voice and Vision in Postcolonial Literature and Film* (Abingdon: Routledge).

—— (2009) 'British Muslim Identities and Spectres of Terror in Nadeem Aslam's *Maps for Lost Lovers*', *Postcolonial Text* 5(2): 1–19.

Moore-Gilbert, Bart (2001) *Contemporary World Writers: Hanif Kureishi* (Manchester: Manchester University Press).

Moors, Annelies and Emma Tarlo (2007) 'Introduction', *Fashion Theory* 11(2/3): 133–42.

Moran, Joe (2002) *Interdisciplinarity* (London: Routledge).

Morey, Peter and Amina Yaqin (2011) *Framing Muslims: Stereotyping and Representation After 9/11* (Cambridge, MA: Harvard University Press).

Mori, Aoi (2000) *Toni Morrison and Womanist Discourse* (New York: Peter Lang).

Moseley, Merritt (2001) 'Britain's Women-Only Orange Prize for Fiction Magazine Article', *World and I* (16 July), http://www.worldandi.com/specialreport/2001/july/Sa21348.htm

Muslim Writers Awards (2009) 'Unpublished Categories', http://muslim writersawards.org.uk/submit-work/unpublished-categories

Naipaul, V.S. (1969 [1967]) *The Mimic Men* (London: Penguin).

—— (1981) *Among the Believers* (London: Deutsch).

—— (1987) *The Enigma of Arrival* (Harmondsworth: Penguin).

—— (1999 [1998]) *Beyond Belief: Islamic Excursions Among the Converted Peoples* (London: Abacus).

—— (2009 [1999]) *Letters Between a Father and Son* (London: Picador).

Naoko, Sugiyama (2007) '"Blessed Malelessness" as Womanist Critique: Toni Morrison's Representation of Goddess in *Paradise*', *Nanzan Review of American Studies* 29: 177–85.

Naqvi, H. M. (2009) *Home Boy* (New York: Shaye Areheart).

Nash, Geoffrey (2007) *The Anglo-Arab Encounter: Fiction and Autobiography by Arab Writers in English* (Bern: Peter Lang).

Nasta, Susheila (ed.) (2004) *Writing Across Worlds: Contemporary Writers Talk* (Abingdon: Routledge).

NBCC (2007) 'Critical Outakes: Mohsin Hamid on Camus, Immigration and Love', *Critical Mass* (30 March), http://bookcritics.org/blog/archive/critical_outakes_mohsin_hamid_on_camus_immigration_and_love/

Nelan, Bruce W. *et al.* (1993) *Time Magazine* (5 July).

Nielan, Catherine (2006) 'Tahmima Anam: Golden Girl', *The Bookseller* (12 December), http://www.thebookseller.com/control/?p=1&msgCode=2

—— (2010) 'Canongate Wins Auction for Anam', *The Bookseller* (2 July), http://www.thebookseller.com/news/122493-canongate-wins-auction-for-anam.html

O'Ballance, Edgar (2000) *Sudan, Civil War and Terrorism, 1956–99* (Basingstoke: Macmillan).

Obituaries (2008) 'Persian professor, Ann Lambton', *Times* (23 July), http://www.timesonline.co.uk/tol/comment/obituaries/article4379464.ece?token=null&offset=0&page=1

Office of National Statistics (2001) 'Population Size', http://www.statistics.gov.uk/cci/nugget.asp?id=455

Ondaatje, Michael (1993 [1992]) *The English Patient* (London: Picador).

Page, Benedicte (2010) 'V. S. Naipaul Withdraws from Turkish Event after Row over Islam Comments', *Guardian* (25 November), 11.

PalFest (2009) 'Closing Night Press Release' (28 May), http://www.palfest.org/Closing%20Night%20Press%20Release.pdf

—— (2009) 'English Press Release', http://www.palfest.org/Palfest_English_Press_Kit.pdf

—— (2010) 'Report', http://www.palfest.org/downloads/PalFest%202010%20Report.pdf

Pamuk, Orhan (2006) 'My Father's Suitcase', http://nobelprize.org/nobel_prizes/literature/laureates/2006/pamuk-lecture_en.html

Patel, Sujata and Alice Thorner (eds) (1995) *Bombay: Mosaic of Modern Culture* (Bombay: Oxford University Press).

Pavese, Cesare (1952 [1950]) *The Moon and the Bonfire*, trans. Louise Sinclair (London: Peter Owen).

Pawson, Lara (2009) 'Aamer Hussein's *Another Gulmohar Tree*', *Times Literary Supplement* (29 May), 19.

Pickthall, Mohammad Marmaduke (2000) *The Meaning of the Glorious Qur'an: An Explanatory Translation* (London: Albirr Foundation).

Pipella, Lawrence (2007) *The Mahdi: The Expected One* (Bloomington, IN: Authorhouse).

Pipes, Daniel (2003) *The Rushdie Affair: The Novel, the Ayatollah, and the West* (London: Transaction).

Pipl (2011) 'Shaheen Anam', http://pipl.com/directory/people/Shaheen/Anam

Pirnajmuddin, Hossein (2008) 'Milton's "Dark Divan" in *Paradise Lost*', *The Explicator* 66(2): 68–71.

Plath, Sylvia (1963) *The Bell Jar* (London: Heinemann).

Poole, Elizabeth (2002) *Reporting Islam: Media Representations of British Muslims* (London: I. B. Tauris).

Potter, Dennis and Melvyn Bragg (2007) 'Great Interviews of the 20th Century: Dennis Potter Interviewed by Melvyn Bragg', *Guardian* (12 September), http://www.guardian.co.uk/theguardian/2007/sep/12/greatinterviews

Prakash, Gyan (2010) *Mumbai Fables* (Princeton: Princeton University Press).

Pratt, Mary Louise (1981) 'The Short Story: The Long AND the Short of It', *Poetics* 10: 175–94.

Procter, James (2003) *Dwelling Places: Postwar Black British Writing* (Manchester: Manchester University Press).

Project for the New American Century (2000) *Rebuilding America's Defenses: Strategies, Forces, and Resources for a New Century* (Washington, DC: Project for the New American Century), http://www.webcitation.org/5e3est5lT

Prono, Luca (2005) 'Abdulrazak Gurnah: Biography', http://www.contemporarywriters.com/authors/?p=auth46

Rahim, Sameer (2008) 'In Search of an Authentic Arab Self', *Telegraph* (26 July), http://www.telegraph.co.uk/culture/books/fictionreviews/3557254/In-search-of-an-authentic-Arab-self.html

Ramadan, Tariq (2005) 'An International Call for a Moratorium on Corporal Punishment, Stoning and the Death Penalty in the Islamic World' (5 April), http://www.tariqramadan.com/An-International-call-for.html

Randall, Lee (2010) 'Interview: Leila Aboulela' (4 December), http://living.scotsman.com/books/Interview-Leila-Aboulela-author .6649588.jp

Rashid, Ahmed (2001 [2000]) *Taliban: The Story of the Afghan Warlords* (London: Pan Macmillan).

Razzaq, Rana (2007) 'Abul Mansur Ahmad', *Banglapedia*, http://www.banglapedia.org/httpdocs/HT/A_0107.HTM

Richardson, John E. (2004) *(Mis-)Representing Islam: The Racism and Rhetoric of British Broadsheet Newspapers* (Amsterdam: John Benjamins).

Richardson, Robin (2008) 'Islamophobia and Anti-Muslim Racism: Concepts and Terms, and Implications for Education', *Race, Equality, Teaching* 27(1): 11–16.

Roberts, Alison (2007) 'Is Tahmima the new Monica Ali?' *Evening Standard* (9 March), http://www.thefreelibrary.com/Is+Tahmima+the+new+Monica+Ali%3B+She%27s+been+hailed+as+a+major+talent,...-a0160375694

Rothschild, Matthew (2009) 'Israel Sends Soldiers to Try to Shut Down Literature Festival', *The Progressive* (25 May), http://www.progressive.org/wx052509.html

Roy, Arundhati (1998) 'The End of Imagination', *Guardian* (1 August), http://www.ratical.org/ratville/nukes/endOfImagine.html

Runnymede Trust (1997) *Islamophobia: A Challenge for us All* (London: Runnymede).

Rushdie, Salman (1981) *Midnight's Children* (London: Jonathan Cape).

—— (1983) *Shame* (London: Picador).

—— (1988) 'Minority Literatures in a Multi-cultural Society', in Kirsten Holst Petersen and Anna Rutherford (eds) *Displaced Persons* (Sydney: Dangaroo), 33–42.

—— (1988) *The Satanic Verses* (London: Viking).

—— (1991) *Imaginary Homelands* (London: Granta).

—— (1996) *The Moor's Last Sigh* (London: Vintage).

Ruthven, Malise (1990) *A Satanic Affair: Salman Rushdie and the Rage of Islam* (London: Chatto & Windus).

Said, Edward W. (1975) *Beginnings: Intention and Method* (New York: Basic).

—— (1995 [1978]) *Orientalism: Western Conceptions of the Orient* (Harmondsworth: Penguin).

—— (1997 [1981]) *Covering Islam: How the Media and the Experts Determine How we See the Rest of the World* (London: Vintage).

Salih, Tayeb (2003 [1966]) *Season of Migration to the* North, trans. Denys Johnson-Davies (London: Penguin).

Sánchez-Arce, Ana Maria (2007) '"Authenticism", or the Authority of Authenticity', *Mosaic* 40(3): 139–55.

Sandars, N. K. (ed. and trans.) (1987 [1960]) *The Epic of Gilgamesh* (Harmondsworth: Penguin).

Sandhu, Sukhdev (2003) *London Calling: How Black and Asian Writers Imagined a City* (London: HarperCollins).

Saracino, Maria Antonietta (2004) 'Hanif Kureishi: Biography', in Alba Amoia and Bettina L. Knapp (eds) *Multicultural Writers Since 1945: An A–Z Guide* (Westport, CT: Greenwood), 305–8.

Sardar, Ziauddin (2006) 'Books of the Year', *New Statesman* (27 November), http://www.newstatesman.com/200611270051

Sciascia, Leonardo (2001) *Sicilian Uncles*, trans. N. S. Thompson (London: Granta).

Sethi, Ali (2009) *The Wish Maker* (London: Hamish Hamilton).

Sethi, Sunil (2011) *The Big Bookshelf: Sunil Sethi in Conversation with Thirty Famous Authors* (Delhi: Penguin/NDTV).

Shackle, Christopher, Shahrukh Husain, and David J. Matthews (2003) *Urdu Literature* (Karachi: Alhamra).

Shahraz, Qaisra (2001) *The Holy Woman* (London: Black Amber).

—— (2003) *Typhoon* (London: Black Amber).

Shamsie, Kamila (1998) *In the City by the Sea* (London: Bloomsbury).

—— (2001 [2000]) *Salt and Saffron* (London: Bloomsbury).

—— (2002) 'Agha Shahid Ali, Teacher', *Urdu Studies* 17: 23–7.

—— (2003 [2002]) *Kartography* (London: Bloomsbury).

—— (2005) *Broken Verses* (London: Bloomsbury).

—— (2009) *Burnt Shadows* (London: Bloomsbury).

—— (2009) 'A Long, Loving Literary Line', *Guardian G2* (1 May), 16.

—— (2009) *Offence: The Muslim Case* (Kolkata: Seagull).

—— (2010) 'Pop Idols', in John Freeman (ed.) *Granta 112: Pakistan* (London: Granta), 197–214.

—— (n.d.) 'With the Ear of a Poet', http://www.kashmiri.info/index2. php?option=com_content&do_pdf=1&id=23

Shamsie, Muneeza (ed.) (1997) *A Dragonfly in the Sun: An Anthology of Pakistani Writing in English* (Oxford: Oxford University Press).

—— (2002) 'Maki Kureishi', *Literary Encyclopedia* (20 June), http://www. litencyc.com/php/speople.php?rec=true&UID=4995

—— (2003) 'Tariq Ali', *Literary Encyclopedia* (20 June), http://www. litencyc.com/php/speople.php?rec=true&UID=4964

—— (2007) 'Nadeem Aslam', Literary Encyclopedia (2 March), http:// www.litencyc.com/php/speople.php?rec=true&UID=11771

—— (2009) '*The Reluctant Fundamentalist*', *Literary Encyclopedia* (21 May), http://www.litencyc.com/php/sworks.php?rec=true&UID=23135

—— (2009) 'Sunlight and Salt: The Literary Landscapes of a Divided Family', *Journal of Commonwealth Literature* 44(1): 135–53.

Shamsie, Saman (2010) *The Adventures of Slothful Slough-off* (Karachi: Oxford University Press).

Siddique, John (2011) 'John Siddique: Poet and Author', http://www. johnsiddique.co.uk/

Sidhwa, Bapsi (1988) *Ice-Candy Man* (London: Heinemann); later published in the US as *Cracking India* (Minneapolis, MN: Milkweed, 1991).

Soueif, Ahdaf (1996 [1983]) *Aisha* (London: Bloomsbury).

—— (1996) *Sandpiper* (London: Bloomsbury).

—— (1999 [1992]) *In the Eye of the Sun* (London: Bloomsbury).

—— (1999) *The Map of Love* (London: Bloomsbury).

—— (2000) 'Under the Gun: A Palestinian Journey', *Guardian G2* (18 December), 2.

—— (2002) 'Egyptian Memories', *Open Democracy*, http://www.open democracy.net/faith-europe_islam/article_403.jsp

—— (2004) *Mezzaterra: Fragments from the Common Ground* (London: Bloomsbury).

—— (2008) 'Visions of the Harem: John Frederick Lewis', *Guardian Review* (5 July 2008), 16.

Soueif, Ahdaf and Joseph Massad (1999) 'The Politics of Desire in the Writings of Ahdaf Soueif', *Journal of Palestine Studies* 28(4): 74–90.

Soueif Official Web Site (2010) '*Aisha*', http://www.ahdafsoueif.com/ Books/aisha.htm

—— (2010) 'Home', http://www.ahdafsoueif.com/

—— (2010) 'Information', http://www.ahdafsoueif.com/about.htm

—— (2011) speaking on Riz Khan 'The Political Power of Literature', *Al-Jazeera* (23 February), http://english.aljazeera.net/programmes/rizkhan/2011/02/201122374815992508.html

Soyinka, Wole (1976) *Myth, Literature and the African World* (Cambridge: Cambridge University Press).

Spivak, Gayatri Chakravorty (1988) 'Can the Subaltern Speak?', in Cary Nelson and Lawrence Grossberg (eds) *Marxism and the Interpretation of Culture* (Basingstoke: Macmillan Education), 271–313.

—— (1989) 'In Praise of *Sammy and Rosie Get Laid'*, *Critical Quarterly* 31(2) (Summer): 80–8.

—— (1999) *A Critique of Postcolonial Reason: Toward a History of the Vanishing Present* (Cambridge, MA: Harvard University Press).

Squires, Claire (2007) *Marketing Literature* (Basingstoke: Palgrave Macmillan).

Srivastava, Neelam (2008) *Secularism in the Postcolonial Indian Novel: National and Cosmopolitan Narratives in English* (Abingdon: Routledge).

Stanley, Liz (1992) *The Auto/biographical I: The Theory and Practice of Feminist Auto/biography* (Manchester: Manchester University Press).

Stanton, Gregory (1996) 'The 8 Stages of Genocide', *Genocide Watch*, http://www.genocidewatch.org/aboutgenocide/8stagesofgenocide.html

Steele, David (1998) 'Lord Salisbury, the "False Religion" of Islam, and the Reconquest of the Sudan', in Edward M. Spiers (ed.) *Sudan: The Reconquest Reappraised* (London: Frank Cass), 11–33.

Straw, Jack (2006) 'I Felt Uneasy Talking to Someone I Couldn't See' (full text of Straw's article originally in the *Lancashire Telegraph*), *Guardian* (6 October), 1.

Sue, D. W., A. I. Lin, G. C. Torino, C. M. Capodilupo, and D. P. Rivera (2009) 'Racial Microaggressions and Difficult Dialogues on Race in the Classroom', *Cultural Diversity and Ethnic Minority Psychology* 15(2): 183–90.

Suhrke, Astri (1995) 'Refugees and Asylum in the Muslim World', in Robin Cohen (ed.) *The Cambridge Survey of World Migration* (Cambridge: Cambridge University Press), 457–60.

Tarlo, Emma (2010) *Visibly Muslim: Fashion, Politics, Faith* (Oxford: Berg).

Taylor, Charles (1997 [1994]) 'The Politics of Recognition', in Ajay Heble, Donna Palmateer Pennee, and J. R. Tim Struthers (eds) *New Contexts of Canadian Criticism* (Peterborough, ON: Broadview), 98–131.

Tew, Philip, Fiona Tolan, and Leigh Wilson (eds) (2008) *Writers Talk: Conversations with Contemporary British Novelists* (London: Continuum).

Thorpe, Vanessa and Mahtab Haider (2006) 'New Fiction Star Taps Bangladeshi Roots', *Observer* (26 November).

Travelsi, Hechmi (2003) 'Transcultural Writing: Ahdaf Soueif's *Aisha* as a Case Study', *Jouvert* 7(2), http://english.chass.ncsu.edu/jouvert/v7i2/trabel.htm

University of Leeds (2010) 'Community Religions Project' (9 November), http://www.leeds.ac.uk/trs/irpl/crp.htm

Varadarajan, Tunku (2010) 'Wole Soyinka's British Problem', *The Daily Beast* (31 January), http://www.thedailybeast.com/blogs-and-stories/2010-01-31/wole-soyinkas-british-problem/?cid=hp:mainpromo5

Von Franz, Marie-Louise (1996 [1987]) *The Interpretation of Fairy Tales* (Boston, MA: Shambhala).

Waheed, Mirza (2011) *The Collaborator* (London: Viking).

Walcott, Derek (1992 [1979]) 'The Schooner *Flight*', in *Collected Poems* (London: Faber), 345–61.

—— (1993) *The Antilles: Fragments of Epic Memory* (New York: Farrar, Straus and Giroux).

Walder, Dennis (2011) *Postcolonial Nostalgias: Writing, Representation and Memory* (Abingdon: Routledge).

Waliullah, Shah (1982) *The Sacred Knowledge of the Higher Functions of the Mind: The Altaf al-Quds of Shah Waliullah*, trans. G. N. Jalbani and David Pendlebury (London: Octagon).

Walker, Alice (1984 [1983]) *In Search of our Mother's Garden: Womanist Prose* (London: Women's Press).

Walter, Natasha (2006) 'Continental Drift', *Guardian Review* (20 May), 16.

Weldon, Fay (1989) *Sacred Cows: A Portrait of Britain, Post-Rushdie, Pre-Utopia* (London: Chatto & Windus).

Werbner, Pnina (2006) 'Seekers on the Path: Different Ways of Being a Sufi in Britain', in Jamal Malik and John Hinnells (eds) *Sufism in the West* (Abingdon: Routledge), 127–41.

Wikipedia (n.d.) 'List of Countries by Sex Ratio', http://en.wikipedia.org/wiki/List_of_countries_by_sex_ratio

Williams, Nigel (1993) *East of Wimbledon* (London: Faber).

Williams, Rowan (2008) 'Civil and Religious Law in England: A Religious Perspective', guardian.co.uk (7 February), http://www.guardian.co.uk/uk/2008/feb/07/religion.world2

Wyatt, Andrew (2005) 'Building the Temples of Postmodern India: Economic Construction of National Identity', *Contemporary South Asia* 14(4): 465–80.

Yassin-Kassab, Robin (2007) 'Review of *The Reluctant Fundamentalist*', *Qunfuz Blog* (1 December), http://qunfuz.com/2007/12/01/the-reluctant-fundamentalist/

—— (2008) 'Dawkins or McIntosh?', *Qunfuz Blog* (21 August), http://qunfuz.com/2008/08/21/dawkins-or-mcintosh/#more-86

—— (2008) 'Flooding the Swamp' *Qunfuz Blog* (27 April), http://qunfuz.com/2008/04/27/flooding-the-swamp/

—— (2008) 'Leaving Oman', *Qunfuz Blog* (30 June), http://qunfuz.com/2008/06/30/leaving-oman/

—— (2008) 'Maps for Lost Lovers and Writerly Responsibility', *Qunfuz Blog* (6 February), http://qunfuz.com/2008/02/06/%E2%80%9Cmaps-for-lost-lovers%E2%80%9D-and-writerly-responsibility/#more-63

—— (2008) 'My Wife Wears the Hijab. I Wish She Didn't', *Observer Woman* (2 November), 38.

—— (2008) *The Road from Damascus* (London: Hamish Hamilton).

—— (2008) 'Two Reviews', *Qunfuz Blog* (22 September), http://qunfuz.com/2008/09/23/two-reviews/

—— (2009) 'Muslim Writer', *Qunfuz Blog* (21 May), http://qunfuz.blogspot.com/2009/05/muslim-writer.html

—— (2010) 'Defamation and Binary Idiocy', *Qunfuz Blog* (22 February), http://qunfuz.com/2010/02/22/defamation-and-binary-idiocy-2/

Yassin-Kassab, Robin and Claire Chambers (2010) 'Ghoshwood's Mendacity', *Pulse* (11 May), http://pulsemedia.org/2010/05/11/ghoshwoods-mendacity/

Yeats, W. B. (2000 [1916]) 'Easter 1916', in *Selected Poems*, ed. and intro. Timothy Walsh (London: Penguin), 119–21.

Zangen, Britta (2003) 'Women as Readers, Writers, and Judges: The Controversy about the Orange Prize for Fiction', *Women's Studies: An Inter-disciplinary Journal* 32(3): 281–99.

Index